Environmental Politics and Policy

For Ashley, Leanna, and Karly

Environmental Politics and Policy

Ninth Edition

Walter A. Rosenbaum
University of Florida

Los Angeles | London | New Delhi
Singapore | Washington DC

Los Angeles | London | New Delhi
Singapore | Washington DC

FOR INFORMATION:

CQ Press

An Imprint of SAGE Publications, Inc.

2455 Teller Road

Thousand Oaks, California 91320

E-mail: order@sagepub.com

SAGE Publications Ltd.

1 Oliver's Yard

55 City Road

London EC1Y 1SP

United Kingdom

SAGE Publications India Pvt. Ltd.

B 1/I 1 Mohan Cooperative Industrial Area

Mathura Road, New Delhi 110 044

India

SAGE Publications Asia-Pacific Pte. Ltd.

3 Church Street

#10-04 Samsung Hub

Singapore 049483

Printed in the United States of America

Library of Congress Cataloging-in-Publication Data

Rosenbaum, Walter A.

Environmental politics and policy / Walter A.
Rosenbaum, University of Florida.—Ninth edition.

pages cm.
Includes bibliographical references and index.

ISBN 978-1-4522-3996-5 (alk. paper)
ISBN 978-1-4833-0163-1 (web pdf : alk. paper)

1. Environmental policy—United States. I. Title.

GE180.R66 2013
363.7′0560973—dc23   2013009505

This book is printed on acid-free paper.

Acquisitions Editor: Charisse Kiino

Production Editor: Libby Larson

Copy Editor: Pam Schroeder

Typesetter: C&M Digitals (P) Ltd.

Proofreader: Wendy Jo Dymond

Indexer: Kathleen Paparchontis

Cover Designer: Michael Dubowe

Marketing Manager: Jonathan Mason

Permissions Editor: Jennifer Barron

Certified Chain of Custody
SUSTAINABLE Promoting Sustainable Forestry
FORESTRY   www.sfiprogram.org
INITIATIVE   SFI-01268

SFI label applies to text stock

13 14 15 16 10 9 8 7 6 5 4 3 2 1

Contents

Figures, Tables, Boxes, and Maps

Tables

Boxes

Maps

Preface

We are well past the threshold of the 21st century. It is a time to measure distances: How far have we come in the last decade? How far must we go? It is a time to talk about time and change: What have we lost? What have we gained? How far have we traveled since that rapidly receding Earth Day 1970, the big bang of the nation's environmental era? This book is addressed to an audience who will live well into the new century, a generation with its ambition and imagination resolutely fixed on tomorrow, so it is also a time to talk about what might be: What might this generation accomplish? What ideas and visions will challenge its imagination and come to fruition? In short, an author should write accurately and responsibly not only about what has happened but also about its meaning in social and historical time. Therefore, this is a book about the more enduring institutions and processes of American environmental policy making as well as their ongoing transformation and implications.

Readers familiar with *Environmental Politics and Policy* will recognize a continuity with previous editions in conceptual framework and substantive policy concerns. They will notice, as well, some significant editorial improvements and an emphatic focus on many remarkable changes in the last decade that already forecast compelling issues on the nation's emerging environmental agenda. The foundational chapters that explain and illustrate the essential components of the policy-making process (Chapters 2 and 3) still cover these key areas, but they have been carefully reorganized for greater clarity and continuity. Chapter 2 now focuses entirely on the policy-making process, whereas Chapter 3 covers the institutions and politics of policy making. Throughout the book, case studies and other examples have been updated comprehensively, where appropriate, to ensure timeliness and relevance. Each chapter has been edited rigorously to eliminate material from previous editions that is no longer essential. The result is a more concise narrative that does not sacrifice fundamentals such as the conceptual design, the careful explanation of substantive policy, and the abundant illustrations that have appealed to the readers of previous editions. As always, a major subtext is the continuing challenge, inherent to environmental policy making, of reconciling sound science with practical politics.

This edition also records significant events and illuminates the strategic transformations that have taken place in domestic environmental politics and policy throughout the Barack Obama administration. These include the following:

- A fresh discussion in Chapters 1 and 8 of the energy policy agenda of the Obama administration, with particular attention to the administration's long-term renewable energy proposals and their environmental significance.
- An examination of the now chronic partisan polarization within Congress, its impact upon domestic environmental policy, and its implications for the Obama administration's environmental agenda following the 2012 presidential election.
- An updated narrative about the shifting texture and discontinuities of public opinion concerning the environment and its impact on environmental policy making. Chapter 2, for example, examines a number of potentially significant aspects of public opinion trends since the 2008 presidential election. These include the increasing polarization of opinion between Republican and Democratic partisans over important domestic energy issues such as climate change, the credibility of science and scientists in environmental policy making, the importance of environmental regulation compared to economic growth in national policy making, and the continuing failure of environmentalism to become a salient factor in presidential voting.
- A recognition of continuing change in environmental trends and indicators. The shelf life of environmental data is short. Data need continual updating and pruning to remain relevant. Tables and figures from earlier editions that are no longer useful have been removed. The remaining tables and figures presenting the most essential data—current trends in national air pollution emissions, water quality, and toxic waste discharges, for example—have been updated as much as possible.
- A discussion of environmental justice in Chapter 4, expanded to emphasize the growing domestic infrastructure of the movement.
- An identification of new issues and the evolving status of old ones. The introductory and concluding chapters bracket the entire narrative with attention to the impact of the Obama presidency and its environmental agenda on understanding both our domestic environmental politics and our international environmental diplomacy.
- A contrast, in Chapter 4, between domestic risk assessment methods with the precautionary principle, an alternative approach widely used in the European Union (EU) and receiving increasing attention

in the United States. This chapter also updates the continuing controversy over the human cancer risk associated with exposure to the chemical dioxin and to chemical plasticizers in materials used in making children's toys. The discussion of water pollution regulation in Chapter 6 includes a description of the technically complex, economically expensive problem now confronting the states in dealing with contaminants in runoff water from agriculture and other sources of nonpoint pollution.

- Exploration in Chapter 8 of several recent, rapid, environmentally profound transformations in America's energy economy created by the onrushing development of fracking technology, the sudden surge in domestic petroleum production, and the failing vision of a commercial nuclear power "renaissance." This chapter updates the discussion of mountaintop removal, a growing and increasingly controversial method of coal surface mining, and the newly emerging challenge posed by coal ash disposal from power-generating plants.
- A greatly expanded exploration in Chapter 10 of global climate change as a domestic policy issue and the implications of its international setting. That discussion includes an assessment of the relevance for the United States of the highly contentious meetings, in 2011 and 2012, of the global Conference of Parties (COP) to the Kyoto Protocol and the crucial role of the Intergovernmental Panel on Climate Change (IPCC) in the domestic climate policy debate. The most widely advocated domestic emissions control strategy to control climate warming emissions, carbon capture and sequester (CCS), is critically assessed.

I have tried to keep faith with colleagues, students, reviewers, and others who have found the narrative design informative, accessible, and durable. That includes an implicit commitment to material that is interesting as well as balanced and teachable—in the end, a book that is both a good read and a fair read.

Acknowledgments

As usual, the talents of many other people were enlisted in the writing of this new edition, and I am deeply indebted to them for the continuing acceptance of this book. Like most teachers, I recognized long ago that my students are often my best instructors and critics. To them, I express my continuing gratitude. A number of reviewers made constructive suggestions during the revision and writing of this edition. I thank Damian C. Adams, University of Florida; Jennifer Allen, Portland State University; Craig Allin,

Cornell College; Donovan Finn, SUNY-Stony Brook; John Freemuth, Boise State University; Marjorie Hershey, Indiana University; James Hill, Central Michigan University; Stephen Nelson, University of Utah; Shannon O'Lear, University of Kansas; Michelle Pautz, University of Dayton; and Dennis Pirages, University of Nevada-Las Vegas, for their thorough reviews. To my current CQ Press editors Charisse Kiino and Libby Larson, and to copy-editor Pam Schroeder, I offer a well-deserved thanks for the many hours of planning, reviewing, and patience invested in the work. Faults of omission and commission—alas!—are my own.

—*Walter A. Rosenbaum*

About the Author

Walter A. Rosenbaum is professor emeritus of political science at the University of Florida and director emeritus of the University of Florida's Bob Graham Center for Public Service. His recent activities include an analysis of the EPA's capacity for climate change regulation, prepared for the Brookings Institution; an examination of the data requirements for a new Federal Environmental Legacy Act; and preparation of an energy policy text for CQ Press. He has also served as a staff member of the U.S. Environmental Protection Agency and an adjunct professor in the School of Public Health, Tulane University Medical College. In addition to his teaching and research, he has been a consultant to the EPA, the U.S. Department of Energy, the Federal Emergency Management Agency, and the South Florida Ecosystem (Everglades) Restoration Project. He is currently the Editor-in-Chief of the *Journal for Environmental Studies and Sciences*.

Chapter 1

After Earth Day

> *The difficulty of converting scientific findings into political action is a*
> *function of the uncertainty of the science and the pain generated by*
> *the action.*
>
> —William D. Ruckelshaus, former administrator
> of the U.S. Environmental Protection Agency (EPA)

It was a humid evening in late July 2010 at Canonsburg, Pennsylvania, a small, historic community resting upon the rich coal seams underlying much of southwestern Pennsylvania. Things were not going quite as planned at The Hilton Garden Inn. The inn expected 800 visitors that evening, not the 1,200 who showed up. Many were very worried and very angry. They crowded every seat and spilled into the aisles and doorways of the inn's most expansive conference room. They were there because the EPA was there to hear their opinions about a mining technology that sounded like a bad joke.

The technology was hydrologic fracturing, commonly called *fracking*. The EPA was preparing to study the national environmental impact of fracking, a technology used to create well sites for natural gas, a practice virtually unregulated and rapidly spreading at an accelerating pace across Pennsylvania and almost every other state. In Pennsylvania, there were already 4,000 new fracking sites. Some experts predicted an annual growth of 2,500 more sites until more than 100,000 facilities would sprawl across the Pennsylvania countryside.

A few years earlier, few people living in that historic coal country or anywhere else had heard of fracking. The EPA's administrators were well aware, however, that fracking had become increasingly familiar and bitterly controversial, especially across rural Pennsylvania. They also thought they knew what to expect at the hearing because, in a sense, they had been there before. This was their third meeting across the nation with other stakeholders similarly embroiled in the fracking issue. They had not anticipated,

1

however, the size of the agitated audience who heard 100 mostly furious speakers flail state and local government, the EPA, the gas industry, and other federal agencies for irresponsibly allowing fracking to continue in Pennsylvania.

According to the *New York Times*, "streams of people came to the public meeting . . . armed with stories of yellowed and foul-smelling well water, deformed livestock, poisoned fish and itchy skin. One resident invoked the 1968 zombie thriller *Night of the Living Dead . . .*" (by a goulash coincidence, the film was produced nearby). To accompanying applause, one speaker charged that EPA's proposal was *"the equivalent of studying the flammability of Rome while the city was burning."* A few "Fracking Is Our Future" signs appeared, but most speakers warned that Pennsylvania was becoming a showcase for the environmental contamination that lay in the wake of fracking's rapid invasion of most other states.[1]

A month later, the EPA had to postpone temporarily its final hearing in Syracuse, New York, when no facility could be readily found to accommodate the estimated 8,000 people anticipated to attend.[2] By then there was no doubt, however, that the EPA's research would proceed. The final report is scheduled to appear in 2014. Meanwhile, Canonsburg and Syracuse are signposts pointing toward a continually enlarging and intensely controversial issue certain to beset almost every state—a reminder that, a generation after the first Earth Day 1970, environmental protection remains fundamental on the American policy agenda and enduringly important to the nation's public health, economic future, and national security. Most importantly, the fracking conflict is American environmental politics in the present tense. The rapidly enlarging contention is a showcase for many issues inseparable from environmental policy making and certain to appear in variation throughout later chapters.

"Frack, Baby, Frack"

Fracking itself is not a new technique for producing natural gas and petroleum. But, a relatively recent innovation called *high-volume hydraulic fracturing and horizontal drilling* has greatly increased the technology's efficiency and economic profitability, thus dramatically accelerating its growth across the natural gas industry into what many industry experts now call a *fracking boom*. Like almost all environmental issues, fracking is a complex mix of politics, economics, technology, science, and health risks—in this case, with a generous seasoning of culture conflict and American energy security.

Fracking has grown most explosively across states overlying the Marcellus, Green River, and Baaken oil shale formations. The massive Marcellus formation underlies large portions of Alabama, Tennessee, all of Kentucky, West Virginia, most of Pennsylvania, and a large wedge of southwestern New York State. The Green River and Baaken formations lie below large portions of North Dakota, Montana, Colorado, Wyoming, and Utah. More than 30 other economically significant oil shale formations exist beneath the United States and the Gulf of Mexico. In short, virtually every American state is, or may be, a fracking site for natural gas.

An Evolving Technology

Oil shale is a densely packed sedimentary material formed millions of years ago containing oil and natural gas combined like an egg in cake batter within the densely packed rock. A much more complicated and expensive technology is required for this extraction and refinement than for traditional petroleum reserves found in underground "pools" of liquid petroleum and natural gas. Fracking technology is designed especially to reach and capture the petroleum resources locked in these deep sedimentary layers.

Fracking involves igniting underground explosives to fracture oil shale. Engineers then combine a vertical pipe, often miles deep, with a horizontally drilled pipe to pump into the shale millions of gallons heated, salty water mixed with numerous chemicals to produce a brine under pressure high enough to penetrate the fractures. The heated brine releases petroleum and natural gas embedded in the shale. The whole mix is captured, pumped to the surface, and separated into petroleum materials and wastewater.[3] The "water comes back up, mixed with salts and other substances more toxic than the chemicals in the original fluid. The resulting mixture, called 'flowback' is . . . a bubbly mix that looks like muddy champagne."[4]

Fracking requires massive water consumption, the potential contamination of surface and subsurface water resources by the drilling brine, and disposal of the millions of gallons of wastewater. Most drilling companies assert that the drilling brine is environmentally safe and that the brine's diffusion through the oil shale and its eventual disposal above ground pose few ecological hazards. (One mining company executive even publicly—and harmlessly—drank a small glass of the drilling brine to demonstrate its safety.)[5] Most drillers believe that any additional environmental regulation, when needed, can be provided by the relevant state or local governments. Almost all drilling companies, however, insist that the content of their brine is a legally protected trade secret and refuse to disclose the formulas.

Contested Environmental Impacts

There is little doubt, however, that the newest fracking technology can pose significant health risks and create potentially severe ecological damage unless properly managed by mining companies and carefully regulated by government. An extensive review of the available research, reported by the highly respected National Academies of Science, concluded that oil shale mining "is much more costly, energy intensive, and environmentally damaging than drilling for conventional oil. The processes . . . involve significant disturbance of the land, extensive use of water (a particular concern in dry regions where oil shale is often found), and potential emissions of pollutants to the air and groundwater. In addition, more energy goes into these processes than into extracting and refining conventional oil, and more CO_2 is emitted."[6]

Fracking's potential impact upon the nation's rivers, lakes, streams, and underground water has become especially contentious. Even a relatively small drilling site pours millions of gallons of chemically treated water into a fracking well. Fracking sites currently operating or planned near large urban drinking water sources or infrastructure, for instance, might create significant contamination and extremely costly remediation. The U.S. Geological Survey has warned that fracking could penetrate and contaminate a major underground aqueduct in the Catskill Mountains, only one of many transporting water to New York City from the Marcellus formation. If the city's water supply is contaminated by drilling, the estimated expense for "cleaning up the water would require a water filtration plant costing at least $8 billion, with a yearly operating expense of $200 million. Even then, city officials have said there is no guarantee that the water could be purified."[7] Small, repeated earthquakes have occasionally been linked to fracking operations. Pennsylvania dairy farmers near fracking operations have complained about methane-contaminated wells, poisoned cattle, and drilling access roads destroying timber and isolating croplands. Many farmers assert that fracking chemicals have impaired their health and their ability to manage their properties.

Clear and convincing evidence of these and other environmental impacts attributed to fracking technology, however, is fragmentary and controversial—a major reason for the EPA's own research initiative. Some limited university studies have found no evidence of groundwater contamination at a few southwestern fracking sites; other research reveals no earthquakes associated in other regions. Illness directly linked to fracking-contaminated soil and water among farmers and ranchers remains unproven. Thus, the fracking boom advances even as government regulators, property owners, the drilling companies, health scientists, and environmentalists debate when, where, and how to regulate it.

Politics: Neighbor against Neighbor, Government versus Government

Whatever else fracking's impact, it divides communities and governments and sets neighbors against each other. It also produces substantial royalty income that can deliver economic security for a property owner living atop an oil shale formation. In DeSoto Parish, Louisiana, noted a mayor, people "went to bed one night poor and woke up the next day rich, enabled to buy and Cadillac and pay cash. . . . It's kind of like the show 'The Beverly Hillbillies.'" Parish homeowners could typically earn "signing bonuses of $350 to as much as $30,000 an acre from gas companies, as well as royalties that can last for decades."[8] Gas companies in Pennsylvania have paid in excess of $1,000 per acre plus royalties to some landowners for the right to drill on their properties. But, such money comes at the cost of exposing the home and land (and perhaps the neighbor's) to fracking's possibly substantial environmental and health risks. New York has become a showcase for the divisiveness attending fracking technology.

Divided Communities, Conflicted Farmers, Contentious Federalism. The decision to sell or lease property for fracking divides farmers and communities. New York farmers, reluctant to lease or sell their property for fracking and struggling to survive financially, can look across to Pennsylvania and see others profiting from their drilling royalties. "I go over the border and see people planting orchards, buying tractors, putting money back in their land," observed one New York farmer. "We'd like to do that too, but instead we struggle to pay the taxes and to hang onto our farms."[9] One New York farming cooperative that annually buys $3 million in New York farm products refuses to purchase from any region that permits fracking. But, New York's large and influential Farm Bureau supports fracking when done safely. In Cooperstown, New York, a reporter observed that the battle over fracking "has pitted neighbor against neighbor, and has often set people who live in the suburbs or villages against the farmers and landowners who live outside them."[10]

Environmental regulation involves federalism, which usually proceeds with considerable cooperation among federal, state, and local governments. But, federalism has raw edges often exposed when federal and state governments disagree about regulation. Some New York communities have refused to wait for the EPA or the state government to decide how to regulate fracking and have enacted their own varied and sometimes conflicting local laws. State officials insist that there must be consistent state regulations, not a patchwork of different local laws. At the same time, New York and federal regulators are contentious about how regulatory authority should be divided between the state and the federal governments. Similar disagreements between local and state governments, and between state and federal regulators, have spread across the United States including Ohio, North Dakota, California, Texas, Virginia, and Colorado. It not uncommon to hear state governors and regulatory officials complain that "you can't trust the EPA" when it comes to regulating petroleum and natural gas production.

"A Tremendous Benefit to Our Nation"

Like most environmental issues, fracking commonly provokes disagreement between proponents and advocates over the scientific and economic credibility of the data each side amasses to support its claims. Virtually none of this data is undisputed. Fracking would be considerably less contentious, however, if it were not freighted with plausible advantages, including potentially enormous economic, political, national security, and consumer benefits.

Economically, some plausible estimates suggest that the construction of pipelines and other infrastructure associated with fracking could annually add $56 billion to the U.S. economy and create an average of 132,000 new jobs annually by 2017.[11] Even if various optimistic predictions of fracking's economic impact are exaggerated, the existing evidence is that fracking is producing thousands of new jobs and infusing many millions of dollars into state and national economies. Moreover, all states with fracking sites also receive royalty income. Many economically blighted communities have revived, and new boomtowns have appeared across the nation as fracking technology proliferates. At a time when the United States remains mired in a severe recession, fracking's real and asserted economic attractions are especially potent.[12]

When John Deutsch, a former Obama administration official who led a special federal panel that studied shale oil fracking in 2011, affirmed that fracking represented "a tremendous benefit to our nation," he echoed a theme frequently heard in many variations among political leaders at all national levels.[13] Given a lingering economic recession and the traditional pressure upon public officials in American politics to promote economic growth, it is inevitable that political leaders will often warily approve the growth of shale oil fracking, especially when—and if—its risks can be acceptably minimized. Thus, while many environmentalists and other fracking critics were disappointed, the Obama administration's refusal to propose a regulatory ban or moratorium to fracking operations and, instead, to advocate a careful evaluation of fracking's risks and benefits was understandable.

Fracking has important implications for national energy supply, national security, and even for mitigating climate warming. Many economists and national security experts predict that an abundance of new natural gas will significantly reduce U.S. dependence upon imported petroleum, thus promoting domestic energy independence while also reducing materially the cost of natural gas to consumers. A substantial decrease in both the price of natural gas and the volume of imported petroleum between 2010 and 2013, argue fracking advocates, demonstrates the potential of a fracking boom.

Ironically, many advocates assert that fracking has plausible environmental advantages. They predict that a fracking boom could drive down the price of natural gas to the point that many existing and new electric utilities will replace coal with cheaper, less environmentally polluting gas as a primary fuel. Moreover, they add, natural gas creates far less climate warming emissions than does coal—at least when burned at utility sites.

Thus, what begins as an innovation in petroleum technology transforms Pennsylvania oil fields into a stage on which are displayed national issues, actors, and institutions that characteristically converge in national environmental policy making, marking its continuing transformation and setting the agenda for the chapters to follow. These are a permanent legacy of an American Environmental Era hardly a generation old.

The Environmental Legacy

By the time Barack Obama first pledged his administration to create a "new energy superhighway," America's environmental movement had already transformed the nation's environment and its politics in many enduring ways. The evidence of important gains in environmental quality is substantial. One influential report card on international environmental performance, for example, commended the United States for its continuing improvement in environmental management between 1996 and 2004, especially in regulating air, water, and pesticide pollutants during a period when the U.S. economy was vigorously growing. In addition, the report noted that, although the United States was disengaging from international negotiations to regulate climate warming during the George W. Bush administration, the United States still continued its support of numerous other international programs.[14]

Perhaps most impressive has been the improvement of the nation's air quality. Ambient concentrations of sulfur oxides, carbon monoxide, nitrogen oxides, and particulates—all associated with serious human health disorders—have been reduced significantly, and many more acutely dangerous ambient air toxics, especially formaldehyde and lead, have been reduced drastically or virtually eliminated. Dangerous chemical and biological pollutants of major U.S. waterways, such as the Mississippi, Potomac, and Ohio rivers, have been reduced sharply. Aggressive regulatory programs have reduced significantly the number of abandoned hazardous waste sites across the United States and, for the first time, compelled the manufacturers and distributors of hazardous or toxic chemicals to comply with national standards for their transport and disposal. National testing programs now require more rigorous screening and testing of newly manufactured chemicals to protect human health and the environment. Numerous plant and animal species that were threatened with extinction, including the American bald eagle and the American panther, have been protected and, in some instances, restored to vitality. Equally important, the United States is committed to numerous regional and international treaties, such as the Montreal Protocol, to reduce the global ozone hole, testifying to a growing recognition that the quality of the nation's domestic environment and global environmental quality have become interdependent. Most important politically, these transformations are grounded in a durable national consensus that environmental protection must now be a first-order public concern—a remarkable emergence of a national ecological consciousness that was nonexistent a few decades ago.

Substantial though these transformations are, the American environment remains significantly degraded in critical respects. More than 60 percent of the U.S. population—more than 186 million Americans—live in 390 counties where unhealthful levels of either ozone or particulate pollution still prevail.[15] More than half the total area of the nation's biologically essential estuaries and almost half the nation's river miles are considered unacceptably polluted. The primary cause of this water degradation is still largely unregulated. Although testing may now be required to assess the public health risk from newly manufactured chemicals, surprisingly little information is available about the extent to which Americans are exposed to thousands of existing chemicals or about the possible health risks involved. Federal government estimates suggest that information on public exposure is available for less than 6 percent of more than 1,400 naturally occurring and manufactured chemicals considered to pose a human health threat.[16] The EPA has been able to assess the public health risks for an even smaller proportion of the about 700 new chemicals introduced annually into commerce and industry. "EPA's review of new chemicals provides only limited assurance that health and environmental risks are identified," according to a report by the U.S. Governmental Accountability Office (GAO; formerly the Government Accounting Office), "because the agency has limited information with which to review them."[17] In fact, one of the most compelling national environmental problems is the pervasive lack of reliable scientific information about current environmental quality and human exposure to environmental contaminants—data that are absolutely essential for sound environmental policy making. When environmental scientists convened in 1998 to create the first comprehensive, detailed assessment of the nation's environmental conditions, they discovered that they lacked sufficient information for almost half of the indicators considered essential to adequately characterize national environmental quality.[18]

It is increasingly apparent that the scope and scale of this ecological degradation were often gravely underestimated and that the social and economic costs of pollution regulation were frequently miscalculated badly when the nation's major environmental policies were enacted. For instance, when Congress wrote legislation in 1976 requiring the EPA to ban or regulate any chemicals posing an unreasonable risk to human health, it did not anticipate that more than 62,000 chemical substances might have to be evaluated to determine their toxicity. Nor did Congress predict when it wrote the Comprehensive Environmental Response, Compensation, and Liability Act of 1980 (CERCLA, popularly known as Superfund) to clean up the nation's worst abandoned chemical waste sites that more than 40,000 sites would be discovered by 2007, that 500 new sites would be identified annually, and that the initial funding would be virtually exhausted by the mid-1990s, thus requiring annual additional appropriations of $1.2 billion through at least 2010.[19] Similar examples of this sort are found in every domain of environmental concern. We know now that the seemingly inexorable expansion in the scale and costs of environmental restoration is often the consequence of better environmental monitoring and research revealing, often to considerable surprise, the true reach and complexity of environmental problems. These issues, and more, are inevitable yet essential to policy making in a democratic society. Thus, environmental protection is a work in progress.

The Evolution of American Environmentalism

"When President [Richard] Nixon and his staff walked into the White House on January 20, 1969," writes a Nixon adviser, "we were totally unprepared for the tidal wave of public opinion in favor of cleaning the nation's environment that was about to engulf us." What followed was no less a surprise. "Only 17 months after the election, on April 22, 1970, the country celebrated Earth Day, with a national outpouring of concern for cleaning up the environment. Politicians of both parties jumped on the issue. So many politicians were on the stump on Earth Day that Congress was forced to close down. The oratory, one of the wire services observed, was "as thick as smog at rush hour."[20]

That first Earth Day in April 1970 was the big bang of U.S. environmental politics, launching the country on a sweeping social learning curve about ecological management never before experienced or attempted in any other nation. No challenge has been more fundamental to American environmentalism since Earth Day 1970 than the constructive adaptation of the original vision of environmental conservation and a renewal, once written into law and embedded into the political and economic structure of American life, to domestic and global changes.

The Environmental Decade: From Richard Nixon to Ronald Reagan

The 1970s, the decade spanning the presidencies of Richard Nixon, Gerald Ford, and Jimmy Carter, remains the most remarkably creative legislative period in the history of American environmentalism.[21] During this decade, almost all of the major environmental laws, federal environmental regulatory institutions, and environmental interest groups that now define the contours of the nation's environmental politics and policy appeared.

Richard Nixon's contribution to American environmentalism is enormously important and curious. A Republican, Nixon himself was no environmentalist, nor were most congressional Republicans. But, both congressional parties recognized the enormous political capital to be gained by riding the crest of the upwelling public concern for environmental protection. In Congress, a vigorous, broad coalition of Democrats and Republicans in both chambers collaborated in creating the legislative majorities essential to firmly establish the legal and political foundations of the U.S. environmental era.[22]

By the time Richard Nixon's presidency abruptly ended in 1974, Congress had written the National Environmental Policy Act of 1969 (NEPA), which required all federal agencies to prepare environmental impact statements for any significant actions affecting the environment, declared a national policy "to encourage productive and enjoyable harmony between man and his environment," and created the Council on Environmental Quality (CEQ) within the White House to advise the president on environmental matters. During this period, the Clean Air Amendments of 1970 for the first time mandated national air pollution standards and regulatory laws to enforce them. Two years later, the Federal Water Pollution Control Act Amendments of 1972 (Clean Water Act) set national water quality goals, established a national pollution discharge permit system, and created federal grants to the states to improve municipal waste treatment plants. To administer these new laws, Nixon created by executive order the EPA, the largest federal regulatory agency and the first of its kind in any national government.

This cascade of environmental legislation continued with the Coastal Zone Management Act (1972), creating federal grants to the states to establish coastal zone management plans under federal guidelines. The Endangered Species Act (1973) broadened federal authority to protect all endangered and threatened species; the Safe Drinking Water Act (1974) authorized the federal government for the first time to set standards protecting the quality of the nation's drinking water. During Jimmy Carter's tumultuous presidential term (1977–1981), the catalog of federal environmental legislation was further enlarged with the addition of the Toxic

Substances Control Act of 1976 (TSCA), requiring premarket testing of chemical substances and authorizing the EPA to regulate or ban the manufacture, sale, and use of chemicals posing "an unreasonable risk of injury to health or to the environment," and the Resource Conservation and Recovery Act of 1976 (RCRA), requiring the EPA to set national standards for hazardous waste treatment, storage, and disposal.

By the time Jimmy Carter entered the White House in 1977, public support for environmental protection had become so broadly and deeply founded that it was, in effect, now part of the national consensus—that array of issues publicly accepted as an essential and priority concern of government. Jimmy Carter portrayed himself firmly as environmentalist and actively courted the environmentalist vote in his 1976 campaign. Environmentalists, however, anticipated an outpouring of successful new White House environmental initiatives and legislative accomplishments that never quite materialized.[23] Carter's term began well enough with his successful promotion of the Surface Mining Control and Reclamation Act (1977), establishing for the first time federal standards for strip mining and requiring mine operators to environmentally restore mined lands. Carter was also instrumental in the congressional passage of amendments to the Clean Air Act (CAA) and Clean Water Act in 1977. Powerfully aided by national revelation of the extensive, buried, toxic waste dump discovered under the suburban settlement at New York's Love Canal, Carter was able to collaborate with Congress in the creation of CERCLA (or Superfund).

Carter's administration was beset from the outset by the energy crisis, created earlier when the Organization of Petroleum Exporting Countries (OPEC) in 1973 imposed an embargo on American imports of Middle Eastern petroleum.[24] The economic shock of the embargo and the political turbulence in its aftermath compelled the federal government for the first time since World War II to regulate domestic petroleum prices and supply, to set energy-efficiency standards for transportation and consumer products, and to create a national energy plan. Carter proposed and Congress enacted legislation establishing the new Department of Energy (DOE). The energy crisis also plunged the Carter administration into the inherently contentious and unpopular business of regulating national energy consumption, thus setting the stage for the bitterly adversarial environmental politics of the 1980s.

The Politics of Deadlock: From Ronald Reagan to George W. Bush

The Reagan and George Bush presidential years (1981–1993) rise like a great divide between environmental eras. The environmental movement had prospered through the 1970s. That changed with the advent of the Reagan administration (1981–1989). Reagan and his advisers, abetted by a new cadre of sympathetic congressional Republicans and the collapse of bipartisan congressional environmentalism, believed they had been elected to bring regulatory relief to the U.S. economy, and environmental regulations were an early priority on their hit list of laws needing regulatory reform. The environmental movement regarded the Reagan administration as the most environmentally hostile in a half century and Reagan's regulatory reform as the cutting edge of an implacable assault on the institutional foundations of federal environmental laws enacted during the 1970s.[25]

The environmental movement, thrown on the defensive, expended most of its energy and resources defending the legislative and administrative achievements of the Environmental Decade from President Reagan's regulatory relief. The Reagan years severely tested the foundations of the environmental movement. Although the foundations held, little was done to advance the implementation of existing policies or to address new and urgent environmental issues.

Accompanied by polarizing partisan infighting and protracted legislative delays, Congress was able to pass important amendments to the Clean Water Act, the Safe Drinking Water Act, Superfund, and the RCRA. What seemed perhaps the most significant legislative achievement of the turbulent Reagan years was the Nuclear Waste Policy Act of 1982, which established a national plan for the highly contentious, permanent disposal of high-grade nuclear waste and authorized the Energy Department to implement a strategy for constructing and operating geological repositories for the mounting volume of domestic commercial nuclear power wastes. The act soon proved so politically vexing—no state wanted the waste—that Congress abandoned the strategy in 1987 and awarded the waste site to a very unhappy Nevada. The future of commercial nuclear power seemed to plunge from bleak to barren when the deadly 1984 reactor meltdowns at the Soviet Union's Chernobyl nuclear power facility released a catastrophic cloud of high levels of atmospheric radioactivity over the Soviet Union and its adjacent European neighbors.

President George Bush (1989–1993) awakened in the environmental movement expectations of major reform and seemed to bring to the White House a more sympathetic and active environmentalism after the Reagan years. Bush's performance never kept his promise to be the environmental president, but his administration ended the pernicious policy impasse of the Reagan years. The EPA's morale and resources, severely depleted during the Reagan years, improved. The Bush administration sponsored and adeptly promoted the CAA Amendments of 1990, a long-overdue reform of the CAA of 1970. The Energy Policy Act of 1992 for the first time created a comprehensive federal energy plan to reduce U.S. dependence on imported oil, encouraged energy efficiency and conservation, and promoted renewable energy.

The environmental movement expected much of Bill Clinton, especially as then-Vice President Al Gore was an outspoken environmentalist and Clinton had cultivated the environmentalist vote. In the end, the Clinton administration was distinguished more by its ambitions than by its accomplishments.[26] Clinton generally reinvigorated environmental regulation and installed aggressive environmentalist administrators in strategic executive agencies such as the Department of the Interior and the EPA. He revived U.S. engagement in international environmental policy making, eventually committing the United States to the Kyoto Protocol to control global climate warming (which the U.S. Senate, for its part, refused to ratify).

But, Clinton confronted throughout most of his administration a hostile Republican congressional majority that thwarted most of his legislative initiatives. Moreover, during his second term (1997–2001), Clinton was increasingly preoccupied with the bitterly divisive congressional battle over his impeachment, and the White House environmental agenda was all but ignored. [27]

Confrontation Renewed: The Second Bush Presidency

Then came Republican George W. Bush (2001–2009). To the wary environmental movement, Bush's succession to the White House seemed to announce a profoundly unsettling new regime emerging from the shadows of the bitterly remembered Reagan administration and enthusiastically embracing its environmental attitudes. The environmental movement and most passionate environmentalists vigorously opposed Bush's election, even though Bush strongly represented himself as a moderate environmentalist, a prudent reformer rather than an antienvironmental zealot.

Nonetheless, Bush's relationship with the environmental movement was confrontational from the outset. His appointment of individuals closely associated with energy production and natural resource consumption to strategic leadership positions in the executive branch, especially in the Department of the Interior and the DOE, and the close association of Vice President Dick Cheney with the oil and gas industry provoked deep misgivings among environmentalists. Subsequent events, including the president's energy plan; his persistent efforts to open federal lands, particularly the Arctic National Wildlife Refuge, to energy exploration; and his repudiation of an earlier commitment to an international agreement combating global climate warming seemed to confirm the dark suspicions about his environmental sensibilities already pervasive among environmental organizations.[28] The Energy Policy Act of 2005 and the subsequent Energy Independence and Security Act of 2009 exemplified the Bush administration's ambitious effort to create a long-term energy strategy for the United States. The 2005 legislation was intended to increase the supply of energy resources; improve energy efficiency; and accelerate energy research, development, and exploration with a heavy reliance on fossil fuels and nuclear power. The Energy Independence and Security Act set the mandated national automobile fuel-economy standard at 35 miles per gallon by 2020 and sought to increase the availability of alternative fuels, especially biofuels. Although the environmental community generally welcomed the initiatives aimed at increasing energy efficiency and developing renewable energy resources, environmentalists continued to criticize the heavy emphasis on accelerated fossil fuel exploration, new commercial nuclear power, and coal-fired utilities in the Energy Independence and Security Act.

During the Bush administration, the EPA did strengthen national air pollution controls on particulates and mercury emissions, but to environmentalists, these and other administration initiatives were too laggard and limited. Environmentalists also complained that the Bush administration routinely suppressed or rewrote scientific data to satisfy its ideological prejudices on environmental issues. As U.S. involvement and public frustration with the war in Iraq escalated, environmental affairs seemed increasingly marginalized in the White House—Republican strategists, in any case, had largely conceded the environmentalist vote to the Democrats. Christie Todd Whitman, Bush's first EPA administrator, had complained at the end of her term that the Bush administration seemed condemned to "an eternal fistfight" with environmental groups.[29] Her remark became prophetic.

A Collision of Expectations: The Obama Presidency

The election of Barack Obama and the return of Democratic majorities to both congressional chambers in 2009 seemed to signify a renewed White House commitment to innovative, new environmental initiatives and a relief from the adversarial, polarizing environmental legislative politics of the Bush administration. Obama had actively and successfully cultivated the environmentalist vote, pledging his administration to new policy initiatives concerning global climate change, energy conservation, and domestic pollution regulation. This generous agenda of ambitious environmental programs, legislation, and regulations anticipated by environmentalist leaders, however, never quite materialized. The Obama administration was confronted from its beginning with a daunting cascade of political and economic events that confounded Obama's environmental agenda and compelled the White House to invest enormous political capital and energy in resolving compelling issues that often conflicted with the expectations of environmentalist leaders.

Despite the steady drumbeat of frustrated environmentalist criticism, the Obama administration did create a substantial record of environmental achievements. Obama's early appointment of Lisa P. Jackson, director of the New Jersey Department of Environmental Protection and an experienced EPA official, as EPA administrator seemed to environmentalists a sure portent that the Obama White House meant to give environmental issues a high priority. This was followed by the administration's American Recovery and Reinvestment Act of 2009, the massive economic recovery program that included more than $100 billion in spending, tax incentives, and loan guarantees to promote energy efficiency, renewable energy development, fuel-efficient cars, and control of climate-warming emissions, among other programs appealing to environmentalists. The administration aggressively promoted new congressional initiatives to create a regulatory program to control domestic climate-warming emissions. The EPA enacted numerous new and revised environmental regulatory programs, including revised regulations to limit mercury emissions from industrial fossil fuel combustion, further regulations to improve control of other toxic air pollutants, and new, stricter mileage standards for automobiles and light trucks. White House guidelines were written to strengthen protection of federal scientific research and regulation from White House political interference—an issue of great concern to the environmentalist and scientific community throughout the previous Bush administration.

Obama, however, confronted massive challenges in achieving the ambitious environmental record he envisioned and environmentalists expected. The president inherited the most severe economic recession since the Great Depression and was compelled to weaken or eliminate many regulatory and legislative environmental initiatives in order to reduce federal expenditures and regulatory costs. Federal budget appropriations that might have underwritten new environmental initiatives had to be invested, instead, in promoting economic growth and generating new jobs. Moreover, the 2010 congressional elections returned to the House of Representatives a Republican majority largely hostile to most White House environmental initiatives and preoccupied with reducing federal spending and regulation. A divided congress virtually assured legislative deadlock and the failure of almost all Obama's environmental legislative proposals. Adding to these potent impediments to White House environmental initiatives was the steeply rising cost of gasoline at the pump, a sluggish economic recovery, new public concerns about the adequacy of domestic carbon fuels, and a compelling pressure on the White House to deal with steeply rising domestic health costs.

Thus, the Obama administration, caught between conflicting demands to revive a severely weakened economy, to invent strategies to achieve legislative leadership in a bitterly divided Congress, and to satisfy the environmentalist expectations it had so diligently cultivated, was almost predestined to create disappointment and division within the environmentalist community. Among other matters, the White House effort to enact new legislation to control climate-warming emissions was a complete failure despite an enormous investment of time and political resources. The EPA postponed its widely anticipated reform of regulations controlling atmospheric ozone and weakened its initial plan to strengthen regulation of atmospheric soot (particulates). The White House continued to support limited development of new commercial nuclear power and failed to prevent continued planning of the Keystone XL pipeline to transport petroleum from shale oil from Canada across to the United States to the Gulf of Mexico. Facing continuing budget deficits, the administration reduced the EPA's budget for three successive years.[30]

As the 2012 presidential election approached, it seemed apparent that Obama faced a considerable challenge in inspiring environmentalists and their allies to rally to his reelection campaign with the strength and enthusiasm of 2008. Despite division and dissensus among themselves concerning Obama's accomplishments; however, environmentalist leaders also found little appealing about Republican presidential candidate Mitt Romney or his platform.

Ongoing Challenges: Present and Future

On that first Earth Day in 1970, more than half the Americans living today had not been born. A whole new generation has since matured, and with that generation, U.S. environmental politics has been, and continues to be, transformed. More than a decade into the 21st century, Americans now have more than 40 years of collective experience with unprecedented experimentation in environmental management. The ultimate test of the ambitious U.S. regime of environmental regulation will be not how well it was conceived but how well it endures. That endurance depends largely on how well American science, political culture, and environmental leadership can learn from past experience and creatively apply the lessons learned to several profound problems now recognized as inherent in all environmental policy making—issues that run as deep and defining themes throughout every chapter in this book.

Keeping Environmentalism Contemporary

The environmental movement is now almost a half century old. Environmentalism is no longer the fresh, growing, politically ascending force that propelled environmental issues to unprecedented importance in national politics and policy. While environmental pollution in all respects remains an imperative national problem, environmental organizations face challenges that come with a now-familiar presence among the nation's major advocacy groups: assuring that environmental issues remain a priority on the national policy agenda, sustaining a large, politically robust membership base, and keeping their messages politically relevant to a new generation of Americans.

These challenges are especially significant because the memberships of many major environmental organizations are aging. (One of the largest and most influential conservation organizations, for example, reported that the average age of their membership is 65, and only 5 percent of its million members are younger than 50.)[31] In politics, moreover, public perceptions can be as important—often more important—than environmental realities in creating priority for environmentalism on the national policy agenda. Many environmental problems, such as visibly polluted air and water, public health alarms about pesticide exposures, and threatening toxic waste sites that effectively dramatized the immediate need for environmental regulation now may seem—whatever the reality—less publicly important. Many newer, profoundly important environmental issues such as global climate warming or the relentless decline in the quality and quantity of freshwater are difficult to characterize with a powerful, persuasive imagery that makes them immediately important and relevant to the public. Moreover, a sustained economic recession has meant less membership and diminished financial contributions to many important environmental organizations.

Thus, among the nation's environmental leadership, a growing, often heated discussion has evolved concerning whether environmentalist language is stale, the issues no longer compelling, and the major advocacy groups too unimaginative and complacent about delivering their political messages. A vigorous constituency within the environmental community is advocating new strategies and a fresh language to inspire a more contemporary image and wider public appeal for environmentalism, especially among the young, ethnic minorities, the economically underprivileged, and middle-income Americans economically struggling through the recession. The transcendent issue is ultimately the continuing vitality and importance of environmentalism in shaping future American public policy.

Implementation Issues

The character and pace of policy implementation change continually in response to shifting public moods; to ebbs and flows in crucial resources such as money and personnel invested in carrying out environmental policies; to changes in political party control of Congress, the White House, and state governments; and to other changes discussed in later chapters. In short, policy implementation is unfolding and variable, powerfully driven by economic, political, and cultural forces. Practically every important environmental ill has been targeted by a major federal law, but delays and difficulties in program implementation routinely impede enforcement. The majority of important environmental laws have been implemented at a plodding pace, and portions of all the laws exhibit regulatory rigor mortis. Although practically all factions agree on the need for a remedy, a laggardly pace is the norm.

One reason for this plodding pace is the growing complexity of the regulatory process. The average size of major environmental statutes has inflated from about 50 pages in the 1970s to more than 500 pages currently. The original CAA (1970) was 68 pages, the CAA Amendments of 1990 weighed in at 788 pages, and the regulations required for their implementation will exceed 10,000 pages. Like an augury of the future, the American Clean Energy and Security Act (2009), the first climate change regulatory legislation to be proposed by the House of Representatives, bloated to more than 1,400 pages. To create the elephantine regulations necessary to implement these complex laws and to apply the procedures in the appropriate instances can consume an enormous amount of time, as subsequent chapters in this book reveal. The regulation of toxic substances provides an illustration. The average time needed for the complete testing of 16 common chemicals required by TSCA (1976)—a small fraction of the total that must be evaluated under the law—from their initial selection through the final EPA review of the test data has been eight years.[32]

Another important source of regulatory delay is the increasing mismatch between the responsibilities assigned to environmental agencies and the budgetary resources required to accomplish them. Although the EPA's workload has increased enormously since its creation in 1970, its budget has failed to keep pace. At the beginning of George W. Bush's administration, for instance, the EPA's annual appropriations were 25 percent below the 1980 level and shrank an additional 12 percent by 2009, when measured in constant dollars (that is, after adjustment for inflation).[33] Decades of underfunding has left the EPA overwhelmed by the scientific and administrative complexity of its regulatory tasks. For example, by 1990, the EPA was able to reassess and register only 31 of more than 20,000 older pesticides whose reevaluations had been ordered by Congress as long ago as 1972 and again in 1988. Despite a congressionally mandated deadline of 1997 to complete the job, the GAO reported that "the program may not be completed until 2006"—and it wasn't completed then.

Enforcement of most environmental legislation also depends on voluntary compliance by regulated interests, public and private, but the responsible federal and state agencies often lack the resources to monitor compliance with the law. Few states, for example, routinely inspect public and private drinking water systems, even though such inspections are required by the Safe Drinking Water Act (1974). One half of the nation's 59,000 large water systems and one fifth of the 139,000 small ones are not monitored to ensure that water is not contaminated by sewage or pesticide runoff.[34] Quite often, the information essential to effective regulation is missing or fragmentary, and the available information is often surprisingly haphazard. Many states, for instance, lack the technical resources to develop numerical standards for many groundwater contaminants and, instead, depend on evidence of environmental damage or public health risks before acting to control these substances.

Economic growth and population expansion often diminish the effectiveness of pollution controls over time. The automobile emission controls and reduced lead levels in gasoline required by the CAA together have lowered the average new car's hydrocarbon and carbon monoxide emissions significantly. But, the number of automobiles in the United States has increased from 80.4 million in 1970 to 250 million by 2010. This vehicle population explosion counteracts the emission reductions achieved for individual vehicles and leads eventually to widespread urban violations of federal air-quality standards.

Other potent impediments to program implementation include the litigation virtually predestined for any major regulation, difficult coordination between state and federal governments, bureaucratic infighting, and more. Collectively, these implementation problems constitute one of the most urgent, and daunting, political and administrative tasks of the 21st century.

Rising Costs

By most estimates, the national cost of environmental regulation does not seem excessive, particularly when compared with estimated economic benefits, or likely to inhibit healthy economic growth.[35] Currently, the United States spends about $120 billion annually for environmental control or about 2 percent of the gross national product.[36] Overall, the annual proportion of national expenditures invested in pollution control appears to have decreased since 1990.[37] Although aggregate expenditures increased only moderately after 2000, these expenditures conceal troublesome details. The cost of individual regulatory programs is soaring, often inflicting heavy, unanticipated costs on specific economic sectors, depleting regulatory resources, and compelling a search for scarce, new funding sources, as the following list exemplifies:

- *Superfund* was created to clean up the nation's numerous abandoned hazardous waste sites. After originally authorizing $1.6 billion for the project, Congress was compelled in the mid-1980s to increase spending to $15.2 billion, and estimates now suggest the program will require annual congressional supplements of at least $1.5 billion after 2010.[38]

- *Diesel fuel regulations for school buses* are soon to be proposed by the federal government and are already required in some states. Meeting the standard can cost from $7,500 to $100,000 per bus. California, the first state to require stricter standards, reportedly spent $715 million to implement the regulations.[39]
- *Federal storm water runoff regulations* will require the District of Columbia to spend $1.9 billion to completely renovate its antiquated sewer system.[40]

The roster of inflationary programs has become a virtual catalog of the nation's major environmental laws. Unanticipated environmental problems, unexpected scientific complexities, and inexperience with new regulations are the common causes of massive cost overruns. Proponents of regulatory programs, particularly the congressional committees and staff writing the laws, are often ignorant (sometimes intentionally) about hidden costs. The litany of other inflationary provocations includes administrative delay, litigation, bureaucratic bungling, waste, missing information, and political obstruction. Whatever the reasons, excessive costs divert public and private capital from more productive investment, promote economic inefficiency, impair competitiveness in some industries, and increase consumer costs. Bloated budgets become a cudgel in the hands of opponents eager to beat back demands for essential improvements in environmental management.

Environmentalists traditionally have approached discussions about the cost of environmental regulation with considerable wariness. They suspect, often correctly, that the estimates of regulatory costs produced by businesses or other regulated interests are inflated deliberately. (However, they are not equally dubious about the considerably lower estimates they usually produce.) They also believe that benefit–cost comparisons applied to environmental policies are usually biased because it is much easier to monetize the costs of regulation than the benefits. Even more controversial is the problem of ecological valuation—assigning a value to wetlands, for example, when deciding whether to convert them to commercial development or to protect an endangered species whose habitat is threatened. Moreover, many environmentalists consider it ethically irresponsible to allow economic costs to weigh heavily in making environmental regulations.

But, spiraling costs are changing traditional environmental attitudes. Leaving aside predictable and usually unresolvable arguments over the "real" costs of environmental regulations, the fact of sharply rising costs has compelled many major environmental leaders to seek creative strategies for reducing the expense and to collaborate in this effort with the businesses and industries being regulated. This search for creative, new approaches has affected the current policy debate in several ways. First, proposals to shift the primary objective of many current pollution laws, such as the CAA, from eliminating pollution to *reducing* exposure to the pollutants have become a major reform issue. Proponents of reform believe that reducing the risk of exposure, rather than attempting to eliminate pollutants, is a far less expensive and more technologically feasible objective. Second, rising regulatory costs have focused more attention on eliminating pollutants (referred to as pollution prevention) in production processes as an alternative to "end-of-the-pipe" pollution treatment. Finally, many environmental leaders and organizations have become more receptive to economic incentives and other market strategies as substitutes for traditional administrative procedures in securing compliance with environmental regulations on the assumption that market approaches may be more economically efficient and environmentally effective. Recently, national and international trading in "emission rights" has become an increasingly popular proposal by those favoring market-oriented strategies for pollution control.

Still, any debate about the importance of economic considerations in environmental regulation excites an ideological passion among many environmental leaders and groups that profoundly believe environmental values must never be compromised by marketplace logic. The environmental movement probably will remain divided over the wisdom of economic reform. Reform will come anyway, slowly and divisively.

Evolving Science and Technology

When the political leadership of American environmentalism set out its initial policy agenda following Earth Day 1970, the ozone hole, global climate warming, genetically altered foods, endocrine disrupters, leaking underground toxic storage tanks, ionizing radiation, indoor air pollution, and a multitude of other environmental issues—as well as many thousands of chemicals now common in U.S. commerce and industry—were unimagined or unknown. All these matters, and many more currently on the environmental movement's priority list, are largely the product of scientific research in the past several decades. In later chapters, we observe how science contributes constructively to environmental management through, for example, the discovery of environmentally benign substitutes for more harmful chemicals such as chlorofluorocarbons (CFCs). But, the relentless evolution of scientific research can also frustrate, confuse, and discredit existing environmental policy by producing all sorts of new and unexpected discoveries. For example, 25 years after the EPA set the original air pollution standard for airborne particulates, a serious public health problem, the agency had to revise the standard, making it significantly more stringent. The result was enormous new public and private costs, attended by a nasty political backlash, largely because later research convincingly demonstrated that the earlier standard had been based on insufficient data—although it was the best available at the time.

Ironically, the environmental movement's success often contributes inadvertently to this disruptive research. Environmental advocacy has greatly enlarged the resources and productivity of U.S. environmental science, thereby accelerating the pace of new discoveries that often reveal deficiencies in the scientific basis of existing environmental policy.

This rising tide of ecological science poses several continuing challenges to environmental scientists and policy makers. First, it can produce new data indicating that prior policy decisions may have been based on inadequate information and must be revised—perhaps with great political or legal difficulty and at considerable expense. Policy makers can easily and unjustly appear to have been ignorant, or impetuous, for having made decisions (although often based on the best currently available information and frequently under strong public pressure) that later and better research shows were incorrect. For example, to meet the public health standards of the CAA, the EPA in 2006 slightly lowered the short-term threshold for public exposure to particulates (soot) as a result of scientific research conducted since the original standard had been set several decades ago. Although the new standard, described by the EPA as "the most health-protective in U.S. history," is assumed to create from $9 billion to $70 billion in long-term health and visibility benefits, it is also estimated to cost electric utilities alone about $400 million yearly to implement.[41]

Scientific research can also produce ambiguous, fragmentary, or contradictory data concerning the existence or extent of an environmental problem—especially at an early stage in the research—at a time when policy makers feel compelled to do something about the issue. Sometimes a solution—or the appearance of one—seems so urgent that policy makers believe that they cannot wait for additional research, or perhaps that additional research may never satisfactorily resolve the issue because the impact of an environmental regulation will remain inconclusive. The continuing scientific ambiguity about the ecological impact of human-made chemicals mimicking human hormones (often called endocrine disrupters) and the persisting controversy about the ecological impact of species loss illustrate this sort of science problem.

Finally, scientific research can complicate environmental policy making and, in the process, drive up the cost and time involved in remedying environmental ills by disclosing, instead of timely or quick answers to an ecological problem, the unanticipated need for new information. Pentagon planners call these discoveries the *unk-unks*—the unknown unknowns, the kinds of information we don't know are needed until a problem is investigated. Consider, for instance, the experience of scientists trying to explain the sudden dramatic increase in fish kills between .1991 and 1993 in North Carolina's vast estuaries. Unprecedented millions of fish were floating to the water surface with large, bleeding sores, often accompanied by a strange smell that burned the eyes and throat—not the smell of decaying fish. At first, investigators assumed the familiar explanation—lack of dissolved oxygen in the water, a seasonal deficiency in the estuarine environment that is sometimes fatal to fish. But, additional study disclosed no severe oxygen deficiency. Instead, extensive fish biopsies gradually revealed something wholly unexpected—the presence of enormous quantities of a tiny, one-celled creature, a dinoflagellate of the species *Pfiesteria piscicida,* an apparently harmless organism seldom studied and never associated with extensive fish kills. So, biologists began to observe *Pfiesteria* habits intensively. They discovered that, when estuarine nutrient levels of nitrogen and phosphorous increased significantly, *Pfiesteria* can transform into a murderous organism with a personality akin to the star of the science fiction movie *Alien,* multiplying in staggering numbers and aggressively attacking and consuming huge fish populations. The *Pfiesteria,* in turn, were stimulated to multiply by the high nutrient levels in the water, apparently caused by agricultural and animal feedlot runoff. Thus, an unk-unk—in this case, the complete life cycle of *Pfiesteria*—was unexpectedly uncovered in the course of investigating a fish kill and became a critical component in understanding and eliminating the problem itself.[42]

Sustainable Development and Ecosystem Management

Presently underway between the Florida Keys and Orlando, Florida, is what is predicted to be the largest, most expensive, and most scientifically complex environmental restoration project ever attempted anywhere. The South Florida Ecosystem Restoration Project, popularly called the Everglades Restoration, intends to restore and protect for future generations the ecologically endangered Everglades, a globally unique, irreplaceable, subtropical ecosystem gravely damaged by urban development and agricultural cultivation. The project embraces 25,000 square miles of Florida's interior, coastal lands, and water. It will cost more than $10.9 billion and require at least 30 years to complete—if the plan is successful.[43] The Everglades Restoration is one of a half dozen massive federal ecosystem management projects underway across the United States. These projects are markers along the way of a profound transformation in environmental policy associated with the growing importance of sustainable development as a foundation for environmental management.

The Challenge of Sustainability

The 1987 publication of *Our Common Future* (often called the Brundtland Report) by the World Commission on Environment and Development (WCED) rapidly advanced an already growing concern with sustainable development into a transcendent goal for the international environmental movement. The WCED's definition of *sustainable development* as "meeting the needs of the present without compromising the ability of future generations to meet their own needs"[44] has become virtually synonymous with the concept itself. Over time, as Jonathan M. Harris, an international environmental scholar, has observed, this definition has been interpreted to include three components:

- *Economic:* "An economically sustainable system must be able to produce goods and services on a continuing basis, to maintain manageable levels of government and external debt, and to avoid extreme sectoral imbalances which damage agricultural and industrial production."
- *Social:* "A socially sustainable system must achieve distributional equity, adequate provision for social services including health and education, gender equality, and political accountability and participation."
- *Environmental:* "An environmentally sustainable system must maintain a stable resource base, avoiding over-exploitation of renewable resource systems . . . and depleting non-renewable resources. . . . This includes maintenance of biodiversity, atmospheric stability, and other ecosystem functions."[45]

A multitude of governmental entities, private institutions, and advocacy organizations worldwide (most created since 1990) testify to the expanding impact of sustainable development as a strategic goal for environmental policy and politics. In 1992, the United Nations Commission on Sustainable Development was created, and the next year President Clinton signed an executive order creating the President's Council on Sustainable Development, directed by then Vice President Gore.[46] In 1996, the EPA created its Sustainable Communities Network. The global salience of sustainability as an environmental concern was reaffirmed in 2002 by the United Nations World Summit on Sustainable Development in Johannesburg, South Africa. By 2007, an international directory listed 51,500 organizations claiming some concern for sustainable development. A U.S. national directory cited more than 2,700 private or public entities involved with environmental sustainability.[47]

The concept of sustainable development, however, is also loaded with ambiguities that can reduce it to a cliché weighted with goals that can seem competitive, even contradictory. Protection of nonrenewable resources, for instance, may appear inconsistent with sustained economic production. Adequate provision of health and education services may appear to require reduction of public spending to protect biodiversity. Some of the most divisive political controversies within the environmental movement arise over these issues.

Implementing Sustainability: Ecosystem Management

Despite the difficulties, policies intended to promote sustainability are being created and implemented through public policy at all U.S. governmental levels. One significant illustration is the growing importance of ecosystem management in federal resource planning. The rapid development of environmental science and increasing experience with environmental policy making has compelled a realization that a greater emphasis must be given to the inherent ecological value of natural resources and that successful ecological restoration often requires planning on a vast spatial and temporal scale never previously attempted.

A fundamental principle of ecosystem management is that wise resource use must involve "the integration of ecological, economic, and social principles to manage biological and physical systems in a manner safeguarding the long term sustainability, natural diversity, and productivity of the landscape." This means that the primary goal of natural resource planning should be "to develop and implement management that conserves, restores and maintains the ecological integrity, productivity, and biological diversity of public lands."[48] In short, a natural resource should not be managed primarily to satisfy human economic interests nor valued mostly in dollar terms. From this perspective, forests, rivers, wetlands, and other natural resources such as the Everglades should be administered in a manner protecting *all* their natural benefits, including as habitats for fish and wildlife; as clean drinking water for communities; and for wood, fiber, forage, and ecological functions as well as for human recreational and economic uses.

A second premise of ecosystem management is that large, endangered natural systems such as river valleys, forestlands, and wetlands—often the most ecologically valuable natural resources—should be restored or protected as whole, interrelated ecosystems, even if they are geographically enormous, rather than divided geographically and managed by different agencies and governments with different missions and often conflicting policies.

Sustainable development through ecosystem management is also politically contentious and inherently risky in the United States. It seems to defy 200 years of past federal, state, and local natural resource planning, with its deeply embedded assumption that government should manage natural resources primarily for their economic value and human utility. Powerful private interests, such as energy producers, timber companies, livestock managers, land developers, recreation industries, and their allies, compete relentlessly for access to natural resources administered by public agencies. Indeed, almost every economic interest associated with natural resource consumption strives persistently to preempt competing claims on such resources. Furthermore, numerous governmental bureaucracies responsible for public resource management, agencies whose historical mission has been to facilitate private access to resources in the public domain, cannot easily adapt their deeply rooted organizational cultures to the newer ideas of ecosystem management and sustainable development. Moreover, many states are at best ambivalent about the new planning principles because the traditional economic exploitation of their natural resources, however ecologically disruptive it might be, also brought new jobs, increased tax revenues, and accelerated local economic development.

Plan for the Book

This chapter has introduced, broadly and briefly, the major themes that later chapters explore in more depth and detail. It has also provided a review of many significant events since Earth Day 1970 that define the political setting for environmental policy making today, thus creating a present sense of place in the rapidly evolving politics of American environmentalism. The chapters that follow progress from a broad overview of the major governmental institutions, private interests, and political forces shaping all environmental policy today to an increasingly sharp focus on the distinctive issues, actors, and interests involved with specific environmental problems.

Chapter 2 (Making Policy: The Process) describes the phases of the policy cycle that shape all major environmental policies. Included is an exploration of the influence of the U.S. Constitution and U.S. political culture on this process. Also discussed are the nature of environmental pressure groups and other stakeholders in the policy process and the important role of public opinion and the scientific community in policy making.

Chapter 3 (Making Policy: Institutions and Politics) describes the specific U.S. governmental institutions, private interests, and political forces engaged in environmental policy making. The narrative includes a discussion of the presidency, the important bureaucracies, Congress, and the courts. Also discussed is the importance of political events such as changing congressional majorities, economic growth or recession, and shifting public moods.

Almost all environmental policy making entails some common issues. Chapter 4 (Common Policy Challenges: Risk Assessment and Environmental Justice) explores two of the most scientifically contentious and politically controversial of these issues: risk analysis and environmental justice. Risk analysis is concerned with determining whether specific chemicals, industrial processes, consumer products, and environmental contaminants, among many other things, pose a significant threat to public health or the environment and, if they do, how they should be regulated. Environmental justice investigates whether various social groups, particularly minorities of color and economically disadvantaged individuals, are disproportionately exposed to environmental risks or denied reasonable opportunity to protect themselves from such risks.

Among the longest-running and least-resolvable conflicts in environmental policy making is over the economic cost and fairness of environmental regulations. Chapter 5 (More Choice: The Battle Over Regulatory Economics) looks at two major aspects of this issue: the use of benefit–cost analysis (BCA) to evaluate environmental regulations and proposals to replace current methods of environmental regulation with policies that rely on market forces to achieve results. Discussed are the major arguments and interests aligned on different sides of these issues together with evidence about the impact of proposed economic reforms when they have been instituted.

Chapter 6 (Command and Control in Action: Air and Water Pollution Regulation) describes the nation's major air and water pollution control laws and evaluates their impacts. The chapter explains how these laws illustrate the command-and-control style of regulation now common in the United States. Also described are the substantive elements of the CAA (1970) and the Federal Water Pollution Control Act Amendments (1972). The accomplishments and deficiencies resulting from these major air and water pollution laws are reviewed together with characteristic policy making challenges created by the scientific and economic requirements of air and water pollution control.

Chapter 7 (A Regulatory Thicket: Toxic and Hazardous Substances) focuses on the major regulatory legislation to control environmental dangers posed by chemical, biological, and radioactive agents. The major laws examined include the TSCA (1976), the RCRA (1974), and Superfund legislation. The chapter briefly describes the major elements of these important laws and examines their impacts in the context of determining whether they have accomplished their purpose to control the manufacture and distribution of ecologically harmful chemicals and to safely regulate toxic waste from the cradle to the grave.

Chapter 8 (Energy: America's Energy Politics in Transformation) describes the nation's primary energy resources and increasing reliance on fossil fuels together with the ecological, economic, and political risks entailed. The chapter focuses special attention on diminishing petroleum supplies, the attractions and environmental dangers associated with increased coal production, and the environmental problems linked to nuclear power. Also explored are future energy policy options and the ecological implications, especially in the contentious trade-off between coal and nuclear power as future energy sources and the challenges created by greater reliance on energy conservation and energy efficiency as alternatives to major reliance on traditional energy sources.

Chapter 9 (635 Million Acres of Politics: The Battle for Public Lands) focuses on the historic political battle over the use of more than 700 million acres of public land, mostly controlled by the federal government. The narrative examines the major economic and environmental interests engaged in a century-long battle over access to timber, natural gas, petroleum, grazing land, hydroelectric power, and other important resources on federal land. Described are the major federal agencies caught in the middle of these conflicts, such as the Department of the Interior and the U.S. Forest Service. The chapter also discusses the major legislation these agencies are expected to implement in managing these resources and the resulting problems, including the obstacles to achieving ecosystem management on federal lands.

Chapter 10 (Climate Change, Domestic Politics, and the Challenge of Global Policy Making) explains why the United States can no longer satisfactorily regulate or protect its own environment without a growing engagement in regional and international environmental policy making; it then reviews the nation's erratic involvement in global environmental policy making. Discussed are the ozone hole, acid precipitation, global climate warming, and sustainable development; these illustrate the compelling need for this international involvement and illuminate some of the major political opportunities and difficulties posed for the United States by international environmental diplomacy. Finally, the chapter identifies the implications of U.S. environmental diplomacy for achieving sustainable national and international development.

Conclusion

In calendar time, the presidential election of Barack Obama preceded the fifth decade of the American Environmental Era proclaimed in the 1970s. In political time, it commenced an uncertain season for environmentalists now deep into that era, a season of conflicting implications and richly contradictory experiences. From the perspective of policy making, a sense of frustration and impasse nurtured by the bitterly divisive conflict between organized environmentalism and the White House has permeated the era, yet evidence is abundant that environmental leaders have enormously enlarged the temporal and geographical scope of their policy vision to embrace sustainable development, ecosystem management, and global ecological restoration. Improvements in environmental quality have become increasingly apparent, and sometimes impressive, yet regulatory achievements fall gravely below expectations. Environmentalism has matured to the point where its organizational advocates can reflect critically on past experience and accept the need for rethinking and reforming their policy agendas, especially the need to moderate the escalating cost of environmental protection and to find more effective ways to implement pollution regulation. At the same time, the rapid progress of environmental science reveals with increasing acuteness the need to improve significantly the quality of the science base on which environmental policy is grounded. Environmentalism is now firmly rooted in U.S. political culture, yet its electoral force often seems surprisingly feeble.

In many ways, it is the best of times and the worst of times for environmentalism. In no other period has environmentalism seemed more politically potent, armed with powerful, organized advocacy, legislative authority, public approval, and scientific credibility and seasoned with political experience. Nevertheless, as this chapter amply demonstrates, at no time have the scientific and political challenges confronting the environmental movement seemed more formidable.

Suggested Readings

Andrews, Richard N. L. *Managing the Environment, Managing Ourselves: A History of American Environmental Policy.* 2nd ed. New Haven, CT: Yale University Press, 2006.

Daynes, Byron W., and Holly O. Hughes, *White House Politics and the Environment: Franklin D. Roosevelt to George W. Bush.* College Station: Texas A&M University, 2010.

Graham, Mary. *The Morning after Earth Day: Practical Environmental Politics.* Washington, DC: Brookings Institution Press, 1999.

Lomborg, Bjorn. *The Skeptical Environmentalist: Measuring the Real State of the World.* New York: Cambridge University Press, 2001.

Mazmanian, Daniel A., and Michael E. Kraft. *Toward Sustainable Communities: Transition and Transformations in Environmental Policy.* 2nd ed. Cambridge, MA: MIT Press, 2009.

Merchant, Carolyn. *American Environmental History: An Introduction.* New York: Columbia University Press, 2007.

Ophuls, William, and A. Stephen Boyan, Jr. *Ecology and the Politics of Scarcity Revisited: The Unraveling of the American Dream.* New York: W. H. Freeman, 1992.

Shabecoff, Philip. *A Fierce Green Fire: The American Environmental Movement.* Washington, DC: Island Press, 2003.

Simon, Julian L. *Hoodwinking the Nation.* Washington, DC: Cato Institute, 2000.

Notes

1. Tom Zeller, Jr., "Passions on Display at E.P.A. Meeting," available at http://green.blogs.nytimes.com/2010/07/23/passions-on-display-at-e-p-a-meeting/ (accessed February 10, 2012).
2. Mireya Navarro, "8,000 People? E.P.A. Defers Hearing on Fracking," available at http://green.blogs.nytimes.com/2010/08/10/8000-people-e-p-a-defers-hearing-on-fracking/ (accessed February 20, 2012).

3. U.S. Department of the Interior, 2012 Oil Shale and Tar Sands Programmatic EIS Information Center, "About Oil Shale," available at http://ostseis.anl.gov/guide/oilshale/ (accessed January 10, 2012).

4. Steve Kastenbaum, "Fracking in New York: Risk vs. Reward," *CNN News,* March 9, 2012, available at http://www.cnn.com/2012/03/09/us/new-york-fracking/index.html (accessed April 19, 2012).

5. Catherine Tsai, "Halliburton Executive Drinks Fracking Fluid," *Huff Post Green,* August 22, 2011, available at www.huffingtonpost.com/2011/08/22/halliburton-executive-drinks-fracking-fluid_n_933621.html (accessed January 28, 2012).

6. The National Academies, *Our Energy Sources: Emerging Technologies Alternatives to Conventional Oil,* available at http://needtoknow.nas.edu/energy/energy-sources/emerging-technologies/conventional-oil-alternatives.php (accessed October 5, 2011).

7. Dusty Horwitt, "Federal Scientists Warn NY of Fracking Risks," Environmental Working Group, February 29, 2012, available at www.ewg.org (accessed March 10, 2012)

8. Clifford Krauss and Tom Zeller, Jr., "When a Rig Moves in Next Door," *New York Times,* November 7, 2010, BU1.

9. Ibid.

10. Peter Applebome, "Drilling Debate in Cooperstown, N.Y., Is Personal," *New York Times* (New York Edition), October 29, 2011, A1.

11. Elana Schor, "Pipeline Projects Pack Economic Wallop for U.S.—Study," *E&E Reporter,* February 17, 2012, available at www.eenews.net/Greenwire/rss/2012/02/17/20 (accessed April 4, 2012).

12. U.S. DOE, "Producing Natural Gas From Shale," January 26, 2012, available at http://energy.gov/articles/producing-natural-gas-shale (accessed February 10, 2012).

13. Elizabeth Rosen, "Benefits of Fracking Could Be 'Magnificent,' Former Obama Administration Official Says," *Cornell Chronicle Online,* May 9, 2012, available at www.news.cornell.edu/stories/May12/DeutchCover.html (accessed July 10, 2012).

14. Norman J. Vig, "Making the Grade? OECD Environmental Performance Reviews: United States," *Environment* 48, no. 7 (2006): 40–43.

15. American Lung Association, "Executive Summary," *State of the Air 2009* (Washington, DC: American Lung Association, 2009), 6–10.

16. U.S. General Accounting Office (GAO), "Chemical Risk Assessment: Selected Federal Agencies, Procedures, Assumptions and Policies," Document no. GAO 01–810, Washington, DC, August 2001, 16.

17. GAO, *Chemical Regulation: Options Exist to Improve EPA's Ability to Assess Health Risks and Manage Its Chemical Review Program,* Report no. GAO-05–2005, Washington, DC, June 13, 2005, 1.

18. Robert O'Malley, Kent Davender-Bares, and William C. Clark, "'Better' Data: Not as Simple as It Might Seem," *Environment Magazine* (March 2003): 9–18.

19. Katherine Probst and David Konisky, *Superfund's Future: What Will It Cost? Executive Summary* (Washington, DC: Resources for the Future, 2001).

20. John C. Whitaker, "Earth Day Recollections: What It Was Like When the Movement Took Off," *EPA Journal* (July–August 1988), available at www.epa.gov/history/topics/earthday/10.htm (accessed December 7, 2009).

21. A comprehensive summary of federal environmental legislation since 1970 is found in Norman J. Vig and Michael E. Kraft, "Major Federal Laws on the Environment, 1969–2008," in *Environmental Policy: New Directions for the Twenty-First Century,* ed. Norman J. Vig and Michael E. Kraft (Washington, DC: CQ Press, 2010), App. 1.

22. Useful analyses of the presidency's role in environmental policy making can be found in Dennis L. Soden, ed., *The Environmental Presidency* (Albany, NY: SUNY Press, 1999); Norman J. Vig, "Presidential Powers and Environmental Policy," in *Environmental Policy: New Directions for the Twenty-First Century,* ed. Norman J. Vig and Michael E. Kraft (Washington, DC: CQ Press, 2010), 75–98.

23. On the Carter presidency's environmental policies and politics, see Peter G. Bourne, *Jimmy Carter: A Comprehensive Biography From Plains to Post-Presidency* (New York: Scribner, 1997); Burton I. Kaufman, *The Presidency of James Earl Carter, Jr.* (Lawrence: University Press of Kansas, 1993).

24. The Carter administration's difficulties with energy policy are examined from different perspectives in Richard H. K. Vietor, *Energy Policy in America since 1945* (Cambridge: Cambridge University Press, 1984); Pietro S. Nivola, *The Politics of Energy Conservation* (Washington, DC: Brookings Institution, 1986).

25. More detailed analyses of Reagan's environmental policies are found in Michael E. Kraft and Norman J. Vig, "Environmental Policy in the Reagan Presidency," *Political Science Quarterly* 99 (Fall 1984): 414–439; Barry D. Freedman, *Regulation in the Reagan-Bush Era: The Eruption of Presidential Influence* (Pittsburgh, PA: University of Pittsburgh Press, 1995); V. Kerry Smith, *Environmental Policy Under Reagan's Executive Order: The Role of Cost–Benefit Analysis* (Chapel Hill: University of North Carolina Press, 1984); Robert V. Bartlett, "The Budgetary Process and Environmental Policy," in *Environmental Policies in the 1980s,* ed. Norman J. Vig and Michael E. Kraft (Washington, DC: CQ Press, 1984); J. Clarence Davies, "Environmental Institutions and the Reagan Administration," in *Environmental Policies in the 1980s,* ed. Norman J. Vig and Michael E. Kraft (Washington, DC: CQ Press, 1984).

26. On the Clinton presidency, see Campbell Colin and Bert A. Rockman, eds. *The Clinton Presidency: First Impressions* (Chatham, NJ: Chatham House, 1995); "GOP Sets 104th Congress on New Regulatory Course," *Congressional Quarterly Weekly Report,* December 10, 1994, 1693–1719.

27. During Clinton's first term, however, Congress passed the important Food Quality Protection Act of 1996. The act created a new approach to regulating pesticides used in food, fiber, and other crops by requiring the EPA to determine the health risk in foods by considering all the ways in which people were exposed to harmful chemicals and created a reasonable risk health standard for raw and processed food that replaced the earlier standard barring processed food containing even a trace of chemicals thought to cause cancer.

28. The environmentalist indictment of George W. Bush's administration is summarized in Natural Resources Defense Council, *Rewriting the Rules, Year-End Report 2002: The Bush Administration's Assault on the Environment* (Washington, DC: Natural Resources Defense Council, January 2003); U.S. Congress, House of Representatives, Committee on Government Reform—Minority Staff, Special Investigations Division, "Politics and Science in the Bush Administration: Prepared for Rep. Henry W. Waxman," Washington, DC, August 2003.

29. Quoted in Katherine Q. Seelye, "Whitman Quits as E.P.A. Chief," *New York Times,* May 22, 2003, 1A.

30. Jeremy P. Jacobs and Jean Chemnick, "Obama Proposes Agency's 3rd Consecutive Budget Cut," *E&E Reporter,* February 13, 2012, available at: http://www.eenews.net/Greenwire/rss/2012/02/13/2 (accessed May 20, 2012).

31. Paul Voosen, "Myth-Busting Scientist Pushes Greens Past Reliance on 'Horror Stories,'" *E&E Reporter,* April 23, 2012, available at www.eenews.net/public/Greenwire/2012/04/03/1 (accessed April 29, 2012).

32. GAO, "Status of EPA's Reviews of Chemicals Under the Chemical Testing Program," Report no. GAO/RCED 92–31FS, Washington, DC, October 1991, 27.

33. J. Clarence Davies, *Nanotechnology Oversight: An Agenda for the New Administration* (Washington, DC: Woodrow Wilson Center, 2008), 10.

34. Michael Decourcy Hines, "Survey Finds Flaws in States' Water Inspections," *New York Times,* April 15, 1993, A14; GAO, "Widening Gap Between Needs and Available Resources Threatens Vital EPA Program," Report no. GAO/RCED 92–184, Washington, DC, July 1992.

35. See, for example, The White House, Office of Management and Budget, *Draft 2012 Report to Congress on the Benefits and Costs of Federal Regulations and Unfunded Mandates on State, Local, and Tribal Entities,* available at http://www.whitehouse.gov/ omb/inforeg_regpol_reports_congress (accessed July 21, 2012), for estimated costs and benefit of EPA regulations between 2002 and 2012.

36. U.S. Department of Commerce, Bureau of the Census, *Statistical Abstract of the United States, 1996* (Washington, DC: Government Printing Office, 1997).

37. For estimates on national pollution expenditures and their impact, see William A. Pizer and Raymond Kopp, "Calculating the Costs of Environmental Regulation," Discussion Paper 03–06, Resources for the Future, Washington, DC, March 2003; U.S. Environmental Protection Agency, Office of Policy Planning and Evaluation, *The Costs of a Clean Environment* (Washington, DC: EPA, 1990), v–viii.

38. Johnathan L. Ramseur, Mark Reisch, and James E. McCarthy, "Superfund Taxes or General Revenues: Funding Policy Issues for the Superfund Program I," Document RL 31410, Congressional Research Service, Washington, DC, February 4, 2008, 9.

39. Janet Wilson, "Aging U.S. School Buses Still Fouling Air," *Los Angeles Times,* May 25, 2006, A14.

40. Lisa Rein, "As Pressure Increases, So Do Ways to Control Pollution," *Washington Post,* May 23, 2006, A01.

41. Andrea Fischer, "EPA Tightens Particulate Matter Rule; Manufacturers Concerned With Costs," *Transport Topics,* October 2, 2006, 4, 35.

42. Chris Reuther, "Microscopic Murderer: Pollution May Be Motivating *Pfiesteria* to Kill Fish by the Thousands," Academy of Natural Sciences, Philadelphia, May–June 1999, available at www.acnatsci.org/research/kye/pfiester.html (accessed August 1999).

43. For a comprehensive description of the South Florida project, see Working Group of the South Florida Ecosystem Restoration Task Force, *Success in the Making: An Integrated Plan for South Florida Ecosystem Restoration and Sustainability* (Washington, DC: U.S. Government Printing Office, 1998).

44. WCED (Brundtland Commission), *Our Common Future* (New York: Oxford University Press, 1987), 43.

45. Jonathan M. Harris, "Basic Principles of Sustainable Development," Working Paper 00–04, Global Development and Environment Institute, Medford, MA, 2000, 5–6.

46. The Clinton administration's ecosystem management initiative is discussed in GAO, "Ecosystem Management: Additional Actions Needed to Adequately Test a Promising Approach," Document no. GAO/RCED 94–111, Washington, DC, 1994.

47. Thaddeus C. Trzyna, Elizabeth Margold, and Julia K. Osborn, *World Directory of Environmental Groups,* 7th ed. (Sacramento, CA: International Center for the Environment and Public Policy, 2005); Harbinger Communications, *National Environmental Directory* (Santa Cruz, CA: Harbinger Communications, 2005), available at www .environmentaldirectory.net/search.htm (accessed February 20, 2007).

48. U.S. Department of the Interior, Bureau of Land Management, "Ecosystem Management in the BLM: From Concept to Commitment," Publication no. BLM/SC/Gi-94/005 Washington, DC, 1994, 1736.

Chapter 2

Making Policy
The Process

> *"You never want a serious crisis to go to waste," [Rahm] Emanuel, the incoming White House chief of staff, said at a Wall Street Journal conference last month. "And what I mean by that is an opportunity to do things that you think you could not do before. . . . What used to be long-term problems, be they in the health care area, energy area, education area—things . . . that were long-term are now immediate and must be dealt with."[1]*
>
> NPR *News,* December 23, 2008

James E. Hansen is a senior scientist at the National Aeronautics and Space Administration (NASA), director of NASA's Goddard Institute for Space Studies, and one of the nation's best-known and most respected atmospheric scientists. One October day in 2004, Hansen sent an angry message from Iowa to the White House and received a predictably disagreeable response. It was the opening public round in an often acrimonious disagreement between Hansen and the White House that prevailed throughout the George W. Bush and Barack Obama administrations over the federal government's response to the issue of climate warming. The struggle exposed deep, persistent, and fundamental disagreements within the federal government over which institutions and officials should shape the government's environmental policies.

The White House and the Greenhouse

The George W. Bush administration's approach to climate change policy was contentious from the beginning. Bush retracted an earlier pledge to restrict power plant discharges of carbon dioxide (CO_2), the major gas associated with climate warming, and also rejected participation in the

Kyoto Protocol, the 1997 global treaty in which 149 other nations pledged to a scheduled reduction in their CO_2 emissions. Bush strongly promoted voluntary industrial cutbacks in CO_2 emissions, endorsed a gradual and moderate decrease in national greenhouse gas reductions, and repeatedly emphasized the scientific uncertainties involved in predicting future climate change, provoking vigorous opposition from segments of the scientific community, sharp congressional debate, and division among policy experts.

A Public Challenge

That October day in 2004, Hansen directly contradicted the White House position by assuring the University of Iowa audience that the scientific community generally agreed that temperatures on Earth are rising because of the greenhouse effect—emissions of CO_2 and other materials into the atmosphere that trap heat. Moreover, he noted, scientists believed these rising temperatures could damage crops and human health, cause sea levels to rise, and trigger other problems.[2]

Hansen's presentation infuriated the White House. Hansen told his audience that the George W. Bush administration wants to hear only findings that "fit predetermined, inflexible positions" and that the Bush administration "consistently downplayed" information confirming global climate warming. If these remarks were not sufficiently inflammatory, Hansen turned to the forthcoming November presidential election between Bush and John Kerry. "Speaking as a private citizen," he said, he believed that "John Kerry has a far better grasp than President Bush on the important issues that we face, as far as the area for which I have expertise, climate change and its relation to energy use."[3]

The Bush administration responded by increasing its already substantial pressure on the administration's political appointees to control the flow of scientific information from NASA by delaying or altering public documents released by the agency. Until mid-2004, however, the simmering conflict between Hansen and the Bush White House seldom erupted publicly. The Iowa speech revealed the widening depth of their disagreement about climate warming.

Dire Consequences?

Rising White House irritation at Hansen's continuing outspoken views throughout 2005 on climate warming policy culminated in December. That month, Hansen warned the American Geophysical Union that, without leadership in the United States, climate change would eventually leave Earth "a different planet" and, later, released information that 2005 was probably the warmest year in at least a century. Hansen soon received

telephone warnings from NASA's public affairs office that "dire consequences" might follow if his statements continued, including the possibility that public affairs officials might stand in for him at news media
interviews. About the same time, a novice NASA public affairs officer,
remarking that his job was to "make the president look good," rejected a
request from National Public Radio to interview Hansen.[4]

Conflict between the White House and agency scientists over where
science ends and politics begins was not peculiar to the Bush administration. However, Hansen reported to several national newspapers, that
"nothing in 30 years equated the push made since early December to keep
him from publicly discussing what he says are clear-cut dangers for further
delay in curbing carbon dioxide."[5] What followed revived public controversy over two of the enduring issues in American environmental policy
making: which government institutions and leaders should shape the
nation's environmental policies and what role science, and the scientific
community, should assume in this process.

Competing Interests and Institutions

Hansen found important allies. Shortly after the revelation of "direct
threats," NASA Administrator Michael D. Griffin issued a message to
NASA's 19,000 employees reassuring them it was not the job of NASA's
public affairs officers "to alter, filter or adjust engineering or scientific
material produced by NASA's technical staff."[6] The public affairs officer
who wanted to "make the president look good" was fired. The influential
chair of the House Science Committee, himself a Republican, warned that
the Hansen affair revealed "NASA is clearly doing something wrong"
because "good science cannot exist in an atmosphere of intimidation."[7]
And, the prestigious American Association for the Advancement of Science
hastily convened a crowded session at its 2006 annual conference to
denounce political interference in governmental science.

Others saw the controversy differently. "It seems that Dr. Hansen, once
again, is using his government position to promote his own views and
political agenda, which is a clear violation of governmental procedure in
any administration," said a spokesperson for James M. Inhofe, the Republican chair of the Senate Committee on the Environment and Public
Works.[8] NASA's deputy assistant administrator for public affairs noted
that public affairs officials routinely reviewed the public statements of
employees in most federal agencies, and such reviews were essential to
ensure an orderly flow of information and to avoid surprises. And, he
added—in words heard often among Bush White House officials and
agency leaders—"while governmental scientists were free to discuss scientific findings, policy statements should be left to policy makers and

appointed spokesmen."[9] Undaunted, Hansen warned a House committee in mid-2008 that it is almost, but not quite, too late to start defusing what he called the "global warming time bomb." He offered a plan for cuts in emissions and also a warning about the risks of further inaction.[10]

The controversy churned into the twilight of the Bush administration, drawing more partisans into the fray and enlarging the conflict. Hansen's supporters were delighted when the nonpartisan GAO, responsible to Congress for oversight of the executive branch, reported in 2007 that communications policies at NASA were inhibiting some scientists from openly discussing their research.[11] Predictably, scientific and environmental interest groups sympathetic to Hansen aggressively rose to his defense. As if to publicly embarrass the Bush administration, early in 2009, the American Meteorological Society, the leading professional association of climate scientists, awarded Hansen its highest honor for "outstanding contributions to climate modeling . . . and for clear communication of climate science in the public arena." And, the National Audubon Society followed several months later with an award established to recognize "demonstrated courage and integrity in defense of the environment."[12]

Environmentalists expected the relationship between Hansen, the scientific community, and the White House to improve dramatically with the election of Barack Obama. Obama had emphasized throughout his 2008 campaign his commitment to eliminating political interference in federal agency science decision making and to initiating an aggressive, new regulatory program to control U.S. climate warming emissions. Moreover, Hansen sent a personal (but highly publicized) letter to the president and his wife just prior to Obama's inauguration, reminding the president of the "urgent need to tackle global warming."

By 2010, however, Hansen was also taking on Obama when it came to national climate policy. Moreover, he spoke for many scientific and environmentalist spokespeople increasingly dissatisfied with Obama's administration's failure to pass new congressional legislation to regulate climate warming emissions and his delay in issuing new air and water pollution regulations. When Obama approved a portion of the controversial XL Keystone pipeline intended to transport Canadian petroleum from oil sands into the United States, Hansen's public response was acid. "If Obama chooses the dirty needle," he remarked, "it will confirm that Obama was just greenwashing all along, like the other well-oiled, coal-fired politicians, with no real intention of solving the addiction [to petroleum]."[13] Soon thereafter, Hansen and 141 other demonstrators were arrested during a sit-in demonstration at the White House to protest Obama's pipeline approval. By mid-2012, Hansen—again signaling the mood of a large and highly critical constituency of environmentalists and scientists—warned in a *New York Times* op-ed essay that the Obama administration's pipeline decision meant "Game Over For the Climate." "President Obama speaks of a 'planet in peril,'" Hansen asserted, "but he does not provide the leadership to change the world's course . . ."[14]

The *New York Time,* article provoked an angry counterattack by former NASA employees. In a widely publicized letter to the director of NASA, the former employees requested that NASA refuse to include Hansen's "unproven remarks" in public releases and NASA websites and reject Hanson's "unbridled advocacy" of climate warming regulation when "the science is *not* settled."[15] The president responded, as he had to Hansen's earlier criticism, by refusing to engage in a public debate.[16]

The public discord between Hanson, his allies inside and outside the federal government, and the Obama White House was alive and well throughout the 2012 presidential election. Nothing the president had done could disguise a deep disagreement between governmental institutions, public officials, and scientists over their appropriate roles in environmental policy making nor guarantee that the next White House occupant would avoid a similar problem. These conflicts arise from the many divisions of power embedded in the U.S. Constitution and the ambiguities of authority that result from these divisions. The White House–Hansen dispute, for example, fed on historic controversies over the limits of the president's power as the nation's chief executive and major public policy maker and on conflicting understandings about the responsibility of federal administrators to the White House and to their own professions or agency missions. In addition, to many scientists inside and outside Washington, the Hansen controversy was the raw edge of the always-contentious dispute over how much policy makers should defer to scientific data and opinions.

Policy Making Is a Process

The Hansen controversy exemplifies the multitude of actors and institutions, the complex fabric of decisions, and the sometimes glacial, disjointed, and frequently contentious sequence of events involved in the making of national environmental policy.

Although environmental policies usually develop less tumultuously, this incident features some characteristics common to environmental policy making. First, policy making is a process that involves a number of related decisions originating from different institutions and actors ranging across the whole domain of the federal government and private institutions. As policy analyst Hugh Heclo observes, policy is "a course of action or inaction rather than a specific decision or action."[17] Moreover, policy making is continuous; once made, decisions rarely are immutable. Environmental policy is therefore in some respects fluid and impermanent, always in metamorphosis. Second, policy makers—whether of the legislative, White House, or bureaucratic type—can seldom act without restraint. Their discretion is bounded and shaped by many constraints: the constitutional separation of powers, institutional rules and biases, statutory laws, shared understandings about the rules of the game for conflict resolution, political realities, and more. These constraints collectively are a given in the policy setting, which means government resolves almost all issues in a predictable style. Third, environmental policy making is a volatile mixture of politics and science that readily erupts into controversy among politicians, bureaucrats, and scientists over their appropriate roles in the process as well as over the proper interpretation and use of scientific data in policy questions.

One useful way to understand public policy, and environmental policy specifically, is to view the process as a cycle of interrelated phases through which policy ordinarily evolves. Each phase involves a different mix of actors, institutions, and constraints. Although somewhat simplified, this approach illuminates particularly well the interrelated flow of decisions and the continual process of creation and modification that characterizes governmental policy development. This chapter begins by describing the significant phases of environmental policy making and then examines important constitutional and political influences, deeply embedded in U.S. political culture, that continually animate and shape the environmental policies emerging from this policy cycle.

The Policy Cycle

Public policies usually develop with reasonable order and predictability. Governmental response to public issues—the business of converting an issue into a policy—customarily begins when an issue can be placed on the governmental agenda. The successful promotion of issues to the agenda does not ensure that public policies will result, but this step initiates the policy cycle. An environmental issue becomes an environmental policy as it passes through several policy phases.

Agenda Setting

Political scientist Charles O. Jones aptly calls agenda setting "the politics of getting problems to government."[18] It is the politics of imparting sufficient importance and urgency to an issue so that the government will feel compelled to place the matter on the official agenda of government— that is, the "set of items explicitly up for the serious and active consideration of authoritative decision-makers."[19] This means getting environmental issues on legislative calendars, before legislative committees, on a priority list for bill introduction by a senator or representative, on the schedule of a regulatory agency, or among the president's legislative proposals. In brief, getting an issue on the agenda means placing it where institutions and individuals with public authority can respond and feel a need to do so. Especially if an environmental issue is technical and somewhat esoteric, its prospects for making the agenda are bleak unless political sponsors are attracted to it. Former EPA assistant administrator and environmental activist Clarence Davies observes, "New technical information by itself does not significantly influence the political agenda. It must be assisted by some type of political propellant," such as an interest group, congressional committee, or the president.[20] Thus, the discovery of the stratospheric ozone hole and the ability of scientists to portray it in the most literal way—scientific photography enabled the public to see a hole—immensely hastened the Montreal Protocol to completion.

Formulation and Legitimation

The governmental agenda also can be a graveyard for public problems. Few issues reaching the governmental agenda (environmental or otherwise) reach the phase of policy formulation or legitimation. Policy formulation involves setting goals for policy, creating specific plans and proposals for these goals, and selecting the means to implement such plans. Policy formulation in the federal government is especially associated with the presidency and Congress. The State of the Union address and the avalanche of bills introduced annually in Congress represent the most obvious examples of formulated policies. Policies, once created, must also be legitimated and invested with the authority to evoke public acceptance. Such legitimation usually is done through constitutional, statutory, or administrative procedures, such as voting, public hearings, presidential orders, or judicial decisions upholding the constitutionality of laws—rituals whose purposes are to signify that policies have now acquired the weight of public authority.

Implementation

Public policies remain statements of intention until they are translated into operational programs. Indeed, the impact of policies depends largely on how they are implemented. What government is doing about environmental problems relates primarily to how the programs have been implemented. Policy analyst Eugene Bardach compares the implementation of public policies to "an assembly process"; according to him, it is

> as if the original mandate . . . that set the policy or program in motion were a blueprint for a large machine that has to turn out rehabilitated psychotics or healthier old people or better educated children. . . . Putting the machine together and making it run is, at one level, what we mean by the "implementation" process.[21]

Policy implementation involves especially the bureaucracy, whose presence and style shape the impact of all public policies.

Impact and Reformulation

All the procedures involved in evaluating the social impact of governmental policies, in judging the desirability of these impacts, and in communicating these judgments to the government and the public can be called impact assessment. Often, the federal courts assume an active role in the process, as do the mass media. The White House, Congress, and the bureaucracy continually monitor and assess the impacts of public policy. As a consequence, once a policy has been formulated, it may pass through many phases of reformulation. All major institutions of government may play major roles in this process of reformulation.

Termination

The "deliberate conclusion or succession of specific governmental functions, programs, policies or organizations" amounts to policy termination, according to political scientist Peter deLeon.[22] Terminating policies, environmental or otherwise, is such a formidable process that most public programs, in spite of intentions to the contrary, become virtually immortal. Policies usually change through repeated reformulation and reassessment.

Policy Making Is a Combination of Phases

Because policy making is a process, the various phases almost always affect each other, an important reason why understanding a policy often requires considering the whole development pattern. For instance, many problems encountered by the EPA when enforcing the Federal Water Pollution Control Act (1956) arose from the congressional failure to define clearly in the law what was meant by a *navigable waterway,* to which the legislation explicitly applied. Congress deliberately built in this ambiguity to facilitate the passage of the extraordinarily complicated legislation. In turn, the EPA sought early opportunities to bring the issue before the federal courts—to compel judicial assessment of the law's intent—so that the agency might have reliable guidance for its implementation of the provision. Also, many aspects of environmental policy may occur simultaneously. While the EPA was struggling to implement portions of the Superfund legislation allocating grants to the states for cleaning up abandoned toxic waste sites, Congress was considering a reformulation of the law to increase funding authorization to support more state grants.

Constitutional Constraints

The design of governmental power intended more than two centuries ago for a nation of farmers still rests heavily on the flow of policy making in a technological age. Like other public policies, environmental programs have been shaped, and complicated, by the enduring constitutional formula.

Checks and Balances

The Madisonian notion of setting "ambition against ambition," which inspired the constitutional structure, creates a government of countervailing and competitive institutions. The system of checks and balances disperses power and authority within the federal government among legislative, executive, and judicial institutions and thereby sows tenacious institutional rivalries that are repeatedly encountered in discussions of specific environmental laws. Yet, as former presidential adviser Richard E. Neustadt has observed, these are separated institutions sharing power; effective public policy requires that public officials collaborate by discovering strategies to transcend these institutional conflicts.[23]

The U.S. federal system disperses governmental power by fragmenting authority between the national and state governments. Despite the growth of vast federal powers, federalism remains a sturdy constitutional buttress supporting an edifice of authority—shared, independent, and countervailing—erected from the states within the federal system. "It is difficult to find any governmental activity which does not involve all three of the so-called 'levels' of the federal system."[24] No government institution monopolizes power. "There has never been a time when it was possible to put neat labels on discrete 'federal,' 'state' and 'local' functions."[25]

Regulatory Federalism

Federalism introduces complexity, jurisdictional rivalries, confusion, and delay into the management of environmental problems. Authority over environmental issues inherently is fragmented among a multitude of governmental entities. Moreover, almost all new federal regulatory programs since 1970 permit, or require, implementation by the states. For instance, 35 states currently administer water pollution permits under the Clean Water Act. State implementation of federal laws may vary greatly in scope and detail. Management of water quality in the Colorado River basin, for instance, is enormously complicated because seven states have conflicting claims on the quantity and quality of Colorado River water to which they are entitled. No overall plan exists for the comprehensive management and protection of the river, and none can exist in this structure of divided and competitive jurisdictions. The federal government often attempts to reduce administrative complications in programs administered through the states by the use of common regulations, guidelines, and other devices to impose consistency on implementation. However, the practical problems of reconciling so many geographical interests within the arena of a single regulatory program often trigger major problems in implementing the programs.

Federal and state collaboration in environmental regulation is often cooperative but can often be contentious. Many state authorities believe that numerous environmental problems now federally regulated would be best managed by state and local governments. Often, as in the emerging national controversy over the environmental impact of fracking to obtain petroleum from oil shale, many states want exclusive authority to regulate and often protest federal plans to assume that responsibility. Many state governments also resent the expense and administrative difficulty they must endure to implement the numerous environmental laws and regulations they believe the federal government has negligently piled on them. In the decade ending in 2010, for example, the EPA's major new environmental regulations imposed a minimum cost upon state governments of at least $23 billion.[26]

Organized Interests

The Constitution encourages a robust pluralism of organized interests. Constitutional guarantees of freedom of petition, expression, and assembly promote constant organization and political activism at all governmental levels among thousands of economic, occupational, ethnic, ideological, and geographical interests. To make public policy in the United States requires public officials and institutions to reconcile the conflicting interests of organized groups whose claims not only to influence but also to authority in making public policy have resulted in an unwritten constitutional principle. The constitutional architecture of the U.S. government also provides numerous points of access to public power for such groups operating in a fragmented governmental milieu. The political influence broadly distributed across this vast constellation of organized private groups clouds the formal distinction between public and private power.[27] Instead, the course of policy making moves routinely and easily between public institutions and private organizations mobilized for political action.

These constitutional constraints have important implications for environmental policy. It is easier to defeat legislation and other governmental policies than to enact them and to frustrate incisive governmental action on issues than to create it. Furthermore, most policy decisions result from bargaining and compromise among institutions and actors all sharing some portion of diffused power. Formulating policy usually means coalition building in an effort to engineer consensus by reconciling diverse interests and aggregating sufficient strength among different interests to support effective policies. As economist James V. DeLong observes, agencies "like to achieve consensus on issues and policies. If they cannot bring everyone into the tent, they will try to get enough disparate groups together so as to make the remainder appear unreasonable. If the interested parties are too far apart for even partial consensus, then the agency will try to give everybody something."[28]

Bargaining and compromise often purchase consensus at the cost of disarray and contradiction in the resulting policies. "What happens is not chosen as a solution to a problem but rather results from compromise, conflict and confusion among officials with diverse interests and unequal influence," notes presidential adviser Graham Allison.[29]

Incrementalism

Public officials strongly favor making and changing policy incrementally. "Policy making typically is part of a political process in which the only feasible political change is that which changes social states by relatively small steps," writes social analyst Charles A. Lindblom.[30] Gus Speth, a former chair of the Council on Environmental Quality and a veteran environmental policy maker, describes incrementalism as "working within the system." He explains:

> When today's environmentalism recognizes a problem, it believes it can solve that problem by calling public attention to it, framing policy and program responses for government and industry, lobbying for those actions, and litigating for their enforcement. It believes in the efficacy of environmental advocacy and government action. It believes that good-faith compliance with the law will be the norm. . . . Today's environmentalism tends to be pragmatic and incrementalist—its actions are aimed at solving problems and often doing so one at a time. . . . In the end, environmentalism accepts compromises as part of the process. It takes what it can get.[31]

In general, such incrementalism favors relying on past experience as a guide for new policies, carefully deliberating before changing policy, and rejecting rapid or comprehensive policy innovation.

Incrementalism is politically seductive. It permits policy makers to draw on their own experiences in the face of unfamiliar problems and encourages the making of small policy adjustments at the margins to

reduce anticipated, perhaps irreversible, and politically risky consequences. But, incrementalism also can become a prison of the imagination
by inhibiting policy innovation and stifling new solutions to issues. Especially when officials treat new policy issues as if they were familiar ones
and deal with them in the customary ways, a futile and possibly dangerous repetition of the past can result in the face of issues requiring fresh
approaches.

NEPA (1969), the CAA (1970), and the other innovative legislation of
the early 1970s came only after Congress repeatedly failed when dealing
with environmental issues incrementally.[32] For more than 30 years previously, and despite growing evidence of serious environmental degradation, Congress had continued to treat pollution as a "uniquely local
problem" requiring a traditional "partnership" between federal and state
governments in which Washington gently prodded the states to deal more
effectively with pollution. Finally, Congress put an end to this incrementalism with the avalanche of new, forceful federal environmental laws in
the 1970s mandating national pollution standards and regulations that
compelled state compliance and enforcement. To many observers, this
was a sudden outburst of environmental reform. In fact, its rise to the
national policy agenda had been achieved by years of increasingly skilled,
patient, and persistent promotion by a multitude of groups. The CAA, for
instance, had been supported for almost five years by a national environmental alliance, the Clean Air Coalition, before it achieved national attention. Nonetheless, the time consumed in attempts to attack problems
incrementally, the degree of environmental damage necessary to convince
Congress that new approaches were needed, and the effort invested by the
environmental movement in political action all testify to the tenacity of
incrementalism in the policy process. Incrementalism, moreover, can
degenerate into deadlock and stalemate, especially when ideological or
partisan cleavages are wide and antagonistic in governmental institutions
requiring a large measure of accommodation and moderation to function
effectively—the sort of partisan deadlock evident in Congress's chronic
failure to enact new environmental legislation following Barack Obama's
2008 election.

Interest Group Politics

It is an implicit principle in U.S. politics, assumed by most public officials as well as those groups seeking access to them, that organized interests affected by public policy should have an important role in shaping
those policies. Few special interests enjoy such pervasive and unchallenged
access to government as business, but almost all major organized groups
enjoy some measure of influence in public institutions. Many officials, in

critic Theodore Lowi's terms, conduct their offices "as if it were supposed to be the practice of dealing only with organized claims in formulating policy, and of dealing exclusively through organized claims in implementing programs."[33]

Structuring Groups into Government

Arrangements exist throughout governmental structures for giving groups access to strategic policy arenas. Lobbying is accepted as a normal, if not essential, arrangement for ensuring organized interests major roles in lawmaking. More than 1,000 advisory committees exist within the federal bureaucracy to give interests affected by policies some access and voice in agency deliberations. Hundreds of large, quasi-public associations bring together legislators, administrators, White House staff, and private-group representatives to share policy concerns, thereby blurring the distinction between public and private interests. The National Rivers and Harbors Congress, for example, looks after water resource projects; the Highway Users Federation for Safety and Mobility diligently promotes the interstate highway system; and the Atomic Industrial Forum pursues the interests of commercial nuclear power corporations. Successful organized groups so effectively control the exercise of governmental power that, in historian Grant McConnell's words, significant portions of the U.S. government have witnessed "the conquest of segments of formal state power by private groups and associations."[34] In effect, group activity at all governmental levels has been practiced so widely that it has become part of the constitutional order.

Business: Secure and Effective Access

No interest has exploited the right to take part in the governmental process more pervasively or successfully than has business. In environmental affairs, the sure access of business to government assumes enormous importance because business is a major regulated interest whose ability to represent itself and secure careful hearing before public agencies and officials often delays or complicates such regulation. In 2008, for instance, about 70 percent of the more than 770 companies and organizations hiring 2,340 lobbyists to work on climate change and spending at least $90 million on lobbying were business groups.[35] But, historically and institutionally, the influence of business on government has transcended the agencies and officials concerned with environmental affairs.

Business traditionally has enjoyed what Lindblom calls a "special relationship" with government.[36] Business weighs especially heavily in the deliberations of public officials because its leaders collectively manage

much of the economy and perform such essential economic functions that
the failure of these businesses would produce severe economic disorder
and widespread suffering. According to Lindblom,

> government officials know this. They also know that widespread failure of
> business . . . will bring down the government. A democratically elected gov-
> ernment cannot expect to survive in the face of widespread or prolonged
> distress. . . . Consequently, government policy makers show constant concern
> about business performance.[37]

So great is this concern that public officials usually give business not
all it desires but enough to ensure its profitability. Out of this grows the
privileged position of business in government and its widely accepted
right to require that government officials often "give business needs precedence over demands from citizens through electoral, party, and interest-
group channels."[38]

Business also enjoys practical political advantages in competition with
other interests for access to and influence on government: far greater
financial resources, greater ease in raising money for political purposes,
and an already existing organization available for use in political action.
These advantages in strategic resources and salience to public officials do
not ensure the uncompromised acceptance of business's demands on government, nor do they spare business from defeat or frustration by opponents. But, business often, if not usually, is able to exploit its privileged
status in U.S. politics to ensure that its views are represented early and
forcefully in any policy conflicts, its interests are pursued and protected
carefully at all policy phases, and its forces are mobilized effectively for
long periods of time. These are formidable advantages, often enough to
give a decisive edge in competitive struggles with environmental or other
interests that do not have the political endurance, skill, or resources to be
as resolute in putting pressure on government when it counts.

Environmentalism's Enlarging Access

Prior to the 1970s, environmentalists were at a considerable disadvantage in achieving effective access to government compared to the environmentally regulated interests, particularly business. The environmental
lobby could claim, with considerable justification, to be political outsiders
compared to business. However, environmental groups—along with
public-interest groups, consumer organizations, and others advocating
broad public programs—were quick to promote a number of new structural
and legal arrangements that enlarged their governmental influence. Indeed,
Congress and administrative agencies often created these structural and

legal arrangements deliberately for the advantage of environmental interests. These new arrangements, defended ferociously by environmental
organizations against continuing assaults by their political opposition,
have diminished greatly the disparities in political access and influence
that once so conspicuously distinguished environmentalists from their
political opponents. Environmental groups, in fact, have acquired the
finesse to be formidable adversaries in traditional political confrontations
with well-endowed opponents. "The perception is that environmentalists
are a bunch of unwashed kids tying themselves to trees," remarked a
political media expert observing environmental activists promoting
national climate warming regulation. "That's not the case anymore. These
are very sophisticated and well-funded campaigns."[39] In a reversal of
form, for instance, during the opening congressional battle over the president's climate warming program shortly after Barack Obama's election,
environmentalist supporters of a proposal to limit greenhouse-gas emissions outspent their opposition in the media $8 million to $7.4 million.
However, environmentalists gain no advantage when the skilled legislative advocacy of lobbyists is involved. During the early months of the
Obama administration, oil and gas interests spent more than $82 million
on lobbying concerned with climate warming regulation; environmental
groups spent $9.8 million.[40] Still, the political season has turned. In the
rough calculus of governmental influence, environmentalists may not yet
claim parity with organized business, but environmentalism no longer
wears comfortably the rags of the politically disadvantaged and the establishment outsider. In the vernacular of Washington, DC, environmentalists
are now major players—so major that a closer look at organized environmentalism and its impact on public opinion is essential to understand the
fundamental driving forces of environmental policy making.

The Environmental Movement: Confronting the Challenge of Change

In mid-2012, the EPA sent photographers across the United States to
once again photograph some of the most dramatic examples of pollution
that inspired the environmental movement and dramatized the environmental crisis during the era of the first Earth Day. However, "the clouds
of smoke billowing from industrial smokestacks, raw sewage flowing
into rivers that had galvanized public concern were gone."[41] And, that
creates a problem, observed William Ruckelshaus, the EPA's first administrator, who commissioned those early, powerful photographs. "To a certain extent, we are a victim of our own success," he observed. "Right
now, EPA is under sharp criticism partly because it is not as obvious to
people that pollution problems exist and that we need to deal with

them."[42] However, this is one among several other compelling issues facing environmental organizations as the environmental movement ages into a changing political era.

As a political profile of the environmental movement illustrates, environmentalism's political vitality has been sustained by the continuity and political skill of its organizational base. While this has enabled environmentalists to be major players in American politics, these organizations now confront the considerable challenges in staying politically relevant and effective for a new American generation in an era of political change. Among these important challenges are effectively dramatizing emerging environmental problems to the public, recruiting and retaining organizational membership, confronting growing partisan division within Congress over environmental regulation, resolving sometimes intense conflicts within the movement itself, and competing successfully for financial resources in economically difficult times.

Strategies and Tactics

Organization is the bedrock on which the politics of successful environmental policy making is built. Estimates of environmentalism's organizational membership vary. About 5 percent of Americans report membership in an environmental organization, and between 15 and 21 percent customarily report they have been active in an environmental group. Careful estimates suggest that perhaps 5,600 organized environmental groups are nationally active, together with thousands more transient state, local, and regional organizations defying enumeration.[43] The thousands of organized national, state, and local groups, collectively enrolling millions of members, arm the movement with absolutely essential political resources that only organized groups provide—dependable, active, informed, and experienced advocacy.[44] Organized groups create the kind of constant pressure on policy makers and the continual aggressive surveillance of policy administration required for effective policy influence in government.

Over the years since Earth Day 1970, the number of U.S. environmental and conservation advocacy groups[45] has grown steadily. Accurate estimates of their number are elusive, but these groups, regardless of size and resources, probably exceed 26,000.[46] The number of these organizations has increased annually since at least 1996 as well as the collective membership of the large and nationally important organizations (see Figure 2–1). However, most environmental organizations are quite small in membership and financial resources.[47] No more than a few thousand have incomes sufficient to enable significant, national-scale activities, and

Figure 2–1 Total Reported Members of 25 National Environmental
Organizations, 1950–2008

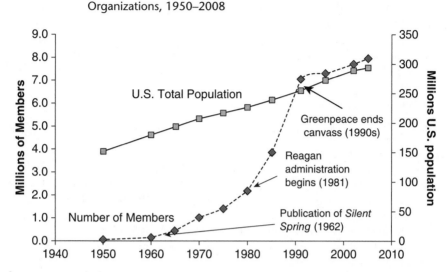

Source: Baird Straughan and Tom Pollak, *The Broader Movement: Nonprofit Environmental and Conservation Organizations, 1989-2005* (Washington, DC: The Urban Institute, 2008), 37. Copyright © 2008. The Urban Institute.

the political core of environmentalist organizations—those with the political clout and income to be major presences in national or international environmental policy making—probably does not exceed 100 organizations. Most of these highly influential groups, often characterized as the environmentalist establishment or BINGOs (big, influential nongovernment organizations) have been important presences since the first Earth Day.

A politically significant change since that Earth Day has been the continuing growth in number of and activism among environmentalist groups at the state and local governmental levels—in fact, these constitute most of the environmental and conservation groups currently active. This growth in membership has enlarged the political clout of environmental interests at the state and local levels at a time when state and local governments have become increasingly important actors in American environmental policy making.[48] Even though federal environmental leadership lapsed during the George W. Bush administration, many innovative initiatives, particularly concerning climate warming, emerged from numerous state and regional governments. Between 2000 and 2008, for instance, environmental organizations successfully promoted three unprecedented regional agreements to regulate climate warming emissions: the Regional

Greenhouse Gas Initiative (RGGI), among northeastern states; the Midwest Climate Initiative; and the Western Climate Initiative.[49] Many leading environmental groups are also moderating the habitually contentious political style that once characterized their confrontations with business and industry groups in favor of a more cautious exploration of the opportunities for collaboration and compromise.[50]

Ideological Consensus and Cleavage

Environmentalism has never been a church of one creed. The reformist politics of the 1990s exacerbated ideological, programmatic, and tactical disagreements that have always existed among the faithful. Although pluralism, and the conflicts born of it, are inherent in environmentalism, this pluralism is still bounded by general values, attitudes, and beliefs—a way of looking at nature, humanity, and U.S. society—widely shared with many nuances by environmental leaders and activists. Although this pluralism lacks the coherence of an ideology, it sets environmentalists apart from mainstream American culture.

Essential Principles

Reduced to essentials, environmentalism springs from an attitude toward nature that assumes humanity is part of the created order, ethically responsible for the preservation of the world's ecological integrity, and ultimately vulnerable, as are all Earth's other creatures, to the good or ill that humans inflict on nature. In the environmentalist perspective, humans live in a world of limited resources and potential scarcities; like the good stewards of an inheritance, they must use their scientific genius to manage global resources. An enlightened approach to managing nature, the environmentalists argue, should stress the interdependency of all natural systems (the ecosystem concept), the importance of ecological stability and resource sustainability, and the enormously long time span in which the impact of ecological change occurs. In its approach to nature, environmentalism emphasizes the sanctity of the created order as a warning against the human assumption that we stand above and apart from the created order by virtue of our intelligence and scientific achievements. All this is summed up for many ecologists in the metaphor of spaceship Earth, the image of a unique and vulnerable ecosystem traveling through space and time, dependent on its crew for survival.

In its cultural stance, environmentalism sharply criticizes marketplace economics generally and capitalism particularly, and it denigrates the growth ethic, unrestrained technological optimism, and the political structures supporting these cultural phenomena. Such an attitude places environmentalists on a collision course with dominant American values. Environmentalism challenges U.S. confidence in market mechanisms to allocate scarce resources for several reasons. Environmentalists assert that market economics esteem economic growth and material consumption above concern for ecological balance and integrity. Therefore, the market cannot be relied on to signal resource scarcity efficiently enough to prevent possibly catastrophic resource exhaustion. Many, like environmental philosopher William Ophuls, believe marketplace economies are ecologically reckless:

> An unregulated market economy inevitably fosters accelerated ecological degradation and resource depletion through ever higher levels of production and consumption. Indeed, given the cornucopian assumptions upon which a market system is based, it could hardly be otherwise; both philosophically and practically, a market economy is incompatible with ecology.[51]

Environmentalism is less hostile to technology itself than to blind faith in the power of technology to cure whatever ecological ills it begets and to bland confidence in technological expertise to meet humanity's material and spiritual needs. Environmentalists regard the public's confidence in American know-how as responsible for many of the nation's most difficult environmental problems, such as the management of commercial nuclear technologies. The environmental movement's initial political agenda arose from these attitudes toward the natural world and contemporary culture. From its inception, the movement has expressed an ambivalence toward the nation's dominant social structures that frequently translates into calls for major institutional as well as policy reforms. Many environmentalists believe that the nation's dominant political institutions and processes must be reformed because they are committed to the preservation of ecological, economic, and technological values that are hostile to prudent ecological management. For some, this is summed up as suspicion of the establishment and the traditional institutions and processes associated with it. Political scientist A. Susan Leeson argues that "If American political ideology and institutions have been successful in encouraging the pursuit of happiness through material acquisition, they appear incapable of imposing the limits which are required to forestall ecological disaster."[52] Many fear the power of an interlocking economic and political structure committed to controlling technology in environmentally reckless ways.

Until the 1980s, the national organizations representing the environmental movement were largely untroubled by impassioned, divisive ideological cleavages. During the 1980s, however, an emergent radicalism and ideological conflict within the movement cohered into a multitude of newly dissident organizations and opened acrimonious schisms within many of the older, established groups. The environmental movement has now become an uneasy alliance of numerous, often discordant political camps spread across a widening ideological terrain.

The Ideological Mainstream

Organized environmentalism today is divided into several ideological enclaves. The movement's dominant ideological and political style has been crafted by pragmatic reformers, the largest, most politically active, and publicly visible organizations, represented by national groups such as the Sierra Club and the National Wildlife Federation. These large organizations emphasize political action through government; traditional styles of politics such as bargaining and coalition building; and national environmental agendas focusing on pollution, resource conservation, and land use. Their priorities are "influencing public policy in incremental steps, forging pragmatic alliances issue by issue with those with whom they could agree," explains Michael McCloskey, former executive director of the Sierra Club. McCloskey emphasizes that the pragmatists do not believe "that the entire political or economic system needed to be changed and were confident that environmental protection could be achieved within the framework of existing institutions of governance."[53]

The robust ideological diversity among the pragmatists, however, makes them appear more an ecumenical movement than a denomination. One important factional conflict pits preservationist groups, such as the Sierra Club and the Wilderness Society, which emphasize the preservation of resources rather than their economic or recreational exploitation, against groups such as the Izaak Walton League and the National Wildlife Federation, which favor prudent resource development for public use and economic growth. Another significant cleavage divides the pragmatists from antiestablishment groups such as Friends of the Earth and Environmental Action, which are impatient with the moderation and slowness of political action among the leading national groups but still committed to traditional forms of political activity. The national leadership in almost all mainstream environmental organizations, in fact, contends with their own grassroots factions, which, in the words of critic Brian Tokar, believe "the voices of 'official environmentalism' [are] hopelessly out of step with the thousands of volunteers who largely define the leading edge of locally based environmental activism."[54] To these critics, the leaders of official environmentalism have become just another political elite, absorbed in promoting their careers and accommodating the corporate interests that they should be opposing. When the World Wildlife Fund, for instance, selected a former executive of Weyerhaeuser Company, an international timber industry giant, for a major management position, the organization was bitterly flayed by one grassroots environmentalist publication:

> The World Wildlife Fund functions more like a corporate enterprise than public interest group. It . . . has made millions upon millions hawking its panda logo, a brand as zealously marketed as Nike's "swoosh." But, of course, it's done almost nothing to save the panda . . . except peddle pictures to trophy wives and innocent third graders. Call it Panda porn. . . . The World Wildlife Fund also rakes in millions from corporations. . . . As a result, WWF's budget has swelled to over $100 million a year. . . . Most of it goes to pay for plush offices, robust salaries, and a tireless direct mail operation to raise even more money.[55]

These critics, who agree on little else, complain about the amount of foundation money flowing into the coffers of pragmatic environmental groups. Such generous underwriting—often by large donors such as the Pew Memorial Trusts and the Heinz Foundation—has sometimes exceeded $400 million annually and, in the opinion of the critics, compels mainstream environmentalism to compromise its programs and tactics to suit its foundation patrons. Undoubtedly, foundations do prod their environmentalist clientele toward political moderation, but such influence is highly variable. The hard-liners, moreover, have had their own foundation angels, such as the Turner Foundation, created by broadcast entrepreneur Ted Turner, which contributed millions of dollars annually during the 1990s to aggressive antiestablishment environmental organizations. And, many odd-couple alliances exist between relatively moderate foundation sponsors and aggressive environmental activists, such as the one between the Ford Foundation and Environmental Defense. Even without these other provocations, differing organizational agendas and constituencies are themselves divisive to environmentalism. Which organizational agendas will prevail in the competition among environmental organizations for political primacy? Will the movement's priorities be air or water pollution, land preservation, hazardous waste management, national land-use planning, species preservation, global environmental problems, recreational development, indoor air pollution, or something else?

Deep Ecologists

Another highly vocal faction within environmentalism comprises individuals and groups ideologically committed to deep ecology or lifestyle transformation. Deep ecologists believe humans are, at best, only a part of nature—and not necessarily the most significant part. They believe that all forms of life have equal claims on existence; that social, political, and economic institutions should promote the ecological vitality of all created orders; and that fundamental changes in national institutions and life-styles are essential to preserve global ecological integrity. The fundamental political problem, from the deep ecologists' perspective, is that social institutions have become instruments for the human exploitation of the created order for the primary benefit of humans, often through technologies that threaten to destroy essential aspects of the natural order. Deep ecology inherently challenges the fundamental institutional structures and social values on which governments, economies, and societies are presently constituted. Thus, between deep ecologists and what they call the shallow ecology of mainstream environmentalism, there abides a profound philosophical tension, nourished by antagonistic principles and a sharply disparate political imagination.[56]

Deep ecologists, lacking the political leverage of organizational or numerical strength, are presently a vocal, aggressive, and dissenting minority within the environmental movement. Many within the movement, preferring social to political action, have adopted individual and collective lifestyles outside conventional American culture. Nonetheless, deep ecologists continue to be politically active, often to greatest effect at the state and local levels. They also constitute a persistent, opportunistic minority in many national environmental organizations with considerable potential to become a creative as well as a disruptive influence in national environmental politics.

Radical Environmentalism

Militant and alienated from the movement's organizational mainstream, *radical environmentalism* emerged in the 1980s among environmentalists disillusioned with establishment styles and accomplishments. According to environmental historian Bill Devall, the radical environmentalists

> were discouraged by the compromising attitude of mainstream groups, by the bureaucratization of the groups, by the professionalization of leaders and their detachment from the emerging concerns of grassroots supporters, and by the lack of success of mainstream organizations in countering the Reagan anti-environmental agenda.[57]

Radical environmentalists favor direct-action tactics, including the street politics of civil disobedience, nonviolent demonstrations, and political obstruction. To environmental radicals, the harassment of commercial whaling vessels on the high seas by Greenpeace protest vessels, carefully orchestrated to attract media attention worldwide, was better politics than the inhibited, reformist style of the mainstream organizations.

Radical environmentalists share a common sensibility that all life is mortally threatened by an ecological degeneration created by advanced, modern cultures. Thus, radicals espouse a fundamental cultural transformation that rejects the dominant political and economic institutions of most advanced societies as incompatible with global ecological vitality. This preoccupation with transformational politics usually involves a belief in "bearing witness" through lifestyle changes emphasizing harmony with nature, conservation of resources, and cooperative living in reconstructed, ecologically sensitive societies.[58]

Despite a commitment to nonviolence, radicals betray ambivalence about, if not tolerance of, forms of violence—*ecotage* and *monkey-wrenching* are euphemisms—condemned from within and outside the environmental movement. Shadowy groups such as the Animal Liberation Front (ALF) and the Earth Liberation Front (ELF) are suspected of violent property destruction. (The ALF website has contained information on making arson devices, and the ELF claimed responsibility for burning down a Boise Cascade Corporation office in Oregon, causing $1 million in damages.)[59] The small but aggressive movement Earth First!, created by former staff members of mainstream environmental groups, epitomizes this tendency despite its many other conventional activities. For instance, Earth First! spokespeople sometimes assert that, in defense of nature and to save old-growth trees from the lumberyards, it may be permissible to spike these trees with metal rods that are likely to fragment and cause injuries when shattered by commercial logging chain saws.

Other groups, such as Greenpeace and the Sea Shepherd Society, have been accused of nonviolent direct action that provokes violence, such as disabling the nets of commercial fishing vessels whose crews refuse to protect dolphins during deep-sea tuna harvesting. In light of the profound cultural alienation inherent in many radical ideologies, an ambivalence about political violence is inevitable, although radical environmentalism's political strategies still remain—sometimes barely—within the tradition of nonviolent direct action.

Organizational Structures and Strategies

The number and size of environmental organizations expanded through the mid-1990s, but membership subsequently declined, evidence of a familiar up-and-down cycle common to environmental organizations as public perceptions of environmental crises ebb and flow. Strong membership growth throughout the early 1990s was largely a response to aggressive organizational recruiting and the highly publicized confrontations between the White House and environmentalists during the Reagan–Bush period. By the end of the 1990s, the largest environmental organizations had collectively lost more than a million members. Nonetheless, the major national organizations retain the numbers and resources needed to ensure their influential presence in national policy making. Moreover, to the national membership rolls should be added the thousands of grassroots state and local groups. For instance, one national organization concerned with solid waste identifies 7,000 collaborating state and local groups. Altogether, the number of national, state, and local environmental organizations is estimated to exceed 10,000.

Membership. Although social support for environmentalism is broadly based in the United States, the organizational membership is mostly middle to upper class, white, well educated, and well-off.[60] Such a socially select membership exposes environmentalists to the frequent criticism that the so-called greens are too white and too well-off and that they are racists or elitists indifferent to minorities and the economically disadvantaged. To support these accusations, critics argue that environmentalism fights for clean air but not for equal employment opportunities, promotes wilderness preservation for upscale recreationists but not better schools for the disadvantaged, and condemns pollution in national parks but not inner-city decay. In short, the agenda of environmentalism is largely a wish list from the book of middle-class white lifestyles. Mainstream environmental organizations, increasingly sensitive to such criticism, have struggled to broaden their social constituencies and policy agendas. A number of national organizations have initiated joint action with labor and minority groups intended to make environmentalism relevant to the workplace and neighborhood. Most national environmental organizations, responding to initiatives from minority groups, also have supported the emerging environmental equity movement intended to end discrimination against the economically disadvantaged in environmental policy making. The emergence of environmental racism as a mainstream environmentalist concern is discussed in Chapter 4.

The Organizational Mainstream. The environmental movement's national leadership is concentrated in a small number of highly visible, politically skilled, and influential organizations. Most of these organizations are included in the Group of Ten, an informal alliance of mainstream organizations that often collaborate on national issues. The Group of Ten comprises the National Wildlife Federation, the Sierra Club, the National Audubon Society, the Wilderness Society, Friends of the Earth, Environmental Defense, the National Parks and Conservation Association, the Izaak Walton League, the Natural Resources Defense Council, and the Environmental Policy Institute. These large, mainstream groups, the movement's political pragmatists, are thoroughly professionalized and sophisticated in staff and organization. They are armed with the same high-technology tools and modern techniques of policy advocacy as any other powerful national lobby. The large membership rolls of the national organizations demonstrate an aptitude for direct-mail solicitation that is as good as can be found in Washington, DC.

The economic recession beginning in 2009 has created sometimes serious funding problems for most environmental organizations. This has often become a major crisis for the middle-sized and smaller organizations especially vulnerable to hard economic times, but most of the large "establishment" organizations have felt the recession's impact in declining membership numbers, diminished contributions, and reduced income from foundation and government grants.[61] Moreover, as a later discussion illustrates, public concern about environmental and energy conservation, and support for their priority on the national policy agenda, often wanes during hard economic times, creating a challenge for the large organization to sustain a politically engaged and effective constituency.[62]

Growing professionalization of the leadership of the mainstream groups also continues to provoke accusations from many environmentalists that the national organizations have lost their fire and vision. The critics charge that the national leadership is more bureaucratic than charismatic and that it has lost touch with the movement's grassroots and become too preoccupied with bargaining and compromise.

The Essential Politics of Procedure. Rep. John Dingell, D-MI, a legislator of legendary political skill, once shared a lesson gleaned from 30 years in Congress: "I'll let you write the substance on a statute and you let me write the procedures, and I'll screw you every time."[63] Dingell's axiom illuminates a law as fundamental to policy making as gravity is to physics—the decision-making rules, as much as the policy outcomes, enlarge or diminish group power. The environmental movement, always respectful of Dingell's axiom, has been as aggressive in promoting advantageous policy procedures as in creating substantive environmental laws.

The politics of procedure is always a fundamental consideration in environmentalist political agendas. Indeed, the movement's power flows, in good part, from success in procedural politics, from aggressively exploiting advantages through the intricate manipulation of policy process. Because so many environmental laws are implemented largely through bureaucracy and the courts, environmental organizations have been especially sensitive to the importance of protecting, or enhancing, decision-making procedures that work to their benefit in these institutions. The success of this strategy depends on securing these procedural advantages through law: statutory, administrative, or judicial. The public politics of environmentalism could not have succeeded so well, and perhaps not at all, had environmentalism's political power not been anchored in procedural law during the movement's rise to influence in the 1970s. "To a great extent, environmental group power . . . was legal power," observes political scientist George Hoberg, and environmentalism survived because the new legal arrangements "granted environmental groups institutional and legal foundations that to a large extent solidified their power status within the regime."[64]

Environmental groups have benefited especially from changes in law and administrative procedure that enhance their access to information and their opportunities to participate in the implementation of environmental laws. A major environmental reform was the enactment of NEPA in 1969, requiring federal agencies to prepare environmental impact statements that have become a major source of substantive information and procedural influence in federal environmental policies. Other important reforms include provisions in almost every major environmental law to greatly expand citizen participation in administrative decision making and to make it easier for citizens to sue administrative agencies for failure to implement environmental laws. Equally important has been increased activism among federal judges in reviewing critically the regulatory decisions of environmental agencies—called the *hard-look doctrine*—that often works to the environmentalists' advantage.

Environmentalism and Its Critics

The mainstream groups are now acknowledged Washington insiders, part of the interest-group establishment. Although environmentalist organizations are committed to defending the public interest and public values, they also represent a constituency with its own ideological and material interests. As environmentalism becomes increasingly organized and politicized nationally, critics assert that it has also assumed the narrow, self-interested viewpoint of every other interest group while promoting policies that often serve no public ends.

Public Interest or Self-Interest?

Critics frequently allege that environmentalism is largely the voice of a social elite hostile to U.S. capitalism, distrustful of science inconsistent to its own viewpoint, and obsessed with imagined or exaggerated ecological problems. In one such indictment, the editors of the *Detroit News* complained that environmentalists were "a small band of environmental doomsayers, mostly upper middle-class whites, who are quick to forecast disaster but never see an upside to technology and economic progress."[65] To fortify such arguments, critics assert that the environmentalists' passion for controlled economic growth will deprive the economically disadvantaged domestically and internationally, that wilderness preservation usually benefits a handful of naturalists but deprives the average American of access to and enjoyment of wilderness resources, and that locking up resources costs jobs and inhibits economic progress. Moreover, continues the indictment, environmentalists often selfishly obstruct valuable public or private projects like power-generating plants, waste landfills, and even apparently environmentally friendly projects when these might threaten their lifestyles or property values—the same NIMBY-ism (not-in-my-backyard-ism, the uncompromising public opposition to living next to any potentially hazardous facility) that environmentalists criticize in others. Critics have delightedly seized on events that seem proof of perverse environmentalism, such as the opposition by some environmental spokespeople to a proposed 130-tower wind farm in Horseshoe Shoal, a shallow portion of Nantucket Sound south of Cape Cod and the vehement environmentalist battle against a vast solar-energy plant in the Mojave Desert, a very remote and reliably sunny location.[66] In these and many similar instances, however, plausible reasons exist for concern about the biological and ecological impacts of such projects and—as often happens—the environmentalist community itself is often divided over the issues. Nonetheless, to such critics, environmentalism speaks not for the public interest but for a public interest, and often a social strata that excludes millions of Americans.

The white, comfortably middle-class ambiance of most environmental organizations does nothing to diminish such criticism, as a former executive director of the Natural Resources Defense Council, John H. Adams, acknowledges: "There is much to criticize—the predominantly white staffs, the cultural barriers that have damaged and impeded joint efforts with activists of color."[67] Many environmental organizations are striving diligently for greater social diversity in membership and programs. National environmental organizations, for example, are actively seeking, with some success, to build durable alliances with labor unions anchored by a shared concern about workplace safety and worker health, but the stigma of social exclusivity still clings to the movement.[68] In addition, increased professionalization and competition among environmental groups breeds a preoccupation with organizational needs. "There's tremendous competition out there for money," observes Les Line, a former editor of *Audubon Magazine*. "And we've gotten top-heavy with bureaucrats and accountants and fund-raisers who are all good professionals but I don't think you'd catch them sloshing through the marsh."[60] Critics frequently add that environmentalism's hidden agenda is antibusiness, maybe even economic revolution.[70]

Environmental leaders also resort to the rhetoric of crisis so habitually that environmentalism's mother tongue may seem to be the Apocalypse. This hyperbolic style begets the kind of misstatements on which critics often seize to demonstrate environmentalism's distorted vision. There have certainly been errors, as the discussion of the controversies over the chemicals disononyl phthalate (DINP) and dioxin demonstrate (see Chapter 4). In addition, the seriousness of many ecological issues declared to be crises may be, at most, a matter of unresolved scientific controversy. Nonetheless, environmentalists have aroused an appropriate sense of urgency about numerous ecological issues such as air and water pollution, groundwater contamination, radioactive wastes, and surface mining, to cite but a few. The crisis style, however, eventually becomes trite and unappealing when it is habitual.

The mainstream environmental organizations are sometimes condemned as shrewd opportunists, promoting policies that enlarge their own political power at public expense. The environmentalist attitude toward the Superfund program is often cited as a flagrant case in point. The major environmental groups generally insist on the strictest possible standards for all Superfund site cleanups, as required in the original law. Others have suggested that some relaxation of standards would enormously shrink the huge program costs and greatly facilitate site cleanups without significantly increasing risks to public health. But, the critics assert, environmentalists insist on the stringent standards because it draws to their side the waste treatment industry and the legal profession, for whom the strictest standards ensure the greatest income.

Constructive Opposition or Destructive Obstruction?

It is a political axiom of organized environmentalism that only unremitting pressure on the government will ensure that environmental laws are implemented effectively. This informal ideology of countervailing power is animated by the conviction that government officials cannot be trusted to implement environmental regulations without the coercive force of pressure politics. Distrust of bureaucrats runs so deeply through environmentalism that, next to saving nature for humanity, environmentalists often seem most dedicated to protecting the public from its public servants. This sour assault on environmental regulators, for instance, comes not from regulation's embittered foes but from Michael McCloskey, the former executive director of the Sierra Club:

> [Regulatory programs] need endless follow-through and can go wrong in a thousand places. The relevant bureaucracies have minds of their own and very little loyalty to the ideas of those who lobbied the programs through.

Although the bureaucracies are somewhat responsive to Presidential direction, they are not very responsive to outside lobbying and are subject to no self-correcting process if they fail to be productive.[71]

The reliance by those within organized environmentalism on countervailing power is manifest in their customary resistance to the relaxation of strict pollution standards, which critics consider to be stonewalling. Countervailing power also means the continual resort to litigation, administrative process, citizen involvement, and any other procedures that equate with group pressure on government. More than half of all litigation initiated against federal agencies involving compliance with NEPA and the majority of all legal challenges to EPA regulations originate with environmental organizations, often in collaboration with labor unions, consumer groups, and private interests. Environmental organizations are extremely aggressive in challenging federal, state, and local agencies over compliance with Superfund cleanup standards and over the licensing of hazardous waste disposal sites and nuclear utilities, among many other issues. Citizen involvement activities at all governmental levels are exploited, if not dominated, by environmental groups and their allies to considerable advantage.[72]

The skilled exploitation of these and other political processes has invested environmentalists with political power they probably would not otherwise have. Moreover, countervailing power often forces administrative agencies and their regulated interests to comply with laws they might prefer to ignore and frequently improves the quality of regulatory decision making. But, countervailing power also has produced enormous delays in the implementation of regulations and increased significantly the cost of environmental regulation through litigation and administrative processes. In addition, countervailing power at state and local levels can virtually immobilize the process of licensing hazardous waste facilities. Whether the use of countervailing power has become dangerously disruptive to environmental governance is a concern to many within the environmental movement as well as to its critics because such power can be subverted into the chronic obstruction of the processes it was intended to safeguard.

The continuing controversy over environmentalism, whatever its admitted merits, reveals some political realities—environmentalist organizations have institutional dogmas and self-serving agendas that may not always be compatible with the larger interests of the movement or even with their own professed goals. Although environmental organizations frequently speak in the name of an encompassing public interest and may unselfishly pursue it, they also speak for a distinctive social and ideological constituency that often does not include the whole public or even a majority of the public. Environmentalism itself is increasingly divided over the goals and social constituencies to which it should be responsive. The rancorous pluralism already inspired by these conflicting convictions will continue to expand during the 21st century. In addition, the professionalization of national organizational leadership—inevitable if environmentalism is to survive the fiercely competitive struggle among interest groups for political resources—is also likely to breed a growing disunity between the national leadership and grassroots environmentalism.

The Public and Environmentalism

Whatever its internal dissonances, the environmental movement has been largely responsible for a remarkable growth in public environmental consciousness and acceptance of environmental protection as an essential public policy. These are public assets, essential to the movement's continuing political vitality, and environmental organizations are extremely adept at arousing public concern on environmental matters and turning it into political advantage. How durable and deep this public support may be, especially in times of severe political or economic hardship, is a different matter.

A Core Value

"The transformation of the environment from an issue of limited concern to one of universal concern is now complete," observed opinion analyst Everett Carll Ladd in mid-1996.[73] The strength of public support for environmental protection early in the 21st century, as measured by public opinion polls, certainly appears vigorous and widespread (see Table 2–1).

It might even appear superficially that the United States was becoming a nation of environmentalists. From the early 1970s to the exit of George W. Bush's presidency, public opinion polls generally exemplified strong public support for environmental protection throughout most American social, ethnic, and regional groups.[74] In 2008, for example, an opinion poll by Duke University's Nicholas Institute posed this question to a representative sample of American voters: "Now, let's say you heard about a proposal that would create stronger national standards to help protect our land, air and water. Not knowing any of the specifics, but just generally, does that sound like something you would favor or oppose?" Almost 80 percent of respondents reported they would favor such a proposal, responses consistent with other polls that regularly exemplified strongly favorable public support for numerous environmental protection measures. Another national poll the same year reported that 41 percent of respondents thought of themselves "as an environmentalist."[75]

Table 2–1   *Citizen Environmental Activities Reported to Gallup, 2000–2010*

"Which of these, if any, have you, yourself, done in the past year?"

	2000 %	2003 %	2007 %	2010 %	Change since 2000 %
Voluntarily recycled newspapers, glass, aluminum, motor oil, or other items	90	89	89	90	0
Reduced your household's use of energy	83	80	85	85	+2
Bought some product specifically because you thought it was better for the environment than competing products	73	72	70	76	+3
Contributed money to an environmental, conservation, or wildlife preservation group	40	42	43	36	-4
Voted for or worked for candidates because of their position on environmental issues	28	30	35	28	0
Contacted a public official about an environmental issue	18	15	17	17	-1
Been active in a group or organization that works to protect the environment	15	20	19	17	+2
Contacted a business to complain about its products or policies because they harm the environment	13	n/a	9	8	-5

Source: Pew Research Center for the People & the Press, a project of the Pew Research Center, Riley E. Dunlap, "At 40, Environmental Movement Endures, With Less Consensus," *Gallup Politics,* April 22, 2010, available at http://www.gallup.com/poll/127487/environmental-movement-endures-less-consensus. aspx (accessed August 10, 2011).

Note: n/a = not asked.

Critics sometimes assert that environmental interest groups speak for only a small portion of the public, but these polls seem to suggest otherwise. In general, opinion polls consistently report that substantial majorities in almost all major socioeconomic groups support the environmental movement and governmental programs to protect the environment and have supported them since Earth Day 1970.[76] Environmental activists have been especially gratified that the polls offer little support to the once widespread notion that concern for environmental quality is a "white thing."[77] As long as environmental questions are lofty abstractions, the public's answers can easily imply that environmentalism's roots run deeply as well as broadly across the nation. Certainly, when the political bedrock of environmental regulation seems threatened—when fundamental laws such as the CAA or Clean Water Act seem imperiled—public support for environmentalism has been impressive.

Environmentalists have also accomplished what amounts to a massive raising of the public's ecological consciousness through public education about environmental issues facing the United States and the world. On the first Earth Day, ecology and the environment were issues foreign to most Americans. Today, most Americans have a rudimentary understanding of many basic ecological precepts, including the importance of resource conservation and the global scale of environmental problems. The movement has educated the public and itself into embracing a progressively larger conception of the environment.

However, environmental organizations also have sometimes encouraged, greater public skepticism about the credibility and managerial skills of the scientists, technicians, and other spokespeople for science and technology involved in public affairs. Since the mid-1970s, environmental organizations have repeatedly challenged the competence of scientific experts and the quality of science supporting opponents in political and administrative battles. These unrelenting technical controversies over the management of commercial nuclear power, the regulation of pesticides, the setting of appropriate air- and water-quality standards, and much else have educated the public about the limits of scientific expertise. Many environmental groups have promoted local citizen involvement in decisions about the siting of real or potential environmental hazards. Critics charge that these groups are entirely too successful at grassroots activism. They blame environmentalists for the rapid spread of NIMBY-ism. This issue is discussed more fully in Chapter 7.

How Deep and Broad Is Public Environmentalism?

Despite the public's ecological concern, environmentalism's public impact is still restricted in politically important ways. Environmentalism may now be a consensual value in U.S. politics, but it is what public opinion analyst Riley E. Dunlap calls a "passive consensus"—a situation of "widespread but not terribly intense public support for a goal [in which] government has considerable flexibility in pursuing the goal and is not carefully monitored by the public."[78]

By 2012, several durable patterns had emerged suggesting that the other things to which Americans are turning seldom include sustained interest or reflection about environmental issues at home, at work, or at the voting booth. First, environmental issues have rarely risen to compelling importance or remained among the issues that most concern the public. Thus, while the public often names the environment among issues about which they concerned, when it comes to voting, the environment seldom ranks among the public's consuming concerns. When the Pew Research Center, for example, asked a sample of the American public in early 2012 which issues they considered most important in the presidential election, the most important concerns were economy, jobs, the budget, and health care—not unexpectedly during an economic recession—while the environment ranked 11th among 18 issues, mentioned by a bare majority (see Table 2–2 below). More, as Table 2–2 also illustrates, environmentalism has remained a relatively low-priority electoral issue during the last several presidential elections.

Table 2–2 *Percent of Voters Saying Each Issue Is "Very Important" to Vote, 2004–2012*

% of voters saying each is "very important" to vote	Aug 2004 %	May 2008 %	Aug 2010 %	Apr 2012 %	2010–2012 Change
Economy	76	88	90	86	−4
Jobs*	76	78	88	84	−4
Budget deficit	55	69	69	74	+5
Health care	72	78	78	74	−4
Education	70	78	–	72	–
Medicare	–	–	–	66	–
Energy	53	77	62	61	−1
Taxes*	59	68	68	61	−7
Terrorism	75	68	71	59	−12
Foreign policy	–	–	–	52	–
Environment	55	62	57	51	−6
Iran	–	–	–	47	–
Gun control	45	–	–	47	–
Afghanistan	–	–	59	46	−13
Immigration	–	54	58	42	−16
Abortion	–	40	43	39	−4
Birth control	–	–	–	34	–
Gay marriage	34	28	31	28	−3

Source: Pew Research Center for People and the Press, *Social Issues Rank as Lowest Priorities, April 17, 2012,* available at www.people-press.org/2012/04/17/with-voters-focused-on-economy-obama-lead-narrows/4-17-12-11/ (accessed May 23, 2012).

Note: Based on registered voters, surveyed April 4–15, 2012.

*2004 data is from mid-October.

Second, this low electoral priority for environmental issues prevails even though the public consistently rates Democrats, and especially Democratic presidential candidates, much higher than Republicans on environmental stewardship. In none of the past six presidential elections, for instance, did more than 11 percent of voters ever state that the environment was the most important issue in casting their ballots.[79] Asked in 2008 if they were likely to vote for a president who was "a strong environmentalist," 54 percent of the poll respondents reported it would matter little or not at all, and another 6 percent were uncertain.[80] Despite Bill Clinton's efforts in 1996 to wrap his campaign in an environmentalist mantle with the presence of self-proclaimed environmentalist Al Gore as his running mate, fewer than 1 percent of those who voted for him cited environmentalism as the most important reason, and fewer than 10 percent cited environmentalism among any reason for supporting him.[81] Conversely, environmentalists may have fiercely criticized George W. Bush's record on environmental regulation, but this did not appear to harm him at the polls.[82] Massive environmentalist criticism of George W. Bush's environmental policies following his 2000 election, moreover, did not appear to change significantly the public's evaluation of Bush as an environmental protector (indeed, in mid-2003, more than half the public polled by Gallup reported that the nation's environmental protection policies were "about the same" as when Bush was elected).[83]

Third, the disconnect between the voters' environmental values and their candidate preferences, especially in presidential elections, seems to result from several enduring assumptions about environmental issues. Duke University's Nichols Institute concluded from a careful survey of voter behavior that most voters

- believe significant progress has been made in environmental protection.
- perceive the environment as "long-term issues that did not warrant the same priority as more 'immediate' concerns such as jobs and health care."
- assume that environmental policies would have negative economic impacts such as lost jobs and higher taxes.[84]

Sudden surges of public interest or apprehension about the environment predictably rise in the aftermath of widely publicized environmental disasters or emergencies, but public concern is usually evanescent unless the issue is repeatedly dramatized and personalized. At best, it appears that deep public engagement with environmental issues is a sometime thing. "While the environment has enjoyed remarkable staying power on the national political agenda over the past thirty years," concludes political scientist Deborah Lynn Guber after studying public environmental attitudes, "public commitment to those issues can be somewhat fickle, moving in cycles that visibly advance and retreat over time."[85]

Fourth, a deep, apparently growing partisan cleavage now runs like a fault line across public alignments on most domestic environmental matters. On most major issues related to environmental policy—how to regulate, what to regulate, and whether to regulate—Republican and Democratic partisans persistently disagree.[86] The breadth and depth of this gap is evident in the Gallup poll found in Figure 2–2 reflecting voter attitudes early in the 2012 presidential election year concerning the environment and other important issues.[87]

This gap is not surprising, considering that Democratic Party identifiers attribute much greater importance to environmental issues and to environmental regulation than Republicans.[88]

Figure 2–2   *Partisan Differences among Voters on Major Political Issues, 2012*

% of voters saying each is "very important" to vote	Total %	Rep %	Dem %	Ind %	R-D diff
Budget deficit	74	86	63	76	R+23
Taxes	61	74	60	53	R+14
Abortion	39	51	40	29	R+11
Economy	86	92	83	86	R+9
Foreign policy	52	58	49	50	R+9
Iran	47	56	47	43	R+9
Gay marriage	28	36	27	24	R+9
Terrorism	59	66	60	52	R+6
Immigration	42	47	42	37	R+5
Gun control	47	51	50	41	R+1
Jobs	84	85	86	81	D+1
Afghanistan	46	45	49	43	D+4
Energy	61	59	68	57	D+9
Health care	74	74	84	66	D+10
Medicare	66	62	77	58	D+15
Birth control	34	31	47	25	D+16
Education	72	63	66	65	D+23
Environment	51	26	74	43	D+48

Source: Pew Research Center for People and the Press, "Wide Partisan Gaps Over Environment, Deficit, Education," April 17, 2012, available at www.people-press.org/2012/04/17/with-voters-focused-on-economy-obama-lead-narrows/4-17-12-12/ (accessed July 20, 2012).

Moreover, the intensity of this partisan division about environmental policy is apparently greater than that found among public attitudes on most, if not all, other issues of concern during the presidential elections and has been increasing. Table 2–3, for example, illustrates the growth of this gap in environmental attitudes among public opinions concerning governmental economic regulation. The breadth and persistence of this partisan divisiveness among the public mirrors the enlarging partisan cleavage about environmental issues in Congress. This pervasive and continuing, if not growing, political division among the public and within government implies a threat of persistent, and perhaps dangerous, impasse of governmental decision making on compelling environmental issues such as global climate warming.

Finally, an important trend since 2000 has been increasing public concern about the possible adverse economic impact of environmental regulation. One symptom has been a gradual increase in the proportion of the public that, when asked to make a choice, agreed that economic growth

Table 2–3   *Partisan Differences Concerning Federal Economic Regulation, 2012*

What should the federal gov't do when it comes to regulating . . .		Feb 2012 %	Rep %	Dem %	Ind %	D–R gap %
Food production & packaging	Strengthen	53	44	63	52	+19
	Keep same	36	43	29	36	−14
	Reduce	7	9	3	9	−6
Environmental protection	Strengthen	50	28	64	53	+36
	Keep same	29	30	28	32	−2
	Reduce	17	36	6	15	−30
Car safety & efficiency	Strengthen	45	33	57	44	+24
	Keep same	42	49	35	44	−14
	Reduce	9	14	5	10	−9
Work place health & safety	Strengthen	41	25	52	43	+27
	Keep same	45	52	42	43	−10
	Reduce	10	18	4	11	−14
Prescription drugs	Strengthen	39	31	41	40	+10
	Keep same	33	37	36	31	−1
	Reduce	20	24	16	21	−8
	N	730	222	224	254	

Source: Pew Research Center for People and the Press, Views of Government Regulation, February 23, 2012, available at http://www.people-press.org/2012/02/23/section-2-views-of-government-regulation (accessed June 3, 2012).

Figure 2–3 Public Preferences: Economic Growth versus Environmental Protection, 1985–2011

Higher Priority for Economic Growth or Environmental Protection

With which one of these statements about the environments and the economy do you most agree—[ROTATED: protection of the environment should be given priority, even at the risk of curbing economic growth (or) economic growth should be given priority, even if the environment suffers to some extent]?

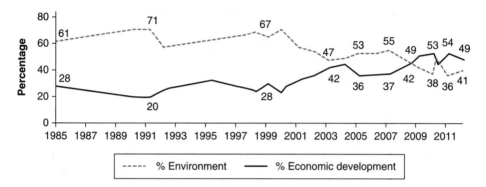

Source: Pew Research Center for the People & the Press, a project of the Pew Research Center, Dennis Jacobe, "Americans Still Prioritize Economic Growth Over Environment," *Gallup Economy,* March 29, 2012, available at www.gallup.com/poll/153515/Americans-Prioritize-Economic-Growth-Environment.aspx (accessed June 19. 2012).

should take precedence over environmental protection—evidence of the nation's growing economic malaise during these years. By 2012, as Figure 2–3 illustrates, Gallup reported after 27 years of repeated polling that, since 2009, in a sharp departure from all past polls, a public majority almost consistently responded that it believed economic growth should be favored over environmental protection if a choice must be made

The severe recession, which began in late 2007, undoubtedly has fueled the public's growing preoccupation with the economy and demonstrated, once again, the potency of economic issues in commanding public attention and setting national policy priorities. Does this imply that environmental protection has become a hostage to the economy? Not necessarily. It is not yet apparent how opinions similar to those expressed to Gallup translate into decisions by the public and public officials concerning specific policies. Such polls are reminders, however, that environmentalism has yet to prove its political toughness by surviving the brutal test of a prolonged recession or a depression. In broader perspective, these polls exemplify what most public officials know from experience—the enormous difficulty in persuading the public to accept the sometimes substantial costs of environmental management in terms of dollars or lifestyle.

(Jimmy Carter, battered by a nasty public backlash after his efforts to manage the 1970s energy crisis with a portfolio of new controls on public energy consumption, compared that struggle to "gnawing on a rock.")[89] It may sometimes appear to environmental leaders that an environmental equivalent of the 9/11 terrorist attack on New York is required to arouse sustained public attention and acceptance for even modest personal costs that might be involved.

Perhaps another common but unstated reason that environmental policy does not engage the public more broadly and deeply is the inherent scientific complexity of the issues, which may often confound the average person. No matter, science and science disputes are unavoidable in environmental policy discourse.

The Special Place of Science in Policy Making

What often distinguishes environmental policy making from other policy domains is the extraordinary importance of science, and scientific controversy, in the policy process. The growth of environmental legislation since the 1970s is evidence of the federal government's increasing concern with science and technology after World War II. Legislation concerning atomic power, air and water pollution, workplace and consumer safety, and hazardous wastes has put before public officials and agencies the need to make determinations of public policy by depending heavily on scientific evidence and scientific judgments. Indeed, environmental issues routinely require administrative agencies, Congress, judges, the White House staff, and even the president to make these determinations.

Science as Law

The range of scientific judgments required of administrative agencies in implementing environmental programs seems to embrace the whole domain of ecological research. For instance, the Coast Guard is authorized "in order to secure effective provisions . . . for protection of the marine environment . . . to establish regulations for ships with respect to the design and construction of such vessels . . . and with respect to equipment and appliances for . . . the prevention and mitigation of damage to the marine environment."[90]

The EPA is to set effluent standards for new sources of water pollution so that each standard reflects "the greatest degree of effluent reduction . . . achievable through application of the best available demonstrated control technology, process, operating methods, or other alternatives, including, where practicable, a standard permitting no discharge of pollutants."[91] The EPA is also required to establish "standards of performance" for classes and categories of new air pollution sources "which contribute significantly to air pollution or contribute to endangerment of public health or welfare."[92]

Congress, and particularly the congressional committees writing legislation, also may have to resolve a multitude of technical issues. When regulating hazardous substances, for instance, what is a reasonable period to specify for chemical manufacturers to produce reliable data on the human effects of potentially dangerous substances? Is it necessary to regulate air emissions from diesel trucks to reduce harmful air pollutants? Is it appropriate to include heavy metals in the list of water pollutants for which standards must be created by the EPA? Eventually, judges will be compelled to weigh scientific evidence and render judgment on environmental issues. For example, did the Department of the Interior have sufficient information to file a valid environmental impact statement on a proposed coal-mining lease on federal lands, as required by NEPA? Or, do federal standards for nuclear reactors adequately protect public safety as required by regulations created by the Nuclear Regulatory Commission?

Science as Politics

In policy conflicts, data become weapons, and science becomes a bastion against critics. Indeed, torturing the technical data to fit some partisan position has become an art form in policy debates. Environmental issues frequently place scientists in a highly charged political atmosphere in which impartiality and objectivity, among the most highly esteemed scientific virtues, are severely tested and sometimes fail.

Scientists are consulted by public officials in good part because the scientists' presumed objectivity, as well as their technical expertise, makes them trustworthy advisers. But, impartiality can be an early casualty in highly partisan and polarizing policy conflicts. Even if scientists maintain impartiality, they cannot prevent the partisans of one or another policy from distorting the technical information to gain an advantage. Scientists suspect (with justification) that their work will often be misrepresented in political debate and their credibility consequently diminished.

In any case, it is characteristic of environmental policy that scientific evidence and opinion frequently are divided for political reasons and, thus, that expert disagreements will reinforce political conflicts. Especially when political conflict tends to polarize views and force division over issues, an expert can intentionally, or unwittingly, shade opinions to fit a favored position or manipulate materials until they fit a simplistic policy position. "Experts tend to behave like other people when they engage in a controversy," Allan Mazur, a sociologist and physicist, observes. "Coalitions solidify and disagreements become polarized as conflict becomes more acrimonious."[93] Mazur further observes that experts favoring nuclear power tend to support the notion that a threshold of radiation exposure exists below which human risks are negligible; experts opposing nuclear power plants, in contrast, favor a linear conception of risk that permits no such threshold.[94] When scientific disputes erupt in the course of environmental decision making, we need not assume willful deceit on any side to suggest that political and economic bias could, and probably does, play some part in convincing experts of the truth of a position. Unfortunately, few executives or legislative agencies are innocent of data manipulation, deliberate or not, at some time.

Policy Pressures and the Scientific Method

Few public officials are scientists. Faced with the technical questions inherent in environmental policy, officials customarily turn to scientists and technicians for answers or at least for definitions of alternative solutions to clarify choices. As a matter of practical politics, solving issues by resorting to credible scientific evidence can also deflect from officials the criticism they might otherwise endure—sometimes science alone legitimizes policy. But, the politician and the scientist live in fundamentally different decision-making worlds.

For instance, significant differences exist in the time frames for problem solving. "In his search for truth," biologist Roger Revelle observes, "the scientist is oriented toward the future; the politician's orientation is usually here and now. He desires quick visible pay-offs for which he often seems willing to mortgage the future. For the politician in a democratic society, infinity is the election after the next one."[95] Often, public officials are compelled to act swiftly. The CAA, for example, required the EPA administrator to set standards for sulfur oxides and nitrogen oxides within two years. The Superfund Amendments and Reauthorization Act, passed in 1986, included among its 150 deadlines a requirement that the EPA issue a plan to implement the act's radon research program, produce an annual report on radon mitigation demonstration programs, and provide a report on its national assessment of the radon problem in less than two years after the legislation was passed.[96]

If a crisis erupts—a newly discovered, leaking hazardous waste dump or a potentially catastrophic oil spill, for instance—information is needed immediately. But, scientific information rarely appears on demand, even in urgent situations and especially when it must be sufficiently accurate to point to a clear direction for policy.

Public officials, moreover, often must craft environmental policies amid continuing disagreement between experts and the public over the degree of risk associated with various environmental problems. For instance, whereas the public rated chemical waste disposal as the highest environmental risk, the experts ranked it considerably lower. In contrast, the experts assigned much greater risk to stratospheric ozone depletion and indoor radon than did the public. Chemical plant accidents were rated a major risk by the public but not by the experts. In effect, these differences amount to two different agendas of priority for environmental regulation. Critics of current environmental regulation, pointing to these disparate views of ecological risk, often argue that public opinion has intimidated policy makers into following the wrong environmental priorities.

Still, decisions must be made, thus often confronting policy makers with an unwelcome choice between a scientifically risky decision and a politically risky one.[97] Consider, for example, the decision facing EPA Administrator Lisa Jackson and her staff in mid-2012 when confronting a legal requirement that the EPA review the national air-quality standard for fine particulates, often called *soot,* and recommend change from an older standard if more recent scientific research justified it. Particulates are extremely small, solid particles found in air and produced by dust, smoke, fuel combustion, agriculture, and forest cultivation, among other sources. Soot is a recognized public health hazard associated with significant deaths, chronic respiratory illness, infant mortality, and other illness. Confronted with an approaching legal deadline and based upon available EPA research, Jackson had informed the White House that she would recommend that existing permissible particulate levels be reduced—in effect, made more rigorous—from the current 15 micrograms per cubic meter of air to 12 micrograms, a decision the EPA estimated would prevent thousands of premature deaths and other illness. The White House responded to the EPA's recommendation with a suggestion that the particulate requirement be less rigorous but still tougher than the existing standard. Jackson subsequently responded with a new proposal for a less rigorous standard than she had originally advocated.

The EPA's revised decision incited an intense, public political and scientific controversy. Critics, including many public health organizations, charged that the White House was interfering with EPA science. Environmentalist organizations were almost unanimously opposed to the White House response. In that spirit, the Clean Air Director of the Natural Resources Council, a major national environmental organization, considered it "obnoxious and untoward that a bunch of economists and politicos in the [White House] evidently told EPA that it had to propose a [weaker standard] as a formally endorsed preference, contrary to EPA's wishes and scientific views."[98] Congressional Republicans, major spokespeople for the petroleum industry such as the American Petroleum Institute, and organizations representing major industries subject to the regulation asserted that the EPA's initial recommendation had been scientifically questionable and economically damaging; many opposing the EPA's new standard asserted that there was no compelling need to change the standard at all, especially at a time when the regulated industries were enduring an economic recession. Moreover, the EPA was aware of concern from political spokespeople from a number of populous urban U.S. counties who expressed displeasure because their counties would be out of compliance with any newly revised standard, resulting in potentially serious political and economic impacts.

As the debate evolved, it became clear that setting the new standard also involved substantial scientific uncertainties. EPA scientists had long acknowledged that setting the particulate standard was difficult because any standard except total elimination of airborne particulates—a political and economic impossibility—would still create significant public health risks.[99] In short, no scientifically "safe" standard could be created, and any decision would have to be made on the basis of how much estimated risk to public health was considered acceptable.

While the EPA had until December 2012 to make a decision and was not necessarily compelled to heed the White House recommendations, as a practical matter, the agency would almost certainly have to abide by White House preferences. In the end, whatever decision Jackson and her staff eventually made concerning the final standard, there was no safe harbor from a decision loaded with both scientific and political risk and uncertainty—and the same problem will likely arise when the standard has to be reviewed in the future.

Conclusion

In an important sense, environmental degradation is a 21st century problem resolved according 18th-century rules. Fundamental government arrangements, such as institutional checks and balances, interest-group liberalism, federalism, and much else reviewed in this chapter, are explicitly created by the Constitution or are implicit in its philosophy. The explosive growth of federal environmental legislation and the distinctive role of science in environmental policy making add distinctly new elements to the federal policy cycle and indicate that environmental management has become a permanent new policy domain within federal and state governments with its own set of institutional and political biases.

Suggested Readings

Cohen, Richard E. *Washington at Work: Back Rooms and Clean Air.* New York: Macmillan, 1992.
Gruber, Deborah Lynn. *The Grassroots of a Green Revolution.* Cambridge, MA: MIT Press, 2003.

Layzer, Judith. *The Environmental Case: Translating Values Into Policy.* 2nd ed. Washington, DC: CQ Press, 2005.

Lindblom, Charles A., and Edward J. Woodhouse. *The Policy-Making Process.* 3rd ed. Englewood Cliffs, NJ: Prentice Hall, 1993.

Marzotto, Toni, Vicky Moshier Burnor, and Gordon Scott Bonham. *The Evolution of Public Policy: Cars and the Environment.* Boulder, CO: Lynne Rienner, 2000.

Notes

1. Quoted in Mara Liasson, "On Obama's Team, Ex-Clinton Staffers Get Do-Over," *NPR News,* December 23, 2008, available at http://www.npr.org/templates/story/story .php?storyId=98593976 (accessed October 10, 2010).

2. Andrew C. Revkin, "Climate Scientist Says NASA Tried to Silence Him," *New York Times,* January 29, 2006, A1.

3. Quoted in Chuck Schoffner, "NASA Expert Says Bush Administration Stifles Evidence on Global Warming," Associated Press State and Local Wire, October 27, 2004, available at www.ap.org (accessed January 5, 2007).

4. Quoted in Revkin, "Climate Scientist," A1.

5. Ibid.

6. Andrew C. Revkin, "NASA Chief Backs Agency Openness," *New York Times,* February 4, 2006, 1.

7. Quoted in Andrew C. Revkin, "Lawmaker Condemns NASA Over Scientist's Accusations of Censorship," *New York Times,* January 31, 2006, A15.

8. Quoted in ibid.

9. Quoted in Revkin, "Climate Scientist," A1.

10. Andrew C. Revkin, "Years Later Climatologist Renews His Call for Action," *New York Times,* June 23, 2008, A18.

11. Andrew C. Revkin, "NASA Office Is Criticized on Climate Reports," *New York Times,* June 3, 2008, A16.

12. States News Service, "James Hansen and David Foster Share Inaugural Peter A. A. Berle Environmental Integrity Awards," April 30, 2009; PR Newswire, "NASA Climate Scientist Honored by American Meteorological Society," January 14, 2009.

13. Christa Marshall, "Hansen Says Obama Will Be 'Greenwashing' About Climate Change If He Approves Keystone XL Pipeline," *Climate Wire,* August 26, 2011, available at www.nytimes.com/cwire/2011/08/26/26climatewire-hansen-says-obama-will-be-greenwashing-about-72041.html (accessed February 17, 2012).

14. James Hansen, "Game Over for the Climate," *Reviewers' New York Times,* May 9, 2012, available at www.nytimes.com/2012/05/10/opinion/game-over-for-the-climate .html?_r=3&ref=opinion (accessed March 20, 2012).

15. Quoted by *The Atheist Conservative,* April 12, 2012, available at http://www.theatheist conservative.com/tag/james-hansen-one-of-the-worlds-leading-global-warming-alarmists/ (accessed May 4, 2012).

16. Jann S. Wenner, "Ready For the Fight: Rolling Stone Interview With Barack Obama," *Rolling Stone,* April 25, 2012, available at www.rollingstone.com/politics/news/ready-for-the-fight-rolling-stone-interview-with-barack-obama-20120425?print=true (accessed June 1, 2012).

17. Hugh Heclo, "Issue Networks and the Executive Establishment," in *The New American Political System,* ed. Anthony King (Washington, DC: American Enterprise Institute, 1979), 89.

18. Charles O. Jones, *An Introduction to Public Policy* (North Scituate, MA: Duxbury Press, 1978), 38.

19. Roger W. Cobb and Charles D. Elder, *Participation in American Politics* (Baltimore: Johns Hopkins University Press, 1972), 86.
20. J. Clarence Davies III, "Environmental Regulation and Technical Change," in *Keeping Pace With Science and Engineering: Studies in Environmental Regulation,* ed. Myron F. Uman (Washington, DC: National Academies Press, 1993), 255.
21. Eugene Bardach, *The Implementation Game* (Cambridge, MA: MIT Press, 1971), 36.
22. Peter deLeon, "A Theory of Termination in the Policy Process: Rules, Rhymes and Reasons," paper delivered at the annual meeting of the American Political Science Association, Washington, DC, September 1–4, 1977, 2.
23. Richard E. Neustadt, *Presidential Power* (New York: John Wiley, 1960).
24. Morton Grodzins, "The Federal System," in *American Federalism in Perspective,* ed. Aaron Wildavsky (Boston: Little, Brown, 1967), 257.
25. Ibid. See also Charles E. Davis and James P. Lester, "Federalism and Environmental Policy," in *Environmental Politics and Policy: Theories and Evidence,* ed. James P. Lester (Durham, NC: Duke University Press, 1989), 57–86; James P. Lester, "A New Federalism? Environmental Policy in the States," in *Environmental Policy in the 1990s,* ed. Norman J. Vig and Michael Kraft (Washington, DC: CQ Press, 1990), 59–80.
26. Executive Office of the President, Office of Management and Budget, Office of Information and Regulatory Affairs, *2011 Report to Congress on the Benefits and Costs of Federal Regulations and Unfunded Mandates on State, Local and Tribal Entities,* 13, available at www.whitehouse.gov/sites/default/files/omb/ . . . /2011_cba_report.pdf (accessed July 11, 2012). Some of these costs were offset by other federal grants. The estimated benefits of these regulations were also estimated to exceed $81 billion.
27. This mingling of private and public power is well explored in Grant McConnell, *Private Power and American Democracy* (New York: Vintage, 1967). See also Helen M. Ingram and Dean E. Mann, "Interest Groups and Environmental Policy," in *Environmental Politics and Policy: Theories and Evidence,* ed. James P. Lester (Durham, NC: Duke University Press, 1989), 135–157.
28. James V. DeLong, "How to Convince an Agency," *Regulation* (September–October 1982): 31.
29. Graham Allison, *The Essence of Decision* (Boston: Little, Brown, 1971), 163.
30. Charles A. Lindblom, "The Science of Muddling Through," *Public Administration Review* (spring 1959): 86.
31. James Gustave Speth, "Environmental Failure: A Case for the New Green Politics," *Environment 360: Opinion,* October 20, 2008, available at http://e360.yale.edu/ content/ feature.msp?id=2075 (accessed November 3, 2008).
32. The reasons for this departure are examined carefully in J. Clarence Davies III and Charles F. Lettow, "The Impact of Federal Institutional Arrangements," in *Federal Environmental Law,* ed. Erica L. Dolgin and Thomas G. P. Guilbert (St. Paul, MN: West, 1974), 26–191.
33. Theodore Lowi, "The Public Philosophy: Interest Group Liberalism," *American Political Science Review* 61 (March 1967): 18.
34. McConnell, *Private Power and American Democracy,* 162.
35. Center for Public Integrity, "Investigations: The Climate Change Lobby Heating Up," available at www.publicintegrity.org/projects/entry/1182/ (accessed August 28, 2009).
36. Charles E. Lindblom and Edward J. Woodhouse, *The Policy-Making Process,* 3rd ed. (Englewood Cliffs, NJ: Prentice-Hall, 1993), 90.
37. Charles A. Lindblom, *The Policy Making Process,* 2nd ed. (Englewood Cliffs, NJ: Prentice Hall, 1980), 73.
38. Ibid.
39. Fredreka Schouten, "Big Greens and Friends Spend $2.9 million in Aug 09 Pushing Self-Dealing Climate Bills," *USA Today,* September 2, 2009, available at http://www.usatoday .com/news/washington/2009-09-02-climateads_N.htm (accessed February 17, 2010).

40. Fredreka Schouten, "Backers of Climate Bill Spend More on Ads," *USA Today,* September 3, 2009, available at www.usatoday.com/news/washington/2009-09-02-climateads_N.htm (accessed December 23, 2009).

41. Dina Cappiello, "Politics Replaces Pollution as Agency's Top Foe," *Atlanta Journal-Constitution,* April 22, 2012. Quoted in *Greenwire,* April 23, 2012, available at http://www.eenews.net/Greenwire/2012/04/23/6/ (accessed April 25, 2012).

42. Ibid.

43. Robert Brulle, Liesel Hall Turner, Jason Carmichael, and J. Craig Jenkins, "Measuring Social Movement Organization Populations: A Comprehensive Census of U.S. Environmental Movement Organizations," *Mobilization: An International Quarterly Review* 12 (July 2007): 195–210.

44. Dunlap, "State of Environmentalism in the U.S.—Diagnosis: Neither Dead nor Rejuvenated," April 26, 2007, available at www.ecoamerica.typepad.com/blog/2007/04/the_state_of_en.html (accessed August 28, 2008).

45. Identified as nonprofits by the U.S. Internal Revenue Service.

46. Based on estimates for 2005 in Baird Straughan and Tom Pollak, *The Broader Movement: Nonprofit Environmental and Conservation Organizations, 1989–2005* (Washington, D C: The Urban Institute, 2008).

47. Ibid., 37.

48. Katrina Darlene Taylor, "The Broadening Strategy of Environmental Organizations on the Issue of Global Warming," paper presented at the annual conference of the Western Political Science Association, San Diego, CA, 2008.

49. Committee on Energy and Commerce, "Climate Change Legislation Design White Paper: Appropriate Roles for Different Levels of Government," February 2008, available at http://energycommerce.house.gov/Climate_Change/white%20paper%20st-lcl%20roles%20final%202-22.pdf (accessed June 23, 2008).

50. Tom Price, "The New Environmentalism: Can New Business Policies Save the Environment?" *CQ Researcher* 16, no. 42 (2006): 985–1008.

51. William Ophuls, *Ecology and the Politics of Uncertainty* (San Francisco: Freeman, 1977), 171.

52. Susan Leeson, "Philosophic Implications of the Ecological Crisis: The Authoritarian Challenge to Liberalism," *Polity* 11 (spring 1979): 305.

53. Michael McCloskey, "Twenty Years of Change in the Environmental Movement: An Insider's View," in *American Environmentalism: The U.S. Environmental Movement, 1970–1990,* ed. Riley E. Dunlap and Angela G. Mertig (Philadelphia: Taylor and Francis, 1991), 78–89, quotation on 78.

54. Brian Tokar, "Questioning Official Environmentalism," *Z Magazine* (April 1997): 38.

55. Jeffrey St. Clair, "Panda Porn: The Marriage of WWF and Weyerhaeuser," *Counterpunch Magazine,* December 5, 2002, available at http://www.counterpunch.org/stclair1205.html (accessed April 2, 2010).

56. Bill Devall, "Deep Ecology and Radical Environmentalism," in *American Environmentalism: The U.S. Environmental Movement, 1970–1990,* ed. Riley E. Dunlap and Angela G. Mertig (Philadelphia: Taylor and Francis, 1991), 51–61; G. Sessions, "The Deep Ecology Movement," *Environment Review* 11 (June 1987): 105–125; Rick Scarce, *Eco-Warriors: Understanding the Radical Environmental Movement* (Chicago, IL: Noble Press, 1992).

57. Devall, "Deep Ecology and Radical Environmentalism," 55.

58. David Foreman, *Ecodefense* (Tucson, AZ: Abbzug Press, 1988); G. Grossman, *And on the Eighth Day We Bulldozed It* (San Francisco: Rainbow Action Network, 1988); S. Obst Love and D. Obst Love, eds., *Ecotage* (New York: Bantam, 1972); D. Day, *The Environmental Wars: Reports From the Front Lines* (New York: St. Martin's, 1989).

59. John H. Cushman Jr. and Evelyn Nieves, "In Colorado Resort Fires, Culprits Defy Easy Labels," *New York Times,* October 24, 1998.

60. Robert Cameron Mitchell, "From Conservation to Environmental Movement: The Development of the Modern Environmental Lobbies," in *Government and Environmental Politics,* ed. Michael J. Lacey (Washington, DC: Wilson Center Press, 1989), 81–114; Michael deCourcy Hinds, "The Politics of Pollution," *American Demographics* 22 (2000): 26.

61. John M. Bridgeland, Mary McNaught, Bruce Reed, and Mark Dunkelman, *The Quiet Crisis: The Impact of the Economic Downturn on the Nonprofit Sector* (Washington, DC: W. K. Kellogg Foundation, 2009); Training Resources for the Environmental Community (TREC), *Moving to Higher Ground: Funding Strategies in Challenging Times,* available at http://www.trec.org/resource/page-report.asp?nMode=1&nLibraryID=32# (accessed June 18, 2012).

62. See, for example, Lyle Scruggs and Salil Benegal, "Declining Public Concern About Climate Change: Can We Blame the Great Recession?," *Global Environmental Change* 22, no. 2 (2012), available at sp.uconn.edu/~scruggs/gec11.pdf (accessed September 20, 2012).

63. George Hoberg, *Pluralism by Design: Environmental Policy and the American Regulatory State* (New York: Praeger, 1992), ix.

64. Ibid., 198–199.

65. Warren T. Brookes, "Here Comes Flat Earth Day," *Detroit News,* March 8, 1990, 13.

66. Amanda Little, "RFK Jr. and Other Prominent Enviros Face Off Over Cape Cod Wind Farm," *Grist,* January 12, 2006, available at www.grist.org/article/capecod (accessed July 10, 2009); Jeffry Ball, "Power Shift: Renewable Energy, Meet the New Nimbys— Solar and Wind-Power Proposals Draw Opposition From Residents Fearing Visual Blight; a Dilemma for Some Environmentalists," *Wall Street Journal* (eastern ed.), September 4, 2009, A13.

67. John H. Adams, "The Mainstream Environmental Movement," *EPA Journal* 18, no. 1 (1992): 25–26.

68. Bryan Mayor, *Blue-Green Coalitions: Fighting for Safe Workplaces and Healthy Communities* (Ithaca, NY: Cornell University Press, 2009).

69. Quoted in *New York Times,* June 9, 1993, 7.

70. Marc K. Landy and Mary Hague, "The Coalition for Waste: Private Interests and Superfund," in *Environmental Politics: Public Costs, Private Rewards,* ed. Michael S. Greve and Fred L. Smith (New York: Praeger, 1992), 75.

71. McCloskey, "Twenty Years of Change," 86.

72. Michael J. McCann, "Public Interest Liberalism and the Modern Regulatory State," *Polity* 21 (winter 1988): 373–400.

73. Everett Carll Ladd and Karlyn Bowman, "Public Opinion on the Environment," *Resources* 124 (summer 1996): 5.

74. See, for example, Riley E. Dunlap, "An Enduring Concern," *Public Perspective* (September–October 2002): 10–15.

75. Nicholas Institute for Environmental Policy Solutions, *A Presentation of Key Findings From a National Survey of 800 Likely Voters Conducted August 25–28, 2005* (Durham NC: Nicholas Institute, 2005), 2.

76. Steven R. Brechin and Daniel A. Freeman, "Public Support for Both the Environment and Anti-Environmental President: Possible Explanations for the George W. Bush Anomaly," *Forum* 2, no. 1 (2004), Berkeley Electronic Press, available at http://www.bepress.com/forum (accessed October 20, 2005).

77. Paul Mohai, "Dispelling Old Myths: African American Concern for the Environment," *Environment* 45 (June 2003): 11–26.

78. Riley E. Dunlap, "Public Opinion and Environmental Policy," in *Environmental Politics and Policy: Theories and Evidence,* ed. James P. Lester (Durham, NC: Duke University Press, 1989), 131.

79. Ibid.

80. ABC News/Planet Green/Stanford University poll.

81. Ibid., 7.

82. Brechin and Freeman, "Public Support."

83. Riley E. Dunlap, "No Environmental Backlash Against Bush Administration," April 19, 2007, available at http://www.gallup.com/poll/27256/state-environmentalism-us.aspx (accessed August 1, 2007).

84. Jim DiPeso, "The 2006 Midterm Elections: An Environmental Perspective," *Environmental Quality Management* (spring 2006), available at www.interscience.wiley.com (accessed January 20, 2007).

85. Deborah Lynn Guber, *The Grassroots of a Green Revolution* (Cambridge, MA: MIT Press, 2003), 177.

86. See, for example, Riley E. Dunlap, "Climate Change Views: Republican-Democratic Gaps Expand," May 29, 2008, available at http://www.gallup.com/poll/107569/Climate Change-Views-RepublicanDemocratic-Gaps-Expand.aspx (accessed February 13, 2010).

87. Pew Research Center for People and the Press, *Social Issues Rank as Lowest Priorities* (Washington, DC: Pew Research Center), 12, available at http://www.people-press .org/2012/04/17/with-voters-focused-on-economy-obama-lead-narrows/ (accessed May 16, 2012).

88. For example, nearly three quarters of Democratic voters (74 percent) say that the environment will be very important to their vote this fall. Just 43 percent of independents and 26 percent of Republicans rate the environment as very important. The environment ranks near the top of the Democrats' agenda; for Republicans, it ranks last among 18 issues tested in Figure 2–2.

89. Quoted in Neil King, Jr., "A Past President's Advice to Obama: Act With Haste—Jimmy Carter Says New Administration Needs to Harness the Benefits of a Crisis Mentality to Tame Energy Policy," *Wall Street Journal* (eastern ed.), December 11, 2008, A16.

90. Ports and Waterways Act of 1972, Pub. L. No. 92–340.

91. Federal Water Pollution Control Act Amendments of 1972, Pub. L. No. 92–500.

92. CAA, Pub. L. No. 84–159 (1955), Pub. L. No. 91–604 (1970), Pub. L. No. 101–549 (1990).

93. Allan Mazur, *The Dynamics of Technical Controversy* (Washington, DC: Communications Press, 1981), 29.

94. Ibid., 27.

95. Roger Revelle, "The Scientist and the Politician," in *Science, Technology, and National Policy*, ed. Thomas J. Kuehn and Alan L. Porter (Ithaca, NY: Cornell University Press, 1981), 134.

96. U.S. General Accounting Office, "Superfund: Missed Statutory Deadlines Slow Progress in Environmental Programs," Report no. GAO/RCED 89–27, Washington, DC, November 1988, chap. 2.

97. The epitome of this decision-making problem is explored in Riley Dunlap, *DDT: Scientists, Citizens, and Public Policy* (Princeton, NJ: Princeton University Press, 1981), esp. chap. 8.

98. Gabriel Nelson, "White House Change to EPA Soot Standards Stirs Debate," *E&E Reporter,* July 18, 2012, available at www.eenews.net/Greenwire/2012/07/18/2 (accessed July 20, 2012).

99. Quoted from U.S. EPA, *Draft Proposal for the Particulate Matter (PM) National Ambient Air Quality Standards (NAAQS): Briefing for Interagency Review, June 4, 2012* (Washington DC: EPA), available at Gabriel Nelson, op cit.

Chapter 3

Making Policy
Institutions and Politics

The White House—any White House—doesn't want to hear an awful lot from the EPA. It's not an agency that ever makes friends for a president.[1]
— William K. Reilly, former administrator of the EPA

It was May 2003. Christine Todd Whitman, administrator of the EPA, and Gale Norton, secretary of the Interior, were meeting for lunch. Neither suspected they were about to plunge unwittingly and unwillingly into an acrimonious environmental controversy that would eventually entangle their agencies, span three presidencies, endure for 18 years, and end—perhaps—with the presidency of Barack Obama. The lunch was a convenient way for two of President George W. Bush's most important environmental administrators to facilitate cooperation between their departments by sharing common concerns and exchanging important information. The year so far had gone badly for Whitman. There were continued public disagreements with the Bush White House and pervasive rumors in Washington, DC, that Whitman had fallen from White House favor and might quit her job or be fired. However, the lunch with Norton—a monthly arrangement—should have been unremarkable. The lunch was civil enough, but even as they ate, the EPA was publicly announcing its support for a ban on snowmobiles in Yellowstone National Park, which Norton, the Department of the Interior (DOI), and the Bush White House had all vigorously opposed since the president's inauguration.

Norton was irritated, and a "blunt conversation" followed. She telephoned the EPA administrator that same afternoon to complain: Why had Whitman failed to tell her about the announcement while they were at lunch? Whitman was surprised because she had not been notified either.

81

In fact, the EPA "announcement" was just a letter written by a relatively low-level regional EPA administrator to the National Park Service (NPS) merely recommending the replacement of snowmobiles. Someone with a distaste for snowmobiles in the Denver EPA office had released the letter to the media, thus creating public confusion about the Bush administration's controversial snowmobile policy, adding to Whitman's discomfort and annoying Norton. "All the people who should have been notified on the snowmobile issue weren't," explained an EPA media spokesperson unhelpfully. Shortly thereafter, Whitman held a conference call with agency employees across the nation to remind them that politically sensitive information like the Denver letter should be cleared with her office.[2]

The EPA letter was merely one episode along a convoluted path left by the snowmobile policy as it labored through the federal government's policy making labyrinth for more than a decade. The trail began when President Bill Clinton, late in his second term, recommended that the DOI ban snowmobiles from Yellowstone and Grand Teton national parks, and the department's NPS sought to comply. When the snowmobile industry and its many allied interests vigorously protested the ban, President Bush, who opposed the Clinton decision, announced on his first day in office that he would encourage the NPS to continue allowing the vehicles in Yellowstone and Grand Teton. The EPA's embarrassing letter appeared while the NPS was preparing to follow Bush's initiative. Opponents of the snowmobiles responded to Bush's announcement by taking their case to the federal courts and, in December 2003, the Washington, DC, district court ordered the DOI to reinstate the Clinton ban on snowmobiles. The Republican majority in the House of Representatives then unsuccessfully attempted to counter the district court by passing a bill, ultimately unsuccessful, that would have permitted continued use of snowmobiles in the parks.[3]

The snowmobile issue now motored back into the federal judiciary and through the federal bureaucracy. In August 2004, the NPS proposed to permit snowmobiles in the parks for at least three years while it studied the conflicting scientific and economic data about snowmobiles. Two months later, the NPS publicly released its plan to allow limited, guided daily treks for 750 snowmobiles in Yellowstone—about twice the average entering the previous year. Environmentalists and other opponents of the snowmobiles now moved to another venue, persuading the Washington, DC, federal district court in September 2004 to order the DOI to restore the Clinton administration's snowmobile ban. The snowmobile industry and its allies countered by initiating other litigation in the Wyoming federal district court, resulting in an October 2004 court injunction in effect forbidding the DOI to enforce the Clinton ban on snowmobiles in Yellowstone and Grand Teton national parks.[4]

The Bush administration seemed to have won. It was "a common sense solution for snowmobile use that protects resources while also allowing appropriate access for employment by the public," exalted Secretary of the Interior Norton. To underscore her point, Norton appeared at Yellowstone Park in February 2005 "with a jaunty orange pennant waving from the back of her black snowmobile," reported the *New York Times,* "[and] tootled through a snowscape of hills, steaming rivers and indifferent bison this week giving an unusual personal endorsement to the machines that some consider a blight and others a blessing."[5] Even though many western political leaders in both parties, and a substantial portion of the western public, were less enthusiastic about snowmobiles—one opinion poll reported that 80 percent of the western public favored more limits on snowmobiles in the two parks—snowmobiles seemed to have overrun the opposition.[6]

But, that was not the end of the story. When Norton resigned from the DOI in mid-2006, she was succeeded by former Idaho governor Kirk Kempthorne, whose nomination was vigorously opposed by environmentalists who considered him an archopponent and a sure partisan for more snowmobiles in the parks. Contrary to predictions, however, the DOI's proposed new park regulations in November 2006 rejected the increased use of snowmobiles in the parks, limited snowmobile access to 518 vehicles daily (less than the NPS quota originally proposed in 2003), and suspended additional snowmobile regulations for three years while a fourth environmental impact statement on the issue was created. This decision satisfied neither the proponents nor opponents of snowmobiles (snowmobiling had become "the most managed experience known to man" growled a snowmobile industry spokesman[7]), and both sides now shifted the controversy back to the federal courts, so often the last resort in environmental policy contention.

From September 2008 until December 2009, the snowmobile issue shuttled between various federal court jurisdictions as each side went venue shopping for an advantage. In September 2008, the Washington, DC, district court rejected the NPS limit of 518 vehicles daily in Yellowstone and Grand Teton national parks, and the NPS responded with a new temporary regulation limiting the snowmobiles to 318 daily. Almost immediately thereafter, another federal district court, in Denver, Colorado, considered the issue from a different legal perspective, rejected the new limit of 318 daily vehicles, and ordered the NPS to reinstate its quota of 720 snowmobiles daily. There the matter stood until mid-July 2009 when Ken Salazar, the new Obama administration's secretary of the Interior, announced that the 318-vehicle limit at Yellowstone and Grand Teton would prevail temporarily, while the NPS spent the next two years working out a final snowmobile plan for both parks. Wyoming's congressional delegation, whose state's recreation industry depended substantially on park patronage, promptly blasted the new arrangement as "an insult to our state and gateway communities." A spokesperson for the snowmobile industry complained that snowmobilers were "incredibly frustrated."[8] Snowmobile opponents like the National Parks Conservation Association complained that the whole process had taken too long and had been inconclusive. The NPS went to work on another environmental impact statement.

Although the discordant progress of its snowmobile policy undoubtedly annoyed the Bush White House, similar instances of publicly confused policy making, often ending with problematic solutions, can be found in the history of any presidency and will surely appear before the end of the Obama presidency. Policy making in the federal government is inherently time-consuming, frequently highly contentious, and often mined with surprises and uncertainties. This situation arises in large part because different institutions, often with conflicting missions, are involved in the policy making process. It could hardly be otherwise in a government of checks and balances, where institutions exercise competing and shared powers concurrently. In addition, history resonates through the policy-making process. Today's policy discussions are infused with institutional memories of past events and nuanced with expectations for the future. This chapter examines the most important of the institutions involved in this process to exemplify how competing constitutional authority, shared powers, and historical experience shape the character of policy making in Washington.

The Presidency

"Mothers all want their sons to grow up to be president," President John Kennedy once remarked, "but they don't want them to become politicians in the process."[9] The president wields vast constitutional authority and powerful leverage over public opinion, enlarged by a century of growing public tolerance for presidential assertions of additional inherent powers. But, to be a successful policy maker, the president must still be a proficient politician. The essential politics of presidential leadership in environmental affairs, as with other policy issues, requires, among other things, the will as well as the ability to bargain and compromise with Congress, to know how to shape public opinion and when to be governed by it, and to know when to respect judicial independence and when to challenge it—in short, a capacity to move a government of divided powers and competitive institutions in the direction that presidential policies require.

Occupants of the White House since Earth Day 1970 have varied greatly in their concern about environmental protection and their ability to translate environmental commitments into practical policy. So-called green presidents have often been the least successful environmental policy makers. It is a lesson repeated endlessly in Washington that even presidents committed to the politics of policy making discover they cannot always command the ends even when they summon the means for policy leadership (see Chapter 1).

Presidential Resources

Environmentalists, long irate at what they perceived to be the Bush administration's dismal environmental record, had awaited prompt signals that the new Obama administration would bring the anticipated friendlier environmentalist agenda to Washington, and they weren't disappointed. Within days of taking office, Obama had, among other welcome initiatives, exercised his constitutional authority as chief executive to revoke Bush administration policies promoting resource exploration near Utah public lands, to suspend other Bush measures facilitating increased timber production from the national forests, and to order regulators to write stringent new rules for auto emissions and fuel economy. This followed a high-profile "green inauguration" featuring a carbon-neutral ball (another was celebrated on a green carpet made from recycled rug), hybrid Lexuses for transportation, organic menus, recycled paper invitations, and valet bicycle parking. All of this demonstrated early the president's intention to summon both the inherent constitutional powers of his office and his unrivalled ability to command media attention to advance his environmental agenda. Here were potent presidential resources, a few among many, that could effectively shape the course of White House environmental policy making—if presidential skill, historical opportunity, congressional and judicial collaboration, the economy, the public, and luck also permitted.

Constitutional Powers

As the nation's chief executive, the president can bring to environmental policy making a vast array of constitutional powers. A short list of these resources includes the following:

- The authority to propose and to veto legislation
- The ability to propose policy priorities and initiatives to Congress and the nation simultaneously in the constitutional State of the Union message
- The power to draft and to present to Congress the annual federal budget

- The authority to appoint a cabinet of executive department heads and to designate other executive leadership of most major federal environmental bureaucracies, such as the DOI and the EPA
- The power to appoint federal judges when judicial vacancies occur
- The prerogative to issue executive orders, which require no congressional approval, to all federal executive agencies
- An ability to appoint policy advisers to the president's personal staff and to White House advisory committees required by Congress
- The authority to negotiate and to propose international agreements and treaties for congressional approval[10]

This inventory excludes a great deal, such as the talent of creative presidents to transmute traditional authority into new modes of influence (such as President Clinton's technique for frustrating congressional Republican opposition to new federally protected forests by creating them through executive orders immune to congressional veto). Moreover, presidential power also resides in the president's decision not to use his or her resources of policy leadership—inaction is also a form of policy making.

In practice, presidential ability to capitalize on the presidency's political resources for environmental purposes has varied greatly. One explanation for this variability is the many ways in which circumstances can alter the political climate surrounding the White House—events such as economic recessions, changing congressional majorities, and other changes in the political "seasons." Moreover, some presidents, such as Jimmy Carter, have been less skilled than others at Washington politics.

Surprise, Crisis, and the Presidency

Sometimes, presidential policy making is blessed or plagued by the unexpected and the unpredictable—as, for instance, when the first Earth Day arrived to the complete surprise of President Richard Nixon and his staff. Often, presidents discover that their policy agendas and priorities become captive not only to unexpected events but to crises that force the pace and substance of White House politics, however much the president may wish otherwise. Crises of various kinds have compelled many crucial White House environmental initiatives such as the Superfund legislation in 1980 regulating abandoned hazardous waste sites and the creation of the Toxics Release Inventory (TRI) in 1984 to track toxic industrial air and water emissions.

The disastrous 2010 oil spill in the Gulf of Mexico is a textbook illustration of how events can shape White House policy. The Deepwater Horizon oil rig exploded and incinerated into the Gulf of Mexico on April 20, 2010. It unleashed a catastrophic oil spill, quickly accelerating into an environmental crisis and spilling 210,000 gallons of crude oil daily into the gulf. Within a month, the spill had created a vast, underwater oil plume ten miles long and one mile wide, a surface slick visible to astronauts in the International Space Station, hundreds of miles above Earth. For British Petroleum, the rig's owner, it rapidly became a financial and political crisis exacerbated by the global media's relentless dramatization of the event and its potentially catastrophic environmental consequences.

The Deepwater Horizon disaster was an acute embarrassment and a potential political disaster for the Obama administration. Exactly a month before the rig explosion, Obama had announced that he would propose that Congress increase significantly the scale of oil and natural gas exploration in a large portion of the eastern Gulf of Mexico. A month later, the Deepwater Horizon disaster compelled Obama to announce that his administration would stop further offshore energy exploration indefinitely—an abrupt policy reversal enthusiastically advertised by his critics as evidence of his bad judgment and poor political leadership. Obama's decision to propose new offshore exploration had been a reluctant concession made to Senate Republicans, many of whom had campaigned decades for increased exploration; it was the price he had to pay for Republican support of the administration's important climate-warming legislation. But, the Deep Horizon disaster now compelled Obama, and Congress as well, to focus not on getting more oil from the gulf but on preventing further offshore drilling crises.

The Executive Office of the President

The president may be an individual, but the presidency is also an institution surrounding the Oval Office with an array of administrative resources, collectively called the Executive Office of the President (EOP), which includes the president's personal staff and has become essential for the president to fulfill his constitutional responsibilities. Most of the EOP's 1,800 employees are permanent civil service appointees, such as the critically important personnel in the Office of Management and Budget (OMB), who provide expert administrative advice, oversee the implementation of presidential policies, and provide continuity from one presidency to the next.[11] In addition, within the EOP is an entity called the White House, containing other, personally appointed presidential staff and advisers, such as speechwriters and congressional liaison specialists, whom the president selects and who serve at his or her pleasure. Much of the daily work involved with the president's environmental policy making is done by the individuals and offices within the EOP and by his or her personal staff. Equally important, presidents routinely turn to their personal staff and the professionals in the EOP for advice and assistance.

Thus, what appears to be a presidential decision often turns out, on close inspection, to be a collaborative White House staff creation. Indeed, it is often an OMB official, not the president, who interprets and represents White House policies to Congress and the federal bureaucracy.

Within the EOP, several offices are especially strategic in environmental policy making. Perhaps the most important (although virtually unknown to the public) is the OMB, which assists the president in preparing his annual budget, oversees the implementation of that budget within all the executive agencies including the environmentally related bureaucracies, assists the president in drafting his legislative proposals, reviews congressional legislation to determine its compatibility with the president's environmental agenda, and oversees the work of the environmental regulatory agencies such as the EPA and the Nuclear Regulatory Commission (NRC). The OMB, and particularly its director, who is appointed by the president, can become an especially powerful presence in environmental policy making when invested by the president with considerable responsibility and discretion in implementing the president's legislative policies and budget priorities.

Because the OMB is so frequently the agent for implementing presidential policy within the executive branch, the OMB readily becomes a focus for conflict over White House environmental policy making. During the G. W. Bush administration, the OMB was repeatedly criticized—with justification—by environmentalists and scientists, for excessive, inappropriate political interference in scientific research supporting EPA regulatory decisions. President Obama emphasized during his presidential campaign that the OMB, during his administration, would be free of such accusations. Still, despite Obama's subsequent efforts to keep the OMB free of criticism for "political" influence in EPA science, we noted in Chapter 2 that environmentalists unhappy with the White House disapproval of the EPA's initial proposal for new particulate regulations were quick to accuse the OMB of "political" interference with the EPA. In fact, most of the OMB's essential work is uncontroversial, but its placement at the intersection of so many environmental issues within the executive branch assures its continuing visibility in the inevitable controversies bound to arise.

Other environmentally important entities within the EOP are the CEQ and the Office of Science and Technology Policy (OSTP). The mission of the OSTP, created in 1976, includes the following:

- Advise the president and others within the EOP on the impacts of science and technology on domestic and international affairs
- Lead an interagency effort to develop and implement sound science and technology policies and budgets

- Work with the private sector to ensure federal investments in science and technology contribute to economic prosperity, environmental quality, and national security
- Build strong partnerships among federal, state, and local governments; other countries; and the scientific community
- Evaluate the scale, quality, and effectiveness of the federal effort in science and technology

Like the OMB, much of the OSTP's continuing responsibilities are uncontroversial and often commendable in the view of environmentalists—for example, promoting federal support for green energy technologies. Inevitably, however, the OSTP's daily involvement in science, technology, energy, and environmental policy within the White House often implicates it in controversial issues together with the OMB and the CEQ.

Council on Environmental Quality

NEPA created a commission to advise the president on environmental matters. Headed by three members appointed by the president, the CEQ was to be part of the president's staff. Among the major responsibilities prescribed for the council were (1) to gather for the president's consideration "timely and authoritative information concerning the conditions and trends in the quality of the environment both current and prospective," (2) "to develop and recommend to the President national policies to foster and promote the improvement of environmental quality," and (3) "to review and appraise the various programs and activities of the Federal Government" to determine the extent to which they comply with, among other things, the requirement for writing environmental impact statements.[12] The CEQ was created, like other major presidential advisory commissions, primarily to provide policy advice and evaluation from within the White House directly to the president.

The CEQ is a small agency with no regulatory responsibilities or major environmental programs beyond modest research activities, but early on, it assumed symbolic importance and political value to environmental interests. Its presence within the White House implied a high national priority given to environmental programs, and the council's opportunities to influence the president directly meant that it might act, in the words of environmental leader Russell Peterson, as "the environmental conscience of the executive branch."[13] The council has a statutory mandate to administer the process of writing and reviewing environmental impact statements within the federal government and to advise other executive agencies on environmental issues. As with all other presidential advisory bodies, the CEQ exercises no more influence in White House decisions than the president cares to give it; it may carry on its NEPA-mandated activities, but the president is always free to ignore any of its recommendations or other initiatives.

By 2000, the CEQ's early political clout had vanished. The CEQ's rapid decline in status since the Carter administration illustrates how much its effectiveness depends on presidential favor. Its influence plummeted rapidly beginning with the Reagan administration. The CEQ experienced no reversal of fortune under the Bill Clinton and George W. Bush administrations. Although the environmental community should have been its natural constituency, the CEQ often became the target of environmentalist criticism for its apparent passiveness, if not complicity, during the Bush administration's frequent attempts to influence science policy within the executive branch. "There is evidence," concluded a report written near the end of the Bush presidency by a panel including several past chairs and numerous members of the CEQ, "that the Council has been used to undermine the statutory environmental protection responsibilities of other federal agencies. There is also a perception that the Council has been used to gainsay the scientific conclusions of federal agencies on climate change and other issues." At the same time, the panel emphasized the CEQ's potential to become again a highly influential and visible presence—"the President's voice on the environment"—during the Obama administration.[14] Whether CEQ has revived its influence during the Obama years has yet to be demonstrated.

Congress: Too Much Check, Too Little Balance

The president may propose, but it is often Congress that ultimately disposes. In a Madisonian government of separated institutions sharing powers, presidents and environmental administrators have good reasons to look warily toward Congress. The Constitution invests Congress with enormous authority over the daily conduct of the president and the executive branch. Under ordinary circumstances, few aspects of presidential and bureaucratic behavior are untouched directly or indirectly by congressional authority and politics.

Despite a panoply of party organizations, legislative leaders, and coordinating committees, Congress is still largely an institution of fragmented powers and divided geographical loyalties. Legislative power is dispersed in both chambers among a multitude of committees and subcommittees; local or regional concerns often tenaciously claim legislative loyalties. The electoral cycle intrudes imperiously on policy deliberations. The public interest and legislative objectivity compete with equally insistent legislative concerns to deliver something from Washington to the folks back home. In environmental affairs, Congress is an assembly of scientific amateurs who must enact programs of great technical complexity to ameliorate scientifically complicated environmental ills that most legislators only dimly understand.

The Statutory Setting. The most fundamental congressional responsibility is to craft environmental law. Current federal environmental legislation is a patchwork of several hundred congressional enactments written since the 1950s. Legal scholar Christopher Schroeder's verdict about federal toxic substance laws—that they have "resulted not in a well-designed cabin, but in a pile of logs"[15]—applies as well to the whole of federal environmental legislation. Many controversies prominent since the 1970s result from the inconsistencies, contradictions, confusions, and inadequacies of this statutory welter. At the same time, each law memorializes the success of a major environmental coalition in waging a battle for environmental protection that may have lasted decades. Each law acquires a politically vocal and potent constituency from congressional factions, private interests, bureaucratic agencies, and program beneficiaries. A huge volume of judicial opinions girding each law with court-derived interpretations and justifications further institutionalizes the legislation. These laws are the legal edifice on which environmental policy has been erected.

The major legislative enactments currently on the federal statute books relating to just one category of environmental pollutant—toxic substances—include more than 15 major laws. Cataloging just this one among the many categories of environmental law is sufficient to emphasize two realities about environmental policy controversies: (1) The existing law becomes a conservative force in policy debate because it is difficult to change, and (2) the incompatibilities and omissions in current environmental legislation are a continuing cause of difficulties in policy implementation and enforcement.

Committee Decentralization. Congress has been described as a "kind of confederation of little legislatures."[16] In both chambers, the committees and subcommittees—those little legislatures wielding the most consistently effective power in the legislative system—are dispersed and competitive in environmental matters. William Ruckelshaus, the first EPA administrator, complained in the early 1970s that he had to deal with 16 different congressional subcommittees.[17] The situation has gotten more complicated since then. In the 110th Congress (2009–2011), the box score for committees with EPA jurisdiction came to 7 full committees including 13 subcommittees in the Senate and 8 full committees with 18 subcommittees in the House of Representatives. Any major environmental legislation, depending on its content, is predestined to arrive on several, perhaps many, different committee and subcommittee tables during a customarily labored progress through congressional deliberation. Congressional jurisdiction over ocean issues, for instance, is very generously dispersed; the 109th Congress included 50 committees and subcommittees in both chambers with jurisdiction over related research and policy.

With authority over environmental policy fragmented among a multitude of committees in each chamber, competition and jurisdictional rivalry commonly occur as each committee attempts to assert some influence over environmental programs. The result is that, as a rule, environmental legislation evolves only through protracted bargaining and compromising among the many committees. This time-consuming process often results in legislation that is vague or inconsistent. Divided jurisdictions, however, provide different interest groups with some point of committee access during environmental policy formulation; as a consequence, these groups resist efforts to reduce the number of committees with overlapping jurisdictions and concentrate authority in a few major committees.

Localism. When the national taxpayer organization Citizens Against Government Waste (CAGW) noted in its annual *Pig Book* that Mississippi ranked sixth among the 50 states in the amount of political pork (a common term for wasteful federal spending) its congressional delegation had delivered to the state. Sen. Trent Lott, R-MS, seemed almost pleased with his state's ranking. "The definition of wasteful 'pork' is in the eye of the beholder," he responded. "In my eye, if its south of Memphis, it sure isn't pork. . . . If we must use our political acumen to get part of our money back, then so be it. In this regard, CAGW's report indicates Mississippi is doing very well."[18] Many of his Senate colleagues would have added, "Amen." Senators are unapologetically loyal to the practice of voting for each other's local public works projects, the most common political pork.

Localism is driven by a powerful tradition in congressional voting. In U.S. political culture, legislators are treated by constituents—and regard themselves—as ambassadors to Washington, DC, from their own geographical areas. They are expected to acquire skills in the practice of pork-barrel politics, capturing federal goods and services for their constituencies. They are also expected to be vigilant in promoting and protecting local interests in the national policy arena. Congressional tenure is more likely to depend on a legislator's ability to serve these local interests than on other legislative achievements. Political localism is perhaps the most deeply rooted and most compelling force in shaping voting decisions.

This localism affects environmental policy in different ways. By encouraging legislators to view environmental proposals first through the lens of local interests, localism often weakens sensitivity to national needs and interests. At worst, it drives legislators to judge the merits of environmental policies almost solely by their impact on frequently small and atypical constituencies.

Localism also whets the congressional appetite for federal distributive programs freighted with local benefits. An aroma of political pork can add appeal to an environmental program, especially if other important local issues are involved. This lesson is not lost on the environmental bureaucracies. For instance, when opposition by the powerful House Ways and Means Committee appeared to threaten defeat for the initial Superfund legislation, a program strongly supported by the EPA, the agency worked with sympathetic congressional staff members to create a list of prospective Superfund sites in each committee member's district. The committee members were then reminded of the "ticking time bombs" in their districts and of the potentially great financial benefits from cleanup activities—an almost irresistible double dose of localism.[19] It is not surprising that federal grants to build pollution control facilities, such as sewage treatment plants, also have instant appeal. The robust political pork packaged with the federal government's original program to improve national wastewater quality, for instance, enormously enhanced its congressional appeal because it contained massive funding for local public works. "The huge $18 billion waste treatment facilities program, first authorized in 1972, [was] the second largest public works program in U.S. history . . . EPA estimated that for every $1 billion spent, about 50,900 worker-years of employment would be generated in plant and sewer construction."[20]

Public works are not the only legislative bargaining chips, however. It is axiomatic that legislation often enlists congressional votes because sponsors are alert to write in diverse benefits or projects of all sorts that are attractive to important colleagues and pressure groups. Conversely, pressure groups—including environmentalists—are perpetually vigilant for opportunities to advance their agendas through legislative benefits. For example, the massive Waxman–Markey climate warming legislation approved in 2009 by the House of Representatives provoked a virtual feeding frenzy among organized groups intent on gaining a share of the benefits from provisions proposing an auction of greenhouse gas emission rights. "Every line of the text [had] billions and billions of dollars riding on it," observed economist Peter Dorman. "People will do and say anything," he asserted, to get a share of the money, including environmentalists who hope that federal revenues from the eventual auction of emissions permits will help their cause.[21]

Elections. The electoral cycle also dominates the legislative mind. The constitutionally mandated electoral cycles of the federal government—two years, four years, and six years—partition the time available for legislative deliberation into periods bounded by different elections. Within these time frames, policy decisions are continually analyzed for their electoral implications and often valued largely for electoral impacts. This affects congressional policy styles in several ways. First, the short term becomes more important than the long term when evaluating programs; legislators often attribute more importance to a program's impact on the next election than to its longer-term effects on unborn generations. Second, policies are tested continually against public opinion. Although a weak or badly divided public opinion often can be ignored, a coherent majority opinion related to an environmental issue usually wields significant influence on congressional voting, especially when legislators can associate the opinion with their own constituencies. Hazardous waste cleanup programs, for example, are hard to oppose whatever their actual merits because the "ticking time bomb" has become a durable, powerful public metaphor in practically every constituency.

Preoccupation with elections, localism, and the other aspects of congressional culture are the givens of policy making. And, congressional policy making, as much as presidential leadership, has been responsible for creating and maintaining the entire foundation of federal environmental governance—one of Congress's greatest historical achievements. However, Congress has also become a rich source of delay, confusion, and waste in making and implementing environmental policy. These problems arise from excesses and exaggeration in the authority the constitutional framers prudently invested in Congress—a case of checks and balances gone awry. Many of these difficulties could be eliminated or mitigated by a self-imposed discipline of which Congress may be incapable.

"Ready, Fire, Aim": Crisis Decision Making. The congressional response to environmental problems is highly volatile, waxing and waning according to changing public moods, emerging environmental crises, economic circumstances, or today's front-page ecological disasters. Congress easily falls into a pollutant-of-the-year mentality, mandating new programs or sudden changes in existing ones according to what environmental problems currently seem most urgent or according to the public's current mood.

The Ocean Dumping Act of 1988, for example, is the very model of crisis-inspired legislation. During summer 1988, popular bathing beaches along New York's eastern coast frequently were fouled with medical wastes, raw sewage, and other dangerous debris apparently washed ashore from New York City sewage dumped more than 100 miles offshore. Closed beaches and public revulsion at the widely publicized pollution quickly persuaded Congress to pass, without one dissenting vote, the Ocean Dumping Act, which prohibited additional ocean disposal of urban waste within a few years. Congress was unmoved by expert testimony that held the real cause of the contamination to be the continual overflow from New York City's antique sewer system, which would be hugely expensive to repair. Nor was Congress in the mood to evaluate alternatives. "There is no question," argued the chief engineer of the regional waste management agency, "that the New York City sewer system is the greatest cause of water pollution in the region. But a sewer system isn't sexy. It's expensive to fix, and nobody wants to hear about it. So people focused on what they understand . . . and they understand that sewage and the sea don't seem nice together."[22] Local representative Thomas J. Manton, D-Queens, initially opposed to the act, soon capitulated to political realities. "Nobody wanted to discuss the relative risks or merits," he later explained. "It had been a bad summer, and we all wanted to be able to say we did something. So we passed a law. I tried to have a debate. And it was like I was trying to destroy the planet."[23] As a result of the act, the city of New York will have spent at least $2 billion on facilities to convert sewage into fertilizer and $300 million annually for a decade thereafter to dispose of its sludge, although many experts believe an equally effective and much cheaper solution would have been possible if Congress had not ordained that ocean dumping be eliminated entirely but, instead, had renovated the existing sewer system to remove the harmful pollutants from the affluent before ocean release.

Environmental policies are seldom so poorly conceived, but this reactive policy making ensures an environmental agenda in which place and priority among programs depend less on scientific logic than on political circumstance. Often, the losers are scientifically compelling environmental problems unblessed with political sex appeal. Moreover, once a program is legislatively attractive, it usually acquires a mandated budget that virtually ensures its survival. Most environmental scientists, for instance, consider indoor air pollution a more compelling health risk than abandoned hazardous waste sites or even some currently regulated forms of air pollution, but most of the EPA's air pollution budget is mandated for ambient air regulation, and Congress lacks enthusiasm to tackle indoor air pollution in the absence of a perceived crisis.[24]

Another result of this crisis mentality is administrative overload. The EPA and other environmental agencies have often had to implement quickly a multitude of new programs, hastily enacted without sufficient time or resources provided for the required tasks. As a result, the EPA has struggled continually and unsuccessfully to find the means to carry out all the program mandates. This crisis mentality also begets constantly mandated changes in regulatory priorities and program deadlines.

Guidance: Too Much and Too Little. Behind the facade of high purpose and ambitious action of every major environmental law probably stretches a terrain mined with muddled language, troublesome silences, and inconsistent programs. Some of this is inevitable. Mistakes in statutory design occur because federal environmental regulations address problems of great scientific and administrative complexity with which legislators have had no prior experience. Moreover, members of Congress are typically lawyers, business executives, or other nonscientific professionals who depend on the expertise of administrators to clarify and interpret the law appropriately in regard to specialized environmental programs. The constant pressure of legislative affairs discourages most members of Congress from giving considerable attention to environmental issues or from developing an adequate understanding of them. "It's tough to get Congress to focus on bills with sufficient time to develop an adequate depth of understanding," observed John A. Moore, former acting deputy director for the EPA. "You've got 1 or 2 Congressmen who truly know it; there are 400 others that are going to vote on it."[25] Even conscientious legislators can be easily intimidated when they attempt to unravel the technical complexities of environmental legislation. During congressional debate over passage of the Safe Drinking Water Act (1974), for instance, proponents argued that 12,000 contaminants existed with unknown causes. Debate raged within the EPA and Congress about whether the agency needed to regulate 20 to 30, 100, or even 1,000s of water pollutants—even the Public Health Service's traditionally undisputed standard for selenium was made suspect. Finally, Congress had to give the EPA the final responsibility for identifying most of the appropriate pollutants for regulation.[26]

Environmental legislation is often vague and contradictory because Congress cannot or will not resolve major political conflicts entailed in the law. Instead, Congress often papers over the conflict with silence or deliberate obscurity in the statutory language. This approach results in a steady flow of political hot potatoes to the bureaucracy, which must untangle and clarify this legal language—often to the accompaniment of political conflict and legislative criticism—or leave the job to the courts. The EPA becomes enmeshed in protracted litigation and political bargaining, program regulations essential to implementing the laws often become hostage to these procedures, and Congress frequently avoids a risky political bloodletting. "Congress outsources the rulemaking to the EPA," asserts regulatory critic David Schoenbrod, "so that the legislators can claim credit for protecting health while the agency bears the inevitable blame for delays, disappointments, and costs."[27] True or not, so it often appears.

Congressional frustration with the continual delay in implementing environmental laws has led to the habitual use of extravagant, extraordinarily detailed, and inflexible language in new environmental laws; to the constant mandating of precise deadlines for completing various programs; and to prescription, in excruciating detail, of how administrators are to carry out program activities—in effect, to a cure as bad as the disease. The CAA Amendments of 1990, for instance, were packed with a multitude of new programs accompanied by hundreds of mandatory deadlines seldom carefully considered. The predictable result was that the EPA missed 198 of the 247 deadlines it was required to meet by 2000 and will miss more than half the 108 deadlines that remain to be met later.[28]

Partisan Polarization and Political Stalemate. Beginning in the mid-1990s, party polarization in both congressional chambers has gradually intensified to the point where it has become extremely difficult, if not impossible, for Congress to respond incisively and expeditiously on a growing agenda of imperative environmental issues, including global climate change, the EPA's chronically underfunded regulatory responsibilities, energy conservation, long overdue revisions of federal air and water pollution legislation, and much else. While partisan stalemate and deadlock has permeated virtually every agenda of legislative policy to an extent unprecedented for at least a century, no issue now incites a more tenacious polarization than environmental regulation.[29] Congressional polarization, moreover, compounds the inherent political and institutional challenges to presidential leadership inherent in the constitutional checks and balances between Congress and the White House. Presidents of both parties have been thwarted by this chronic congressional incapacity to find consensus on the White House environmental policy agenda. Often, the solution has been to make an end run around Congress and to create policy by resorting to authority assumed to be inherent to the presidency—a predictably contentious strategy—as Barack Obama did in 2011when he countered congressional failure to enact regulations to control climate warming emissions by initiating regulation using the EPA's existing regulatory powers.

The Bureaucracy: Power through Implementation

Federal agencies concerned with environmental affairs and closely related matters such as energy, consumer protection, and worker health have grown explosively since 1970. More than 150 major new federal laws, most concerned with the broad regulation of business and the economy in the interest of public health and safety, have been enacted since then. More than 20 new regulatory agencies have been created to implement these programs, including the EPA, the Occupational Safety and Health Administration (OSHA), and the DOI's Office of Surface Mining. An understanding of such bureaucracies, and especially the more environmentally important among them, is essential to explaining the logic of federal environmental policy making.

The Power of Discretion

The significance of the environmental agencies rests less on their size and budget than on the political realities obscured by a constitutional illusion. The Constitution appears to vest the power to formulate policy primarily in Congress, while leaving to the president and the executive branch the task of seeing that the laws are "faithfully executed." Although implemented and enforced principally in the bureaucracy, public policy actually develops in both branches of the government.

Delegated authority and administrative discretion are the wellsprings of bureaucratic power. Congress routinely invests administrators with responsibility for making a multitude of decisions it cannot or will not make itself about the implementation of policy; often this becomes legislative power delegated to the executive branch. Even when delegation is not clearly intended, administrators assume the power to make public policy when they choose how to implement policies permitting different options—hence, the existence of administrative discretion.

Congress and the president, using a variety of constitutional and statutory powers, attempt to discipline the exercise of administrative discretion. Still, this oversight holds no certain rein on administrative discretion, particularly in light of the vast number and complexity of environmental programs, the elephantine size of the bureaucracy, and competing demands on presidential and congressional time.

A commonplace example can illustrate the pervasive problem of controlling administrative discretion. In 1981, President Reagan ordered all federal administrative agencies to prepare a regulatory impact analysis—a type of benefit–cost assessment—for most of their new regulatory proposals and left to his own administrative management agency, the OMB, the responsibility of drafting guidelines for the agencies. The OMB, in turn, interpreted the president's order as requiring the responsible agencies, such as the EPA, to include in each of its assessments an evaluation of alternatives to the proposed regulation. The EPA, for its part, issued guidelines to each of its offices recommending that at least four alternatives be considered for each proposed new regulation. A review of regulatory impact analyses prepared by one EPA office in mid-1997 suggests that the intent of the original White House directive had been significantly adulterated by this trickle down of discretionary authority from the White House to the EPA. Of the 23 assessments studied, 6 examined only 1 alternative to the proposed regulation. The rest compared 2 or more alternatives to the proposed regulation but were not always clear about how many alternatives or which types were involved. In no instance had any agency in the chain of command violated law nor was there evidence of intent to do so.[30] Still, the documents ultimately prepared by the EPA appeared to disregard in many respects the intent of the original White House directive. Whatever the interpretation, the flow of discretionary authority and its compounding influence throughout government, for good and ill, will be reality, in all seasons, for all presidents, and for all parties. The federal bureaucracy, assured of generous discretionary authority well into the future, will continue to be an independent and largely self-regulated influence in environmental policy.

Bureaucratic Competitiveness

The bureaucracy is no monolith. Its powers in environmental affairs, although collectively vast, also are dispersed and competitive. One source of this fragmentation is the federalizing of environmental administration. Many major environmental laws enacted in Washington, DC, are administered partially or wholly through state governments; others give states an option to participate. Under the Federal Water Pollution Control Act, for instance, 27 states currently administer their own water pollution permit systems; all but 6 states and the District of Columbia administer the Safe Drinking Water Act. The CAA permits the states to participate in several major aspects of the program, including the control of pollutants and the establishment of emission standards for stationary sources.

Another cause of fragmented administrative authority is the chronic division of and overlapping responsibility for environmental programs among federal agencies. Twenty-seven separate federal agencies share major regulatory responsibility in environmental and occupational health. Regulating even a single pollutant often necessitates what might appear to be a bureaucratic convention. Toxic substances currently are regulated under 20 different federal statutes involving five agencies. To address all the problems in human exposure to vinyl chloride, for example, would require the collaboration of all five agencies working with 15 different laws.[31]

Dispersed authority breeds conflict and competition among agencies and their political allies over program implementation, authority, and resources—the turf wars familiar to students of bureaucracy. The story of Whitman and Norton's lunch recounted at the beginning of this chapter affirms a bureaucratic reality—collaboration is common but never dependable. And, in environmental affairs, federal agencies are notoriously fitful collaborators. In this milieu of dispersed and competitive agency authority, policy implementation often becomes a continual process of collaboration and conflict between coalitions of agencies and their allies shaping and reshaping policy as the relative strengths of the conflicting alignments change. Moreover, administrative conflict crosses the institutional divisions of the federal government, spreading downward through the federal system to state and local governments and outward from government to organized private groups. Indeed, agencies failing to enlist diverse and active allies in their policy struggles may frustrate their own missions and leave their futures hostage to more politically skilled opponents.

The Environmental Protection Agency

The EPA, created by an executive order of President Nixon in 1970, is the largest federal regulatory agency in terms of budget and personnel. Its responsibilities embrace an extraordinarily large and technically complex set of programs ranging across the whole domain of environmental management. Asked if his job had been rewarding, a former administrator for the EPA replied that it was "like beating a train across a grade crossing— if you make it, it's a great rush. If you don't, you're dead."[32] Political controversy is the daily bread of the EPA's leadership. "The Administrator rarely goes to the President with good news and is more often the bearer of bad news," observed Lee Thomas, EPA administrator from 1985 to 1988. "You almost never have a decision where many people applaud it."[33] In such a politically charged setting, the EPA administrator's office has often been a revolving door through which a succession of executives pass, unwilling or unable to manage the inherited political turbulence. Such was the case during the George W. Bush administration, when Whitman, Michael O. Leavitt, and Stephan L. Johnson all occupied the administrator's office within a five-year period.

Statutory Responsibilities. The size of the EPA's regulatory burden is suggested in Box 3–1, which summarizes the EPA's current statutory responsibilities. These regulatory programs represent the major environmental legislation of the past three decades. The EPA grew steadily in staff and budget until 1981, when the Reagan administration severely reduced both budget and personnel. The EPA has never fully recovered from the budgetary austerity that followed throughout the1980s. While its administrative responsibilities have constantly increased, and despite periods of occasional improvement, its budget measured in dollars (and not discounted for inflation) had increased relatively little through the end of the 2012 (see Figure 3–1). Even though the Obama administration initially created a substantial increase in the EPA's resources during the president's first years in office, by the end of 2012, the continuing economic recession compelled Obama to propose a 13 percent reduction in the EPA's FY 2013 budget, reducing it to a level approaching its status in 2001.[34]

The agency presently has about 17,000 employees and an annual budget exceeding $8 billion, of which less than half supports its administrative activities (most of the money underwrites water treatment and Superfund grants).[35] When adjusted for inflation, the EPA's proposed budget for FY 2013 will equal about 60 percent of its 1980 level.[36] The agency, whose administrator is appointed by the president, consists of a Washington, DC, headquarters and ten regional offices, each headed by a regional administrator. Unlike most regulatory agencies, the EPA administers both regulatory and distributive programs such as the huge federal waste treatment grants, the Superfund program, and various research activities.

Box 3–1 *Major Responsibilities of the EPA*

The following are the major regulatory tasks assigned to the EPA in each important pollution control program.

Air quality
- Establishes national air-quality standards.
- Sets limits on the level of air pollutants emitted from stationary sources such as power plants, municipal incinerators, factories, and chemical plants.
- Establishes emission standards for new motor vehicles.
- Sets allowable levels for toxics such as lead, benzene, and toluene in gasoline.
- Establishes emission standards for hazardous air pollutants such as beryllium, mercury, and asbestos.
- Supervises states in their development of clean air plans.

Water quality and protection
- Issues permits for the discharge of any pollutant into navigable waters.
- Develops effluent guidelines to control discharge of specific water pollutants, including radiation.
- Develops criteria that enable states to set water quality standards.
- Administers grants program to states to subsidize the cost of building sewage treatment plants.
- Regulates disposal of waste material, including sludge and low-level radioactive discards, into the oceans.
- Cooperates with the U.S. Army Corps of Engineers to issue permits for the dredging and filling of wetlands.
- Sets national drinking water standards to ensure that drinking water is safe.
- Regulates underground injection of wastes to protect purity of groundwater.
- With the U.S. Coast Guard, coordinates cleanup of oil and chemical spills into U.S. waterways.

Hazardous waste
- Maintains inventory of existing hazardous waste dump sites.
- Tracks more than 500 hazardous compounds from point of origin to final disposal site.

(continued)

Box 3–1   (continued)

- Sets standards for generators and transporters of hazardous wastes.
- Issues permits for treatment, storage, and disposal facilities for hazardous wastes.
- Assists states in developing hazardous waste control programs.
- Maintains a multibillion-dollar fund (Superfund) from industry fees and general tax revenues to provide for emergency cleanup of hazardous dumps when no responsible party can immediately be found.
- Pursues identification of parties responsible for waste sites and eventual reimbursement of the federal government for Superfund money spent cleaning up these sites.

Chemical regulation, including pesticides and radioactive waste
- Maintains inventory of chemical substances now in commercial use.
- Regulates existing chemicals considered serious hazards to people and the environment, including fluorocarbons, polychlorinated biphenyls (PCBs), and asbestos.
- Issues procedures for the proper safety testing of chemicals, and orders them tested when necessary.
- Requires the registration of insecticides, herbicides, or fungicides intended for sale in the United States.
- Requires pesticide manufacturers to provide scientific evidence that their products will not injure humans, livestock, crops, or wildlife when used as directed.
- Classifies pesticides for either general public use or restricted use by certified applicators.
- Sets standards for certification of applicators of restricted-use pesticides. (Individual states may certify applicators through their own programs based on the federal standards.)
- Cancels or suspends the registration of a product on the basis of actual or potential unreasonable risk to humans, animals, or the environment.
- Issues a "stop sale, use, and removal" order when a pesticide already in circulation is found to be in violation of the law.
- Requires registration of pesticide-producing establishments.
- Issues regulations concerning the labeling, storage, and disposal of pesticide containers.
- Issues permits for pesticide research.
- Monitors pesticide levels in the environment.
- Monitors and regulates the levels of radiation in drinking water, oceans, rainfall, and air.
- Conducts research on toxic substances, pesticides, air and water quality, hazardous wastes, radiation, and the causes and effects of acid rain.
- Provides overall guidance to other federal agencies on radiation protection matters that affect public health.
- Maintains inventory of chemical substances now in commercial use.

Other
- Sets acceptable noise levels for construction equipment, transportation equipment (except aircraft), all motors and engines, and electronic equipment.

Figure 3–1   EPA Budget for Fiscal Years 2001–2013

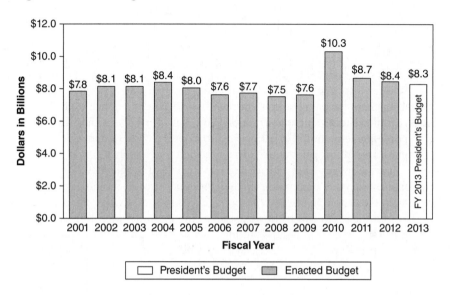

Notes: FY 2002 Enacted Includes $175.6 M provided for Homeland Security in the Emergency Supplemental Appropriations Act. FY 2006 Enacted excludes hurricane supplemental funding. FY 2009 Enacted excludes ARRA funding. All Enacted Budgets include rescissions; President's Budget includes cancellation of prior year funds.

Source: EPA, Office of the Financial Officer, FY 2013 *EPA Budget in Brief*, Pub. No. EPA-190-S-12-001 (February 2012), available at http://www.epa.gov/planandbudget/annual-plan/fy2013.html.

Notwithstanding some significant achievements, the EPA confronts a daunting array of problems in the early years of the 21st century: an unmanageable burden of continually growing regulatory responsibilities, a politically toxic inheritance of chro nic congressional Republican antipathy toward much of EPA's regulatory programs compounded with legislative polarization thwarting congressional action on many overdue EPA reforms, a chronically inadequate budget, and the administrative complexities inherent in complicated environmental regulations. The growing disparity between the EPA's administrative responsibilities and its resources has reached a point at which many observers believe the agency is, or will soon be, mired in "a pathological cycle of regulatory failure."[37]

Micromanaged and Overloaded. By the mid-1980s, it was already obvious, as the CEQ observed, that "the Environmental Protection Agency cannot possibly do all the things its various mandates tell it to do," and conditions have not improved.[38] More than three decades later, the agency is still years, or decades, behind in complying with important requirements in its ten major statutory programs, and new jobs are always ahead.

One reason for the agency's chronic compliance problems is the congressional penchant for packing legislation with a multitude of demanding deadlines, detailed management instructions, and hammer clauses that threaten dire consequences should the EPA fail to comply with various statutory deadlines. The EPA continues to experience what is probably the most relentless legislative oversight of any federal agency. Even though EPA staff grew by approximately 18 percent during the 1990s, this growth has failed to keep pace with the accumulating new responsibilities the agency has inherited.

The cumulative result of this excessive congressional attention is written in the statistics of missed deadlines, lagging research, and impossibly distant completion dates for existing program responsibilities. The doleful litany includes the following two programs:

- The Federal Insecticide, Fungicide, and Rodenticide Act requires the EPA to evaluate more than 50,000 individual pesticide products containing more than 600 active ingredients and 900 inert ingredients. "If EPA has to prepare interim registration standards for all 600 active ingredients," the GAO concluded in 1986, "then the Agency may finish the first round reviews in about 2004."[39] In fact, by 2010 the EPA had not yet completed its first round of reviews.
- The Food Quality Protection Act (1996) requires the EPA to screen all commercial pesticides for estrogenic effects that may affect human health, to develop a screening and testing program by 1998, to implement the program by 1999, and to report to Congress on the program's accomplishments by August 2000. This requires the EPA to review data on 600 pesticides in active commerce, 1,800 inert ingredients in 20,000 pesticide products, and 75,000 industrial chemicals, plus consumer products. None of this, including the report, had been accomplished by the end of 2010.

The EPA frequently resorts to improvised strategies for deciding which programs and pollutants will get priority. Sometimes it depends on litigation initiated by private interests—most often environmental groups—to force its attention to specific programs.

Are Integrated Programs Possible? The EPA has come to resemble a regulatory holding company, a conglomerate of offices, each focused narrowly on problems in a single environmental medium (such as air, land, or water) or on one kind of pollutant (such as toxic waste). Further, each office is responsible for numerous regulatory laws written with little attention to their compatibility. "Each program has staked out an environmental problem that it is required to 'fix,' according to the peculiar rules embodied in its statutory mandate," observed the 1985 CEQ report.[40] The EPA originally was conceived very differently. The advisory council recommending the EPA's creation to President Nixon had argued that environmental policy had a unique character because there were "interactions and trade-offs inherent in controlling different types of pollution."[41] In short, the EPA was intended to synthesize approaches to specific environmental problems into an "integrated and holistic approach"[42]—which is precisely what the EPA has not done.

Circumstances have conspired against this integrated approach from the EPA's inception. Its most grievous fault is lack of political allure. Congress and the White House, needed to promote what seemed the quickest solution to what appeared to be the most urgent problem of the moment. Integrated management, in contrast, seemed strange and complicated, too difficult to explain and too unpredictable in results to appeal to Congress or the public.[43] Also, the program offices concerned with air, water, and land quickly dominated the EPA and defeated most efforts to create more integrated programs; these offices had powerful constituencies:

> Each environmental medium and the separate programs within each medium have attracted politically potent constituencies that are likely antagonists toward any attempt to transform—or integrate—the existing system. They include environmental professionals and agencies, representatives of business and industry, and various policy-making committees and subcommittees that operate in Congress and state legislatures.[44]

The problem with the EPA's present segmented organization is illustrated by the case of toxic metal wastes from coal-fired, electricity-generating plants. These toxic wastes include a multitude of potentially dangerous chemicals, such as arsenic, selenium, lead, radioactive chromium, and barium that scrubbers extract from coal-combustion gases.[45] The resulting coal ash has been stored as solid or liquid waste on power plant sites. While the CAA guides the EPA regulation of these emission gases, the resulting waste has been treated as ordinary solid waste and regulated through the RCRA, a very different law. In December 2008, a Tennessee Valley Authority (TVA) coal ash containment pond at Kingston, Tennessee, collapsed, releasing 1.1 billion gallons of liquid ash waste—the largest industrial waste spill in U.S. history—flooding 300 acres in the small town of Harriman, Tennessee, and leaving a distillation of hazardous chemical residues. Recognizing and regulating these coal wastes as hazardous has been complicated because these pollutants are subject to two federal laws involving different standards and EPA offices and because the EPA lacks authority to achieve the economic and regulatory efficiency that could result from treating coal-combustion pollutants, or most other pollutants, from their source to their disposal as a single regulatory problem—called *integrated management.* The integration issue has become even more compelling as the EPA now needs to incorporate sustainability planning throughout its administrative structure. As the National Research Council observed, this will be a formidable challenge. "It will require a shift toward a systems-based approach that integrates multiple media. . . . In addition to changes in thinking, incorporating sustainability into EPA operations will require integrating and extending existing approaches and, in some cases, developing new approaches."[46]

Needed: Clear Priorities. Like the man who mounted his horse and galloped off in all directions, the EPA lacks a constant course. With responsibility for administering ten separate statutes and parts of four others, the EPA has no clearly mandated priorities and thus no way of allocating scarce resources among different statutes or among programs within a single law. Nor does the EPA have a congressional charter, common to most federal departments and agencies, defining its broad organizational mission and priorities. Although the agency has had to make informal, ad hoc decisions about program priorities to survive, these are much less satisfactory legally and politically than is a clear, congressionally mandated agenda.

Congress has shown little inclination to provide the EPA with a charter or mandated priorities, in good part because the debate sure to arise on the relative merits and urgency of different environmental problems is an invitation to a political bloodletting most legislators would gladly avoid. Intense controversy over which problems to emphasize would be likely among states, partisans of different ecological issues, and regulated interests; the resulting political brawl would upset existing policy coalitions that themselves were fashioned with great difficulty. Many experts inside and outside the EPA have argued that, unless Congress sets priorities enabling the agency to concentrate its resources on a relatively few, feasible, measurable objectives, the nation will be dissipating its environmental resources among a multitude of different programs and objectives with few significant results.

The Reform Struggle. The EPA's administrators have been acutely aware of the agency's managerial problems and initiated many programs throughout the 1990s to encourage greater administrative efficiency and effectiveness when opportunities arose. The difficulties involved in implementing these internal reforms arose, quite often, from conflicts among the agency's numerous stakeholders, both inside and outside the organization, whose buy-in to reform is frequently essential to its success. Even politically skilled administrators, armed with a vigorous reform agendas and administrative expertise, have struggled to overcome the divisive pluralism of interest often evident among the EPA's multiple constituencies. The EPA's major media offices regulating air, water, and hazardous waste, especially, have been the organizational and regulatory centers of power within the agency and have not readily surrendered the significant amount of authority, budgetary resources, and technical expertise required to implement many of the reinvention initiatives. Moreover, many among the large, diverse constituency of outside interests deeply concerned with the EPA's work have preferred to keep the agency's present structure or mildly amend it. The acute partisan polarization in recent years, moreover, has virtually assured that Congress will be incapable of doing what many informed observers believe is the most satisfactory solution to the EPA's organizational challenges: a major revision and rationalization of the stockpile of numerous, inconsistent environmental laws presently loaded upon the agency.

The Department of the Interior

Established as a cabinet-level department in 1845, the DOI is among the oldest and most important of all federal agencies. With a current budget of approximately $12.1 billion and 72,000 employees, the department's responsibilities leave few environmental issues untouched. These responsibilities include (1) protection and management of more than 549 million acres of public land—roughly 28 percent of the total U.S. land area—set aside by Congress for national parks, wilderness areas, forests, and other restricted uses; (2) administration of Native American lands and federal Native American programs, including authority over western tribal lands containing a large proportion of the coal, petroleum, uranium, and other largely unexploited energy resources in the western United States; (3) enforcement of federal surface mining regulations through its Office of Surface Mining; (4) conservation and management of wetlands and estuarine areas; and (5) protection and preservation of wildlife, including endangered species. Headed by a cabinet secretary appointed by the president, the department's programs historically have been a primary concern to environmentalists. The secretary of the Interior has traditionally been a westerner, a political concession to the western states, where most of the public lands are found. During the 1970s, the department secretaries appointed by Presidents Nixon and Carter, although not necessarily outspoken environmentalists or even conservationists, were at least tolerable to the growing environmentalist movement. Since the 1980s, however, the relationship between the environmental community and DOI secretaries has often been combative.

The DOI has always been a battleground between interests seeking to conserve the resources in the public domain and those seeking generous access to them. The DOI's mandate to ensure "balanced use" of resources between conservation and development—a mandate that continually propels the department and its secretary into a storm of controversy concerning which use shall dominate—is a certain source of trouble for every secretary. Moreover, the department's programs serve a clientele including not only environmentalists but also the timber and cattle industries, mining companies, sports enthusiasts, a multitude of private corporations, and many other interests that expect the department to be solicitous of their viewpoints. Finally, the western states historically have maintained that they have not been given a sufficient voice in the administration of the federal properties that often constitute the vast majority of land within their boundaries. The desire of these states to assume greater control over the public domain within their jurisdictions and the resulting tensions with the federal government will outlive any administration.

Although environmentalists were generally delighted with President Clinton's selection of former Arizona governor Bruce Babbitt to be secretary of the Interior, they were not so satisfied with many of Babbitt's early policy initiatives, including the scope of the department's efforts to restrict timbering and other resource development on public lands. The Clinton administration's agenda of slow and cautious environmental reform, especially grating on grassroots environmentalists who expected a bold display of environmental initiatives, nurtured continuing controversy, albeit more temperate than in the 1980s, between the DOI and its environmentalist constituency. In the closing months of his administration, however, Clinton's sudden designation of vast public land tracts for national parks, refuges, wilderness, and other restricted uses enormously gratified conservationists.

Congressional Republicans were hugely annoyed by Clinton's whirlwind designations, which they considered an arrogant unconstitutional exercise of presidential discretion, and vowed unsuccessfully to undo them during President George W. Bush's term. Further complicating the department's relations with Congress was the opposition of environmentalists and most congressional Democrats to Bush's appointment of Gale Norton as the new secretary of the Interior. Norton's political background inspired environmentalist criticism that she was "just Jim Watt in a skirt"[47] and awakened environmentalists' apprehension about another Reagan-style assault on environmentalist legislation, which Norton's successor, former Idaho governor Kirk Kempthorne, did little to relieve. One of President Obama's earliest presidential actions, clearly intended to send a signal, was to suspend numerous DOI decisions made during the Bush administration that had opened federal lands to increased energy exploration and timber production. Kenneth Salazar, Obama's newly appointed secretary of the Interior, has been outspoken in his determination that the DOI's leadership style and agenda will be much more appealing to environmentalists and their allies. The department's mission, however, will inevitably evoke criticism and conflict among its multitude of different constituencies, regardless of which party controls Congress or the White House. Environmentalists themselves are often divided over DOI policies—for example, over the relative importance of recreation and species protection on public lands and over the volume of timber that should be harvested from the national forests.

The Nuclear Regulatory Commission

The NRC was created by Congress in 1976 to assume the regulatory responsibilities originally vested in the Atomic Energy Commission. An independent agency with five commissioners appointed by the president, the NRC regulates most nonmilitary uses of nuclear facilities and materials. The commission's major activities related to the environment include (1) the regulation of the site choice, construction, operation, and security of all civilian nuclear reactors; (2) the designation and supervision of all nuclear waste repositories; (3) the regulation of uranium mining and milling facilities; and (4) the closing of civilian nuclear facilities after they discontinue production (called decommissioning). In 2012, the NRC included a staff of approximately 4,000 and a budget of $1 billion.

Environmental groups have been most concerned with the NRC's supervision of nuclear power plants and repositories for radioactive wastes. Although 104 nuclear plants were operating or approved for construction by 2004, the majority of these have been criticized by environmental groups for alleged deficiencies in structural safety, control of radioactive emissions, and waste storage.[48] In addition, environmental groups have often been aggressive in seeking NRC safety reviews of operating plants and personnel training procedures. The NRC has assumed a major responsibility for the review of site selection and the supervision of waste disposal at the nation's first permanent nuclear waste repository at Yucca Flats, Nevada. Environmental groups still regard the process of site construction and disposal as an issue likely to remain important for several decades.

The NRC and environmental groups have been both adversaries and allies. The environmental movement generally has supported the NRC's stricter enforcement and review of regulations for operating nuclear facilities and its increasingly rigorous standards for new facility licensing. Yet, environmentalists also have criticized the NRC for allegedly siding too often with the nuclear power industry against its critics, for bureaucratic inertia and conservatism, and for ignoring technical criticism and data from sources not associated with the nuclear power industry or the commission. As with other regulatory agencies, the NRC is bound to its own clientele—the nuclear power industry—by professional associations, common technical and economic concerns, and historical sympathies; it is also committed to regulating the industry in the public interest while maintaining sufficient objectivity and disengagement from the nuclear power movement to do that job. These often-conflicting responsibilities lead the NRC into controversies with environmental interests. Nonetheless, the NRC and its mission remain among the most environmentally significant elements in the executive branch.

The Department of Energy

With a current budget exceeding $26.4 billion and more than 20,000 employees, the DOE and its programs and regulatory responsibilities continually involve a great diversity of environmentally related matters. Despite its size and importance, the DOE has been a stepchild of the executive branch. Widely criticized and burdened with difficult, unpopular programs throughout the 1980s, the department struggled through the 1990s with immense new problems—legal, political, economic, and technical—created by the disastrous mismanagement of the military nuclear weapons facilities under its jurisdiction since the late 1970s. These unprecedented difficulties constituted more high-profile bad news for an agency with a talent for collecting misfortune.

The DOE began George W. Bush's administration still mired in high-visibility controversy, struggling against the stigma of flagrant mismanagement and still saddled with responsibility for unpopular policies. The DOE's problems seem almost inevitable in light of its history. The department was created in 1976, when Congress combined a number of independent agencies with programs already operating in other departments to bring the federal government's sprawling energy activities within a single bureaucratic structure. Under the DOE's jurisdiction are regulatory activities and energy programs strongly affecting the environment. The more important of these include (1) promotion of civilian nuclear power activities, (2) regulation of military nuclear facilities and radioactive wastes, (3) administration of the federal government's research and development programs in energy production and conservation, (4) regulation of price controls for domestic petroleum and natural gas, and (5) administration of federal research and development grants for commercial synthetic fuels production in the United States. The DOE is the principal executive agency involved in the regulation and production of many different energy technologies with significant environmental impacts.

Also, by design, it is expected to undertake a volatile agenda of frequently contradictory and inconsistent missions destined to set it at odds with itself and with the environmental community: to promote environmentally risky energy technologies and to minimize the environmental risks, to promote energy use and energy conservation, to stimulate research and development of new energy-consuming and energy-saving technologies, to control energy prices in emergencies, and to avert energy shortages and stimulate long-range energy planning.

By far the most politically and financially costly problem confronting the DOE remains the environmental contamination of the nation's nuclear weapons facilities (discussed in Chapter 8). More than 122 nuclear weapons manufacturing and laboratory sites in 30 states, the Marshall Islands, and Puerto Rico have to be made safe. The cleanup program will probably exceed $250 billion and take perhaps a half century or more to accomplish—if it can be accomplished; no public or private agency has any experience in cleaning up radioactive contamination of such scale and complexity.[49] Spending for the cleanup of these nuclear weapons sites and for other related programs could involuntarily transform the DOE into the nation's largest environmental agency and launch it on the most expensive public works program in U.S. history.[50]

Neither a new century nor a new presidency improved political karma at the DOE. The department was anointed the lead agency for President George W. Bush's ambitious new national energy policy in 2001, intended to combat what the president proclaimed as a new national energy crisis—a situation that set the DOE on a collision course with almost all organized environmental groups that considered the new plan to be extravagantly expensive and environmentally reckless. To environmentalists, the DOE seemed to be promoting hugely accelerated fossil fuel extraction and electricity production when it should be promoting energy conservation, advocating more commercial nuclear power when it should be advocating less, and proclaiming an energy crisis when one didn't exist. Moreover, the DOE was still struggling with an apparently intractable problem of creating a permanent repository for the nation's nuclear waste. And, controversy continued over the DOE's management of military nuclear waste sites.

President Obama's selection of Dr. Steven Chu, a Nobel Laureate physicist, to be secretary of the Interior inaugurated what the administration expected to be a fresh, ambitious agenda of environmentally benign programs. These programs emphasized energy conservation, renewable energy, federal support for innovative energy technologies, and other initiatives that environmentalists generally perceived as a welcome change from the Bush administration's apparent preference for fossil fuels and nuclear power in national energy development.

The Courts: The Role of Appraisal

Federal judges actively participate in the environmental policy process in several ways. They continually interpret environmental law, an inevitable task in light of the ambiguities and silences common to environmental legislation. This statutory interpretation often amounts to policy making by the judicial branch. Judges also attempt to ensure that agencies discharge their mandated responsibilities under environmental legislation and otherwise comply with administrative obligations. In addition, the federal courts enforce the Administrative Procedures Act (1946), the code of administrative procedures applicable to all federal agencies. Finally, the courts ensure that environmental laws and their administrative implementation comply with constitutional standards. As the volume of environmental litigation expands relentlessly, federal judges find themselves increasingly at the pulse points of environmental policy making. Although critics have argued that federal judges are not prepared by a legal education for this pivotal role in adjudicating complex scientific and economic issues, the trend seems inexorable.

The Courts and Environmental Policy. The impact of the federal courts on environmental policy has changed over the decades since Earth Day 1970. In the 1970s, federal court decisions in both substantive and procedural issues generally worked to the advantage of environmental interests. During this period, environmentalists often saw the federal judiciary as the great equalizer, offsetting the previously enormous advantage enjoyed by regulated interests in administrative and judicial forums. Environmental organizations, aggressively exploiting the procedural advantages they had gained during the 1970s to compel federal enforcement of new regulatory programs, achieved some of their most significant judicial victories during this period. The federal courts greatly expanded opportunities for environmental groups to bring issues before the bench by a broadened definition of *standing to sue,* a legal status that authorized individuals or organizations to sue governmental agencies for failure to enforce environmental legislation.

By the late 1980s, however, the federal judiciary was no longer a predictably friendly venue for environmentalism. Business and other regulated interests began to use the federal courts far more effectively than they had previously. The increased effectiveness of business interests also exemplified the great growth in number and activity of specialized not-for-profit legal foundations representing regulated industries in environmental litigation. Reasoning that the devil should not have all the good tunes, business patterned these associations after the successful public-interest legal foundations created in the 1970s to represent environmental interests. As do environmental public interest groups, these business associations maintain that they are suing the government in the public interest and enjoy tax-exempt status. However, business public-interest groups are financed principally by organizations, such as the Adolph Coors Company and the Scaife Foundation, that have fought vigorously against most of the major environmental regulatory programs passed since the 1970s. The tide of judicial favor began to turn more decisively against environmental litigants in the 1990s as an increasing number of federal judges appointed by Presidents Reagan and George Bush came to the bench.[51] The benefit to business interests from this growing strength in environmental litigation does not depend solely on winning cases. Exhaustive and relentless challenges to federal regulation can delay the enforcement of environmental laws for many years and throw environmental groups on the defensive, compelling them to invest their resources in protracted legal battles. Often, battles are won not by the side with the best case but by the side with the most endurance.

Environmental groups anticipated that the election of George W. Bush was the prelude to another round of federal judicial appointments equally unfriendly to environmental interests. Despite its court appointments, however, the Bush administration did not fare nearly as well as predicted in the lower federal courts, where most environmental cases begin and end (the Supreme Court hears fewer than 100 cases a year; the circuit, or appellate, courts hear more than 40,000 appeals annually and often create most of the legal precedents that become the law of the land).[52] Federal judges in the Northwest, Midwest, and Far West were especially critical of the administration's efforts to open up public lands to more energy exploration, its lackluster enforcement of the Endangered Species Act, and its enthusiasm for increasing timber production on federal forests.[53]

The Supreme Court has been a very different matter. The Court ended its 2009 term after a series of decisions that evoked from environmentalist legal scholars verdicts such as "the worst term ever" and "a message of extreme hostility to the goals and methods of environmental law"; in contrast, advocates of more restrained environmental regulation predictably approved what seemed to be the Court's determined direction.[54] In several high-profile cases, for example, the Court limited the ability of five conservation groups to challenge U.S. Forest Service regulations and limited the scope of business liability for Superfund cleanups. Such decisions appeared to reflect the Court's increasingly conservative outlook resulting from the gradual appointment of new justices during the Bush administration and to project a problematic future for environmentalist litigation considered by the highest federal court.

However, the Supreme Court has seldom been wholly predictable about environmental issues. While most environmentalists still regard the Court as an unfriendly venue, the Court announced perhaps the most important of its decisions supporting environmental regulation, ironically, during the latter days of the G. W. Bush administration. A coalition of states, frustrated by congressional inability to pass legislation to regulate climate warming CO_2 emissions and by the Bush EPA's refusal to use the CAA for the same purpose, sued the EPA, asserting the EPA was compelled to regulate CO_2 by the CAA. In a landmark decision, the Supreme Court ruled in *Massachusetts v. Environmental Protection Agency* (2007) that CO_2 could potentially endanger human health or the environment as defined by the CAA. The Court then instructed the EPA to determine whether CO_2 was, in fact, a threat to humans or the environment (the *endangerment finding*) and, if so, to write appropriate regulations to control domestic CO_2 emissions. Shortly after Barack Obama's inauguration, his new EPA Administrator Lisa Jackson initiated action culminating in the EPA's declaration that CO_2 was a human health threat to be regulated by the CAA. The EPA then began preparation of new regulations, anticipated to take effect in 2012, for the first time creating national emissions controls for CO_2.

Litigation as a Political Tactic. The impact of the courts on policy, as the previous discussion suggests, arises not only from the substance of court rulings but also from the use of litigation as a tactical weapon in policy conflict—a weapon used by all sides. Most environmental litigation arises from three sources: major environmental organizations (such as the Sierra Club or the Environmental Defense Fund); business and property interests, including public-interest law firms (such as the highly aggressive Western States Legal Foundation); and federal agencies (such as the EPA or the DOI) with major environmental responsibilities. Quite often, the courts become another political arena in which the losers in prior policy battles fought among Congress, the bureaucracy, and the White House can launch yet another campaign. Litigation is also a stall in the policy process, a frustration to the opposition. Litigation creates a bargaining chip to be bartered for concessions from the opposition. Both environmentalists and their opposition have used the obstructive capacities of litigation to their advantage.

Many critics have pegged NEPA's requirement of environmental impact statements as an especially productive source of lawsuits working to the advantage of environmentalists, but the data suggest otherwise. The number of lawsuits challenging agency actions under NEPA has been diminishing steadily in number and importance as judges have increasingly determined that agencies have prepared and reviewed environmental impact statements properly. In addition, environmental impact statements are fast becoming a bureaucratic rite, meticulously observed but then substantively ignored.

When Should Judges Become Involved? The evolution of environmental politics increasingly embroils federal judges in resolving legal issues that have important policy consequences—in effect, implicating them in environmental policy making through the courts. Moreover, many of these issues embrace highly technical or scientific disputes. Federal judges may, for instance, have to decide whether the EPA considered the proper animal tests in deciding that a chemical constituted a significant risk to human health. Judges are often reluctant participants in these affairs, so heavily weighted with policy or scientific implications. They may be compelled by law to adjudicate such matters, but are acutely aware of their limitations as technical experts. Equally important, as Supreme Court Justice Stephen Breyer observed, when the courts must substitute their judgment for an administrator's, the result is often politically unsatisfactory:

> Regulators must make "legislative-type" decisions, the merits of which depend upon finding, or prying out important general facts about the world; they work in a politically charged environment; they may need to seek compromise solutions acceptable to warring private groups. [But judges must make decisions] the merits of which depend upon the relevant legal norm and a record . . . that need not contain all relevant facts about the world. . . . Given these differences, a compromise solution that a regulator considers reasonable, for practical administrative reasons, might not seem practical to a judge.[55]

Both critics and defenders of existing environmental policies have frequently proposed that some alternative venue to the traditional courts be created for resolving technical and scientific controversies arising from environmental regulation. One common suggestion is the creation of a science court in which technical experts would resolve the scientific and technical issues involved in environmental litigation, leaving the judges free to focus on the largely legal matters. Other proposals involve creating impartial technical advisers to judges when scientific issues confront the court. These and many other alternatives discussed among environmental law activists illuminate not only the evolving impact of environmentalism on U.S. legal institutions themselves but also the larger challenge entailed in integrating the judicial branch effectively and appropriately into the whole environmental policy process.

The Political Environment of Environmental Policy Making

Governmental institutions are fated to work in a political setting that is inconstant, influential, and often fickle. Opportunities to make or change policy shift continually, often unpredictably, with changing political circumstances. At any given time, there will be differences between what policy makers want and what they can accomplish, between what they are compelled to do and what they would prefer to do, and between what is feasible and what is not. This ebb and flow of opportunity are created by different circumstances. The most important of these circumstances includes changes in the partisan control of governmental institutions, transient shifts of public mood, major economic change, and regulatory federalism. These can be called the changing seasons of policy making.

Changing Party Majorities

The balance of party strength within Congress and between Congress and the White House powerfully shapes the substance and opportunities for environmental policy making. In theory, opportunities to make or change policy are greatest when the White House and Congress are controlled by the same party. However, since 1970, Republicans have usually occupied the White House and Democratic majorities have usually controlled at least one congressional chamber. The floodtide of environmental legislation originating in Washington, DC, during the 1970s was largely the result of a broad bipartisan environmental coalition in both chambers that strongly supported innovative environmental programs proposed or accepted by both Republican and Democratic presidents. The political climate for environmentalists darkened dramatically with Reagan's 1980 election and remained unsettled during the 1980s and early 1990s when shifting party majorities in Congress resulted in an environmental gridlock in which the Democratic House frustrated Senate Republican efforts to pass Reagan's sweeping agenda of change in existing environmental laws.

Reagan's enormous impact on environmental policy making in the 1980s is evidence, however, that in the hands of a politically skilled president with a clear policy agenda, White House resources can be a potent policy making instrument, with or without congressional cooperation. During the Reagan years, especially, administrators were able to obstruct and revise many environmental regulations and manipulate their agency budgets so effectively that the administration's environmental goals were at least partially achieved without any congressional cooperation.

With the exception of EPA Administrator William K. Reilly, the environmentally important appointments of George Bush's administration generally went to individuals sympathetic to the Reagan–Bush regulatory reform agenda and thereby objectionable to most environmental organizations. The chill blowing toward the EPA from the White House was unmistakable; it became a continuing and effective obstacle to many environmental policy initiatives from Congress or the bureaucracy.

The Democrats' return to the White House with Clinton in 1992 turned out to be less the prelude to the bright future anticipated by environmentalists than a false dawn. The stunning Republican congressional victories of 1994 returned a Republican majority to both congressional chambers and elevated to its leadership a cadre of Republicans outspokenly unsympathetic to most of the major environmental legislation created by Congress in the previous two decades. The Republican congressional leadership sponsored a multitude of legislative proposals that would become a recurring agenda, continuing through the Obama administration, heavy with proposals to radically recast, and usually enfeeble, most of the major environmental laws written during the 1970s and 1980s.

The first six months of George W. Bush's presidency were additional confirmation that shifting congressional majorities can profoundly—and sometimes abruptly—transform the course of environmental politics. Less than six months after the 107th Congress convened, Republicans lost their tenuous Senate majority. This, in turn, delivered the Senate majority to the Democrats, whose environmental policy agenda differed substantially from that favored by President Bush and Senate Republicans. Control of the Senate's policy agenda and all its committees now belonged to the Democrats. The White House no longer had the policy initiative in the Senate, and the president's whole environmental agenda, like the rest of his legislative program, would become more difficult to promote. Although Republicans temporarily recovered their Senate majority in the 2002 elections, Democrats reclaimed control of both chambers in the startling 2006 elections, much to the satisfaction of most environmentalists, who interpreted the results as a sharp public rejection of the Bush environmental record and a mandate to the Democrats for a more environmentalist agenda.

The election of Barack Obama and return of Democratic majorities to both congressional chambers in 2008 seemed to most environmentalists to imply—quite deceptively—greater collaboration between White House and Congress in promoting environmentalist legislation. In fact, Republicans recaptured control of the House of Representatives in 2010. The political polarization relentlessly growing since the mid-1990s now hardened into the chronic congressional deadlock that practically precluded any significant new environmental legislation by the end of 2012.

Shifting Public Moods

"When President Nixon and his staff walked in the White House on January 20, 1969, we were totally unprepared for the tidal wave of public opinion in favor of cleaning up the nation's environment that was about to engulf us," John C. Whitaker, one of Nixon's close advisers, remembered. Congress was quicker to read the political prophecy in the polls.[56] By Earth Day 1970, recalled the same adviser, "so many politicians were on the stump that Congress was forced to close down."[57] Presidents and Congress alike always feel enormous political pressure to respond when confronted by broad public majorities demonstrating a strong interest, or apprehension, about an environmental issue.

The pressure to do something, or to look as if one is doing something, is almost irresistible when sudden spikes of public apprehension rise in the aftermath of a well-publicized environmental crisis. Many major environmental laws and regulations are direct responses to environmental disasters, real or threatened. The Three Mile Island nuclear reactor accident of 1979 begot new regulations from the NRC increasing the requirements for emergency planning at commercial nuclear power plants. The tragic 1984 chemical plant disaster at Bhopal, India, in which 5,000 nearby residents and plant workers lost their lives, almost alone produced the community right-to-know provision of the Superfund Amendments and Reauthorization Act of 1986, which required industries using dangerous chemicals to disclose the type and amount of these chemicals to individuals living within an area likely to be affected by an accident on site. "The Bhopal train was leaving the station," observed one environmental lobbyist about Congress, "and we got the kind of legislation we could put on the train."[58] When California, in early 2001, suddenly experienced rolling power blackouts and steeply rising electric power costs, President Bush and congressional spokespeople of both political parties quickly proclaimed an energy crisis and produced competing prescriptions for a new national energy plan, even while experts debated whether such a crisis really existed.

Washington's impetuous reaction to any publicly perceived environmental crisis is predictably nonpartisan. This hypersensitivity to public opinion has been criticized frequently because it sometimes results in hastily written laws that are difficult to implement. According to economists Robert W. Crandall and Paul R. Portney, "Congress bears a large share of the responsibility for the problems of environmental regulation. Congress has passed enabling statutes containing unrealistic deadlines and an unnecessary degree of specificity with respect to the standards that [agencies] must issue."[59]

Opinion can also become an obstacle to environmental policy making when the public mood is inhospitable to action. The disappearance of gasoline and petroleum shortages in the late 1970s, and other evidence that the so-called energy crisis was passing, quickly removed energy problems from public concern and thwarted efforts by the Carter administration to pass new energy regulatory programs after mid-1978. By the time the Reagan administration finished its first term, Congress no longer felt pressure to continue mandatory plans for national fuel rationing, to require increased fuel economy standards for automobiles after 1986, or to promote solar technologies and other fuel conservation measures. Advocates of environmental issues often must wait until the opinion climate is ripe to move the White House or Congress to action. Crisis or disaster may sometimes be the only force that moves the political will.

Economic Change

In all environmental policy making, economics is the counterpoint to ecology. The impact of environmental policies on the economy is a continual preoccupation of environmental regulators and the regulated. Economic conditions, in turn, influence environmental policy making.

The economic impact of environmental regulations is continually an issue in all discussions of environmental policy. Concern most often focuses on whether environmental regulation will inhibit the expansion of the gross national product, how regulations will affect business investments and the market positions of firms or industries, and whether regulatory costs are inflationary. Regulated interests frequently assert that specific policies will have most, or all, of these negative effects, whereas proponents of regulation usually claim no such negative effects will occur. Data wars erupt; each side summons its economists and econometrics to vindicate its position and discredit the opposition. Although the result of these conflicts is often inconclusive, the issues are vitally important. Policies that appear (or can be made to appear) to adversely affect economic growth, market positions, or business investment are likely to command greater and more critical attention from policy makers than those appearing more economically benign. In times of economic recession or depression, the economic impact of policies can become the major determinant of their survival.

Environmental regulations, in any case, do create major public and private costs. Between 1980 and 2000, about 60 percent of the cost of national pollution control was paid by the private sector.[60] In general, studies suggest that new capital spending for pollution control by the public and private sectors has not significantly deterred the growth of the gross national product or contributed much to inflation or to a rise in the consumer price index. For most industries, spending for pollution control has been a gradually diminishing portion of new capital investment since 1980. In 1990, business spending on pollution control was estimated at 2.8 percent of all capital investment but was expected to diminish to less than 2 percent by 2004, although final data are unavailable.[61]

Most theorists assume that a major economic recession, depression, or serious bout with inflation will profoundly affect environmental regulation. The United States experienced no major depression and only a few short recessions between 1970 and 2006. However, the economic recession beginning in 1989 and the sluggish recovery in the early 1990s affected the environmental agendas of the Bush and Clinton administrations. The economic malaise all but extinguished the Bush administration's mild enthusiasm for environmental policy innovation after 1990 and—much to the disappointment of environmentalists—inhibited the scope of environmental reforms initiated by the Clinton administration, despite the president's campaign commitment to aggressive environmentalism.

The mild downturn of the economy beginning in 2000 was congenial to G. W. Bush's environmental agenda. Bush and his advisers believed that even a modest economic recession called for a relaxation of environmental regulations that allegedly inhibited economic development in the industrial sector and particularly in the energy industry—a theme that resonated well with congressional Republicans. The Bush administration seized on California's highly publicized energy problems in early 2001 as further proof that massively increased energy production had to be a national economic priority. Asserting that a national energy crisis existed, the president's early legislative agenda capitalized on the sluggish economy and California's energy ills to promote a comprehensive relaxation of environmental regulations and aggressive new energy exploration on public lands.

The severe recession crippling the national economy starting in 2006 is widely expected to have a significant impact on environmental policy making enduring well after 2012. Predictions include a growing public reluctance, shared by national political leaders, to support vigorous new environmental laws and regulations because they might inhibit economic recovery (a symptom of this malaise may be the growing public concern about the economic impact of environmental laws, discussed in Chapter 2). Environmental organizations have experienced a significant decline in assets leading to cutbacks in staff and programs, although many groups have responded with a greater reliance on volunteers and more efficient resource use in the most essential programs.[62] The recession clearly cut deeply into the Obama administration's environmental agenda, promoting increased emphasis on energy development including new commercial nuclear power and carbon fuel production, cutbacks in the EPA's regulatory budget, and greater restraint in promoting new environmental regulations.

Regulatory Federalism

Federalism disperses governmental power by fragmenting authority between national and state governments. Despite the historical enlargement of federal powers, federalism remains a sturdy constitutional buttress supporting the edifice of authority—shared, independent, and countervailing—erected for the states within the federal system. An observer has said, "It is difficult to find any government activity which does not involve all three of the so-called 'levels' of the federal system." Yet no one level monopolizes power. "There has never been a time when it was possible to put neat labels on discrete 'federal,' 'state,' and 'local' functions."[63]

Environmental programs usually are federalized, and sometimes regionalized, in their implementation, thereby introducing another political dimension into the policy process. For instance, federal air and water pollution legislation is administered through the Washington, DC, headquarters of the EPA, its ten regional offices, and the majority of state governments, which assume the responsibility for issuing to pollution dischargers permits specifying the acceptable control technologies and emission levels. In the mid-1990s, for instance, 38 states had authority to issue water permits, and 49 certified pesticides under federal authority. This two- and three-tiered design ensures that state and regional interests take part in the regulatory process and that, consequently, state and local governments, together with their associated interests, actively pursue their individual, often competitive objectives during program implementation. Even if the states are not formally included in the administration of federal environmental regulations, they are likely to insist on some voice in decisions affecting them. Federalism in environmental regulation guarantees voice and influence to the multitude of states involved, providing essential representation for various geographical interests affected politically and economically by federal environmental laws.

The most untiring watchdog over state environmental interests in Washington is the U.S. Senate. The status of the states has altered considerably since the 1970s. At the time of the first Earth Day, only a few progressive states such as California anticipated federal policy makers by initiating needed environmental regulations. Most states seemed unable or unwilling to attack vigorously their own environmental ills. In fact, a major provocation for the array of new federal environmental legislation flowing from Washington during this period was the conviction among federal policy makers that most states had neither the will nor the competence to attack grave environmental problems on their own. Today, the states have often been well ahead of Washington in developing innovative and experimental environmental management and in attacking emerging environmental problems. Aggressive state pressure often forces the EPA's policy implementation and innovation. Thus, a coalition of northeastern states, collaborating in 2006 to sue the EPA for its failure to regulate national CO_2 emissions through the CAA, eventually forced the U.S. Supreme Court to review the scientific evidence for climate warming despite the Bush administration's opposition.

Federalism can also complicate and delay program implementation. Few issues arouse state concern more than federal aid and administrative discretion for the states in program management. Federal aid comes in many forms: grants for program administration, staff training, salary supplements, program enforcement, and pollution control facilities; technical assistance in program development or enforcement; research cost sharing; and much more. The states understandably favor generous federal cost sharing in the administration of federally mandated environmental programs. Many proponents of environmental regulation believe that the amount of federal aid directly affects the quality of environmental protection, particularly in states lacking adequate staff and technical resources to implement programs on their own.

The amount of discretion permitted the states when interpreting and enforcing federal regulations within their own borders begets ceaseless controversy in U.S. environmental administration. In general, the states prefer the federal government to leave state administrators with enough discretion to adapt federal environmental regulations to unique local conditions and to be responsive to local economic and political interests. Assailing the federal government for imposing regulations on the states without respect for local interests is a political mantra among state officials, but the criticism has grown increasingly strident as the states' competence in and resources for pollution regulation improved throughout the 1990s. States now commonly complain that federal regulations force them to conform to rules that are inappropriate, economically wasteful, or politically unfair to local interests—a mood aggravated by mounting regulatory responsibilities imposed by Washington along with diminishing financial support for their implementation.

Another fertile source of controversy in regulatory federalism is the existence of many regional conflicts deeply embedded in the nation's history. Disagreements between the western states, where most of the federal public lands reside, and Washington, DC, over the management of the public domain west of the Mississippi—almost one third of the nation's land area—repeatedly erupt in the course of federal environmental regulation.

Conclusion

In an important sense, all the nation's environmental problems can be solved. There are almost no contemporary environmental problems for which a technical or scientific solution does not exist or cannot readily be found. Even when ensuring environmental quality might require social action—perhaps a major shift of consumer spending away from gas-guzzler vehicles to highly fuel-efficient cars to reduce urban smog—what could solve the problem is usually much easier to imagine than how to accomplish it. With this perspective, perhaps the greatest challenge to environmental policy making is finding the governmental, economic, and cultural arrangements—the institutional means—to achieve the environmental ends. To most Americans, the nation's environmental challenges are epitomized by polluted air, fouled water, dangerously unregulated hazardous and toxic wastes, and a multitude of other ecological derangements. This chapter illuminates the less-obvious dimension of the nation's environmental difficulties—the institutional and economic obstacles to implementing environmental policy effectively. Despite the numerous improvements in environmental quality since 1970, in many critical respects, the governmental institutions on which the nation now depends to reverse its ecological degradation are struggling, and often failing, at the task.

Difficulties with environmental policy making often originate in the fundamental constitutional design of the political system or in deeply rooted political traditions. Among these problems are excessive congressional control of the agencies implementing environmental policy, legislative reluctance to creating clear mandates and priorities within regulatory programs, the extreme fragmentation of committee control over environmental policy, and the resistance of entrenched bureaucracies to structural and policy reform. Although federalism is essential to the political architecture of any environmental regulatory program in the United States, it also complicates policy implementation by introducing competitive pluralistic interests. The institutions, moreover, must function in a volatile political climate of shifting party majorities, economic cycles, fluctuating public opinion, and contentious issues of policy implementation arising from tensions deeply embedded in a federalized regulatory process.

In essence, the quality of the nation's environmental policy making is grounded in an institutional design that shapes and limits outcomes. To understand what policies are made, we inevitably must appreciate how they were created.

Suggested Readings

Kamieniecki, Sheldon, and Michael E. Kraft. *Business and Environmental Policy: Corporate Interests in the American System.* Cambridge, MA: MIT Press, 2007.

Keller, Ann Campbell. *Science in Environmental Policy: The Politics of Objective Advice.* Cambridge, MA: MIT Press, 2009

Lindstrom, Matthew J., and Zachary A. Smith. *The National Environmental Policy Act: Judicial Misconstruction, Legislative Indifference, and Executive Neglect.* College Station: Texas A&M Press, 2001.

National Academy of Public Administration. *Setting Priorities, Getting Results: A New Direction for the U.S. Environmental Protection Agency.* Washington, DC: National Academy of Public Administration, 1995.

Scheberle, Denise. *Federalism and Environmental Policy: Trust and the Politics of Implementation.* Washington, DC: Georgetown University Press, 2004.

Notes

1. John Broder, "E.P.A. Chief Stands Firm as Tough Rules Loom," *New York Times,* July 5, 2011, A13 (New York ed.).
2. For this EPA story, see Katherine Q. Seelye, "EPA Surprises Its Leader and Interior Chief on Snowmobiles," *New York Times,* May 2, 2003, A5.
3. T. R. Reid, "For Snowmobiles, an Uncertain Fate; Future in Parks May Hinge on Election," *Washington Post,* March 15, 2004, A23.
4. Felicity Barringa, "Judge's Ruling on Yellowstone Keeps It Open to Snowmobiles," *New York Times,* October 16, 2004, A9.
5. Felicity Barringa, "Secretary Tours Yellowstone on Snowmobile," *New York Times,* February 17, 2005, A18.
6. Bettina Boxall, "Bush's Grade on Environment Falls," *Los Angeles Times,* August 4, 2006, A1.
7. Jack Welch, "Blue Ribbon Coalition Responds to Yellowstone Debate," August 7, 2009, available at http://cs.amsnow.com/snocs/blogs/news/archive/2009/08/07/blue-ribbon-coalition-responds-to-yellowstone-debate.aspx (accessed October 20, 2009).
8. Ibid.
9. Quoted by Nancy Pelosi, speaker of the House of Representatives, in Ken Root, "Agriculture Still Has Clout With Politicians," *High Plains Journal,* March 21, 2007, B12.
10. Useful illustrations of presidential activism in environmental policy making are found in Dennis L. Soden, ed., *The Environmental Presidency* (Albany, NY: SUNY Press, 1999); Norman J. Vig, "Presidential Leadership and the Environment," in *Environmental Policy: New Directions for the Twenty-First Century,* ed. Norman J. Vig and Michael E. Kraft (Washington, DC: CQ Press, 2003), 103–125.
11. A useful summary of the EOP's development can be found in Harold C. Relyea, "The Executive Office of the President: An Historical Overview," Congressional Research Report to Congress, Order Code 98–606 GOV, Washington, DC, November 26, 2008.
12. National Environmental Policy Act, Title II, 42 U.S.C. § 4321 et seq. (1970).
13. Quoted in Russel E. Train, "The Environmental Record of the Nixon Administration," *Presidential Studies Quarterly* 26, no. 1 (1996): 191.
14. Henry M. Jackson Foundation, "Facing the Future: Recommendations on the White House Council on Environmental Quality: A Report to the President Elect," Tulane Institute on Water Resources, Law, and Policy, Tulane Law School, New Orleans, October 2008, 4.

15. Christopher Schroeder, "The Evolution of Federal Regulation of Toxic Substances," in *Government and Environmental Politics: Essays on Historical Development Since World War II,* ed. Michael J. Lacey (Lanham, MD: University Press of America, 1990), 118.

16. Ralph Huitt, "Political Feasibility," in *Policy Analysis in Political Science,* ed. Ira Sharkansky (Chicago, IL: Markham, 1970), 414.

17. Barry G. Rabe, *Fragmentation and Integration in State Environmental Management* (Washington, DC: Conservation Foundation, 1986), 16–17. See also Michael E. Kraft, "Congress and Environmental Policy," in *Environmental Politics and Policy: Theories and Evidence,* ed. James P. Lester (Durham, NC: Duke University Press, 1989), 179–211.

18. "Mississippi 'Pork' Ranking," Official Trent Lott Press Release, May 2, 2002, available at www.lott.senate.gov/news/2000/502.pork.html (accessed February 8, 2004).

19. Mark J. Landy and Mary Hague, "The Coalition for Waste: Private Interests and Superfund," in *Environmental Politics: Public Costs, Private Rewards,* ed. Michael S. Grave (New York: Praeger, 1992), 72.

20. Lawrence Mosher, "Clean Water Requirements Will Remain Even if the Federal Spigot Is Closed," *National Journal,* May 16, 1981, 874–878.

21. Quoted in Marcia Clemmitt, "Energy and Climate Change: Should Carbon-Based Fuels Be Phased Out?" *CQ Researcher,* July 24, 2009, available at http://library.cqpress.com/cqresearcher/search.php?PHPSESSID=207p8d3i1ek2nbscahp1j5iad3&fulltext=climate+change&action=newsearch&sort=custom%3Asorthitsrank%2Cd&x=15&y=12 (accessed November 14, 2009).

22. Quoted in *New York Times,* March 22, 1993, B8.

23. Quoted in ibid.

24. GAO, "Indoor Air Pollution: Federal Efforts Are Not Effectively Addressing a Growing Problem," Report No. GAO/RCED 92–8, Washington, DC, October 1991, 6.

25. Quoted in Margaret E. Kriz, "Pesticidal Pressures," *National Journal,* December 12, 1988, 125.

26. Jared N. Day, "Safe Drinking Water-Safe Sites: Interaction between the Safe Drinking Water Act and Superfund, 1968–1995," in *Improving Regulation: Cases in Environment, Health, and Safety,* ed. Paul S. Fischbeck and R. Scott Farrow (Washington, DC: Resources for the Future, 2000).

27. David Schoenbrod, "The EPA's Faustian Bargain," *Regulation* (fall 2006): 41.

28. GAO, "Implementation of the Clean Air Act Amendments of 1990: Statement of David G. Wood, Associate Director, Environmental Protection Issues," Report no. GAO/T-RCED 00–183, Washington, DC, February 10, 1990, 9.

29. On American political polarization and its congressional implications, see: Pew Research Center for the People and the Press, *Partisan Polarization Surges in Bush, Obama Years* (Washington, DC: Pew Research Center, June 4, 2012), also available at www.people-press.org (accessed June 20, 2012); Nolan McCarty, "Policy Consequences of Partisan Polarization in the United States," available at bcep.haas.berkeley.edu/papers/McCarty.doc (accessed January 10, 2012; Sean M. Theriault,"Party Polarization in Congress," available at www.ruf.rice.edu/~lmartin/Speakers/Theriault.pdf; and Sean M. Theriault, *Party Polarization in Congress* (New York: Cambridge University Press, 2008); William Galston, "Can a Polarized American Party System Be 'Healthy'? *Issues in Governance Studies* (Washington, DC: Brookings Institution, 2010), available at http://www.brookings.edu/research/papers/2010/04/polarization-galston (accessed July 27, 2012).

30. GAO, "Improving EPA's Regulatory Impact Analysis," Report no. GAO/RCED 97–38, Washington, DC, April 1997.

31. David D. Doniger, *The Law and Policy of Toxic Substances Control* (Baltimore, MD: Johns Hopkins University Press, 1978), 3.

32. Quoted in John H. Trattner, *The Prune Book: The 100 Toughest Management and Policy-Making Jobs in Washington* (Lanham, MD: Madison, 1988), 250.

33. Quoted in ibid., 249.

34. Green Energy News, "Obama Slashes EPA Funding By 13 Percent," February 21, 2011, available at www.renewable-energy-news.info/obama-budget-cuts-funding-for-epa-programs/?wpmp_switcher=mobile (accessed March 10, 2012).

35. EPA, Office of the Chief Financial Officer, "FY 2008: Budget in Brief," Publication no. EPA-205-S-07–001, Washington, DC, February 2007, v.

36. Estimated from data contained in J. Clarence Davies Jr., *Nanotechnology Oversight: An Agenda for the New Administration* (Washington, DC: Woodrow Wilson Center, 2008), 10.

37. Richard J. Lazarus, "The Tragedy of Distrust in the Implementation of Federal Environmental Law," *Law and Contemporary Problems* 54 (autumn 1991): 334. See also Marc K. Landy, Marc J. Roberts, and Stephen R. Thomas, *The Environmental Protection Agency: Asking the Wrong Questions* (New York: Oxford University Press, 1990); Paul R. Portney, ed., *Public Policies for Environmental Protection* (Washington, DC: Resources for the Future, 1990), chaps. 1, 8.

38. CEQ, *Environmental Quality, 1985* (Washington, DC: Council on Environmental Quality, 1986), 14. See also Walter A. Rosenbaum, "Into the Nineties at EPA: Searching for the Clenched Fist and the Open Hand," in *Environmental Policy in the 1990s*, 2nd ed., ed. Norman J. Vig and Michael E. Kraft (Washington, DC: CQ Press, 1994), 121–143.

39. GAO, "Pesticides: EPA's Formidable Task to Assess and Regulate Their Risks," Report No. GAO/RCED 86–125, Washington, DC, April 1986, 35.

40. CEQ, *Environmental Quality, 1985*, 12–13.

41. Richard Harris and Sidney Milkis, *The Politics of Regulatory Change: A Tale of Two Agencies* (New York: Oxford University Press, 1989), 228.

42. EPA, "Ash Council and Creation of EPA," September 21, 2007, available at http://www.epa.gov/history/publications/costle/04.htm (accessed January 19, 2009).

43. Peter W. House and Roger D. Shull, *Regulatory Reform: Politics and the Environment* (Lanham, MD: University Press of America, 1985), esp. 106.

44. Rabe, *Fragmentation and Integration*, 126.

45. EPA, Office of Solid Waste, "Human and Ecological Risk Assessment of Coal Combustion Waste," RTI, Research Triangle Park, NC, August 6, 2007, available at www.earthjustice.org/news/press/007/coal-ash-pollution-contaminates-groundwaterin-creases-cancer-risks.html (accessed November 27, 2011).

46. Nationals Research Council, Committee on Incorporating Sustainability in the U.S. Environmental Protection Agency, *Sustainability the U.S. EPA* (Washington, DC: National Academies Press, 2011), 86.

47. Zachary Coile, "Interior Chief Gale Norton to Step Down," *San Francisco Chronicle*, March 11, 2006, A1.

48. Michelle Adato, James Mackenzie, Robert Pollard, and Ellyn Weiss, *Safety Second: The NRC and America's Nuclear Power Plants* (Bloomington: Indiana University Press, 1987), esp. chaps. 1, 5.

49. GAO, "Department of Energy: Cleaning Up Inactive Facilities Will Be Difficult," Report no. GAO/RCED 92–149, Washington, DC, June 1993; see also GAO, "Much Work Remains to Accelerate Facility Cleanups," Report no. GAO/RCED 93–15, Washington, DC, January 1993.

50. See Christopher Madison, "The Energy Department at Three—Still Trying to Establish Itself," *National Journal*, October 4, 1980, 16–19.

51. Lettie M. Wenner, "Environmental Policy in the Courts," in *Environmental Policy in the 1990s,* 2nd ed., ed. Norman J. Vig and Michael E. Kraft (Washington, DC: CQ Press, 1994), 156.

52. Werner J. Grunbaum, *Judicial Policy Making: The Supreme Court and Environmental Quality* (Morristown, NJ: General Learning Press, 1976), 31. See also Lettie McSpadden Wenner, "The Courts and Environmental Policy," in *Environmental Politics and Policy: Theories and Evidence,* ed. James P. Lester (Durham, NC: Duke University Press, 1989), 261–288.

53. Barton H. Thompson, Jr., "Conservative Environmental Thought: The Bush Administration and Environmental Policy," *Ecology Law Quarterly,* 37 (2005): 307–348; John D. Graham, Paul R. Noe, and Elizabeth L. Branch, "Managing the Regulatory State: The Experience of the Bush Administration," *Fordham Urban Law Journal,* 33 (2006): 903–953; Blaine Harden, "Bush Policy Irks Judges in West; Rulings Criticize Agencies for Not Protecting the Environment," *Washington Post,* October 6, 2006, A3.

54. Jennifer Koons, "Supreme Court: A Rough Term for Environmentalists," *Environment and Energy Daily,* June 25, 2009, available at www.eenews.net/public/Greenwire/2009/06/25/3 (accessed August 14, 2010); Adam Liptak, "Environmental Groups Find Less Support in Court," *New York Times,* July 3, 2009, A10.

55. Stephen Breyer, *Breaking the Vicious Circle: Toward Effective Risk Regulation* (Cambridge, MA: Harvard University Press, 1993), 59.

56. John C. Whitaker, "Earth Day Recollections: What It Was Like When the Movement Took Off," *EPA Journal,* 14 (July–August 1988): 14.

57. Ibid.

58. Quoted in Margaret Kriz, "Fuming Over Fumes," *National Journal,* November 26, 1988, 3008.

59. Robert W. Crandall and Paul R. Portney, "Environmental Policy," in *Natural Resources and the Environment: The Reagan Approach,* ed. Paul Portney (Washington, DC: Urban Institute Press, 1984), 14.

60. U.S. Department of Commerce, Bureau of the Census, *Statistical Abstract of the United States, 1992* (Washington, DC: Government Printing Office, 1993), 217. Figures are given in 1982 dollar values, corrected for inflation.

61. EPA, "Environmental Investments: The Cost of a Clean Environment: A Summary," Washington, DC, 1990, vi.

62. W. K. Kellog Foundation, *The Quiet Crisis: The Impact of the Economic Downturn on the Nonprofit Sector* (Washington, DC: Kellog Foundation, March 2009).

63. Morton Grodzins, "The Federal System," in *American Federalism in Perspective,* ed. Aaron Wildavsky (Boston, MA: Little, Brown, 1967), 257.

Chapter 4

Common Policy Challenges
Risk Assessment and Environmental Justice

> *[The EPA] will need to ensure that it allocates resources to needed research on emerging issues, such as the relative toxicity of particulate matter components, and to assessing which sources of uncertainty have the greatest influence on benefit estimates. While EPA officials said they expect to reduce the uncertainties associated with the health benefit estimates in the final particulate matter analysis, a robust uncertainty analysis of the remaining uncertainties will nonetheless be important for decision makers and the public.*
>
> —U.S. GAO, 2006[1]

> *Risk assessment means never having to say you're certain.*
> —Humor among professional risk assessors

Until 1998, few Americans knew about phthalates nor cared about them. In November 1998, however, the environmental organization Greenpeace International released the first of its many reports demanding that the toy industry worldwide immediately abandon the use of the chemical DINP, an ingredient in vinyl, a material widely used throughout the industry in producing thousands of children's products as varied as pacifiers, rubber ducks, teddy bears, dolls, rattles, and teething rings. The report was another sortie in a militant campaign by environmentalists and public health officials against a large class of chemicals called phthalates, or plasticizers, which bond with vinyl molecules to make plastic products more flexible. In the United States, the announcement unleashed a relentless public controversy that has continued for more than 15 years, a conflict that quickly assumed a pattern common to the contemporary politics of environmental risk assessment

A Toxic Nightmare from Toyland?

First came a dramatic public condemnation of an important industrial chemical. Greenpeace International asserted a major domestic chemical manufacturer used the chemical DINP to manufacture products that children might chew, such as pacifiers and rattles, even though a similar compound caused liver damage in laboratory rats.[2] The accusation and accompanying information, quickly disseminated worldwide by the media, was alarming not only to the chemical producers and to parents whose children might be exposed to the products but also to the hundreds of manufacturers and consumers of other products using plasticizers—products such as medical equipment, food containers, consumer goods, packaging material, and much more—because plasticizers are a global commodity. Within weeks, two major U.S. medical advocacy groups issued a "health alert" warning that intravenous bags and tubing made of vinyl chloride contained a chemical very similar to DINP that previously had been removed from toy products because of suspected toxicity. A story on the popular ABC news program *20/20* in early 1998 repeated many of the Greenpeace International allegations, thus ensuring a huge domestic audience for the controversy. Within a few weeks, the plasticizer debate was a media event.[3]

Next, an acrimonious, highly technical dispute erupted in the public media, abetted by technical publications and professional spokespeople caught up in the controversy, over the extent of the health risks resulting from exposure to the plasticizers. At the same time, the controversy became quickly politicized. Organized groups representing environmentalists, consumers, public health interests, the chemical and toy manufacturers, governmental agencies, parents, political think tanks, and many others rapidly aligned on disputing sides of the issue. Conflict approached the surreal, as exquisitely technical and publicly confounding arguments raged over baby bottle nipples, animal fetuses, Teletubbies, squeeze toys, liver biopsies, monkey testicles, and other exotica. Even Barbie and Dr. C. Everett Koop, the former U.S. surgeon general, appeared. At stake were possibly a billion dollars in worldwide product sales, the ethical and economic stature of the chlorine chemical industry, markets for hundreds of manufacturers using the embattled chemicals, and perhaps the health of uncounted children worldwide.

The Political Front

Within a week of the Greenpeace International announcement, 12 consumer, environmental, and religious groups demanded that the U.S. Consumer Product Safety Commission (CPSC), the federal regulatory agency responsible for ensuring the safety of children's products sold in the United States, ban vinyl toys for small children. Shortly thereafter, 28 members of Congress addressed President Bill Clinton through a letter urging him to ensure that the Department of Commerce was not pressuring European countries to keep their markets open to children's vinyl products. The National Environmental Trust, a coalition of environmental organizations, urged the U.S. government to ban all vinyl baby products. In November 1998, the CPSC also stated that it was uncertain about the risks to babies from DINP but nonetheless advised parents to throw away nipples and pacifiers made with vinyl and asked manufacturers not to use DINP in products children might put in their mouths.

Meanwhile, the manufacturer of DINP and many industrial consumers were rising to DINP's defense. Major toy manufacturers such as Mattel; large toy retailers, including Toys R Us; and the industry's trade association, the Toy Manufacturers of America, all publicly defended the safety of the plasticizers used for decades in children's products. Defenders of DINP were enormously gratified when a nonprofit organization of distinguished scientific experts represented by Dr. Koop asserted that it stood "firmly behind the conclusions drawn from the weight of the scientific evidence [that] consumers can be confident that vinyl medical devices and toys are safe."[4]

A Scientific Enigma

The actual risk to children from exposure to plasticizers seemed anything but clear. One problem was the absence of a standard procedure to determine how much of the suspect chemical a child could realistically be expected to absorb. For example, how much DINP could a child be expected to consume by chewing a toy? In addition, toy components vary considerably in their plasticizer content. For instance, high levels of DINP were found in the arms of the Rugrats Tommy Pickles Ice Cream Face doll and in the shoes of the Cabbage Patch Kids Star Rosie doll but not elsewhere on either doll.

Another major problem involved the reliability of the animal tests indicating that DINP and its predecessor could cause liver damage in humans. Critics of these tests noted that similar damage did not occur in other experimental animals including guinea pigs, hamsters, and monkeys. Also, the age of the test animals might matter. Other disagreements arose over the relative importance to be given to toxic effects observed in different organs of experimental animals.[5]

Finally, there was the unsettling enigma about how long it could take before any health problems might appear among children exposed to plasticizers. Health professionals noted that the damaging effects of such exposure might be latent for many years and that, as a consequence, the current incidence of any suspected damage might greatly underestimate the long-term damage to humans. Thus, it might seem prudent to ban the plasticizers even in the absence of convincing, current evidence of their danger.

Barbie Gets a Green Makeover

With the controversy public, the Toy Manufacturers of America reluctantly advised its members to voluntarily eliminate DINP-based vinyl products even while it maintained their safety.[6] The Chlorine Chemistry Council, representing the users of all chlorine-based products, and toy manufacturers continued to defend DINP. The industry's capitulation was ensured when Mattel, the world's largest toy manufacturer, announced in December 1999 that it would substitute plant- and vegetable-based plastics for chlorine-based vinyls. Barbie was destined for a complete chemical makeover, along with a multitude of other familiar toys and products from other manufacturers, among them Teletubbies, Pony Luv, and Clear and Soft pacifiers and nipples.

And the Winner Is . . .

In 2003, to the considerable satisfaction of the Chlorine Chemistry Council and toy manufacturers, the CPSC voted unanimously to deny the petition to ban phthalates from products for children younger than five years old because there appeared to be "no demonstrable health risk."[7] The CPSC also knew how to defend itself. This decision, it noted, was supported by numerous scientific studies including a meticulous inquiry concerning "mouthing habits" among infants. The "average daily mouthing time" of soft plastic toys for children 12 to 24 months of age was 1.9 minutes, considerably fewer than the 75 minutes per day determined to be the risk threshold.[8] Average daily mouthing time, however, was not the science that satisfied most public health and environmental advocates, who continued to advocate the elimination of phthalates from toys.

By 2006, phthalate opponents had rearmed with a new wave of highly publicized scientific studies once again implying that phthalates might be a human toxic. One university study suggested that mothers exposed during pregnancy to high levels of phthalates found in cosmetics, plastics, and detergents might have "less masculine" boys; another investigation noted that plastic food containers might "contribute" to breast cancer.[9] The Cosmetic, Toiletry and Fragrance Association protested that "an extensive body of science research"[10] proved the safety of cosmetics, but public health and environmental advocates persisted, determined to skewer high-profile industries, such as nail polish manufacturers, with apparently damning scientific research.

Public health and environmental organizations also exploited opportunities to bring pressure on the federal government from other political venues. As early as 2002, the California legislature passed legislation prohibiting baby toys containing phthalates. In December 2006, San Francisco became the first U.S. city to prohibit the sale, manufacture, and distribution of products with high phthalate concentrations.[11] A powerful political blow against phthalates was struck by the European Union (EU), which in late 2006, passed a law regulating the manufacture and use of 30,000 toxic substances, including phthalates, thus creating enormous pressure on U.S. industry to do the same.

By 2010, continuing scientific evidence raised such substantial doubt about phthalate safety that parents and other consumers of phthalate-containing products were no longer left to decide which side—if any—should be trusted. A 2008 report of the National Academy of Sciences voiced considerable concern about phthalate safety and urged Congress and the EPA to promote new studies about the effects of cumulative human exposure to all phthalates.[12] This report, fortified by other accumulating research, created a receptive setting for new regulatory legislation. In September 2008, Congress passed the Consumer Product Safety Reform Act (CPSRA) mandating, among other important provisions, that the CPSC prohibit DINP and certain other phthalates in children's toys and care products and require manufacturers of children's products to test their safety and certify it.

The American Chemistry Council, a major organizational voice of the chemical industry, predictably expressed the industry's dissatisfaction with the CPSRA, arguing that "after all this study and review, no reliable scientific evidence has found phthalates to cause adverse human health effects."[13] In mid-2012, the plasticizer controversy revived on yet another front when the Food and Drug Administration (FDA), the federal agency responsible for assuring the safety of ingredients in domestic food products, proposed to ban another plasticizer, bisphenol A (BPA) from infant-feeding products such as children's sippy cups and baby bottles. However, the FDA also stated that adult food containers could safely contain BPA. The American Chemical Council was content with this decision because plasticizers had already been eliminated from most infant-feeding products anyway. But, public health groups were not satisfied. "To truly protect the public, the FDA needs to ban BPA from all food packaging," declared a spokesperson for the Natural Resources Defense Council, a major public health and environmental advocacy organization.[14] Further political and legal infighting was inevitable.

The continuing plasticizer controversy will likely eliminate a potentially hazardous class of chemicals, and probably others, from infant and children's products and perhaps from adult materials as well. In a broader perspective, moreover, the conflict also introduces the policy making pathway that is common to most risk assessments required by federal law and the focus of this chapter—a path littered with protracted litigation, sustained political infighting, disputed science, and multiple government venues.

Risk Assessment and the Limits of Science

In recent years, the EPA alone has written more than 7,500 risk assessments annually in various forms to carry out its regulatory responsibilities.[15] In 1993, President Clinton further elevated the importance of risk assessment by requiring in Executive Order 12866 that all regulatory agencies, not only environmental ones, "consider, to the extent reasonable, the degree and nature of risks posed by various substances or activities within its jurisdiction" and mandating that each proposed regulatory action explain how the action will reduce risks "as well as how the magnitude of risk addressed by the action relates to other risks within the jurisdiction of the agency."[16]

Traditional risk assessment associated with environmental regulation creates a flow of decisions that starts, as Figure 4–1 indicates, when the EPA or another regulatory agency is required to determine whether a substance—a commercial chemical, for example—constitutes a sufficient hazard to humans or to the environment to require regulation under one of many current environmental regulatory laws. The process begins with research that assembles currently available information about the possible adverse health or environmental effects of a suspected hazard, such as a chemical. If the research suggests possibly adverse effects to humans or the environment, the regulatory agency proceeds to risk assessment, during which additional information is obtained or experiments are conducted concerning the current levels of exposure to a suspected chemical, and an estimate is made of the likely adverse consequences. If this risk assessment indicates that a chemical is sufficiently hazardous to meet the requirements for regulation, the agency proceeds to risk management, during which regulators consider alternative strategies for the chemical's regulation and then propose a regulatory plan. Note that, although Figure 4–1 may imply that this is a dependably neat, deliberate, and timely sequence of decisions, the reality is often more episodic, with many decisions contested and an elapsed time in years or even decades.

Risk assessment has grown increasingly controversial until it now incites the impassioned conflicts once confined to holy wars such as the benefit–cost debate. A major reason for the controversy is that risk

Figure 4–1 The Risk Assessment Process

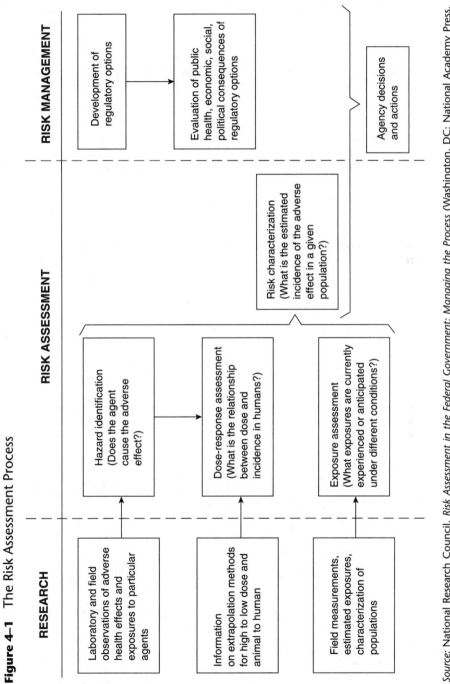

Source: National Research Council, *Risk Assessment in the Federal Government: Managing the Process* (Washington, DC: National Academy Press, 1983), 21. Reprinted with permission from National Research Council. Courtesy of the National Academies Press, Washington, DC.

assessment lies in the treacherous zone between science and politics, where practically all environmental policies reside and where collaboration between public officials and scientists is both essential and difficult. What public officials and scientists involved in policy making want from each other is often unobtainable. Public officials seek from scientists information that is accurate enough to indicate precisely where they should establish environmental standards and credible enough to defend in the inevitable conflicts to follow. Scientists want government to act quickly and forcefully on ecological issues they believe to be critical.[17] Yet, science often cannot produce technical information in the form and within the time desired by public officials. Indeed, science often cannot provide the information at all, leaving officials to make crucial decisions from fragmentary and disputable information.

In short, risk assessment frequently compels public officials to make scientific judgments and scientists to resolve policy issues for which neither may be trained. The almost inevitable need to resolve scientific questions through the political process and the problems that arise in making scientific and political judgments compatible are two of the most troublesome characteristics of environmental politics.

Derelict Data and Embattled Expertise

Controversy among experts commonly arises in environmental policy making. Contending battalions of experts—garlanded with degrees and publications and primed to dispute each other's judgment—populate congressional and administrative hearings about risk assessment. Policy makers are often left to judge not only the wisdom of policies but also the quality of the science supporting the policies.

Missing Data. Why is controversy so predictable? Frequently there is a void of useful data about the distribution and severity of environmental problems or possible pollutants. Many problems are so recent that public and private agencies have only just begun to study them. Many pollutants—hazardous chemicals, for instance—have existed for only a few decades; their ecological impacts cannot yet be measured reliably. The EPA alone receives about 1,500 petitions annually requesting the approval of new chemicals or new uses of existing chemicals for which tests may be required.[18] Quite often, the result is that nobody has the information that somebody should have. For instance, the EPA and the U.S. Department of Health and Human Services together have data reporting the degree of exposure among the general population for less than 7 percent of more than 1,400 chemicals considered to pose a threat to human health.[19] Lacking high-quality data, experts often extrapolate answers from fragmentary information, and plausible disputes over the reliability of such procedures are inevitable.

Late and Latent Effects. Disagreement over the severity of environmental problems also arises because the effects of many substances thought to be hazardous to humans or the environment may not become evident for decades or generations. The latency and diffusion of these impacts also may make it difficult to establish causality between the suspected substances, or events, and the consequences. Asbestos, a hazardous chemical whose malignancy has been documented since 1979, illustrates these problems.[20] Since World War II, approximately 8 million to 11 million U.S. workers have been exposed to asbestos, a mineral fiber with more than 2,000 uses; its heat resistance, electrical properties, immunity to chemical deterioration, and other characteristics made it appear to be ideal to a multitude of major industries. In the past, it was used widely to manufacture brake and clutch linings, plastics, plumbing, roofing tile, wall insulation, paint, paper, and much else. Asbestos is highly carcinogenic. Among those exposed to significant levels of asbestos, 20 to 25 percent died of lung cancer, 7 to 10 percent perished from mesothelioma (cancer of the chest lining or stomach), and another 8 to 9 percent died from gastrointestinal cancer.[21] The toxicity of asbestos became apparent only decades after workers were exposed because the cancers associated with it do not become clinically evident until 15 to 40 years after exposure, and severe illness may appear 2 to 50 years after the cancers first appear in humans. Added to the incalculable cost of human suffering is the immense economic impact of these delayed effects. More than 2,000 new cases of incurable asbestos-related cancer now appear each year in the United States. Presently, 300,000 lawsuits arising from human exposure to asbestos are pending in the nation's courts, and 20,000 to 50,000 lawsuits are predicted annually for several decades. U.S. corporations and insurers have spent more than $30 billion to defend and settle asbestos lawsuits. The total cost of these suits, according to several professional estimates, may exceed $200 billion.[22]

Many other substances used in U.S. commerce, science, and domestic life are suspected of producing adverse impacts on humans or the environment. Yet, conclusive evidence might not appear for decades, whereas government officials must decide whether to regulate these substances now. Difficult as such decisions are, a failure to act, as in the case of asbestos, eventually may prove so costly in human suffering and economic loss that many scientists may be reluctant to wait for conclusive data, even though others may argue the evidence is inconclusive. These issues are illustrated vividly by the federal government's continuing problems with the chemical dioxin.

The Case of Dioxin. Early in the 1990s, the EPA was persuaded by growing scientific evidence to initiate a searching reevaluation of its 20-year-old exposure standards for the chemical dioxin, which it had characterized earlier as one of the most lethal substances on Earth.[23] The most dangerous among the 75 varieties of dioxin was thought to be 2,3,7,8-tetrachlorodibenzodioxin (TCCD), considered so harmful that the EPA's maximum exposure standards had limited human ingestion of TCCD to 0.006 trillionth of a gram per day for every kilogram (2.2 pounds) of body weight over an average lifetime—in other words, an average-size man was limited daily to an amount equal to a grain of sand sliced 1 billion times.

The EPA's original exposure standard for dioxin, as with most risk assessments made by federal agencies, was extrapolated largely from animal experiments. In the late 1970s, the EPA ordered an end to the production of the weed killer 2,4,5-T, also a dioxin, on the basis of its own earlier studies and additional, if circumstantial, evidence of great harm to individuals exposed to high concentrations of the herbicide. When concentrations of dioxin far exceeding levels considered safe were discovered during 1981 in the soil of Times Beach, Missouri—the result of illegal toxic waste disposals—the EPA decided that public safety required the permanent evacuation of the entire Missouri community. All 2,240 residents were removed to new residences and reimbursed for their property at a cost exceeding $37 million, while an additional $100 million was spent to clean up other nearby contaminated sites. During the 1980s, hundreds of lawsuits were filed against the federal government by Vietnam War veterans for alleged health impairment from exposure to dioxin in the defoliant Agent Orange. Meanwhile, the EPA's strict standards were expected to cost the paper and pulp industry about $2 billion for pollution control.

But, a growing number of scientific experts questioned not only the EPA's exposure standards for dioxin but also the reliability of all the animal studies for determining the safe levels of human exposure to hazardous substances.[24] A particularly damning public indictment of the EPA's own standard appeared in 1991 when the federal scientist who had ordered the evacuation of Times Beach admitted to a congressional committee that he made the wrong decision. "Given what we know now about this chemical's toxicity," then assistant surgeon general Vernon N. Houk stated, "it looks as if the evacuation was unnecessary."[25] Additional complications arose in the 1990s. A panel of experts convened by the EPA concluded that, although dioxin was a significant cancer threat to people only when they were exposed to unusually high levels in chemical factories, it wreaked biological havoc among fish, birds, and other wild animals even in minute doses.[26] Shortly thereafter, the agency supervising all federal animal studies used in toxics regulation released another report suggesting that animal studies alone were not reliable for judging the exposure risks to human beings in toxics research.[27] Scientific experts speaking for environmental and public health organizations asserted that the new evidence created no compelling case for a new standard. Nonetheless, the Clinton administration and EPA officials were extremely uneasy with the existing exposure standards, and a thorough restudy of the issue was ordered.

In mid-2000, the EPA released the results of its long-awaited restudy. To the surprise of the White House and most EPA officials, the agency for the first time concluded that dioxin TCCD was a "human carcinogen" and that 100 related chemicals were "likely" human carcinogens. The result was all the more startling because domestic emissions of dioxin had declined by 87 percent since 1984.[28] Some environmental organizations then deduced from the EPA's risk estimates that about 100 of the 1,400 cancer deaths occurring in the United States daily were attributable to dioxin. The EPA knew full well what to expect, warning its senior officials to anticipate that, when the report became public, "many stakeholders [will] take dramatic action" and "pressure from other interests" would grow. Predictably, the EPA's decision was assailed from both sides of the controversy. Major chemical producers involved asserted the EPA was "out of sync" with dioxin regulation in the rest of the world and the report was "counterintuitive to what the facts are." The U.S. Chamber of Commerce suggested the decision wasn't based on "sound science." Greenpeace International, like some other environmental groups, lacerated the EPA for failing to control aggressively the remaining dioxin emissions; "That suggests that [the EPA] can't walk and chew gum at the same time," it sniffed.[29]

Still, the dioxin controversy would not—and still will not—go away. In mid-2003, Congress passed legislation requiring the National Research Council, a part of the National Academy of Sciences, to perform a complete review of the assessment document—a cascade of reviews that environmentalists claimed was a tactic by the George W. Bush administration to stall the implementation of new dioxin regulations indefinitely.[30] In July 2006, the National Academy of Sciences review concluded that the EPA should reassess the risks of dioxin exposure—especially exposure to very low dioxin doses—and issue a revised risk assessment explaining more clearly "how it selects both the data upon which the reassessment is based and the methods used to analyse them."[31] Meanwhile, the existing EPA risk standards would be enforced. In December 2009, the EPA, in accord with new administrator Lisa Jackson's promise to accelerate its dioxin review, initiated a comprehensive restudy of dioxin health risks. By 2012, the EPA had concluded that "generally, over a person's lifetime, current exposure to dioxins does not pose a significant [non-cancer] health risk," but the EPA had yet to release its highly anticipated assessment of cancer risks associated with dioxin.[32]

Animal and Epidemiological Experiments. As the dioxin controversy illustrates, estimates of the health risks from suspected toxics are a source of much controversy. But, having rejected most controlled human studies as ethically repugnant, scientists are left with no certain alternatives in arriving at risk estimates. The common alternative is controlled animal experiments in which test animals are exposed to substances, the effects are monitored, and the risks to human beings are extrapolated from the findings.

These animal studies are particularly controversial when used to estimate the effects of low levels of chemical exposure on humans—for instance, a dose of a few parts per million or billion of a pesticide or heavy metal in drinking water over 30 years. The human risks of cancer or other serious illnesses will be small, but how small?[33] And, how reliable is the estimate? Animal studies do not and cannot use enough animals to eliminate all possibilities of error in estimating the effects of low-level exposure on humans. To demonstrate conclusively with 95 percent confidence that a certain low-level dose of one substance causes fewer than one case of cancer per million individuals would require a "megamouse" experiment involving 6 million animals.[34] Instead, researchers use high doses of a substance with relatively few animals and then extrapolate through statistical models the effect on humans from low-level exposure to the tested substance. But, these models can differ by a factor of as much as 100,000 in estimating the size of the dose that could produce one cancer per million individuals. A litany of other problems is associated with small-animal studies. Failure to observe any response to a substance among a small group of animals does not mean a substance is safe. Moreover, various animals differ greatly in their sensitivity to substances; dioxin is 5,000 times more toxic to guinea pigs than to hamsters, for example.[35]

The Limited Neutrality of Scientific Judgment

Perhaps 50 opportunities exist in a normal risk assessment procedure for scientists to make discretionary judgments. Although scientists are presumed to bring to this task an expertise untainted by social values to bias their judgments, they are not immune to social prejudice, especially when their expertise is embroiled in a public controversy. According to physicist Harvey Brooks, a veteran of many public controversies,

> The more an issue is in the public eye, the more expert judgments are likely to be influenced unconsciously by pre-existing policy preferences or by supposedly unrelated factors such as media presentations, the opinions of colleagues or friends, or even the emotional overtones of certain words used in the debate.[36]

Scientific judgment on environmental issues can be influenced by one's beliefs about how government should regulate the economy, by one's institutional affiliation, or by other social and political attributes.[37] Another study of several hundred risk professionals involved in federal environmental policy making suggests that, once risk professionals become involved in policy making, there is "a weakening of disciplinary perspectives and a strengthening of viewpoints based on politics and ideology."[38] In general, the study concludes that risk professionals working for corporations or trade associations differ from those working for government or academic institutions in their technical judgments about how risk should be determined and when substances should be regulated as well as in broader attitudes about governmental regulation.

Social or political bias can be particularly pernicious when not recognized or admitted by the experts. It is now evident that many technical controversies in policy making may not be resolvable by resort to scientific evidence and argument because scientific solutions will be permeated with social, political, or economic bias. Indeed, political controversy often subverts scientific integrity. Experts can be readily, even unintentionally, caught up in the emotionally and politically polarizing atmosphere of such disputes, their judgment compromised so badly that, as political scientist Dorothy Nelkin remarks, their expertise "is reduced to one more weapon in a political arsenal."[39] Yet, no barrier can be contrived to wholly insulate science from the contagion of social or economic bias. This is a strong argument for keeping scientific and technical determinations open to examination and challenge by other experts and laypersons.

What Risks Are Acceptable?

Risk assessment for environmental policy making is also difficult because no clear and consistent definition of *acceptable risk* exists in federal law. *Acceptable risk* is usually defined in environmental regulation by statutory criteria—that is, by standards written into law to guide regulators in determining when to regulate a substance. Despite repeated congressional efforts at clarification, the only consistency in these statutory standards is their inconsistency.[40]

The EPA, uneasy with the enormous scientific uncertainties inherent in determining acceptable risk, frequently has shrouded its discretionary decisions in a fog of verbal mystification. Nonetheless, determining acceptable risk remains an intensely discretionary—and often political—affair, however much the language of the law may try to conceal it.

A Multitude of Risk Criteria

A multitude of different congressional standards guide regulatory agencies in making determinations of acceptable risk. Different substances often are regulated according to different standards. The same agency may have to use as many as six or seven standards, depending on which substances, or which laws, are involved. The same substance may be subject to one regulatory standard when dumped into a river and another when mixed into processed food. Statutory risk standards are commonly vague and sometimes confusing; congressional intent may be muddled, often deliberately.

In general, regulatory agencies encounter one or more of the following statutory formulas in determining the permissible exposure levels to various substances.[41] The examples are drawn from existing legislation.

- *Health-based criteria.* Regulatory agencies are to set standards based on risks to human health from exposure to a hazard. These standards are usually "cost oblivious" because they seldom permit agencies to use the cost of regulation as a consideration in standard setting. Health-based criteria, however, can involve different levels of acceptable health risk. The CAA (1970) mandates that national primary ambient air-quality standards "shall be . . . in the judgment of the Administrator, based on [air-quality] criteria and allowing an adequate margin of safety . . . requisite to protect human health." The EPA is also left to determine the magnitude of this "margin of safety" and to whom it applies.[42]
- *Technology-based criteria.* The EPA is instructed to ensure that pollution sources will use the best available or the maximum achievable technology, or some other specified technology criteria, to control their hazardous emissions. The Safe Drinking Water Act (1974) and the Federal Water Pollution Control Act (1956) use technology-based standards. In effect, acceptable risks are defined by whatever residual risks to public health may exist after the prescribed control technologies are applied to a pollution source.
- *Balancing criteria.* Congress mandates that an agency consider, to varying extents, the costs of regulation, or the magnitude of threat to human health, alongside the benefits in setting a standard for human or environmental exposure. Or, Congress may permit cost considerations to be among other criteria that an agency may consider. These statutes define how various considerations, such as cost and risk, are to be balanced in determining acceptable risk. For instance, a law may permit an agency to balance the benefits for a given regulatory standard (which may include health as well as monetary benefits) against the costs of its enforcement. In contrast, another law may require agencies to balance the benefits against the economic costs in setting standards for exposure to a substance.

A close reading of these guidelines reveals the enormous discretion customarily left to regulatory agencies in determining how to balance the various statutory criteria. Congress often packs regulatory laws with so many criteria for risk determination—lest any important consideration be ignored—that regulatory decisions become enormously complicated. Consider, for instance, the criteria the EPA was ordered to use under the TSCA (1976) when deciding whether the risks from exposure to a substance are unreasonable:

> The type of effect (chronic or acute, reversible or irreversible); degree of risk; characteristics and number of humans, plants and animals, or ecosystems, at risk; amount of knowledge about the effects; available or alternative substances and their expected effects; magnitude of the social and economic costs and benefits of possible control actions; and appropriateness and effectiveness of TSCA as the legal instrument for controlling the risk.[43]

Agencies spend considerable time working out detailed internal regulations to translate these complexities into workable procedures. They may attempt to reach understandings concerning how criteria will be balanced, with interest groups active in the regulatory process. But, agencies often face imperious deadlines for making regulatory decisions, fragmentary information relevant to many criteria for standard setting, and disputes among interest groups concerning the validity of information and the priorities for criteria in policy making. In the first years of a new regulatory program, an agency can expect virtually every major decision to be challenged through litigation, usually by an interest alleging the agency has failed to interpret its statutory responsibilities properly.[44]

The Disappearing Threshold

One of the most politically controversial aspects of determining acceptable risk remains the problem of the disappearing threshold, a largely unanticipated result of three tendencies among Congress and the agencies concerned with environmental regulation. First, in writing and enforcing most environmental legislation during the 1970s, risk reduction was preferred to risk tolerance. Second, Congress generally assumed that with many, or most, regulated substances, some threshold of exposure would exist below which the risks to humans or the ecosystem were negligible. Congress certainly did not anticipate removing all traces of human or ecological hazards. Third, legislators, who were largely indifferent to regulatory costs, compared to health criteria, in setting regulatory standards, discouraged agencies from using cost–benefit analyses when determining acceptable risks.

Economics and technology now present regulation writers with some difficult decisions as a result of these circumstances. Extremely sophisticated technologies enable scientists to detect hazardous substances in increasingly small concentrations, currently as small as parts per billion or trillion. It is usually impossible to assert scientifically that such low concentrations are wholly innocent of adverse risk, however slight, to humans or the environment. In addition, the cost of controlling hazardous substances often rises steeply as progressively higher standards are enforced; for instance, after reducing 85 percent of a substance in a waterway, it may cost half as much or more to remove an additional 5 to 10 percent. In effect, the risk threshold once presumed by policy makers has vanished; no measurable concentration of a substance apparently can be assumed innocent of potential harm to humans or the environment. To eliminate conclusively any probable risks from such substances, regulators would have to require the total elimination of the substance—an extraordinarily expensive undertaking. Should a trade-off be made between the costs and benefits of risk prevention, and if so, what criteria should govern the choice?

Critics assert that regulators should err in this trade-off on the side of caution by insisting on extremely high standards for controlling risks out of all proportion to the benefits to society or the environment and without sensitivity to the economic burden imposed on regulated interests.[45] This may leave the public with unrealistic expectations about the benefits, which in most cases will be extremely small if not undiscoverable when regulators insist on eliminating even minuscule risks from hazardous substances.[46] Advocates of strict risk management, however, usually respond that the full extent of risk is unknown or may be greater than currently estimated; they also may dispute the accuracy of opposing data. Often, they are indignant at the suggestion that human lives may be endangered if the cost of protection is deemed excessive—an assertion, skillfully delivered, that implies that officials are venal or inhumane for imperiling lives to save money for a regulated interest. Elected officials are understandably wary when dealing with these publicly sensitive issues, especially when the advocates of strict regulation may cast them as the villains. It is easy to make tolerance for even small risks appear to be cruel gambling with the destinies of innocent people, even though risk assessment deals in probabilities, not certainties, of accident, death, or disease.

Risk Assessment Reconsidered: The Precautionary Principle

Considering the challenges involved with traditional risk assessment, is there a better way to deal with environmental risks? Environmentalists, together with many related scientists, public health authorities, and policy professionals have vigorously promoted the precautionary principle as an approach to risk management quite different and, they believe, less complicated and more environmentally protective, than the current federal method of risk assessment.[47] The *precautionary principle,* in one widely accepted interpretation, declares, "when an activity raises threats of harm to human health or the environment, precautionary measures should be taken even if some cause and effect relationships are not fully established scientifically."[48]

The principle has been widely adopted and implemented throughout EU environmental legislation and in such important international environmental agreements as the Montreal Protocol on Ozone (1987), the Rio Declaration (1992), and the EU Stockholm Protocol on Persistent Organic Pollutants. It is the premise undergirding the global movement to control greenhouse gas emissions. Proponents of the precautionary principle assert that it has several advantages over traditional risk assessment:

- It mandates preventive action in the face of uncertainty rather than waiting for the determination of acceptable risk and the resolution of all the many scientific controversies often involved in regulating possible hazards.
- It shifts the burden of proof to the proponents of an activity or chemical, who assume the obligation to establish the safety or acceptability of the suspected hazard.
- It promotes the exploration of a wide range of alternatives to possibly harmful actions, including the possibility of not creating the potential hazard.
- It encourages public participation in decision making by requiring transparency and stakeholder participation.[49]

Proponents of the precautionary principle would contend, for example, that if these principles had been invoked in the regulation of dioxin, much of the previously described political controversy, enormous consumption of time, seemingly interminable litigation, and unresolved (and perhaps unsolvable) scientific disputes about acceptable risk could have been avoided, while the human and environmental danger from dioxin exposure would have been more rapidly reduced. In effect, the precautionary approach insists that, even if errors may occur, is it is better to err on the side of caution when deciding how to manage a suspected hazard.

The precautionary principle, however, also entails potentially significant risks that prompt others to caution against its widespread adoption. Perhaps the most fundamental concern, as one regulatory expert asserts, is that "it seeks to stop innovation before it starts."[50] The precautionary principle may stifle important commercial, scientific, or economic initiatives whose possibly substantial benefits will be lost—what economists call the *opportunity costs*—because real or suspected hazards may also be involved. In addition, some urgent problems may be unsolvable without significant real or anticipated risk. The continually growing volume of radioactive wastes from commercial nuclear electric utilities is sometimes cited as an example. These wastes must be isolated and stored indefinitely as securely as possible even though the containment may itself entail calculated human or environmental risks. Moreover, failure to assume the risks arising from developing and regulating a substance or technology may deliver these into the hands of irresponsible, perhaps dangerous, interests prepared to ignore risks and regulation—an argument sometimes proposed to justify the controversial proposal that the federal government undertake research on human cloning.

The precautionary principle, at the very least, would require policy makers and regulators to learn an unfamiliar way of thinking about risk management. "Teaching ourselves and our leaders a persistent precautionary approach," observes one scientist, "is like learning to tie shoes by following instructions. It's hard to do at first and may require justification, repetition and reassurance."[51]

The Value of Science in Environmental Policy Making

Despite the scientific disputes attending environmental policy making, it remains important to recognize how often science provides useful and highly reliable guidance to policy makers. Often, the scientific data relevant to an issue clearly point to the adverse effects of substances and define the magnitude of their risks. This was certainly evident in the data leading to the federal government's decision to ban most domestic agricultural uses of the pesticides dichlorodiphenyltrichloroethane (DDT), aldrin, and dieldrin, for instance. Furthermore, even when one set of data does not alone provide definitive evidence of human risks from exposure to chemicals, numerous studies pointing to the same conclusion taken together can provide almost irrefutable evidence; such was the case in the epidemiological evidence indicting asbestos as a human carcinogen. Often, the reliability of data will be routinely challenged by those opposed to the regulation of some substance, regardless of the ultimate merit—or lack thereof—of their case. In the end, public officials must make decisions on the basis of the best evidence available. For all their limitations, scientific data often enable officials to define more carefully and clearly the range of options, risks, and benefits involved in regulating a substance, even when the data cannot answer all the questions of risk conclusively.

Even if indisputable data were available on the risks of human exposure to all levels of a substance, controversy over the acceptable level would continue. It is asserted sometimes that science should be responsible for determining the magnitudes of risk from exposure to chemicals and that government should define the acceptability. In other words, defining *acceptable risk* is largely a political matter. Such a division of labor is rarely possible. Scientists, too, are often drawn into the nettlesome problem of determining what levels of exposure to substances ultimately will be acceptable.

Risk and Discrimination: The Problem of Environmental Justice

In October 1997, a jury in New Orleans in a landmark decision awarded $3.4 billion in damages to 8,000 people who had been evacuated a decade previously from their community near a major train route after a tank car filled with the chemical butadiene had caught fire. This award was the largest liability ever assessed in federal court on the basis of environmental discrimination. The fact that most of the plaintiffs lived in a poor, underprivileged neighborhood, and thus were exposed to *environmental racism*, appeared to have been a major consideration in the jury's generous damage award, even though the plaintiffs' attorneys had only alluded to such racism during the trial. "No one said this is racism," explained one of the lawyers for the neighborhood, "but the facts were such that any commonsense appraisal would tell you that the poorer, underprivileged neighborhood was discriminated against."[52]

It is testimony to the present political potency of the environmental justice movement in the United States that, merely a decade previously, the idea of environmental racism was virtually unknown in public discourse and in the language of the courts, let alone as a cause for civil damage claims. Now, issues of environmental justice—or environmental equity—are raised in so many different political and judicial venues that the language has become almost a staple in political discussions involving minorities and health risks. One of new EPA administrator Lisa Jackson's earliest administrative decisions was to declare environmental justice an agency priority. "I want to see a full-scale revitalization of what we do and how we think about environmental justice," she asserted. "This is not an issue we can afford to relegate to the margins. It has to be part of our thinking in every decision we make."[53]

What Is Environmental Justice?

No consensus exists in law or political debate on the meaning of *environmental justice* or about *environmental equity* and *environmental racism*—two terms often used interchangeably with *environmental justice*.

After considerable difficulty, the EPA in 1994 decided that *environmental justice* should be taken to mean "the fair treatment and meaningful involvement of all people regardless of race, color, national origin, or income with respect to the development, implementation or enforcement of environmental laws, regulations, and policies."[54] In February 1994, President Clinton issued Executive Order 12898, Federal Actions to Address Environmental Justice in Minority Populations and Low-Income Populations, which identified environmental injustice as "disproportionately high and adverse human health or environmental effects created by [executive agency] programs, policies, and activities on minority populations and low-income populations . . ." In contrast, Robert D. Bullard, an environmental justice scholar and leading national advocate for the environmental justice movement, equates environmental justice with the elimination of environmental inequity, which he suggests has at least three implications[55]:

- *Procedural inequity.* The extent to which governing rules, regulations, and evaluation criteria are not applied uniformly. Examples of procedural inequity are holding hearings in remote locations to minimize public participation, stacking boards and commissions with pro-business interests, and using English-only material to communicate to non-English-speaking communities.
- *Geographical inequity.* A situation in which the direct benefits, such as jobs and tax revenues, from industrial production are received by some neighborhoods, communities, and regions, but the costs, such as the burdens of waste disposal, are fixed elsewhere. For example, communities hosting waste-disposal facilities receive fewer economic benefits than do the communities generating the waste.
- *Social inequity.* The extent to which environmental decisions mirror the power arrangements of the larger society and reflect the still-existing racial bias in the United States. Institutional racism, for instance, influences the siting of noxious facilities, placing many black communities in so-called sacrifice zones.

Whether or not it is also linked with equity or racism, the concept of environmental justice is commonly evoked in situations in which identifiable minorities have been exposed, deliberately or not, to disproportionate health or safety risks from a known hazard such as a chemical waste dump or an environment-polluting industrial site. Still, practically every definition of *environmental justice* or related terms abounds in ambiguities—what, for instance, constitutes a disproportionate health risk, and how is *minority* defined?

As these definitions demonstrate, the advocates of environmental justice now use the term, or its close relations, to embrace an enormous diversity of political and economic practices far surpassing the human health and safety issues traditionally associated with environmental risk. Here are a few examples:

- In 2012, the North Carolina Environmental Justice Network collaborated with state water conservation organizations to initiate a lawsuit against a Jones County hog farm that discharged into the Trent and Neuse Rivers the animal wastes from a 10,000-hog concentrated feeding operation and, the alliance asserted, exposed local residents and river recreationists to excessive and disproportionate risk from waterborne health hazards.[56]
- In 2010, the EPA, in cooperation with Maryland environmental justice groups and Maryland's Commission for Environmental Justice and Sustainable Communities initiated an aggressive investigation into the scope and risk of local water well contamination created from disposal of toxic coal waste from the Mirant Mid-Atlantic's Chalk Point power plant.[57]
- In Texas, where research suggests Hispanics living near coal-fired electric utilities are disproportionately exposed to hazardous air pollutants, Hispanic environmental justice advocates have joined other state environmental organization in initiating a vigorous campaign to inform and to mobilize Hispanics for political action, demanding more vigorous state and federal regulatory control over such exposures.[58]

It has been left to the courts, legislators, advocacy groups, and scholars to render order from this definitional confusion as they struggle to translate such abstractions into law and political practice. More important than its precise definition, however, is the concept's social impact. From an inauspicious beginning in the mid-1980s, the movement has gradually become a potent political force. Its most important impacts have been to compel government attention at all levels to issues of environmental discrimination, to motivate grassroots political movements nationwide that mobilize minorities against apparent environmental discrimination, and to bring environmental discrimination within the scope of judicial concern and remedy.

A Growing Movement

The environmental justice movement achieved major national attention in 1991 when 600 delegates met in Washington, DC, at the first National

People of Color Environmental Leadership Summit. From its inception, the movement's relationship to mainstream environmental advocacy groups has been ambivalent. "For the most part," observes historian Martin V. Melosi, "the movement found strength at the grassroots, especially among low-income people of color who faced serious environmental threats from toxics and hazardous wastes."[59] Thus, the movement assumes a very different social and economic aspect from the predominantly middle-class, white, and relatively affluent organizations dominating U.S. environmental politics. Moreover, the movement's agenda focuses primarily on local communities, toxic and hazardous waste sites, and new organizational identities. At the same time, environmental justice generates a political gravity that can draw minority advocates into a closer political orbit with organized environmentalism. Mainstream environmental organizations have been quick to recognize that environmental justice offers an opportunity to attract economic and racial minorities to the environmental movement and to overcome persistent criticism that environmentalism is, or appears to be, a "white thing." The Sierra Club's national Environmental Justice and Community Partnerships and the National Resources Defense Council's Environmental Justice Website are two among many illustrations of this strategy. Environmental justice organizations, for their part, often create strategic partnerships with mainstream environmental advocacy groups when this works to their political advantage, yet the movement insists on maintaining an identity apart from mainstream environmentalism.

The environmental justice movement has relied primarily upon three federal enactments to provide a basis for administrative or legal action against governmental or private entities alleged to be responsible for environmental injustice. Two of these measures have been President Clinton's Executive Order 12898, noted earlier, and the EPA's 1994 guidelines for environmental justice (currently called Plan EJ 2014). The executive order requires federal executive agencies to identify and eliminate environmental injustice as part of their mission. While the executive order compels federal administrators to implement a policy of environmental justice, it is also limited because it is not enforceable in court and does not create any rights or remedies.[60] The EPA's Office of Environmental Justice, created also in 1994, has been responsible for promoting the EPA's environmental justice guidelines throughout the agency's organization and programs, although like Executive Order 12898, it neither creates judicially recognizable rights nor authorizes the courts to enforce it. The third foundation for political and legal action, Title VI of the Civil Rights Act (1964), has been interpreted by the federal courts to include a substantive and enforceable right to environmental justice, although Title VI does not mention environmental justice explicitly.

The movement's fundamental conviction that cultural, racial, and ethnic minorities have been exposed disproportionately to health and safety risks throughout the United States has inspired an aggressive campaign to identify and mobilize these minorities, to demand various forms of compensation for those afflicted by such discrimination, and to demand that governmental policy making be redesigned to weigh issues of environmental equity in environmental policy making. The movement has been aided powerfully by active support from numerous social action organizations affiliated with many of the nation's major religious denominations. The movement has also been alert to the environmental justice implications of the global climate change issue, and in mid-2000, a new climate justice movement emerged from the organizational base. "Climate change is the most significant social and political challenge of the 21st Century," a leadership manifesto declares, "and the time to act is now." This new climate agenda "must be just, fair, sustainable, and equitable" and should, among other goals,

- establish a zero-carbon economy and achieve this by limiting and reducing greenhouse gas emissions in accordance with the levels advocated by the scientific community.
- protect all of America's people—regardless of race, gender, nationality, or socioeconomic status—and their communities equally from the environmental, health, and social impacts of climate change.
- ensure that carbon reduction strategies do not negatively impact public health and do not further exacerbate existing health disparities among communities.
- require those most responsible for creating the impacts that arise from climate change to bear the proportionate cost of responding to the resulting economic, social, and environmental crisis.[61]

The environmental justice movement has grown in size, organizational skill, and political influence. In 2000, the movement was estimated to include approximately 400 organizations. By 2010, one directory listed more than 800 groups (many of these are small and transitory, however).[62] This may, however, greatly underestimate the strength of the movement because it does not include a number of other organizations that have actively adopted environmental justice as a part of their larger agendas in recent years. "The last decade has seen some positive change in the way environmental groups in the United States relate to each other around health, environment, economic, and racial justice," notes a 2011 survey of national environmental justice activism. "An increasing number of community-based groups, networks, university-based centers, environmental and conservation groups, legal groups, faith-based groups, labor, and youth organizations have formed partnerships and collaboratives to address environmental and health issues that differentially impact poor people, people of color, and children. The number of people of color environmental groups has grown from 300 groups in 1992 to more than 3,000 groups and a dozen networks in 2011."[63] The movement's impact has been magnified enormously in recent years as the result of an enlarging, increasingly skillful network of collaborating local, state, and national organizations. The Internet has provided a highly congenial, and virtually costless, venue for network development. Especially significant in enlarging the resource base and intellectual breadth of the environmental justice movement has been the rapid expansion of college- and university-based environmental justice research, teaching, and advocacy centers. Among the earliest of these were the Clark Atlanta University's Environmental Justice Resource Center and the University of Michigan's Environmental Justice Program and Multicultural Environmental Leadership Initiative. By 2011, there were "13 university-based environmental justice centers, four of which are located in Historical Black Colleges and Universities . . . 22 legal clinics that list environmental justice as a core area, and six academic programs that grant degrees in environmental justice, including one legal program."[64] Other professionally related programs include the Energy Justice Network; advocacy specialists in the American Bar Association, the Environmental Law Institute, and other professional legal associations; and a multitude of independent legal and paralegal entities at all government levels. The EPA maintains a very substantial environmental justice website. Another website creates an environmental justice scorecard for communities, based on federal toxic emissions reports, that "profiles environmental burdens in every community in the U.S., identifying which groups experience disproportionate toxic chemical releases, cancer risks from hazardous air pollutants, or proximity to Superfund sites and polluting facilities emitting smog and particulates."[65] In addition, specialized environmental justice media are increasing, such as the Inner City Press's *Environmental Justice Reporter*. The movement's leadership now embraces virtually all people of color and all the economically disadvantaged within its mission, so that Native Americans, Latinos, and Asians, among other important domestic minorities, are being recruited.

This growing coalition committed to social equity in environmental regulation illustrates why the creation and solution of environmental risks are often inherently a political issue. In early 1994, President Clinton issued Executive Order 12898, instructing all federal agencies to develop strategies to ensure that their programs "do not unfairly inflict environmental harm on the poor and minorities.[66] Since the EPA created its Office of Environmental Justice in 1992, numerous state and local governments have also declared a commitment to environmental justice by law or executive order. In early 2004, for example, New Jersey's governor issued an executive order that mandated the state's Departments of Environmental Protection and Transportation to develop a strategy to reduce pollution exposure in minority and low-income neighborhoods.

Environmental Justice and the Courts

Despite occasional judgments entailing large financial awards for plaintiffs claiming significant harm as a result of environmental injustice, state and local courts, where such litigation typically originates, have not proven to be a major venue for the environmental justice movement. A major reason is that most states lack appropriate statutory or administrative enactments creating a basis for legally enforceable rights, claims to damage, or other awards based upon evidence of environmental injustice. Only six states, for example, have enacted legislation creating a judicially enforceable right to environmental justice. Nineteen states have not yet enacted any measures to address environmental justice, while the remaining states have taken a variety of actions, such as creating study commissions or state boards to identify issues of environmental injustice and to promote their resolution.[67]

The federal courts, however, have been more receptive to litigation based on claims of environmental injustice, based primarily upon Title VI of the Civil Rights Act (1964), which prohibits major forms of discrimination against racial, ethnic, national, and religious minorities and women.[68] Using Title VI for leverage, environmental justice advocates have achieved modest but important progress in enforcing civil rights, criminal penalties, and civil financial awards against public and private institutions based upon claims of discrimination based upon environmental evidence. The EPA, for instance, is among many federal agencies that have used the Civil Rights Act as well as President Clinton's executive order to initiate environmental justice activities.

Administrative Challenges

Administering laws that mandate environmental justice has been labored and controversial from its inception. Stakeholders may agree on its necessity, yet translating environmental justice into public policy—like implementing other public laws—can manufacture formidable obstacles between the word and the deed.

Laggard Federal Agency Initiative. One major obstacle has been the frequent lack of resources and (sometimes) resolve among federal agencies to implement aggressively their environmental justice mandates. The

EPA, in particular, has constantly struggled with impediments—not all of its own creation—in enforcing its environmental justice regulations and Executive Order 12898. These problems promoted Administrator Lisa Jackson's promise of "a full-scale revitalization" of the environmental justice program.[69] Some of these problems arise from White House failures to fund generously the agency's environmental justice activists and from the meager data sometimes available to characterize environmental justice conditions. Often, however, pressure by environmental justice organizations is required to compel careful attention to these matters from the EPA and other federal agencies. The EPA, additionally, has been continually pressured to apply its environmental justice mandate more aggressively and creatively in interpreting its fundamental regulatory programs. The EPA's National Environmental Justice Advocacy Council, the agency's primary environmental justice advisory group, has asserted that among the compelling reasons the agency should use the CAA to create regulations preventing terrorist attacks and accidents at chemical facilities is that disadvantaged populations constitute a large proportion of the populations at risk at 483 chemical facilities in 43 states.[70]

The Challenge of Data Quality and Availability. While scientific data relevant to environmental justice problems has been improving significantly since the mid-1990s, almost all discourse about environmental justice—whatever the venue—is still likely to ignite controversy over the scientific basis of claims to environmental injustice.[71] Fragmentary evidence accumulating for decades and more deliberate studies in recent years often seem to demonstrate that minorities and poor individuals are disproportionately exposed to health risks from environmental pollutants.[72] The economically disadvantaged may also be more likely than others to have a hazardous waste site for a neighbor. Several studies have suggested as much; for example, one Detroit, Michigan, survey, cited by sociologists Paul Mohai and Bunyan Bryant, indicated that "minority residents in the metropolitan area are four times more likely than white residents to live within a mile of a commercial hazardous waste facility."[73]

Still, significant problems remain in assembling and interpreting the social, economic, and scientific data essential as evidence of environmental injustice. One problem is the frequent difficulty of obtaining basic information about population exposures to environmental risks that is sufficiently rich in detail and covering long-enough periods to satisfy the requirements of common risk assessment methods. With the exception of lead exposure, little reliable evidence has existed before 2000 about the specific relationship of race or class to environmental health measures. Moreover, even when considerable evidence exists that disadvantaged populations have frequently been exposed to higher levels of exposure and risk from environmental hazards when compared to more advantaged groups, the data concerning the long-term health impacts are often meager or missing. Additionally, it is difficult with existing data to demonstrate that adverse health impacts among disadvantaged populations exposed to environmental hazards are caused primarily, or in significant measure, from these exposures among the many other plausible causes of ill health.[74] Especially when there is a possibility of population exposure to multiple environmental hazards—a situation quite common in minority communities—the appropriate scientific protocols for estimating individual or population exposure have seldom existed and almost never existed before 2000 for regulatory decision making.

An additional obstacle is demonstrating that economic or racial minorities have been exposed deliberately to disproportionate environmental risks or that risk exposures were assumed involuntarily. For example, it may be demonstrated convincingly that populations living for decades near a known environmental hazard (such as a petrochemical plant) are largely poor, racial minorities and that they are more heavily exposed to environmental pollutants than nonracial minorities in the same community. Yet, it may be argued in political debate and courtrooms that such individuals often moved to their residences deliberately and with knowledge of the environmental risks so that the environmental exposures were voluntary.

Finally, difficulties arise over the appropriate strategies for identifying how risks may be distributed unfairly in environmental regulation and how this inequity can be solved. Over how long a period, for example, should risk estimates be made? Which populations qualify as disadvantaged? To what extent should the ability of individuals to protect themselves from such risks be taken into account? What sort of environmental risks should be included? How can such issues be introduced early enough in the regulatory decision-making process to influence the outcomes?

For environmental justice advocates, however, the available evidence of injustice seems convincing if not overwhelming. For example, a policy paper by one major advocacy group begins, "Although communities of color, tribes and indigenous peoples, and the poor have been heavily and disproportionately affected by noxious risk producing environmental practices for decades," as if stating common knowledge.[75] At the other extreme, Christopher H. Foreman, Jr. of the Brookings Institution completed an extensive study of claims made by environmental justice advocates and concluded that

[W]hen you clear away all the smoke blown over risk and racism in recent years, there turns out to be remarkably little good evidence indicating that low-income and minority citizens regularly bear a disproportionate share of society's environmental risk, much less that they develop pollution related illnesses more often than other citizens.[76]

Environmental Justice and Politics

Surveying these difficulties, critics have argued that the environmental justice agenda is ultimately a means to much broader political ends. The movement's political potency, so the argument runs, is grounded less on scientific credibility than on the capacity of its grassroots organizers to mobilize minorities and to articulate deeply rooted historical social grievances for which environmental issues are often symbolic. "It effectively speaks to the fear and anger among local communities feeling overwhelmed by forces beyond their control, and outraged by what they perceive to be assaults on their collective quality of life," Foreman concludes.[77] To the movement's leadership, such assertions are likely to appear to be an effort to deflect attention from the evidence of environmental injustice by implicitly attacking the motivation of its leadership.

In any case, the environmental justice movement now claims a salience on the agenda of national environmental policy that is unlikely to decline in the near future. For the nation's governments, one of the most daunting challenges is to find a way to effectively translate lofty goals such as environmental equity or environmental justice into specific policy procedures and specific governmental actions. How do we bring environmental justice to the desktop and conference table of routine governmental regulation? It seems evident that a successful policy translation will require, at least, the rapid development of a science base, which means acquiring and disseminating information about the exposure of minority populations to specific environmental hazards and developing reliable methodologies for estimating individual and population risks from such exposure. Administrative law and procedure must be modified in detail and depth so that considerations of inequitable environmental risk can be considered in a timely and explicit manner in regulatory decision making. Converting prescription into practice will be arduous, however, in light of the current disagreement on appropriate metrics for measuring discrimination and equity and on the degree of difference among populations that constitutes inequity.

Conclusion

The complex new problems of risk assessment in environmental regulation confirm that we live in a historically unique era of technocratic power. U.S. science and industry, in common with those of other advanced industrial nations, now possess the capacity to alter in profound but often unpredictable ways the biochemical basis of future human life and thus to change future ecosystems radically. In its extreme form, represented by nuclear weapons, modern technology has the power to eradicate human society, if not humanity itself. But, modern technologies also can alter the future ecosphere in a multitude of less-dramatic but significant ways: through the deliberate redesign of genetic materials in human reproduction, through the depletion of irreplaceable energy resources such as petroleum or natural gas, through the multiplication of long-lived hazardous substances whose biological impacts on humans and the ecosystem may magnify through hundreds of years, and many more. We are practically the first generation in the world's history with the certain technical capacity to alter and even to destroy the fundamental biochemical and geophysical conditions for societies living centuries after ours. It is, as one social prophet noted, a power that people of the Middle Ages did not even credit to devils.

With this new technocratic power comes the ability to develop technologies, to manufacture new substances, and to deplete finite resources so that the benefits are largely distributed in the present and the risks, for the most part, are displaced into the future. Future societies may inherit most of the burden to create the social, economic, and political institutions necessary for managing the risks inherent in this generational cost transfer. Such technical capacity can become an exercise of power undisciplined by responsibility for the consequences.

The status of nuclear wastes in many ways provides a paradigm for this problem. Because the wastes from civilian nuclear reactors currently cannot be recycled, as was assumed when the nuclear power industry began in the United States during the 1950s, the federal government now must find a safe and reliable way to dispose of the growing amount of nuclear wastes from these facilities.

Among the most dangerous of these substances are high-level wastes—those highly toxic to humans for long periods—found in the spent fuel rods from civilian reactors. Strontium-90 and cesium-137, for instance, must be isolated from human exposure for at least 600 years; other high-level wastes must be isolated for perhaps 1,000 years. Equally dangerous and much more persistent are the transuranic wastes forming over long periods from the decay of the original materials in the spent fuel rods after they are removed from the reactors. Plutonium-239 remains dangerous to most species for at least 24,000 years, perhaps for as long as 500,000 years. This plutonium, noted one commentator generally sympathetic to the nuclear power industry, "will remain a source of radioactive emissions as far in the future as one can meaningfully contemplate."[78] Other transuranics include americum-241 (dangerous for more than 400 years) and iodine-129 (dangerous for perhaps 210,000 years).

Practically speaking, such figures mean that hazardous wastes must be prevented from invading the ecosystem for periods ranging from centuries to hundreds of millennia. Not only must they be securely isolated physically, but also human institutions must survive with sufficient continuity to ensure their responsible administration throughout these eons. Many other chemicals created in the past few decades, including widely used pesticides such as DDT, 2,3,5-T, and dieldrin are not biodegradable and may persist throughout the world ecosystem indefinitely. Although less dangerous than nuclear wastes, these and other substances also represent a displacement of risks to human health and to the ecosystem well into the future.

This transfer of risk raises fundamental ethical and social questions for government. Should public institutions be compelled in some formal and explicit way to exercise regard for the future impact of decisions concerning environmental management today? And, if so, how much regard? When deciding whether to develop dangerous technologies, should government be forced, if necessary, to consider not only the future ecological implications of these technologies but also the ability of future societies to create institutions capable of controlling them?

This issue is significant because government and economic institutions have a tendency to discount the future impacts of new technologies or newly developed chemicals when compared with the immediate impacts. In economic terms, this is done in formal cost–benefit analysis by discounting future benefits and costs rather substantially. In political terms, it amounts to adopting a strategy that favors taking environmental actions on the basis of short-term political advantage rather than long-term consequences. (Elected officials, especially, often treat as gospel the legendary advice of a former House speaker to a new colleague: Remember that when it comes time to vote, most folks want to know, "What have you done for me lately?") It is particularly difficult for public officials to develop a sensitive regard for the distant future when there are no apparent political rewards for doing so. At some time, the political cynic in practically all public officials whispers, "What has posterity done for you lately?"

Suggested Readings

Bryant, Bunyan. *Environmental Justice: Issues, Policies, and Solutions*. Washington, DC: Island Press, 1995.

Davies, J. Clarence, ed. *Comparing Environmental Risks: Tools for Setting Governmental Priorities*. Washington, DC: Resources for the Future, 1996.

Foreman, Christopher H. *The Promise and Peril of Environmental Justice*. Washington, DC: Brookings Institution Press, 1998.

Keller, Ann Campbell. *Science in Environmental Policy: The Politics of Objective Advice*. Cambridge, MA: MIT Press, 2009.

Margolis, Howard. *Dealing With Risk: Why the Public and the Experts Disagree on Environmental Issues.* Chicago: University of Chicago Press, 1997.

Mitchell, Sandra D. *Unsimple Truths: Science, Complexity, and Policy.* Chicago: University of Chicago Press, 2009.

National Research Council. *Science and Decisions: Advancing Risk Assessment.* Washington, DC: National Academies Press, 2009.

Notes

1. U.S. GAO, "Particulate Matter: EPA Needs to Make More Progress in Addressing the National Academies' Recommendations on Estimating Health Benefits," Report no. GAO-06-992T, Washington, DC, July 19, 2006, 8.
2. Matthew L. Wald, "Chemical Element of Vinyl Toys Causes Liver Damage in Lab Rats," *New York Times,* November 13, 1998, A20.
3. Matthew L. Wald, "Citing Possible Dangers, Groups Seek Ban on Vinyl Toys," *New York Times,* November 20, 1998, A24; Scott Allen, "IV Bag Hazards Are Alleged; Trace Toxins Found, Interest Groups Say," *Boston Globe,* February 22, 1999, A3.
4. Holcomb B. Noble, "A Debate over Safety of Softeners for Plastic," *New York Times,* September 28, 1999, B10.
5. Andrea Foster and Peter Fairley, "Phthalates Pay the Price for Uncertainty," *Chemical Week,* February 17, 1999, 54.
6. Ibid.
7. David Kohn, "New Questions About Common Chemicals," *Newsday,* March 3, 2003, available at www.ourstolenfuture.org/Commentary/News/2003/2003-0304-Newsday-phthalates.htm
8. Steven Milloy, "A Toy Story," *Tech Central Station,* February 25, 2003, available at www.techcentralstation.com/022503C.html (accessed February 28, 2004).
9. Seth Borenstein, "Study Links Chemical to Changes in the Womb," *Albany Times-Union,* May 27, 2005, A1; "Plastics," *Houston Chronicle,* June 3, 2005, B10.
10. The Cosmetic, Toiletry, and Fragrance Association, "Cosmetics Containing Phthalates Are Safe," *The Free Library,* July, 10, 2002, available at www.thefreelibrary.com/The Cosmetic, Toiletry, and Fragrance Association: Cosmetics...-a088697872 (accessed February 16, 2013).
11. Jane Kay, "San Francisco Prepares to Ban Certain Chemicals in Products for Tots, but Enforcement Will Be Tough—and Toymakers Question Necessity," *San Francisco Examiner,* November 19, 2006, Al.
12. National Academy of Sciences, Committee on Health Risks, *Phthalates and Cumulative Risk Assessment: The Task Ahead, Report in Brief* (Washington, DC: National Academy Press, 2008).
13. American Chemistry Council, "ACC Believes Amendment to Consumer Products Safety Commission Reform Act Will Not Produce Benefits Envisioned by Authors," March 5, 2008, available at http://phthalates.americanchemistry.com/Media-Room/News/Consumer-Products-Safety-Commission-Reform-Act (accessed December 4, 2012).
14. Elana Schor, "BPA Battle Rages on as FDA Acts to Ban Plasticizer in Infant Products," *E&E Reporter,* July 17, 2012, available at www.eenews.net/Greenwire/customize/2012/7/1 (accessed July 30, 2012).
15. National Academy of Public Administration, *Setting Priorities, Getting Results: A New Direction for EPA* (Washington, DC: Author, 1995), chap. 3.
16. "Executive Order 12866—Regulatory Planning and Review," *Federal Register,* October 4, 1993.

17. For a general discussion of the political and administrative setting of risk assessment, see Committee on Risk Assessment of Hazardous Air Pollutants, National Research Council, *Science and Judgment in Risk Assessment* (Washington, DC: National Academies Press, 1994), chap. 2.

18. GAO, "Chemical Risk Assessment: Selected Federal Agencies' Procedures, Assumptions and Policies," Report no. GAO-01-810, Washington, DC, August 2001, 14.

19. Ibid.

20. See CEQ, *Environmental Quality, 1979* (Washington, DC: CEQ, 1980), esp. 194.

21. Ibid.

22. Gregory Zuckerman, "Specter of Costly Asbestos Litigation Haunts Old Economy Companies," *Wall Street Journal,* December 27, 2000, A3; Alex Berenson, "A Surge of Asbestos Suits, Many by Healthy Plaintiffs," *New York Times,* April 10, 2002, A1.

23. On the controversy over dioxin, see John A. Moore, Renate D. Kimbrough, and Michael Gough, "The Dioxin TCCD: A Selective Study of Science and Policy Interaction," in *Keeping Pace With Science and Engineering: Case Studies in Environmental Regulation,* ed. Myron F. Ulman (Washington, DC: National Academies Press, 1993), 221–242.

24. Ibid.

25. Quoted in Keith Schneider, "Times Beach Warning: Regrets a Decade Later," *New York Times,* August 15, 1991, D23.

26. Keith Schneider, "Panel of Scientists Finds Dioxin Does Not Pose Widespread Cancer Threat," *New York Times,* September 26, 1992, D20.

27. Joel Brinkley, "Many Say Lab-Animal Tests Fail to Measure Human Risk," *New York Times,* March 23, 1993, D20.

28. Cindy Skrzycki and Joby Warrick, "EPA Links Dioxin to Cancer; Risk Estimate Raised Tenfold," *Washington Post,* May 17, 2000, A1. However, TCCDs can accumulate in human body fat from repeated exposures, and thus, the report asserted, dioxin was a significant health risk to humans who ingested it through a normal diet. For the small proportion of the population with extremely high-fat diets, the odds of developing cancer were estimated to be as high as 1 in 100, or ten times the EPA's previous estimate. Low-grade exposure could create other health problems, the report concluded, including hormonal and developmental defects in babies and children.

29. Ibid.

30. U.S. EPA, National Center for Environmental Assessment, "Draft Dioxin Assessment," October 2003, available at http://cfpub.epa.gov/ncea/cfm (accessed March 4, 2004).

31. National Research Council, *Health Risks from Dioxin and Related Compounds: Evaluation of the EPA Assessment* (Washington, DC: National Academies Press, 2006). See also "EPA Assessment of Dioxin Understates Uncertainty About Health Risks and May Overstate Human Cancer Risk," *National Academies News,* July 11, 2006, available at www.nationalacademies.org/onpinews/newsitem.aspx?RecordID=11688 (accessed February 20, 2007).

32. "EPA Administrator Pledges Strong Federal Cleanup Presence at Dow Dioxin Site in Michigan and Accelerated Assessment of Dioxins' Human Health Impacts," May 26, 2009, available at http://yosemite.epa.gov/opa/admpress.nsf/6fa790d452bcd7f585257 50100565efa/3ffa6e8e70763f28852575c20064b26b!OpenDocument (accessed July 16, 2010); Jeremy P. Jacobs and Elana Schor, "EPA Releases Long-Awaited Dioxin Review," *E&E Reporter,* February 17, 2912, available at http://www.eenews.net/ Greenwire/2012/02/17bn (accessed May 20, 2012).

33. On the general problems of animal experiments, see David D. Doniger, *The Law and Policy of Toxic Substances Control* (Baltimore: Johns Hopkins University Press, 1978), pt. I.

34. Animal data are cited in Philip M. Boffey, "The Debate over Dioxin," *New York Times,* June 25, 1983, A10.

35. Ibid.
36. Harvey Brooks, "The Resolution of Technically Intensive Public Policy Disputes," *Science, Technology, and Human Values* 9 (winter 1984): 40. For estimates of discretionary judgments in risk assessment, see National Research Council, Commission on Life Sciences, Committee on the Institutional Means for Assessment of Risks to Public Health, *Risk Assessment in the Federal Government: Managing the Process* (Washington, DC: National Academies Press, 1983), chap. 1.
37. Frances M. Lynn, "The Interplay of Science and Values in Assessing and Regulating Environmental Risks," *Science, Technology, and Human Values* 11 (spring 1986): 40–50.
38. Thomas M. Dietz and Robert W. Rycroft, *The Risk Professionals* (New York: Russell Sage, 1987), 111.
39. Dorothy Nelkin, ed., *Controversy: The Politics of Technical Decisions* (Beverly Hills, CA: Sage, 1984), 17.
40. A comprehensive review of the various statutory standards for risk in federal law is found in John J. Cohrssen and Vincent T. Covello, *Risk Analysis: A Guide to Principles and Methods for Analyzing Health and Environmental Risks* (Washington, DC: Council on Environmental Quality, 1989), 14–15; see also Walter A. Rosenbaum, "Regulation at Risk: The Controversial Politics and Science of Comparative Risk Assessment," in *Flashpoints in Environmental Policymaking: Controversies in Achieving Sustainability,* ed. Sheldon Kamieniecki, George A. Gonzalez, and Robert O. Vos (Albany, NY: SUNY Press, 1997), 31–62.
41. This analysis is based on National Academy of Public Administration, *Setting Priorities, Getting Results,* chap. 3.
42. In contrast, the Food Quality Protection Act (1996) requires, very precisely, that the EPA must set the standard to protect infants and children from allowable pesticide residues in food at ten times the safety factor for adults unless reliable data show that a different factor would be safe.
43. CEQ, *Environmental Quality, 1979,* 218.
44. An agency sometimes invites litigation. By interpreting the manner in which risk determinations should be made by agencies, judges often dissipate the fog of uncertainty about congressional intent and provide agencies with firm guidelines for future determinations.
45. A sampling of this literature may be found in the collection of articles by Peter Lewin, Gerald L. Sauer, Bernard L. Cohen, Richard N. Langlois, and Aaron Wildavsky in *Cato Symposium on Pollution,* special issue of *Cato Journal* 2 (spring 1982).
46. Ibid.
47. The CPSRA—the 2008 legislation that Congress intended to resolve the phthalate controversy mentioned at the beginning of this chapter—does contain a rare example of the precautionary principle in national environmental legislation.
48. Science and Environmental Health Network, "Wingspread Conference on the Precautionary Principle," January 26, 1998, available at www.sehn.org/wing.html (accessed March 14, 2007).
49. Stephen G. Wood, Stephen Q. Wood, and Rachel A. Wood, "Whither the Precautionary Principle? An American Assessment From an Administrative Law Perspective," *American Journal of Comparative Law* 54, suppl. (fall 2006): 581–610.
50. Ronald Bailey, "Precautionary Tale," *Reason Magazine,* April 1999, available at http://reason.com/archives/1999/04/01/precautionary-tale (accessed April 20, 2010).
51. Nancy Myers, "Introduction," in *Precautionary Tools for Reshaping Environmental Policy,* ed. Nancy Myers and Carolyn Raffensperger (Cambridge, MA: MIT Press, 2004), 12.
52. Quoted in *Wall Street Journal,* October 29, 1997, B3.

53. Lisa P. Jackson, "Remarks to the National Environmental Justice Advisory Council, as Prepared 07/21/2009," available at http://yosemite.epa.gov/opa/admpress.nsf/dff15a5 d01abdfb1852573590040b7f7/313ec9a2bc80d677852575fa007b3c42!OpenDocum ent (accessed November 28, 2009).

54. EPA, "Environmental Justice," February 10, 2004, available at www.epa.gov/compliance/ environmentaljustice (accessed March 4, 2004).

55. Robert D. Bullard, "Waste and Racism: A Stacked Deck?" *Forum for Applied Research and Public Policy* 8 (spring 1993): 29–35. On the general problems of defining environmental justice, see Evan J. Rinquist, "Environmental Justice: Normative Concerns and Empirical Evidence," in *Environmental Policy in the 1990s,* 3rd ed., ed. Norman J. Vig and Michael E. Kraft (Washington, DC: CQ Press, 1997), 231–254; EPA, Office of Policy, Planning, and Evaluation, *Environmental Equity: Reducing Risk for All Communities, Vol. 1: Workgroup Report to the Administrator* (Washington, DC: Author, June 1992), 1.

56. Anne Blythe, "Environmental Groups Say 10,000-Hog Farm Pollutes Waterways," *Charlotte News & Observer,* August 6, 2012, available at www.newsobserver.com/ 2012/08/05/2248670/environmental-groups-say-10000.html#storylink=cpy (accessed September 15, 2012).

57. Juliet Eilperin, "Environmental Justice Issues Take Center Stage," *Washington Post,* November 21, 2010, available at www.washingtonpost.com/wp-dyn/content/article/ 2010/11/21/AR2010112103782.html (accessed April 26, 2012).

58. "Air Pollution: An Environmental Justice Issue for Hispanics," *Texas Vox,* June 29, 2011, available at http://texasvox.org/2011/06/29/air-pollution-an-environmental-justice-issue-for-hispanics/ (accessed August 2, 2012).

59. Martin V. Melosi, "Environmental Justice, Political Agenda Setting, and the Myths of History," *Journal of Policy History* (January 2002): 44.

60. EPA, Office of Civil Rights, "Title VI and Environmental Justice at EPA," available at http://www.epa.gov/ocr/t6andej.htm (accessed August 3, 2012).

61. Environmental Justice Leadership Forum on Climate Change, "Principles of Climate Justice," November 2009, available at www.weact.org/Coalitions/EJLeadershipForumon ClimateChange/tabid/331/Default.aspx (accessed January 23, 2010).

62. Environmental Justice Resource Center, "People of Color in the United States and Puerto Rico," *People of Color Environmental Groups Directory* (Flint, MI: C. W. Mott Foundation, 2000), chap. 4; Multicultural Environmental Leadership Development Initiative, "Directory of Environmental Justice Organizations," available at http://meldi .snre.umich.edu/ej_orgs (accessed May 9, 2004).

63. Robert D. Bullard, Glenn S. Johnson, and Angel O. Torres, *The State of Environmental Justice in the United States Since Summit II: Timeline-Milestones 2002–2011* (April 2011): 5, available at http://www.ejrc.cau.edu/featurearticles.htm (accessed August 1, 2012).

64. Ibid, 5.

65. Scorecard, the Pollution Information Site, available at http://scorecard.org/ (accessed April 21, 2010).

66. "Executive Order 12898—Federal Actions to Address Environmental Justice in Minority Populations and Low-Income Populations," *Federal Register,* February 11, 1994.

67. Patricia A. Robert, "The State of the States: Progress in Environmental Justice Law and Policy?," Presented at The State of Environmental Justice in America 2007 Conference, Washington, DC, March 29–31, 2007; and Julie Sze, "The State of the States: Environmental Justice Programs," University of California (2004), commissioned by the Ford Foundation, available at ej.ucdavis.edu/includes/docs/Sze_WhitePaper.pdf (accessed August 5, 2012).

68. Uma Outka, "NEPA and Environmental Justice: Integration, Implementation and Judicial Review," *Boston College Environmental Affairs Law Review* vol. 33, no. 3 (2006): 601–625.

69. See, for example, GAO, "Environmental Justice: EPA Should Devote More Attention to Environmental Justice When Developing Clean Air Rules," Report no. GAO 05-289, Washington, DC, July 5, 2005, 10.

70. Jeremy P. Jacobs, "EPA Action Needed to Avert 'Tragedy of Historic Proportions,'" *E&E Reporter*, April 16, 2012, available at www.eenews.net/public/Greenwire/2012/04/16/1 (accessed May 17, 2012).

71. See, for example, Anita Milman, "Geographic Pollution Mapping of Power Plant Emissions to Inform Ex-Ante Environmental Justice Analyses," *Journal of Environmental Planning and Management* 49 (July 2006): 587–604; Paul Mohai and Robin Saha, "Reassessing Racial and Socioeconomic Disparities in Environmental Justice Research," *Demography,* 43 (May 2006): 383–399.

72. Ivette Perfecto and Baldemar Valazquez, "Farm Workers: Among the Least Protected," *EPA Journal,* 18 (March–April 1992): 13–14; Dee R. Wernette and Leslie A. Nieves, "Breathing Polluted Air," *EPA Journal* 18 (March–April 1992): 16–17.

73. Paul Mohai and Bunyan Bryant, "Race, Poverty, and the Environment," *EPA Journal* 18 (March–April 1992): 8.

74. See, for example, Robert J. Brulle and David N. Pellow, "Environmental Justice: Human Health and Environmental Inequalities," *Annual Review of Public Health* 2006, 103-124; Jean D. Brender, Juliana A. Maantay, and Jayajit Chakraborty, "Residential Proximity to Environmental Hazards and Adverse Health Outcomes," *American Journal of Public Health* 101, no. S1 (2011): S37–S52; and Onyemaechi C. Nweke, Devon Payne-Sturges, Lisa Garcia, et al., "Symposium on Integrating the Science of Environmental Justice Into Decision-Making at the Environmental Protection Agency: An Overview," *American Journal of Public Health* vol. 102, no. S1 (September 2011): S19–S26.

75. Eileen Gauna, Sheila Foster, Carmen Gonzalez, Lisa Heinzerling, Catherine O'Neill, Clifford Rechtschaffen, and Robert R. M. Verchick, "CPR Perspective: Environmental Justice at Stake," Center for Progressive Reform, available at www.progressiveregulation.org/perspectives/environjustice.cfm (accessed March 3, 2004).

76. Christopher H. Foreman, Jr., "The Clash of Purposes: Environmental Justice and Risk Assessment," Brookings Institution: Social Policy, March 20, 1988, available at www.brookings.edu/views/articles/foreman/1998RPP.htm (accessed March 5, 2004).

77. Foreman, "Clash of Purposes."

78. Phil Gailey, "Evacuation Issue Threatening Nuclear Plants," *New York Times,* May 12, 1983, A1.

Chapter 5

More Choice
The Battle over Regulatory Economics

> *Benefit–cost analysis has a solid methodological footing and provides a valuable performance measure for an important governmental function, improving the well-being of society. However, benefit–cost analysis requires analytical judgments which, if done poorly, can obfuscate an issue or worse, provide a refuge for scoundrels in the policy debate.*
>
> —Scott Farrow and Michael Toman,
> *Using Environmental Benefit–Cost Analysis to Improve Governmental Performance*, 1998

> *GAO's recent reviews of four Corps civil works projects and actions found that the planning studies conducted by the Corps to support these activities were fraught with errors, mistakes, and miscalculations, and used invalid assumptions and outdated data. Generally, GAO found that the Corps' studies understated costs and overstated benefits, and therefore did not provide a reasonable basis for decision-making.*
> —GAO, *Corps of Engineers: Observations on Planning and Project Management Processes for the Civil Works Program*, March 2006

Controversy over the economic rationality of environmental regulation has not ceased since the first Earth Day. Critics assert that both the process and the objectives of environmental regulation are flawed by economic inefficiency, irrationality, and contradiction. Spokespeople for the business sector, state and local governments, and other regulated interests often join many economists in advocating fundamental changes in the criteria used in formulating environmental regulations and in the methods used to secure compliance with them. Environmentalists and many economists, among others, believe that economic arguments are often inappropriate, if not deliberately deceptive, when used by critics to evaluate environmental policies.

165

Although some environmental regulatory programs are very costly, the total public and private cost of regulation to the United States appears reasonable. Currently, the United States invests about 0.06 percent of its gross domestic product in environmental protection, an amount varying from 0.08 to 0.06 since 2000, which most economists consider acceptable and comparable with that of other industrialized nations.[1] Spending for environmental regulation also constitutes about 2.5 percent of recent federal budgets, a modest figure when compared with other social programs such as Medicare or Social Security, which account for about 20 and 22 percent, respectively, of recent spending.[2] Moreover, the collective benefit from all this spending, by most estimates, far exceeds the costs. Figure 5–1, for instance, provides an estimation made by the White House OMB of the national costs and benefits from environmental and other federal regulatory programs during the decade 1992 to 2000.[3]

Figure 5–1   Estimates of the Total Annual Benefits and Costs of Major Federal Regulations, 1997–2007 (millions of 2001 dollars)

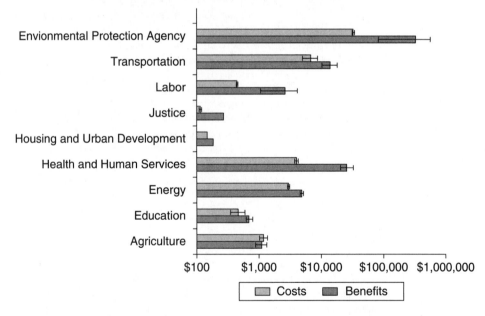

Source: David Anthoff and Robert Hahn, "Government Failure and Market Failure: On the Inefficiency of Environmental and Energy Policy," December 17, 2009, available www.smithschool.ox.ac.uk/wp-content/uploads/2010/02/Hahn_09_online.pdf.

Notes: Data were provided in ranges, which are shown as error bars in this figure; the values for costs and benefits were calculated as the mean of the range for the central values. Note that the horizontal axis uses a logarithmic scale and the origin starts at 100 million dollars.

Still, troubling problems arise. Could the same or better results—perhaps far better—be achieved much less expensively? Could regulated business also save considerable money and invest it in more socially productive activities? Might better results be had by switching to a different form of regulation? Is the average consumer paying too much for environmental protection? As regulatory costs and dissatisfaction over regulatory achievements mount, even the environmental movement, traditionally hostile to proposals for economic reform, has felt compelled to examine critically the economic basis of current environmental laws. The debate can whirl into mind-numbing complexity that only an economist could love, but the answers may powerfully shape future environmental regulation, and the major issues, at least, are clear.

Controversy has traditionally focused on two issues: the use of BCA as a major criterion in writing environmental regulations and the effectiveness of marketplace incentives rather than the current command-and-control methods for securing compliance with environmental standards. This chapter looks at these issues, beginning with a discussion of the BCA controversy, followed by a brief description of the command-and-control approach to regulation and a comparison with some proposed alternatives.

The Benefit–Cost Debate

In theory, BCA seems simple and straightforward. Essentially, it is a process by which federal agencies (usually regulators such as the EPA) compare the net benefits and costs of a proposed action—usually a regulatory law—to determine whether the benefits exceed the costs. Using this procedure, they can also compare alternative proposals to determine which is the more economically desirable. BCA is a constant issue in environmental regulation because a common complaint about almost all environmental regulations written since 1970 is that the congressionally mandated procedures for setting environmental standards are too often insensitive to costs. "Cost-oblivious" laws, such as portions the CAA or the Occupational Safety and Health Act, in which benefit–cost considerations are explicitly forbidden as regulatory criteria, are cited as examples of legislatively ordained disregard for the economic consequences of regulation. Other laws, such as the RCRA, have been criticized for failing to require specifically that regulatory agencies consider costs among other factors in setting environmental standards. In the view of critics, this mandated indifference toward BCA breeds a carelessness about costs among regulators that inflicts economic penalties on regulated interests. Even when Congress has permitted or required some kind of BCA in regulatory decision making, critics assert that, too often, agencies can ignore the results or treat them as a formality.[4]

A Long and Contentious History

The conflict over BCA resonates throughout U.S. regulatory history. Every administration since John F. Kennedy's has attempted to use some institutional arrangement to promote sensitivity to economic costs and benefits in regulatory policy making by federal agencies. Toward the end of the 1970s, the White House and Congress began to pressure federal agencies through executive action and legislative mandates to give economic considerations greater attention in environmental regulation. Jimmy Carter, the most avowed environmentalist of all recent presidents, nonetheless established a White House review entity with the pugnacious acronym RARG (Regulatory Analysis Review Group), whose mission included reducing the cost of federal environmental regulations. The mildly controversial RARG annoyed environmentalists; what replaced it infuriated them.[5]

The Battle over Regulatory Impact Analyses. Ronald Reagan, whose administration was viewed by environmentalists with nearly unanimous disfavor, initiated the most aggressive effort to promote BCA in environmental policy making with Executive Order 12291. The executive order, issued practically the day Reagan was inaugurated, required all federal agencies to prepare a type of BCA, called a regulatory impact analysis (RIA), for any major, new regulatory proposals to demonstrate that the benefit of such proposals would exceed the anticipated costs. Reagan's order unleashed a prolonged, bitter conflict among ideological supporters of Reagan's so-called regulatory reform in Congress, the executive agencies, and the business community on one side and environmentalists, most congressional members, and other White House critics on the other. Proponents of the executive order believed it was long overdue, a sensible remedy to excessively numerous and expensive federal regulatory laws and a blow to increasingly costly governmental interference in economic life. Critics were convinced that Reagan's order was a covert attack on environmental regulation, virtually a subversion of congressionally mandated environmental programs, and that the enforcement of it by the OMB an illegal, if not unconstitutional, represented presidential encroachment on the regulatory process. Contention over Executive Order 12291 became a running theme during the Reagan years, dissipating only when George Bush's administration found the contention too politically costly and quietly backed away from Reagan's aggressive enforcement policies.

Bill Clinton's administration appeared to put the BCA controversy to rest, at least temporarily, when Clinton issued Executive Order 12866 in September 1993, significantly relaxing the requirements for the preparation and review of RIAs in federal agencies and greatly diminishing the OMB's role in the process, much to the satisfaction of environmentalists. Nonetheless, the new order still required federal agencies to prepare and review BCAs frequently, insisting that they remain a formal part of regulatory procedure.

The Second Generation of Benefit–Cost Analysis. When George W. Bush entered the White House in 2001, Congress had already attempted to push BCA well beyond what Clinton or even Reagan had accomplished. Congressional Republicans had unleashed a fusillade of new BCA legislative proposals during the 1990s intended to make regulatory BCA ever more rigorous, and although these measures were (sometimes barely) defeated, the legislative mood was obvious to federal agencies—a Republican Congress would vigorously press BCA on regulatory agencies whenever possible and make economics a major consideration in regulatory policy debate.[6]

By the time of George W. Bush's inauguration, BCA in the form of RIAs had come to stay in environmental regulation. The White House and Congress now accepted the idea that RIAs (or another form of BCA) should be considered frequently, if not routinely, when the EPA or other regulatory agencies proposed new environmental regulations. As Cass Sunstein notes, the second-generation debate raises

> difficult questions about how (not whether) to engage in cost–benefit analysis—how to value life and health, how to deal with the interests of future generations, how to generate rules of thumb to simplify complex inquiries . . . how and when to diverge from the conclusion recommended by cost–benefit analysis. . . . [7]

In his second term, George W. Bush refueled the BCA controversy with Executive Order 13422, which mandated the most substantial and (critics claimed) most aggressive benefit–cost assault on environmental regulations since Ronald Reagan ordained RIAs. Among other major provisions, Executive Order 13422 required all executive agencies writing RIAs to (1) identify in writing the specific market failure or problem that warrants a new regulation, (2) designate a presidential appointee within the agency as a *regulatory policy officer* who can control upcoming rule making activity in that agency, and (3) provide their best estimates of the cumulative regulatory costs and benefits of rules they expect to publish in the coming year—in short, to embed BCA more deeply and pervasively throughout regulatory rule making.[8] An additional provision expanded OMB's authority to issue *guidance documents* and other instructions to regulatory agencies. Environmentalists charged that all this amounted to a White House power grab at environmental regulation. The new RIA makeover, however, gained little traction because the Obama administration quickly nullified its impact with the new Executive Order 13422 in February 2009, largely restoring the earlier Clinton rules and mandating another review of the RIA process.

Many Varieties of Benefit–Cost Analysis. If calculate they must, what kind of BCA should environmental agencies use? Every federal environmental law currently requires, or permits, a somewhat different approach to BCA. The one certainty is that no current federal law compels the EPA or any other environmental regulator to adopt or reject a proposed regulation solely on the basis of a benefit–cost calculation (although such proposals now routinely appear in Congress). One federal law, the CAA, prohibits the EPA from basing any air-quality standards on a consideration of cost. Some federal laws, such as the Safe Drinking Water Act (1974), require the EPA to "consider" benefits and costs when contemplating new regulations; other statutes, such as the Occupational Safety and Health Act, may instruct regulators to consider only regulations that are "economically feasible"; and still others may allow the regulatory agency to consider benefits and costs among other factors when writing regulations, without specifying how much importance the economic considerations ought to assume.[9] Presidential requirements that agencies create an RIA apply only when an agency is not instructed to perform an economic analysis in some other manner by a particular law. It is hardly surprising, then, that environmental regulatory agencies approach BCA in different ways. Sometimes, the same agency must use a different approach to BCA depending on which law it is in effect. Most economists and other regulatory experts believe that, at the very least, the current jumble of procedures for BCA requires radical simplification.

Despite all the differences, a few important common issues arise in virtually all approaches to BCA. These issues concern the general merits of BCA and the procedures by which benefits and costs are calculated.

The Case for Benefit–Cost Analysis

A number of advantages are claimed for BCA. Many regulatory experts believe that BCA can greatly assist Congress and regulatory agencies in setting priorities for pollution control by identifying which regulations are the most economically desirable. "By drawing attention to costs and benefits," argues Sunstein, "it should be possible to spur the most obviously desirable regulations, to deter the most obviously undesirable ones, to encourage a broader view of consequences, and to promote a search for least-cost methods of achieving regulatory goals."[10]

Economists point to transparency as another advantage of BCA in the sense that "the results of a well-executed BCA analysis can be clearly linked to the assumptions, theory, methods and procedures used in it. This transparency can add to the accountability of public decisions by indicating where the decisions are at variance with the analysis."[11] Thus, an argument over the economic impact of a proposed environmental regulation would presumably be clarified considerably because a competent BCA would enable all sides to understand what went into the economic evaluation and to examine the validity of the components of that valuation. In addition, proponents believe that a competent BCA can reveal where important information is lacking about the costs of and benefits from a policy—what has been called *ignorance revelation*. Moreover, it is also argued, BCA gives policy makers a common metric for comparing policies and choosing among them.[12]

Proponents of BCA argue that, at the very least, it can point decision makers to the most economically desirable, or cost-effective, policies for achieving a regulatory goal. "Even if one objects . . . to basing environmental policy on benefit–cost analysis," argues economist A. Myrick Freeman III, "it still makes good sense to be in favor of cost-effective environmental policies. Cost-effectiveness means controlling pollution to achieve the stated environmental quality standards at the lowest possible total cost."[13] Moreover, proponents add, critics of BCA are really objecting to incompetent analysis, especially when created deliberately to produce a desired outcome. Competent BCA sometimes can identify policies that are both economically and environmentally wiser than those currently implemented. According to Freeman, a well-conceived BCA would probably have revealed better alternatives to many federally financed water resource developments such as dams, stream channelization, and flood-control projects that were justified originally by questionable BCAs. Freeman notes that these analyses used techniques that systematically overstated the benefits of water resource development, understated the economic costs, and ignored environmental costs. The result was the construction of a number of economically wasteful and environmentally damaging projects as well as serious consideration of misguided proposals such as the one to build a dam in the Grand Canyon.[14]

When all the regulated sectors of the U.S. economy are considered, the critics reason, a huge inflationary diversion of capital from more economically desirable uses results. Critics frequently allege that excessive regulatory costs will drive some firms out of business or out of the country. Spokespeople for major national business associations, such as the Business Roundtable and the U.S. Chamber of Commerce, have alleged that excessive regulatory costs have depressed significantly the growth rate of the gross national product.

Few proponents of BCA argue, however, that it should be the sole criterion for regulatory strategies. Still, they believe that the routine use of the procedure would make regulators more sensitive to the costs of their regulatory decisions and more likely to select regulatory procedures with net benefits or with the least cost among alternatives. Many supporters also believe that BCA leads to a better quality of decision making. As economist Paul Johnson observes, "The value is that it injects rational calculation into a highly emotional subject. . . . It offers you a range of alternatives. Without stringent analysis, nobody knows whether costs imposed by regulatory programs are money well spent."[15] And, although it is seldom admitted, many advocates hope the publicity given to regulatory costs, especially when net benefits are lacking, will deter agencies from choosing such regulations.

The Case Against Benefit–Cost Analysis

Environmentalists traditionally have opposed the routine use of BCA in setting environmental standards. Some still regard it a categorical evil, wholly inappropriate for the selection of environmental regulations. Others recognize that economic considerations may sometimes merit attention in writing environmental laws but believe benefit–cost calculations are easily distorted to the advantage of regulated interests. Most environmentalists regard BCA as nothing less than a covert assault on environmental regulation whenever it is used. Environmentalists assert that BCA often distorts economic reality by exaggerating the regulatory costs and underestimating the benefits. Regulated interests, the argument continues, often deliberately magnify their compliance costs; it is difficult, in any case, to obtain accurate economic data from them. In addition, regulated interests give little attention to the economic "learning curve," which often yields a substantial savings over the full period of regulation as they gain experience and expertise in controlling their pollutants. Benefits from regulation, in contrast, are often underestimated because they are not easily calculated. For instance, how are the health benefits from significantly cleaner air over the next several decades to be calculated? What value is to be placed on rivers, streams, and lakes made fishable and swimmable again? What is the dollars-and-cents value of an irreplaceable old-growth forest conserved for another generation?

Some benefits almost defy monetizing. For instance, an agency may consider regulatory alternatives involving different levels of risk to populations from exposure to hazardous or toxic substances. What is the appropriate value to be placed on a life saved? A variation of BCA sometimes advocated in such a situation is to compare the costs of regulation with estimates of the lives saved from the different strategies. Such a comparison implicitly requires regulators to decide how much an individual human life is worth.

As a practical example, in 2006, a BCA study conducted by the EPA examined the impact of reducing its recommended air-quality threshold for soot from 15 micrograms per cubic meter to 14 micrograms. This apparently minor reduction would create an estimated $1.9 billion in additional annual control costs among the regulated industries but would also prevent an estimated 24,000 premature deaths. "It's pretty darn obvious," asserted the president of the environmental advocacy group Clean Air Watch, "that better standards would mean fewer premature deaths."[16] Not all experts agree with this regulatory arithmetic. But, a metric that measures lives against dollars spent on pollution controls appears to confront decision makers with a choice that will seem arbitrary, if not morally repugnant: saving dollars or lives.

Critics note, moreover, that BCA traditionally ignores equity considerations—an increasingly potent argument as the environmental justice movement expands (see Chapter 4). In a sense, this is correct; common BCA lacks a social conscience because it is unconcerned with the social distribution of benefits and costs—that is, with which groups are winners and losers in the distribution.[17] "It is often argued," explains economists Raymond J. Kopp, Alan J. Krupnick, and Michael A. Toman, "that [BCA] takes the existing distribution of income as given and does not consider the equity implications of the policies it seeks to evaluate. This criticism points to the anonymous manner in which the welfare changes of individuals are aggregated."[18] It is possible, however, to factor at least some equity considerations into BCA, but such an exercise is uncommon and fraught with difficulties for regulatory agencies that must decide whose equities are to be considered and how to compare equity among different groups.

Perhaps the most persuasive reason for resisting BCA, in the environmentalist's view, is that reducing an environmental value such as clean air or water to a monetary figure makes it appear to be just another commodity that can be priced, bought, and sold. According to Stephen Kelman,

> Many environmentalists fear that subjecting decisions about clean air or water to the cost–benefit tests that determine the general run of decisions removes those matters from the realm of specially valued things. . . . The very statement that something is not for sale enhances and protects the thing's value in a number of ways. . . . [It] is a way of showing that a thing is valued for its own sake, whereas selling a thing for money demonstrates that it was valued only instrumentally.[19]

Environmentalists often believe they stand apart from regulated business through a profound ethical disagreement over the intrinsic worth of wild places, uncontaminated air and water, and other environmental amenities. This conviction of moral purpose imparts to the movement much of its passion and persistence. It also elevates arguments over BCA to the level of ethical principles, making compromise especially difficult.

Reality and Rhetoric

In practice, BCA has often proved to be more paper tiger than bulldog in regulatory affairs. Reagan's BCA initiative never achieved the epic impact that its proponents wished because its implementation was badly flawed. Several major environmental programs, such as the CAA and the Occupational Safety and Health Act, prohibited BCA or severely limited its application in the regulations implementing them (although the EPA spent $2 million preparing an unused BCA for an air-quality standard anyway).[20] Many other regulatory proposals escaped Executive Order 12291 because their impacts did not exceed $100 million. Currently, agencies often prepare BCAs but, lacking confidence in the results, turn to other criteria in writing regulations. Sometimes—perhaps often—agencies do not, despite formal requirements, diligently explore alternatives to their proposed regulations. At the end of a comprehensive, independent 2008 survey of RIA writing at the EPA, Richard Morgenstern, a former high-level EPA economist, concluded that

> One of the things that we found in actually reviewing specific regulations was that despite the mandate that exists and the guidelines that agencies consider alternatives . . . in many instances they do not consider alternatives. So if you think about it, what's the point of doing what's probably a million dollar study in looking into a lot of aspects of regulation if you're not going to give serious consideration to an alternative?[21]

And, agencies showed little consistency in how they prepared their analyses, notwithstanding OMB guidelines. Experience demonstrated at the EPA, as in many other agencies, the severe limitations and inherent bias implicit in data deficiencies.[22]

In some instances, however, the White House has used—or has attempted to use—BCA to stifle environmental regulations objectionable to the president. This was perhaps the most potent impact of Reagan's RIAs. The Reagan administration's use of BCA, in the end, created a pervasive bias against environmental regulation that embittered environmentalists against RIAs and engendered continuing suspicion of the OMB's role in regulatory review.[23] The OMB's review of regulatory agency RIAs, however, was far less aggressive under Reagan's successor, George Bush. Although environmentalist criticism of the OMB's role in regulatory RIAs subsided during the Clinton years, the controversy flared continually through George W. Bush's administration and into the Obama years.

The Controversial Office of Information and Regulatory Affairs. Since George W. Bush's inauguration, a continual flashpoint of cost–benefit conflict has been the OMB's Office of Information and Regulatory Affairs (OIRA), which is responsible for oversight of the RIA process throughout the executive branch. In following Bush's Executive Order 13422, OIRA not only reviewed the RIAs produced by the EPA and related agencies but also examined critically the scientific studies used to justify environmental regulations and their related BCAs. "Once staffed mainly by economists and policy analysts," writes science policy specialist Charles W. Schmidt, "OIRA also employed a variety of health and environmental scientists," which has provoked criticism from environmentalists and others that "OIRA is overstepping its legislative mandate because health and environmental expertise should be concentrated in the agencies that draft legislation."[24] Critics suspected the OIRA was using its newly acquired scientific resources to delay or reject regulatory proposals by challenging the scientific accuracy or credibility of the data supporting the regulations instead of confining itself to examining the relevant BCAs. For example, they asserted, OIRA sometimes attempted to discredit proposed regulations by questioning the qualifications of peer reviewers for the science studies used by the EPA to justify the regulations. Proponents of OIRA's new approach, however, asserted that scientific reviews would improve the quality of the science on which environmental regulations are based and that scientific studies often must be reviewed to determine how RIAs were constructed. Environmentalists, regarding the OIRA's new approach as additional evidence of pervasive White House political interference with the conduct of science, anticipated a major change in OIRA's behavior with the election of Barack Obama, an outspoken proponent of OIRA reform. Not anticipated was Obama's choice of Cass Sunstein, a well-known Harvard scholar and proponent of BCA, as OIRA's new director. Sunstein's appointment left environmentalists uncertain, and many confused if not disillusioned, about the expected OIRA reforms. By 2012, it was apparent that Obama had largely continued the approach to BCA of the Clinton administration in requiring quantification of costs and benefits when evaluating proposed regulation with one significant difference. In May 2012, Obama issued Executive Order 13563, which requires the additional consideration of benefits difficult to quantify such as "equity, human dignity, fairness, and distributive impacts," and strongly emphasizes public participation in the process—thus, it appears to require, when possible, considerations of environmental justice as potential regulatory costs and benefits. The impact of this requirement, however, remains uncertain. Such costs and benefits may frequently be impossible to quantify and regulatory agencies as yet have had no experience, nor detailed White House guidance, in interpreting the order at the end of Obama's initial term.[25]

Benefit–Cost Analysis's Continuing Problem. By now, thousands of regulatory economic analyses have been prepared by federal administrators—more than 1,200 by the EPA alone. Yet, federal agencies continue to struggle when attempting to estimate realistically the benefits or costs of the regulatory programs they implement. Whatever the reason—incompetence, inexperience, creative bookkeeping, or something else—regulatory cost estimates frequently prove to be inaccurate. For example, the EPA's Superfund cost estimates have been unreliably low, and the situation is no better for hazardous waste site remediation required by the RCRA.[26] Often, EPA officials, like other regulatory officials, appear nonchalant about guidelines— or perhaps confounded by them—even when guidance is explicit. For instance, the CAA Amendments of 1990 required the EPA to produce a BCA for any proposed regulations to implement the amendments. Congress specifically required that the EPA describe the key economic assumptions, the extent to which benefits and costs were quantified, and the extent to which alternatives were considered in the BCA procedure. When the GAO evaluated 23 RIAs written under these guidelines, it discovered considerable disparities. Eight RIAs did not identify key economic assumptions such as the value placed on human life. Analyses explicit about economic assumptions were often silent about the reasons for those chosen. All the RIAs assigned dollar values to the estimated costs of proposed regulations, but only 11 assigned dollar values to the benefits.[27]

Regulatory officials, environmental or otherwise, still frequently discount their own agency analyses when making regulatory decisions. This is not necessarily administrative malfeasance—federal agencies are usually required only to consider the benefits and costs in the course of policy making—but the situation bespeaks the considerable practical difficulty in using RIAs and the substantial official uneasiness about the situation. Nonetheless, estimates about policy benefits and costs, some perhaps grievously flawed, continue to pack policy debates.[28]

At least one agency, the U.S. Army Corps of Engineers, seems almost incapable of conquering a historical addiction to "cooked" BCAs.[29] Environmentalists are especially critical of these dubious BCAs because of the Corps's enormous impact on the nation's environmental management. The Corps's budget annually exceeds $4.7 billion for civil works—including, especially, local public works such as levees, dams, and drainage canals, dear to all congressional members even though these projects often become environmental disasters. For almost a century, these projects have frequently been justified by dubious BCAs, which Congress uncritically accepts because doing so works to the advantage of local constituencies. Every president from Jimmy Carter through George W. Bush has vigorously opposed these questionable projects, with mixed success. "On Capitol Hill," writes a veteran political reporter, "it is still considered almost bad form to oppose a water project in another member's district. . . . Corps authorizations have long been viewed as congressional prerogatives, nearly as automatic as the franking privilege or special license plates."[30] Despite repeated promises to swear off "cooked" economics, the Corps still invites suspicion of its BCA math. Few verdicts about the Corps's BCA process have been as blistering as the GAO evaluation toward the end of the George W. Bush administration, which had virtually nothing good to conclude. "The cost and benefit analyses performed by the Corps to support decisions on Civil Works projects or actions were generally inadequate to provide a reasonable basis for deciding whether to proceed with the project or action," stated the GAO. For example, for the Delaware Deepening Project, the GAO found credible support for only about $13.3 million per year in project benefits compared with the $40.1 million per year claimed in the Corps's analysis; and for the Oregon Inlet Jetty Project, the GAO analysis determined that, if the Corps had incorporated more current data into its analysis, the reported benefits would have been reduced by about 90 percent.[31]

In reality, the Corps's resolve to improve its BCAs has often been smothered by the incessant congressional pressure to justify coveted projects. Consider, for example, Louisiana's congressional delegation, the undisputed national champion at harvesting Corps projects, commendable and otherwise. During George W. Bush's first administration, before Hurricane Katrina, Louisiana reaped $1.6 billion in Corps-funded projects and, in the years following Katrina, an additional $14 billion, mostly to reconstruct the New Orleans levees. "We live and die by what the Corps of Engineers does or doesn't do, literally," observed John Breaux, Louisiana's Democratic U.S. senator for 18 years, "The Corps are us."[32] Louisiana's congressional delegation, nonetheless, is distinguished only by its proficiency in collecting Corps projects. Few congressional delegations can long resist the temptation to press the Corps for benefit–cost calculations that justify attractive, local projects.[33]

BCA is not, however, necessarily an administrative charade. Impressive examples of improved economic efficiency and substantial savings due to BCA at the EPA, for instance, exist. Nonetheless, and despite confidence among many economists that BCA quality and influence are improving among regulatory agencies, the evidence still is not convincing.

More persuasive is the conclusion from a meticulous study of 48 major federal health, safety, and environmental regulations between 1996 and 1999: "We find that economic analyses prepared by regulatory agencies do not provide enough information to make decisions that will maximize the efficiency and effectiveness of a rule." Moreover, the findings "strongly suggest that agencies failed to comply with the executive order and adhere to the OMB guidelines."[34]

Some Lessons

Much can yet be learned from the experiences since 1980. The blizzard of econometric data normally accompanying arguments over the cost of regulation should be at least initially considered suspect—by all sides. Willfully or not, regulated businesses will often overestimate the costs of regulation and the proponents of regulation will often underestimate them. Also, as experience with the Reagan and George W. Bush administrations illustrates, BCA is so vulnerable to partisan manipulation that it is often discounted by officials even when they are allowed to consider the economics of regulation. As a former adviser to President Richard Nixon recalls, "In executive branch meetings, the EPA staff repeatedly seemed to minimize pollution costs, while other agencies weighed in with high costs to meet the identical pollution standard. Often, we halved the difference. . . ."[35] Many regulatory decisions made on the basis of political, administrative, or other considerations are sanctified later by economics for the sake of credibility. Sometimes, costs are inflated grossly not so much by individual regulations as by the multiplicity and unpredictability of regulatory procedures.

This discussion should clarify at least a few aspects of the benefit–cost controversy. First, there is no substantial evidence that regulatory costs have become so excessive that BCA must be routinely imposed on all environmental regulation programs. Second, there are doubtless instances, perhaps a substantial number of them, in which BCA might suggest better solutions to environmental regulation than would otherwise be selected. For this reason, such analysis should not be excluded categorically from consideration unless Congress specifically mandates an exclusion. Third, it matters a great deal who does the calculating. All BCAs should be open to review and challenge during administrative deliberations. Fourth, Congress should indicate explicitly in the text of environmental legislation or in the accompanying legislative history how it expects regulatory agencies to weight economic criteria alongside other statutory guidelines to be observed in writing regulations to implement such legislation. Fifth, regulatory costs might be diminished significantly not by using BCA but by using economic incentives in securing the compliance of regulated interests with environmental programs.

The Emerging Problem of Environmental Valuation

The BCA controversy illuminates an especially vexing problem inherent to most debates about environmental policy: How can environmental amenities be valued accurately if some metric must be devised? This issue is at the core of traditional economic theory because it raises profound questions about the assumptions implicit in placing value on nonmarket goods, such as clean air or pristine wilderness. In recent years, this problem has stimulated considerable debate among economists and others concerned with environmental valuation, which has led to several significant proposals for a radical change in the way environmental amenities are evaluated and, as a consequence, in how environmental policy making transpires.

Environmental Accounting. Many economists, recognizing that the continuing development of environmental policy making increasingly confronts policy makers with problems of environmental valuation not addressed by traditional economics, propose the development of environmental accounting as an alternative. In effect, environmental accounting attempts to broaden enormously the scope of environmental amenities to which society attaches significant value and to devise a metric appropriate for comparing these values with other, usually monetary, values involved in policy evaluation. In this perspective, environmental amenities with obvious and immediate human benefits would be valued—clean air and water, for instance—but so would habitats essential to the preservation or proliferation of species, ecological sites essential for biosphere preservation or improvement, environments of unusual beauty, flora and fauna of biological significance, or other aspects of the human environment important for ecological reasons. Identifying these distinctively valued ecological elements will be difficult and challenging but no less so than assigning an appropriate value to them.

Environmental accounting is especially difficult because it requires both economists and ecologists to work at the intellectual margins of their disciplines, where theory and evidence are often tenuous. Ecologists, for instance, may strongly suspect that the eradication of certain species will create a long-term economic disruption of human environments—without being able to prove it or to estimate the scope of the disturbance. Because many environmental amenities are neither bought nor sold in markets, economists would have to construct shadow prices—best estimates of real market value—by a tortuous, inevitably contentious logic. "Demand and supply curves must be constructed," explains economist Roefie Hueting; however, "constructing a complete demand curve is difficult because the intensity of individual preferences for environmental functions cannot be expressed in market behavior or translated into market terms.

This is further complicated by the fact that the consequences of today's actions will often only be manifest in future damage."[36]

Many economists assert, in rebuttal, that a procedure called *revealed preferences* is a reasonable substitute for a market in valuing environmental amenities. Economists Kopp, Krupnick, and Toman offer an example:

> It would be wrong . . . to think of economic values as dollar-denominated values in one's brain to be downloaded when a person is asked the worth of a beautiful sunset; rather, such a value might be inferred from the things that one gives up to see the sunset (e.g., the cost of travel to the ocean). . . . To economists . . . the importance of things (tangible or intangible) is revealed by what a person will give to obtain them. . . . If the thing given up was money, the value can be expressed in monetary units; otherwise, it is expressed in the natural units of the thing given.[37]

Contingent Valuation. One profound consequence of environmentalism's political ascendancy in the United States has been to compel a sustained rethinking of traditional economic and ecological theories to come to terms with the problems of environmental valuation implicit in contemporary environmental regulation. One approach to environmental valuation currently proposed for federal policy makers is a methodology called *contingent valuation,* meaning that a monetary value is to be assigned to an environmental amenity whose use or destruction would deprive others of its future availability. Contingent valuation could be used, for example, to estimate the monetary cost to the public created by haze over the Grand Canyon, by widespread pollution of Alaskan waters caused by oil tanker spills, or by any other event that deprives the public of the passive value in an environmental amenity. In a typical case, a representative segment of the relevant public would be asked how much it would be willing to pay to prevent haze over a national park, to avoid an oil spill, or to preclude some other environmental problem. Through statistical procedures, a monetary value would then be assigned to an environmental amenity based on these public valuations. Alaska's state government used contingent valuation in the early 1990s to discover what value Americans who might never visit Prince William Sound would assign to preventing a catastrophic oil spill there—a strategy used to estimate the monetary damages for which the Exxon Corporation would be held liable for the devastating oil spill by the tanker *Exxon Valdez* in 1989. Based on an average response of $30 per person, Alaskan officials estimated that Americans would collectively pay $2.8 billion to avoid such a disaster.[38] In 1989, the federal courts, apparently influenced by an endorsement of contingent valuation by a panel of distinguished U.S. economists, ordered the Department of the Interior to take into account the losses to people not directly affected by environmental problems when estimating the cost of CAA and Superfund violations in facilities under its jurisdiction.

Contingent valuation remains controversial among economists and other policy makers. Many economists dismiss the methodology as "junk economics" because, they assert, the public cannot accurately assess the value in the passive use of an environmental amenity. Critics argue that the public is overly generous with hypothetical statements about personal outlays, tends to exaggerate the value of an amenity, and is often influenced by the wording of questions. To support these contentions, critics cite studies showing enormous variability in public environmental valuations: Saving an old-growth forest in the Pacific Northwest was valued between $119 billion and $359 billion, and sparing the whooping crane from extinction was valued between $51 billion and $715 billion.[39] Understandably, some of the most aggressive opponents of contingent valuation in federal policy making are corporations, such as Exxon, which feel at considerable financial risk. Neither Bill Clinton nor George W. Bush was willing to issue an executive order explicitly permitting, or encouraging, contingent valuation. Whatever federal agency may adopt the methodology on its own can expect to defend it before a federal judge because it is certain to be challenged legally and, thus, unlikely to be implemented for several years at least.

Environmental Risk. An alternative approach to environmental valuation might be to substitute risk for dollars, thereby avoiding the problem of monetizing environmental amenities. Such an approach might, for instance, compare the risks of losing an environmental amenity with those of preserving it, assuming that a satisfactory risk metric can be created. Or, in another variation, the monetary benefits in altering an amenity might be compared with the risks in losing it. Suppose, for example, that federal regulators must decide whether to open a large portion of wilderness area, the habitat of a rare or endangered species, to oil and gas exploration. The benefits of exploration could be calculated in terms of the potential governmental royalties, new employment, regional economic development, corporate taxes, or other monetized considerations. These might be compared with the expected number of species endangered or lost, the extent of land made unusable for other purposes, the amount of air and water pollution generated, and the special resources affected (such as historic sites, national parks, and recreation areas). These strategies require a comparison of dollars to risks, or risks to risks, each with its own difficulties. Nonetheless, environmental officials often do make such comparisons implicitly or informally in arriving at regulatory decisions, and formalizing the procedure would at least force the comparisons to become explicit and reviewable.

Regulation Strategies: Command and Control versus the Marketplace

The CAA was the first in a long succession of federal environmental laws based on the command-and-control approach to environmental regulation (see the next section). Chapters 6 and 7 illustrate well how this approach has been translated into specific statutes to control air and water pollution, toxic and abandoned waste, drinking water quality, and practically every other environmental hazard currently regulated by Washington, DC. Many economists, regulatory scholars, and policy practitioners, including some environmental leaders, now consider command-and-control regulations to be a statutory antique, too economically flawed and administratively clumsy to cope effectively with many current environmental problems. At the very least, they suggest, command-and-control laws often require refitting with newer economic approaches. The most commonly proposed reform for the command-and-control approach is to substitute or add market-based approaches that rely fundamentally on economic incentives and markets to accomplish the environmental improvements intended.

Market-based regulation, in fact, has become a fundamental standard by which critics judge almost all aspects of command-and-control regulation. Thus, it is helpful to compare briefly the philosophy of command-and-control with market-based regulation before discussing current environmental regulations in greater detail.

Command-and-Control Regulation

The foundation of federal pollution regulation is the command-and-control approach, also called standards and enforcement. The structure and philosophy of this approach create many of the characteristic processes and problems familiar from current governmental management of the environment. Regulatory horror stories abound, convincing believers that a better approach lies in less direct governmental involvement and more economic incentives to encourage pollution abatement. In fact, both approaches have virtues and liabilities, and a combination of both approaches often seems more effective than one alone.[40] The command-and-control approach can best be understood as a set of five phases through which pollution policy evolves: goals, criteria, quality standards, emission standards, and enforcement.

Goals. In theory, the first step in pollution abatement begins with a determination by Congress of the ultimate objectives to be accomplished through pollution regulation. In practice, these goals are often broadly and vaguely worded. Sometimes, as when Congress decides to press technology by setting pollution standards that it hopes will force industry to develop control technologies not currently available, the goals are deliberately made extremely ambitious as an incentive for vigorous regulatory measures by regulated interests. The principal goals of the CAA are, for example, to protect public health and safety. Vague goals are not as important in defining the operational character of a regulatory program as are the more detailed specifications for the setting of pollution standards, emission controls, and enforcement—the real cutting edges of regulation. Statements of goals, however, may be politically significant as signals to the interests involved in regulation about which pollutants and sources will be given priority and how vigorously Congress intends to implement programs. The CAA goal of establishing national air-quality standards for major pollutants, for instance, was an unmistakable signal that Congress would no longer tolerate the continual delays in controlling air pollution caused by past legislative willingness to let the states create their own air-quality standards. It was also evidence that regulated interests had lost their once-dominant position in the formation of air pollution policy.

Criteria. Criteria are the technical data, commonly provided by research scientists, indicating which pollutants are associated with environmental damage and how such pollutants, in varying combinations, affect the environment. Criteria are essential to give public officials some idea of what pollutant levels they must achieve to ensure various standards of air and water quality. If regulators intend to protect public health from the effects of air pollution, they must know what levels of pollution—sulfur oxides, for instance—create public health risks. In a similar vein, restoring game fish to a dying lake requires information about the levels of organic waste such fish can tolerate. Criteria must be established for each regulated pollutant and sometimes for combinations of pollutants.

Obtaining criteria frequently is difficult because data on the environmental effects of many pollutants still may be fragmentary or absent. Even when data are available, there is often as much art as science in specifying relationships between specific levels of a pollutant and its environmental effects because precise correlations may not be obtainable from the information. The reliability of criteria data also may vary depending on whether they are obtained from animal studies, epidemiological statistics, or human studies. Criteria are likely to be controversial, especially to those convinced that a set of data works to their disadvantage. Given the limitations in the criteria data, regulatory agencies often have had to set pollution standards with information that was open to scientific criticism but was still the best available.

Quality Standards. Goals and criteria are preludes to the critical business of establishing air-quality and water-quality standards—the maximum levels of various pollutants to be permitted in air, soil, workplaces, or other locations. As a practical matter, defining standards is equivalent to declaring what the public, acting through governmental regulators, will consider to be *pollution*. An adequate set of quality standards should specify which contaminants will be regulated and what variation in levels and combinations will be accepted in different pollutant categories.

Creating quality standards—in effect, another way of defining acceptable risk—is ultimately a political decision. Criteria documents rarely provide public officials with a single number that defines unambiguously what specific concentration of a pollutant produces precisely what effects. A rather broad range of possible figures associated more or less closely with predictable effects is available; which one is accepted may be the result of prolonged struggle and negotiation among the interests involved in regulation. This battle over numbers is a matter of economics as much as science or philosophy. The difference between two possible pollution standards, only a few units apart, may seem trivial to a layperson. But, the higher standard may involve millions or billions of additional dollars in pollution-control technologies for the regulated interests and possibly many additional years before standards are achieved. Sometimes Congress establishes a standard based on a number's political "sex appeal." The original requirements in the CAA that automobile emissions of hydrocarbons and carbon monoxide be reduced by 90 percent of the 1970 levels by no later than 1975 were accepted largely because the 90 percent figure sounded strict and spurred the auto industry into action. In practical terms, the figure might have been set at 88 percent or 85 percent, or some other number in this range, with about the same results. Air-quality standards created by the EPA for the major criteria pollutants—that is, pollutants that the CAA specifically designates for regulation because of their well-known, pervasive threat to public health—are identified in Table 5–1.

Emission Standards. Standards for clean air or water are only aspirations unless emission standards exist to prescribe the acceptable pollutant discharges from important sources of air or water contamination. If emission standards are to be effective, they must indicate clearly the acceptable emission levels from all important pollution sources and should be related to the pollution-control standards established by policy makers.

Congress has used two different methods of determining how emission standards should be set. In regulating existing air pollution sources under the CAA, Congress requires that emissions be limited to the extent necessary to meet the relevant air-quality standards; determining what emission

Table 5–1   *National Ambient Air-Quality Standards*

Pollutant	Standard value[a]		Standard type[b]
Carbon monoxide (CO)			
8-hour average	9 ppm	10 mg/m^3	Primary
1-hour average	35 ppm	40 mg/m^3	Primary
Nitrogen dioxide (NO$_2$)			
Annual arithmetic mean	0.053 ppm	100 µg/m^3	Primary and secondary
Ozone (O$_3$)			
1-hour average	0.12 ppm	235 µg/m^3	Primary and secondary
8-hour average[b]	0.08 ppm	157 µg/m^3	Primary and secondary
Lead (Pb)			
Quarterly average		1.5 µg/m^3	Primary and secondary
Particulate (PM$_{10}$) *Particles with diameters of 10 µm or less*			
Annual arithmetic mean		50 µg/m^3	Primary and secondary
24-hour average		150 µg/m^3	Primary and secondary
Particulate (PM$_{2.5}$) *Particles with diameters of 2.5 µm or less*			
Annual arithmetic mean[b]		15 µg/m^3	Primary and secondary
24-hour average[b]		65 µg/m^3	Primary and secondary
Sulfur dioxide (SO$_2$)			
Annual arithmetic mean	0.03 ppm	80 µg/m^3	Primary
24-hour average	0.14 ppm	365 µg/m^3	Primary
3-hour average	0.50 ppm	1,300 µg/m^3	Secondary

Source: U.S. EPA, Office of Air Quality Planning and Standards, available at http://www.epa.gov/air/criteria.html.

[a]The two values are approximately equivalent concentrations.

[b]The ozone 8-hour standard and the PM$_{2.5}$ standards are included for information only. A 1999 federal court ruling blocked implementation of these standards, which the EPA proposed in 1997.

controls are necessary depends on where the quality standards are set. In controlling new air pollution sources, and most water polluters, the emission controls are based on the available technologies. This technology-based approach sets the emission levels largely according to the performance of available technologies. A direct and critical relationship exists between air-quality standards and emission controls. For example, once the EPA declares national ambient air-quality standards, each state is required in its State Implementation Plan to calculate the total emissions of that pollutant within an airshed and then to assign emission controls to each source of that pollutant sufficient to ensure that total emissions will meet air-quality standards. In effect, this approach calls for the states to decide how much of the total pollution "load" within an airshed is the responsibility of each polluter and how much emission control the polluter must achieve. This process has become bitterly controversial. Experts often have difficulty in determining precisely how much of a pollution load within a given body of water or air can be attributed to a specific source; this difficulty compounds the problem of assigning responsibility for pollution abatement equitably among a large number of polluters.[41]

Regulated interests, aware of the relationship between air-quality standards and emission controls, will attack both standards and controls in an effort to avoid or relax their assigned emission controls. Regulated industries also chronically complain that insufficient attention is given to the cost of emission controls when government regulators prescribe the acceptable technology. Polluters often balk at installing the specific control technologies prescribed by governmental regulators. The scrubber wars between electric utilities and regulatory authorities, for instance, continued for more than two decades. Alleging that the scrubbers—complex and expensive technologies that remove toxic gases from power plant air emissions—prescribed by the government are inefficient and unreliable, coal-fired utilities fiercely resisted installing the scrubbers until compelled to do so. The battle ended only when the 1990 amendments to the CAA permitted other control alternatives.

The backlash against emission controls often falls on state government officials who, under existing federal law, usually are responsible for setting specific emission levels, prescribing the proper technologies, and enforcing emission restraints on specific sources. Enforcing emission controls is accomplished largely through issuing a permit to individual dischargers specifying the permissible emission levels and technological controls for their facilities. Despite several decades of experience and substantial financial assistance from the federal government, some state regulatory authorities remain understaffed and undertrained. In the late 1990s, however, most state regulatory agencies had become highly professional to the point where failures in state environmental regulation could no longer be routinely attributed to incompetence. The political and economic influence of regulated interests, nonetheless, is often far more formidable in state capitals than in Washington, DC, and state regulators often feel especially vulnerable to these local pressures.

Enforcement. A great diversity of enforcement procedures might be used to ensure that pollution standards are achieved; adequate enforcement must carry enough force to command the respect of those subject to regulation. Satisfactory enforcement schemes have several characteristics: They enable public officials to act with reasonable speed (very rapidly in the case of emergencies) to curb pollution, they carry sufficient penalties to encourage compliance, and they do not enable officials to evade a responsibility to act against violations when action is essential. It is desirable that officials have a range of enforcement options that might extend from gentle prodding to secure compliance at one end all the way to litigation and criminal penalties for severe, chronic, or reckless violations at the other. In reality, when it comes to enforcement, administrative authority is often the power to make a deal. Armed with a flexible variety of enforcement options, administrators are in a position to bargain with polluters that are not in compliance with the law, selecting those enforcement options they believe will best achieve their purposes. This bargaining, a common occurrence in environmental regulation, illustrates how political pressure and administrative discretion concurrently shape environmental policy (enforcement is examined in greater detail in the next section). In the end, an effective pollution abatement program depends largely on voluntary compliance by regulated interests. No regulatory agency has enough personnel, money, and time to engage in continual litigation or other actions to force compliance with pollution standards. Furthermore, litigation usually remains among the slowest, most inflexible, and inefficient means of achieving environmental protection. Administrative agencies prefer to negotiate and maneuver to avoid litigation as a primary regulatory device whenever possible.

What's Wrong with the Command-and-Control Approach? Economists have been the most outspoken critics of command-and-control regulation. However, they are now joined by an increasing number of other critics, including some leading environmental organizations such as Environmental Defense, whose experience with command-and-control regulation since 1970 has demonstrated that it has some severe deficiencies. First, they assert, it offers regulated interests few economic incentives to comply rapidly and efficiently with mandated pollution standards. In the economist's perspective, the standards-and-enforcement approach lacks an appeal to the economic self-interest of the regulated. Even severe penalties for noncompliance with the law often fail to motivate polluters to meet required pollution control deadlines. Penalties are often not assessed or are severely weakened by negotiation with regulatory agencies. Some firms find it more profitable to pay penalties and to continue polluting in violation of the law than to assume the often far-steeper costs of compliance. In addition, polluters have no economic incentive to reduce their emissions below the regulatory requirements.

Second, traditional regulatory approaches require the federal government to specify the appropriate technologies and methods for their use in practically every instance in which pollutants are technologically controlled.

Highly complicated, exquisitely detailed specifications that make poor scientific or economic sense for particular industries or firms can result. One reason for this situation is that neither Congress nor administrators may have sufficient scientific training or experience to make correct judgments about the appropriate technologies for pollution abatement in a specific firm or industry. Also, regulators sometimes lack sufficient information about the economics of firms or industries to know which technologies are economically efficient—that is, which achieve the desired control standards the least expensively. In general, according to economists Allen V. Kneese and Charles L. Schultze,

> Problems such as environmental control . . . involve extremely complicated economic and social relationships. Policies that may appear straightforward—for example, requiring everyone to reduce pollution by the technologically feasible limit—will often have ramifications or side effects that are quite different from those intended. Second, given the complexity of these relationships, relying on a central regulatory bureaucracy to carry out social policy simply will not work: There are too many actors, too much technical knowledge, too many different circumstances to be grasped by a regulatory agency.[42]

Third, proponents assert that incentive approaches can be simply and economically administered. As a National Academy of Public Administration report notes,

> Incentive-based systems are administratively simple because . . . they require much of the regulatory energy to be expended up front in the design state of the regulatory program. If the design is correct, less burdensome administration may be facilitated. Further, once the program is in place, regulators can rely on the energies of the private sector to drive pollution downward.[43]

The alternative seems to require bureaucratic legions toiling endlessly in the regulatory vineyards. "Command-and-control regulation," continues the report, "may impose a never-ending requirement on regulators to develop new and more stringent industry-specific regulations on smaller and smaller discharge points."[44]

Fourth, proponents point out that a market incentive approach is easier for the public to understand and presumably easier to approve. Economic incentives focus on a pollution-reduction goal that the public would presumably find much more comprehensible—hence, easier for government to defend politically—than technology specifications with all the mystifying technical disputation about their appropriateness and efficiency.

Regulation Goes to the Market

Economic incentives are not new to U.S. environmental management. Many familiar forms of environmental control, such as sewage treatment charges, taxes on leaded gasoline, and deposit-refund systems for disposable beer and soft drink containers, use the pulling power of economic incentives to encourage pollution control. Table 5–2 provides a brief summary of the different methods used in the United States.

Not until a decade after Earth Day 1970 did the EPA first experiment warily with economic regulatory incentives. This set in motion a succession of additional economic innovations at the EPA, culminating in the current emissions trading program in the CAA.

Bubbles, Nets, and Offsets. In 1979, the EPA moved away from the traditional standards-and-enforcement approach to air pollution by introducing its *bubble policy* for controlling emissions from existing air pollution sources. This policy assumed "that an imaginary enclosure, or bubble, is placed over an industrial plant. From this enclosure, or bubble, a maximum allowable level of emissions is permitted. A firm in this bubble would be free to use more cost-effective pollution controls than are usually allowed."[45] For example, a firm with three smokestacks emitting pollution might find it least costly to cut back severely on the emissions from one stack while leaving the others only slightly controlled. If the total emissions leaving the imaginary bubble over the plant did not violate air-quality standards, the firm would be free to decide how best to comply with the law. Advocates of the approach assumed that the result would be a substantial cost savings for the firm and quicker compliance with pollution standards because the firm would be free to choose the solution that best suited its economic self-interest. With bubbling, the EPA also allowed emissions banking, which permitted a regulated firm to earn credits for keeping pollutants below the required level. Firms could apply these credits against their own future emission-control requirements, sell them to other firms, or save them.

In any case, few firms seized the opportunity to start emissions trading. Then came Title IV of the 1990 amendments to the CAA, initially permitting many of the nation's biggest fossil-fuel-burning electric utilities to create what could potentially be a huge market for emissions trading. Title IV also allows smaller utilities to join the "big dirties" (the most polluting industries) within a few additional years, thereby expanding the prospective marketplace in emissions. Title IV creates by far the most significant test of market-based regulation since the inception of the environmental era in 1970. Title IV's acceptance by influential spokespeople for mainstream environmentalism—albeit with fingers crossed—betrays a recognition that market-based reform is probably inevitable and perhaps overdue.

Table 5–2   *Economic Incentives Used in Environmental Regulation*

Incentives	Examples	Pros and cons
Pollution charges and taxes	Emission charges Effluent charges Solid waste charges Sewage charges	*Pros:* Stimulates new technology; useful when damage per unit of pollution varies little with the quantity of pollution *Cons:* Potentially large distributional effects; uncertain environmental effects; generally requires monitoring data
Input or output taxes and charges	Leaded gasoline tax Carbon tax Fertilizer tax Pesticide tax Virgin material tax Water user charges Chlorofluorocarbon taxes	*Pros:* Administratively simple; does not require monitoring data; raises revenue; effective when sources are numerous and damage per unit of pollution varies little with the quantity of pollution *Cons:* Often weak link to pollution; uncertain environmental effects
Subsidies	Municipal sewage plants Land use by farmers Industrial pollution	*Pros:* Politically popular; targets specific activities *Cons:* Financial impact on government budgets; may stimulate too much activity; uncertain effects
Deposit-refund systems	Lead-acid batteries Beverage containers Automobile bodies	*Pros:* Deters littering; stimulates recycling *Cons:* Potentially high transaction costs; product must be reusable or recyclable
Marketable permits	Emissions Effluents Fisheries access	*Pros:* Provides limits to pollution; effective when damage per unit of pollution varies with the amount of pollution; provides stimulus to technological change *Cons:* Potentially high transaction costs; requires variation in marginal control costs
Reporting requirements	Proposition 65 Superfund Amendments and Reauthorization Act	*Pros:* Flexible, low cost *Cons:* Impacts may be hard to predict; applicable only when damage per unit of pollution does not depend on the quantity of pollution
Liability	Natural resource damage assessment Nuisance, trespass	*Pros:* Provides strong incentive *Cons:* Assessment and litigation costs can be high; burden of proof large; few applications
Voluntary programs	Project XL 33/50 Energy Star	*Pros:* Low cost; flexible; many possible applications; way to test new approaches *Cons:* Uncertain participation

Source: U.S. EPA, Office of Policy, Economics, and Innovation, "The United States Experience With Economic Incentives for Protecting the Environment," Document no. EPA-240-R-01–001, Washington, DC, January 2001, ix.

Cap and Trade: The Gamble on Sulfur Dioxide Emissions Trading. The most innovative provision of the 1990 amendments to the CAA is the emissions trading scheme created by Title IV. These provisions, sometimes called the Acid Rain Program, aim specifically at emissions of sulfur dioxides associated with human health risks, environmental degradation, and especially acid precipitation. The regulatory approach, known as *cap and trade,* is intended to reduce by the year 2010 the nation's total emissions of sulfur dioxide to 8.5 million tons below the level of 1980 emissions. To accomplish this overall goal, a mandatory cap is established on the total sulfur dioxide emissions annually from the nation's utilities. The program is implemented in two phases.

Phase I began in 1995 and regulated 110 of the nation's electric utilities with the largest sulfur dioxide emissions, primarily coal-burning facilities, and 182 smaller units, all in the East and Midwest.

- A mandatory cap is set on the total sulfur dioxide emissions permitted annually from these sources.
- Each source is granted by the EPA an annual allowance—each allowance equals 1 ton of sulfur dioxide emissions—based on its current emission levels and the overall emission cap.
- At the end of each year, each source must have allowances equal to its emissions for that year.
- Each utility is permitted to bank, sell, or carry over to the following year any emission allowances in excess of its actual emissions.
- Each utility must carefully measure and report its annual emissions and submit to an annual EPA emission audit.
- Each utility is free to select whatever method it chooses to control its emissions and to meet its annual emission cap.

Phase II began in 2000 and regulated electric utilities and other sources of sulfur dioxide emissions nationally. Altogether, more than 2,000 units were affected by this phase by the beginning of 2001. All units are regulated in the same manner as in Phase I.

The early results of cap and trade were keenly scrutinized. The critical tests: Would a market in tradable emission permits develop among the regulated utilities, and would it produce the economic and environmental benefits predicted by its proponents?

By early 1994, the Chicago Board of Trade had created a national emissions trading market for Title IV, and modest trading had occurred there and in California (which has its own version of emissions trading) between some utilities. Several important issues were evident immediately. First, environmental groups in the Northeast expressed a concern that Midwestern utilities would purchase permits from other areas and stockpile them, thus permitting themselves to continue emissions at unacceptably high levels. Proponents of Title IV, however, believe that other utilities will not have enough emission permits to sell to the advantage of the Midwestern facilities. A second concern among environmentalists is that some of the big dirties will abandon their plans to replace existing plants with new, less-polluting facilities and will, instead, stockpile emission permits for older, dirtier facilities. Midwestern utilities and their supporters, in contrast, have been concerned that the emission limits will inhibit economic growth in the economically depressed Ohio River Valley and adjacent areas. Utilities elsewhere have been concerned also with the effect of emission levels on economic growth. Most utilities remain apprehensive about the impact of the new scheme on their own market share and economic future.

By the beginning of Barack Obama's administration, most economic experts had agreed that Title IV had been a success—but not completely. Using three measures for evaluation—environmental quality, the performance of the market, and economic assessment, such as cost savings, innovation, and economic efficiency, one careful summary concluded that Title IV "generally . . . has worked well in achieving its stated goals of achieving emissions targets, resulting in substantial environmental and public health benefits" and a later thorough review concluded optimistically that "the SO_2 allowance trading system had come to be seen as both innovative and successful. It has become exceptionally influential, leading to a series of policy innovations in the United States and abroad to address a range of environmental challenges, including the threat of global climate change."[46] However, the trading program significantly reduced ambient SO_2 concentrations associated with acid rain but had not eliminated them. Moreover, a federal district court in 2008 invalidated most of the Title IV program in a decision concerning a related regional variation of Title IV, resulting in a virtual collapse of the Title IV market in SO_2. By 2012, the EPA had not devised a solution to address the concerns raised by the court.[47]

Conclusion

To most Americans, the nation's environmental troubles are epitomized by polluted air, fouled water, dangerously unregulated hazardous and toxic wastes, and a multitude of other ecological derangements. This chapter illuminates a less-obvious dimension of the environmental crisis that is equally dangerous in its ecological implications—the economic problems in implementing environmental policy effectively. In many critical respects, the institutions and policies the nation now depends on to reverse its ecological degradation are failing, sometimes badly. Equally as imperative as new technological solutions are to ecological ills are new economic and institutional solutions. Finding these solutions will require critical, difficult debate within the environmental movement and among public policy makers at all governmental levels concerned with ecological restoration.

These problems are especially refractory because they often originate in the fundamental constitutional design of the political system or in deeply rooted political traditions. Among these is a historical dependence on traditional policy approaches to environmental problems, particularly the command-and-control method of regulation and the single-media approach to controlling specific pollutants. Although other approaches often seem more appropriate, and in some cases have been tried experimentally, they are strongly resisted by a multitude of institutional, professional, and economic interests with a stake in the status quo. Often, the environmental movement itself has been excessively conservative in resisting policy innovation.

Among the significant economic problems arising from environmental regulation, none is debated more often than the high cost of environmental regulation. As costs continually rise well above expectations, the need to find cost-effective, cost-saving approaches to policy making grows more apparent. Although BCA is sometimes a useful strategy for reducing regulatory costs, its serious political and economic deficiencies suggest that other approaches, involving more economic incentives for pollution abatement in the private sector, are likely to be more broadly effective. None of the problems now associated with regulatory incapacity is likely to be solved easily or quickly.

Suggested Readings

Ackerman, Frank, and Lisa Heinzerling. *Priceless: On Knowing the Price of Everything and the Value of Nothing.* New York: The New Press, 2004.

Harrington, Winston, Richard D. Morgenstern, and Thomas Sterner, eds. *Choosing Environmental Policy: Comparing Instruments and Outcomes in the United States and Europe.* Washington, DC: Resources for the Future, 2004.

Heal, Geoffrey. *Nature and the Marketplace: Capturing the Value of Ecosystem Services.* Washington, DC: Island Press, 2001.

Portney, Paul R., and Robert N. Stavins, eds. *Public Policies for Environmental Protection.* 2nd ed. Washington, DC: Resources for the Future, 2000.

Revesz, Richard, and Paul Livermore. *Retaking Rationality: How Cost Benefit Analysis Can Better Protect the Environment and Our Health.* New York: Cambridge University Press, 2008.

Tietenberg, Tom, and Lynne Lewis. *Environmental & Natural Resources Economics.* 9th ed., Saddle River, NJ: Prentice Hall, 2011.

Notes

1. Current and historic federal budget data can be found at http://www.usgovernment spending.com/spending_chart_2002_2017USp_13s11i111tcn_8Cf (accessed September 3, 2012).

2. Center on Budget and Policy Priorities, "Most of the Budget Goes Toward Defense, Social Security and Major Health Programs," available at http://www.cbpp.org/cms/index.cfm?fa=view&id=1258 (accessed May 2, 2009).

3. Ibid.

4. The arguments for considering costs in environmental regulation are usefully summarized in Allen V. Kneese and Charles L. Schultze, *Pollution, Prices and Public Policy* (Washington, DC: Brookings Institution Press, 1975). See also A. Myrick Freeman III, "Economics, Incentives, and Environmental Regulation," in *Environmental Policy in the 1990s,* 2nd ed., ed. Norman J. Vig and Michael E. Kraft (Washington, DC: CQ Press, 1997), 189–208.

5. On the history of BCA, see Richard A. Liroff, "Cost–Benefit Analysis in Federal Environmental Programs," in *Cost–Benefit Analysis and Environmental Regulations: Politics, Ethics, and Methods,* ed. Daniel Swartzman, Richard A. Liroff, and Kevin G. Croke (Washington, DC: Conservation Foundation, 1982), 35–52; Richard N. L. Andrews, "Cost–Benefit Analysis as Regulatory Reform," in *Cost–Benefit Analysis and Environmental Regulations: Politics, Ethics, and Methods,* ed. Daniel Swartzman, Richard A. Liroff, and Kevin G. Croke (Washington, DC: Conservation Foundation, 1982), 107–136; Norman J. Vig, "Presidential Leadership and the Environment: From Reagan to Clinton," in *Environmental Policy in the 1990s,* 2nd ed., ed. Norman J. Vig and Michael E. Kraft (Washington, DC: CQ Press, 1997), 98–118.

6. For a summary of the issues involved, see Walter A. Rosenbaum, "Regulation at Risk: The Controversial Politics and Science of Comparative Risk Assessment," in *Flashpoints in Environmental Policymaking: Controversies in Achieving Sustainability,* ed. Sheldon Kamieniecki, George A. Gonzalez, and Robert O. Vos (Albany, NY: SUNY Press, 1997), 31–62.

7. Cass Sunstein, "Cost–Benefit Default Principles," AEI-Brookings Joint Center Working Paper no. 00–07/University of Chicago, Law and Economics Working Paper no. 104, Washington, DC, October 2000, 5, available at http://papers.ssrn.com/s013/papers.cfm?abstract_id=247884 (accessed April 23, 2010); see also John D. Graham, Paul R. Noe, and Elizabeth L. Branch, "Managing the Regulatory State: The Experience of the Bush Administration," *Fordham Urban Law Journal,* 33 (May 1, 2006): 953–1001.

8. Curtis W. Copeland, "Changes to the OMB Regulatory Review Process by Executive Order 13422," *CRS Report to Congress,* February 5, 2007 (Washington, DC: Congressional Research Service).

9. Ibid., 10–14.

10. Quoted in ibid., 10.

11. Raymond J. Kopp, Alan J. Krupnick, and Michael A. Toman, "Cost–Benefit Analysis and Regulatory Reform: An Assessment of the Science and Art," Discussion Paper no. 97–19, Resources for the Future, Washington, DC, 1997, 14.

12. Ibid.

13. Freeman, "Economics, Incentives, and Environmental Regulation," 150, 153.

14. Ibid.

15. Paul Johnson, "The Perils of Risk Avoidance," *Regulation* (May–June 1980): 17.

16. Brian Hansen, "New Soot Rules to Cost Power Sector $400 Million Annually, EPA Reckons," *Inside Energy,* October 16, 2006, 6.

17. Kopp, Krupnick, and Toman, "Cost-Benefit Analysis and Regulatory Reform."

18. Ibid.

19. Stephen Kelman, "Cost–Benefit Analysis: An Ethical Critique," *Regulation* (January–February 1981): 39.

20. U.S. GAO, "Cost–Benefit Analysis Can Be Useful in Assessing Regulations, Despite Limitations," Report no. GAO/RCED 84–62, Washington, DC, April 1984, iii.

21. E&E News PM, "RFF's Morgenstern Discusses Cost-Benefit Analysis Reform," *E&ETV's OnPoint* 10, no. 9 (April 2, 2009), available at www.eenews.net/tv/tran script/969 (accessed April 12, 2009).

22. See, for example, World Resources Institute, "For EPA Regulations, Cost Predictions Are Overstated," November 2010, available at www.wri.org/stories/2010/11epa-regulations-cost-predictions-are-overstated (accessed September 1, 2012).

23. On the history of the OMB's use of BCA under the Reagan administration, see W. Norton Grubb, Dale Whittington, and Michael Humphries, "The Ambiguities of Cost–Benefit Analysis: An Evaluation of Regulatory Impact Analysis Under Executive Order 12,291," in *Environmental Policy under Reagan's Executive Order,* ed. V. Kerry Smith (Chapel Hill: University of North Carolina Press, 1984), 121–166; GAO, "Cost–Benefit Analysis Can Be Useful," 7; Edward Paul Fuchs, *Presidents, Managers, and Regulation* (Englewood Cliffs, NJ: Prentice-Hall, 1988), esp. 124; Joseph Cooper and William F. West, "Presidential Power and Republican Government: The Theory and Practice of OMB Review," *Journal of Politics,* 50 (November 1988): 864–895.

24. Charles W. Schmidt, "Subjective Science: Environmental Cost–Benefit Analysis," *Environmental Health Perspectives* (August 2003): A530.

25. Dan Farber, "Obama's Cost–Benefit Executive Order," Legal Planet, the Environmental Law and Policy Blog, University of California, available at http://legalplanet.wordpress .com/2011/01/24/obamas-cost-benefit-executive-order/ (accessed August 20, 2012).

26. GAO, "Much Work Remains to Accelerate Facility Cleanups," Report no. GAO/RCED 93–15, Washington, DC, January 1993, 17.

27. GAO, "Improving EPA's Regulatory Impact Analyses," Report no. GAO/RCED 97–38, Washington, DC, 1997, 2.

28. Traci Watson, "Clean Air: EPA Report Hails Law as Success," *USA Today,* October 21, 1997.

29. The Corps is not required to use an RIA, but it must still produce a BCA for proposed projects.

30. Michael Grunwald, "An Agency of Unchecked Clout: Water Projects Roll Past Econom-ics, Environmental Concerns," *Washington Post,* September 10, 2000, available at www.washingtonpost.com/wp-dyn/content/article/2006/05/12/AR200605120 1550. html (accessed April 23, 2010).

31. GAO, "Corps of Engineers: Observations on Planning and Project Management Processes for the Civil Works Program," Report no. GAO 06–529T, Washington, DC, March 15, 2006, 1.

32. Quoted in Gerard Shields, "Congress and the Corps—Politics, Provincialism, Sometimes Interfere With Priorities, Plans," (Baton Rouge) *Advocate,* November 9, 2008, A01

33. See, for example, the comprehensive report National Academy of Public Administra-tion, "Background: Adapting to Changing Missions and Demands," *Prioritizing America's Water Resources: Budget Reform for Civil Works Construction Projects at the U.S. Army Corps of Engineers* (Washington, DC: National Academy of Public Administration, 2007), chap. 2.

34. Robert W. Hahn, Jason K. Burnett, and Yee-Ho I. Chan, "Assessing the Quality of Regulatory Impact Analyses," Working Paper no. 001, AEI–Brookings Joint Center for Regulatory Studies, Washington, DC, January 2000, executive summary. For similar conclusions, see also Winston Harrington, Richard D. Morgenstern, and Peter Nelson, "On the Accuracy of Regulatory Cost Estimates," Working Paper no. 99–18, Resources for the Future, Washington, DC, January 1999.

35. John C. Whitaker, "Earth Day Recollections: What It Was Like When the Movement Took Off," *EPA Journal,* 14 (July–August 1988): 11.

36. Roefie Hueting, "Correcting National Income for Environmental Losses: A Practical Solution for a Theoretical Dilemma," in *A Survey of Ecological Economics,* ed. Rajaram Krishnan, Jonathan M. Harris, and Neva R. Goodwin (Washington, DC: Island Press, 1995), 248.

37. Kopp, Krupnick, and Toman, "Cost–Benefit Analysis and Regulatory Reform," 30.

38. *New York Times,* September 6, 1993.

39. Ibid.

40. Winston Harrington, Richard D. Morgenstern, and Thomas Sterner, eds., "Overview," in *Choosing Environmental Policy: Comparing Instruments and Outcomes in the United States and Europe* (Washington, DC: Resources for the Future, 2004), 1–22; National Academy of Public Administration, *The Environment Goes to Market* (Washington, DC: National Academy of Public Administration, 1994), chap. 1; Paul R. Portney, ed., *Current Issues in U.S. Environmental Policy* (Baltimore, MD: Johns Hopkins University Press, 1978), esp. chap. 1; Erica L. Dolgin and Thomas G. P. Guilbert, eds., *Federal Environmental Law* (St. Paul, MN.: West, 1974), esp. the articles by Robert Zener, "The Federal Law of Water Pollution Control," 682–791, and Thomas Jorling, "The Federal Law of Air Pollution Control," 1058–1148.

41. On the problem generally, see Kneese and Schulze, *Pollution, Prices, and Public Policy,* chap. 2.

42. Ibid., 116.

43. National Academy of Public Administration, *Environment Goes to Market,* 12.

44. Ibid.

45. Robert W. Hahn and Gordon L. Hester, "EPA's Market for Bads," *Regulation* (December 1987): 48–53.

46. Dallas Burtraw and Sarah Jo Szambelan, *U.S. Emissions Trading Markets for SO$_2$ and NO$_x$,* RFF Research Paper RFF DP 09–40 (Washington DC: Resources for the Future, October 2009, 1, available at http://www.rff.org/Publications/Pages/PublicationDetails.aspx?PublicationID=20925 (accessed August 2, 2012); and Richard Schmalensee and Robert N. Stavins, "The S02 Allowance Trading System: The Ironic History of a Grand Policy Experiment," Joint Center of the Department of Economics, MIT Energy Initiative and MIT Sloan School Management, Paper CEEPR 2012–12, August 2012, available at http://dspace.mit.edu/handle/1721.1/72007 (accessed May 14, 2011).

47. Schmalensee and Stavins, op. cit., 9

Chapter 6

Command and Control in Action
Air and Water Pollution Regulation

> *In environmental history, the twentieth century qualifies as a peculiar
> century because of the screeching acceleration of so many of the
> processes that bring ecological change.*
> —J. R. McNeill, *Something New under the Sun:
> An Environmental History of the Twentieth Century* (2001)

Clean air and clean water are powerful public images. Leaders of the
environmental movement regard the CAA of 1970 and the Federal Water
Pollution Control Act Amendments (FWPCAA) of 1972 as the foundations of the environmental era. Public opinion polls show that Americans
almost universally recognized on the first Earth Day that the nation's
degraded air and waters were major ecological problems. Clean air and
water acquired political chic. Politicians so routinely assured constituents
of their unceasing regard for clean air and clean water that both quickly
become clichés instead of realities.

After more than four decades of sustained effort by government and
the private sector to eliminate air and water pollution, with a cumulative
public expenditure between 2000 and 2012 exceeding $80 billion and an
additional industrial expenditure of $46 billion, the nation's air and
water remain seriously polluted.[1] Some dramatic achievements, many
lesser but impressive gains, and a multitude of marginal improvements
make up the veneer that brightens reports about implementation of the
CAA and the FWPCAA with cosmetic success. But, air and water quality
remain seriously degraded throughout much of the United States. By
2009, the EPA estimated that more than 124 million Americans, mostly
urbanites, lived in counties where pollution levels exceed at least one
national air-quality standard.[2] The water quality in almost two thirds of
the nation's river miles has never been assessed because of deficient state

monitoring resources.[3] The water quality in approximately one third of the nation's surveyed lakes, estuaries, and streams is still considered by the EPA to be significantly impaired.[4]

Why aren't there truly impressive results from so massive a national investment? Many difficulties arise from inexperience in implementing wholly new regulatory programs. To many observers (as noted in the discussion of market approaches to regulation in Chapter 5), the problem is the policy itself, the command-and-control logic so firmly embedded in the two earliest, and most important, national pollution laws of the first environmental era. Other difficulties result from new or unexpected scientific discoveries that complicate pollution control. But, all these difficulties are compounded by political problems. Federal, state, and local governments have been unable or unwilling to invest the enormous resources and to make the politically difficult decisions needed to deal effectively with air and water pollution on a national scale. Public belief about the intensity of pollution and the urgency of further new air and water quality regulation has often wavered and fragmented into partisan polarization in the last several decades. These and other significant influences shaping current air and water pollution regulation will become apparent as this chapter examines the implementation of the CAA and the FWPCAA since the 1980s.

The Political Anatomy of Command-and-Control Regulation

The language and logic of command-and-control regulation is politically innocent. Formally, as observed in Chapter 5, environmental regulators are supposed to follow a legislatively prescribed pathway to pollution control by now built into virtually every federal environmental law: (1) regulate toward the goals identified by Congress, (2) identify the criteria for setting pollution standards, (3) set the quality standards for each regulated pollutant, (4) create the emission standards for regulated pollutants, and (5) see to enforcement of quality and emission standards. In reality, each command-and-control element is a distinctive decision-making arena rich with political implications—often unintended—lurking behind the statutory language and shaping the impact of regulation as much as the formal language of the law.

The technicality of pollution regulation, however, frequently creates a language and a style of action that conceal, sometimes deliberately, the extent to which these political forces operate behind the façade of prescribed regulatory procedures. Nonetheless, regulation is fundamentally a political enterprise, involving considerable negotiation and sometimes conflict magnified by the number and diversity of the actors and institutions involved. (See Figure 6–1.)

Figure 6–1 Key Players in Enforcement of Pollution Control Laws

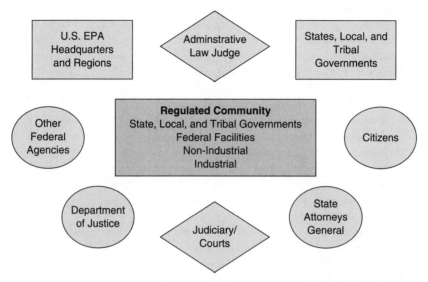

Source: Robert Esworthy, "Federal Pollution Laws: How Are They Enforced?," CRS Report to Congress, Report No. 7-5700-RL34384 (Washington, D C: Congressional Research Service, 2012, available at www.fas.org/sgp/crs/misc/RL34384.pdf (accessed September 20, 2012).

A number of characteristic political processes and issues arise regardless of the specific pollution program involved. Political pressure and conflict flow to wherever administrative discretion exists in the regulatory process. Such administrative discretion ordinarily is found at several points in pollution regulation:

- *When words, phrases, or policy objectives are unclear.* Congress may deliberately shift responsibility to administrators for settling disputes between interests that are in conflict over how a law should be phrased. Tossing this political hot potato to administrators ensures that partisans on all sides of an issue with something to gain or lose by the law's interpretation will scramble to influence however officials or bureaucracies resolve such obscurities. Sometimes, this lack of legislative clarity results less from deliberation than from congressional confusion or ignorance. In any case, regulators usually find themselves caught between competing group pressures to interpret statutes or regulations in different ways. Such pressures, in fact, should be considered routine in the regulatory process.
- *When technical standards must be created or revised.* Existing legislation regulating air pollution, water pollution, and hazardous

substances ordinarily requires the EPA to define the standards and prescribe the appropriate control technologies necessary to meet mandated standards. Often, regulatory agencies also are required by such legislation to review periodically and, if appropriate, revise such standards or technology requirements. Legitimate disagreement often exists (as noted in Chapter 5) over the technical and economic justifications for most regulatory standards. In the presence of expert dissension about such issues, a large measure of discretion rests with regulatory agencies for resolving such disputes. This discretion, and the conflict it invites, will reappear whenever agencies review regulatory standards. In fact, virtually all major technical determinations by regulatory agencies are politicized by the activity of pressure groups, Congress, competing governmental agencies, and other interests seeking to shape discretionary decisions to their respective advantage.

- *When compliance deadlines are flexible.* Pollution legislation may bristle with explicit compliance deadlines, but administrators almost always have authority to extend them. Legislation is particularly generous in granting administrators authority to extend compliance deadlines when, in their opinion, economic hardship or other inequities may result from strict enforcement. Thus, the CAA instructs the EPA to set emission standards for new air pollution sources by considering, among other things, "the degree of emission limitation achievable through the application of the best system of emission reduction which (taking into account the cost of achieving such reduction) the administrator determines has been adequately demonstrated." Such a fistful of discretionary authority in effect permits the EPA to extend compliance deadlines for specific air pollution sources by increasing the time allowed to search for pollution controls meeting these multiple criteria. In many cases, a compliance deadline also may be relaxed if an agency determines that it is beyond the technical ability of a polluter to install the proper controls in the required time. Agencies sometimes can achieve a backdoor extension of compliance deadlines by deliberately delaying the establishment of a standard long enough to permit the regulated interests to make adjustments to the anticipated standard.

Beyond Public View

The implementation of most environmental regulatory programs does not routinely involve the public or public opinion. Unlike the White House and Congress, the federal bureaucracy is neither highly visible nor readily understood by the public; regulation operates, in the words of political scientist Francis E. Rourke, behind an "opaque exterior"[5] that the public seldom cares to penetrate. This dearth of dependable public interest means that the constellation of political forces and actors involved in regulatory politics ordinarily is confined to organized interests, governmental officials, scientists, technicians, and other insiders. Given the complexity and technicality of environmental issues, this situation is not surprising. But, it emphasizes the extent to which regulatory politics tends to involve a process that is highly specialized and commonly closed to public involvement.

When Enforcement Is Discretionary

Few provisions in current pollution legislation compel federal officials to stop a polluting activity. Most often, enforcement actions are discretionary, as in Section 111 of the CAA, which instructs the EPA administrator to regulate any pollutant from a stationary source when, in the judgment of the administrator, it may cause or contribute to "air pollution which may reasonably be anticipated to endanger public health or welfare." Even when enforcement action is initiated, officials are usually given optional methods for securing compliance.

Typically, air and water pollution laws are enforced through state or local agencies with considerable discretion to decide what level of emission controls will be required of an air or water polluter and when emission controls must be achieved. These become conditions for the permits that all air- and water-polluting firms must obtain from state, federal, and local authorities to operate. In air pollution regulation, for instance, this discretion can arise from the regulator's authority under the CAA to decide which emission controls are technically and economically feasible and to issue variances that temporarily waive emissions-control deadlines or technology specifications.[6] Regulators seek voluntary compliance. They want to avoid imposing penalties as a means of ensuring compliance if possible because they know that resorting to administrative or judicial tribunals very likely will involve a protracted, inflexible process with no assurances that the polluter will be compelled to control emissions speedily and efficiently at the conclusion. In fact, polluters often provoke such action, hoping to avoid emission controls indefinitely by exploiting the complexities of the administrative or judicial procedures involved.

Regulated firms often balk at a regulatory agency's initial specification of acceptable control technologies and deadline dates for compliance with emission standards. The usual solution is bargaining between regulator and regulated, particularly when regulatory agencies confront an economically and politically influential firm or group of firms that is capable of creating political pressures on the regulatory agency to reach some accommodation over required control technologies or compliance deadlines. Regulatory agencies typically will make some concession to firms concerning the required control technologies or compliance deadlines. One form of these concessions is the frequently used variance that allows a firm some delay in achieving emission controls that are otherwise required under the law. A firm often is able to negotiate a variance permitting it to discharge on an interim basis at its existing emission levels and to obtain several additional variances that can delay significantly the achievement of required emission controls.

Agencies also depend heavily on firms to monitor and report their own pollution emissions, in part because of the sheer volume of regulated entities. Under the CAA, for instance, more than 3,400 major sources and 45,600 minor sources of wastewater discharge must be controlled. The 1990 amendments to the CAA increased the regulated sources to more than 35,000 major and 350,000 minor facilities.[7]

Most regulatory agencies still lack the personnel and other resources to inspect routinely and monitor all emission controls within their jurisdictions. Voluntary compliance is almost a necessity. Quite often, regulatory agencies monitor only the larger sources of pollution emissions within their jurisdiction, leaving smaller sources to report their own compliance with permit conditions under all but exceptional circumstances. Even monitoring the largest pollution sources does not necessarily ensure that air or water pollutants are satisfactorily regulated. For example, in 2009, the EPA reported that, although it was able to assure that most dischargers of large-volume water pollutants complied with their discharge permits, the compliance of numerous smaller-volume polluters could not be assured because the agency's resources supporting the oversight of compliance and enforcement with the Clean Water Act had progressively diminished since the early 2000s.[8] The EPA has encountered similar problems when monitoring compliance with the CAA's stationary source emission permits. Confronted with a daunting challenge compounded with relentlessly multiplying regulatory responsibilities and insufficient resources, and burdened by episodic White House disfavor, the EPA's efforts to enforce its regulatory duties has been a constant struggle.[9]

Although administrative discretion, limited resources, and political pressure clearly limit the vigor and strictness in enforcement of environmental regulations, these constraints can sometimes be inevitable, even prudent. Often, the use of administrative discretion to make a deal over pollution allows a regulatory agency to achieve more pollution abatement than would be the case if it insisted on extremely stringent emission standards in full and immediate compliance with the law. This is true particularly when the regulated firm either is unable to comply fully and immediately with a strict interpretation of the law or is willing to fight indefinitely in the courts or administrative hearing rooms to prevent any regulation. Many regulatory agencies, limited by staff and funding that are inadequate for their mandated responsibilities, have no practical alternative to relying on voluntary compliance and accommodation. Finally, regulatory agencies often confront regulated interests—including other governmental agencies subject to pollution control—that are too politically or economically powerful to be compelled to comply fully and immediately with the law. Although this should be no excuse for exemption from full compliance with environmental regulation, it is often an immutable political reality with which regulatory agencies must make peace. In such circumstances, agencies may logically conclude that it is better to bargain with the regulated interests in the hope of achieving some limited goals than to adopt what may well become an ultimately futile strategy of insisting on stringent compliance with the law in spite of massive resistance from the polluter.

Discretion in the enforcement of pollution regulation, however inevitable, also means that this discretion at times will be abused. Discretion sometimes leads agencies to yield needlessly and negligently to political pressures that prevent enforcement of essential pollution controls. It is unfortunate that these are among the unavoidable risks inherent in the exercise of discretionary authority, without which environmental administration would be impossible.

Regulating Air Quality

Since Earth Day 1970, the federal government has continually monitored a variety of environmental indicators and has published current assessments of environmental quality using these indicators. These data provide a useful baseline for observing changes in national environmental quality since the major federal environmental programs began in the early 1970s. They are also an essential standard for judging the impact of the CAA and other federal legislation. The CAA, together with its important 1977 and 1990 amendments, constitutes one of the longest, most complex, and most technically detailed federal regulatory programs ever enacted. The CAA creates a standards-and-enforcement program in which the federal government establishes national ambient air-quality standards for major pollutants, the states and local government agencies assume primary responsibility for implementing the program within federal guidelines, and the various levels of government share enforcement responsibilities. However, the states may enact more stringent standards for airsheds in their jurisdictions.

Overall, national air quality has undoubtedly improved—in a few instances, dramatically—since the CAA's enactment in 1970. By 2006, the

EPA was regulating more than 200 air pollutants—most of them toxic air pollutants identified by Congress in 1990. However, the most important of these pollutants in terms of public health and political significance are the so-called criteria pollutants—carbon monoxide, nitrogen oxides, ozone, particulate matter, sulfur dioxide, and lead—whose regulation was mandated in 1970 by the original CAA and whose health effects are summarized in Box 6–1. After 2006, the EPA regulated only so-called small particulates (those smaller than 2.5 microns, $PM_{2.5}$). As Table 6–1 illustrates, the improvement in both air quality and pollution emissions associated with these six pollutants between 1980 and 2010 has been, in most cases, significant and, in the case of lead, dramatic. Airborne lead, which is especially hazardous to children, has been virtually eliminated through the abolition of leaded automobile fuels. Since 1980, sulfur dioxide emissions decreased by more than 76 percent and carbon monoxide emissions by 80 percent. America's urban environment has improved significantly. The data understate the significance of these achievements because they do not estimate what pollution emissions would have been in the absence of regulation during a period from 1990 to 2010, when the U.S. population increased by 24 percent and vehicle miles traveled increased by 40 percent. Improvements in air quality have been especially significant since the mid-1980s, when the cumulative effect of earlier regulation began to appear. Additional improvement is predicted as new regulatory programs are implemented. Here are two examples:

- Recent EPA diesel regulations for trucks are expected to remove 90 percent of the soot from present diesel motor emissions.
- The EPA 2006 Clean Air Mercury Rule is expected to significantly reduce mercury emissions from coal-fired power plants—the largest remaining sources of mercury emissions in the country—from 48 to 15 tons per year, a reduction of nearly 70 percent.

Despite this improvement, the nation's air remains seriously degraded in several respects. First, ground-level ozone, a primary component of urban smog, remains a pervasive problem. This low-level ozone poses significant human health risks and produces more than $1 billion in agricultural crop damage annually. Currently, more than 108 million Americans, mostly urbanites, live in areas that are not in compliance with the ozone standard. Second, emissions of nitrogen oxides, a precursor of acid precipitation and a greenhouse gas contributing to urban smog, have increased since 1970. Third, U.S. releases of greenhouse gases, especially carbon dioxide (CO_2), is predicted to increase by more than 42 percent between 2000 and 2020 under present U.S. air quality policies—a surge in climate-warming emissions that is considered highly undesirable by most climate scientists, unacceptable by environmentalists, and threatening internationally (as discussed fully in Chapter 10).[10] In addition, the control of small particulates, identified as an important public health problem in the early 1990s, has just begun. Fourth, air toxics have yet to be adequately regulated. The 1990 amendments to the CAA required the EPA to regulate 188 air toxics, including well-known health threats such as dioxins, benzene, arsenic, beryllium, mercury, and vinyl chloride. To date, the EPA has established emission standards for only 99 of these pollutants.

Box 6–1   *Human Health and Environmental Effects of Common Air Pollutants*

Ozone (ground-level ozone is the principal component of smog)
- *Source.* Ozone is produced by a chemical reaction involving volatile organic compounds (VOCs) and nitrogen oxides.
- *Health effects.* Ozone causes breathing problems, reduced lung function, asthma, irritated eyes, stuffy nose, and reduced resistance to colds and other infections and may speed up aging of lung tissue.
- *Environmental effects.* Ozone can damage plants and trees; smog can cause reduced visibility.
- *Property damage.* Ozone damages rubber, fabrics, and other materials.

Volatile organic compounds (smog formers)[a]
- *Source.* VOCs are released from burning fuel (for example, gasoline, oil, wood, coal, and natural gas) and from solvents, paints, glues, and other products used at work or at home. Cars are a common source of VOCs. VOCs include chemicals such as benzene, toluene, methylene chloride, and methyl chloroform.
- *Health effects.* In addition to ozone (smog) effects, many VOCs can cause serious health problems such as cancer.
- *Environmental effects.* In addition to ozone (smog) effects, some VOCs such as formaldehyde and ethylene may harm plants.

Nitrogen dioxide (one of the nitrogen oxides, a smog-forming chemical)
- *Source.* Nitrogen dioxide is produced in the burning of gasoline, natural gas, coal, oil, and other fuels. Cars are a common source of nitrogen dioxide.
- *Health effects.* Nitrogen dioxide causes lung damage and illnesses of the breathing passages and lungs (the respiratory system).

---

[a]All VOCs contain carbon, the basic chemical element found in living things. Carbon-containing chemicals are called organic. Volatile chemicals escape into the air easily. Many VOCs are also hazardous air pollutants, which can cause serious illnesses. The EPA does not list VOCs as criteria air pollutants, but they are included here because efforts to control smog also target VOCs for reduction.

(continued)

Box 6–1   *(continued)*

- *Environmental effects.* Nitrogen dioxide is an ingredient of acid rain (acid aerosols), which can damage trees and lakes. Acid aerosols reduce visibility.
- *Property damage.* Acid aerosols can eat away stone used in buildings, statues, and monuments.

Carbon monoxide
- *Source.* Carbon monoxide is produced in the burning of gasoline, natural gas, coal, oil, and other fuels.
- *Health effects.* Carbon monoxide reduces the ability of blood to bring oxygen to body cells and tissues; the cells and tissues need oxygen to work. Carbon monoxide may be particularly hazardous to people who have heart or circulatory (blood vessel) problems and to people who have damaged lungs or breathing passages.

Particulate matter (dust, smoke, soot)
- *Source.* Particulate matter is produced in the burning of wood, diesel, and other fuels; by industrial plants; through agriculture (for example, plowing and burning off fields); and from driving on unpaved roads.
- *Health effects.* Particulate matter causes nose and throat irritation, lung damage, bronchitis, and early death.
- *Environmental effects.* Particulate matter is the main source of haze that reduces visibility.
- *Property damage.* Ash, soot, smoke, and dust can dirty and discolor structures and other property, including clothes and furniture.

Sulfur dioxide
- *Source.* Sulfur dioxide is produced in the burning of coal and oil (especially high-sulfur coal from the eastern United States) and through industrial processes (for example, those involving paper and metal).
- *Health effects.* Sulfur dioxide causes breathing problems and may cause permanent damage to lungs.
- *Environmental effects.* Sulfur dioxide is an ingredient in acid rain (acid aerosols), which can damage trees and lakes. Acid aerosols reduce visibility.
- *Property damage.* Acid aerosols can eat away stone used in buildings, statues, and monuments.

Lead
- *Source.* Lead is found in leaded gasoline (being phased out), paint (used, for example, on houses and cars), and smelters (metal refineries); it is used in the manufacture of lead storage batteries.
- *Health effects.* Lead causes brain and other nervous system damage; children are especially at risk. Some lead-containing chemicals cause cancer in animals. Lead causes digestive and other health problems.
- *Environmental effects.* Lead can harm wildlife.

Source: Adapted from EPA, Office of Air Quality Planning and Standards, *The Plain English Guide to the Clean Air Act,* available at www.epa.gov/oar/oaqps/peg_caa/pegcaa11.html (accessed March 6, 2001).

Table 6–1　*Percent Change in Air Quality, 1980–2010*

	Change 1980–2010	Change 1990–2010	Change 2000–2010
Carbon Monoxide (CO)	–82	–73	–54
Ozone (O_3) (8-hr)	–28	–17	–11
Lead (Pb)	–90	–83	–62
Nitrogen Dioxide (NO_2) (annual)	–52	–45	–38
PM_{10} (24-hr)	—	–38	–29
$PM_{2.5}$ (annual)	—	—	–27
$PM_{2.5}$ (24-hr)	—	—	–29
Sulfur Dioxide (SO_2) (24-hr)	–76	–68	–48

Source: U.S. EPA, *Air Quality Trends*, available at http://www.epa.gov/airtrends/aqtrends.html (accessed September 20, 2012).

Notes: Trend data not available. Negative numbers indicate improvements in air quality.

Improved air quality, like other environmental gains in recent decades, is fragile and highly vulnerable to technological change, economic cycles, and other social impacts.

The Clean Air Act and the 1977 Amendments

In broad outline, the CAA, including the 1977 amendments, mandates the following programs:

1. *National air-quality standards.* The act directs the EPA to determine the maximum permissible ambient air concentrations for pollutants that it found to be harmful to human health or the environment. The EPA was instructed to establish such standards for at least seven pollutants: carbon monoxide, hydrocarbons, lead, nitrogen oxide, particulates, ozone, and sulfur oxides. The agency was to set two types of national ambient air-quality standards without considering the cost of compliance:

   a. *Primary standards.* Primary standards were supposed to protect human health with an adequate margin of safety for particularly vulnerable segments of the population, such as the elderly and infants. Originally, all air-quality control regions in the United States were required to meet primary standards by 1982; this deadline was extended several times and still remains unenforced.

   b. *Secondary standards.* Secondary standards were intended to maintain visibility and to protect buildings, crops, and water.

2. *Stationary source regulations.* The EPA was to set maximum emission standards for new stationary sources, called *new source performance standards.* The following procedures were to be followed:

   a. Standards were to be set on an industry-by-industry basis; the states then were to enforce the standards.
   b. In setting new source performance standards, the EPA was required to take into account the costs, energy requirements, and environmental effects of its guidelines.
   c. For existing sources (those dischargers active at the time the act was passed), the EPA was to issue control-technique guidelines for the states' use.

3. *State implementation plans.* Each state was required to create a plan indicating how it would achieve federal standards and guidelines to implement the act fully by 1982. The plans were to contain information relating to several important elements:

   a. The nation was divided into 247 air-quality control regions for which states were made responsible. The regions were classified as either attainment or nonattainment regions for each of the regulated pollutants.
   b. States were also made responsible for enforcing special air-quality standards in areas with especially clean air. These regions were called prevention of significant deterioration (PSD) regions.
   c. States were required to order existing factories in nonattainment areas to retrofit their plants with control technologies representing "reasonably available control technology."
   d. In PSD areas, all new stationary emission sources were required to install the best available control technology.

4. *Mobile source emission standards (for automobiles and trucks).* Title II of the CAA created a detailed but flexible timetable for achieving auto and truck emission controls:

   a. For autos, there was to be a 90 percent reduction in hydrocarbon and carbon monoxide emissions by 1975 and a 90 percent reduction in nitrogen oxide emissions by 1976, when measured against 1970 emission levels.
   b. The administrator of the EPA was authorized to grant extensions of these deadlines for approximately one year. Considerable extensions have been repeatedly granted by the EPA, and others have been authorized by Congress.

By 1990, the original CAA and its massive 1977 amendments apparently had achieved significant reductions in several ambient air pollutants, particularly suspended large particulates, lead, and carbon monoxide, as Table 6–1 indicates. With the exception of lead, however, reductions in other pollutants still seemed unsatisfactorily slow, and urban air pollution—especially concentrations of nitrogen oxide, ozone, and volatile organic compounds—continued to be a major concern. After almost a decade of bitter impasse, the White House, environmentalists, and Congress collaborated to rewrite comprehensively the 1970 legislation by passing the Clean Air Act Amendments of 1990, the most important and imaginative regulatory reform in more than a decade.

The Clean Air Act Amendments of 1990

The new amendments are a curious mélange of hammer clauses, multitudinous deadlines, and other tread-worn approaches combined with a timely sensitivity to emerging problems and an aggressive new approach to global climate protection based on an innovative, market-inspired scheme for emissions trading. This mix of tradition, invention, and desperation represents what may be the last, best hope for fortifying the original CAA sufficiently to achieve its purpose. The 1990 amendments added to the original act's two titles concerning acid precipitation and ozone protection and substantially amended most of the remaining provisions while keeping the basic command-and-control approach of the original legislation. The major features are outlined in the sections that follow.[11]

Title I: Nonattainment Areas. The amendments established a new classification of areas that failed to meet national air-quality standards for ozone, carbon monoxide, and particulates and created deadlines of from 3 to 20 years for attaining these standards. They also created a graded set of regulatory requirements for each area, depending on the severity of the pollution.

Title II: Mobile Sources. The new amendments set more than 90 new emission standards for autos and trucks. Among the important emission requirements were these:

- Tailpipe emissions of hydrocarbons were to be reduced by 35 percent, and nitrogen oxides were to be reduced by 60 percent for all new cars by the 1996 model year.
- Beginning in 1998, all new cars were required to have pollution control devices with a 10-year, 100,000-mile warranty.
- Auto manufacturers were required to produce by 1996 a fleet of experimental cars available in Southern California that met emission

standards and that were more stringent than the 1996 levels already required by the amendments.

- Petroleum companies were required to produce cleaner-burning fuel to be used in the most-polluted areas by 1992 and in all areas with ozone problems by 1996.

Title III: Hazardous Air Pollutants. The amendments required the EPA to create national emission standards for hazardous air pollutants for all major sources of hazardous or toxic air pollutants and specified 189 chemicals to be regulated immediately. They established a multitude of specific deadlines by which the EPA was ordered to list categories of industrial processes that emit dangerous air pollutants, to establish health-based standards for each hazardous chemical emission, and to ensure that sources of hazardous emission have established safety controls at their facilities.

Title IV: Control of Acid Deposition. The amendments created a new emissions trading program for sulfur oxides, a major precursor of acid precipitation. Under this new approach, the EPA was "to allocate to each major coal-fired power plant an allowance for each ton of emission permitted; sources cannot release emissions beyond the number of allowances they are given. Allowances may be traded, bought, or sold among allowance holders . . . "[12] Title IV required that national sulfur oxide emissions be reduced by half by the year 2000. The 110 largest sulfur oxide sources in the utility industry were required to meet stricter emission standards. In addition, emissions of nitrogen oxides were to be reduced by 2 million tons annually, compared with 1980 levels, through more traditional regulatory methods.

Title VI: Stratospheric Ozone Protection. Title VI listed specific ozone-depleting chemicals and created a schedule for phasing out their production or use. It also pledged the United States to an accelerated phaseout of ozone-depleting chemicals that exceeded the schedule to which the United States had agreed in the 1987 Montreal Protocol on Substances That Deplete the Ozone Layer.

Current Controversies in Air-Quality Regulation

The CAA is the nation's longest, most complex regulatory law. Its legal and technical intricacy seems to ensure employment for a generation of lawyers and judges unborn and unrelenting partisan debate about its wisdom and implications among politicians and economists. At the same time, it is among the most revolutionary and ambitious environmental laws in U.S. history, the foundation of U.S. environmental regulation. Thus, the issues and their embedded controversies have profound implications for the future of the U.S. environment. One of these important matters (discussed in Chapter 5) is emissions trading. Other major issues involved with the CAA concern the impact of federalism, regulatory science, and partisan change in the presidency. Current controversies over urban smog, small particulate regulation, and controls for new air pollution sources illustrate these issues.

Combative Federalism: The Smog Wars. Regulating urban smog has been difficult because so many varied sources contribute to its creation. Large, stationary sources, such as fossil-fuel-burning utilities, factories, mineral smelters, and chemical manufacturers, are major contributors. But, thousands of small sources, most previously unregulated and many until recently unrecognized—including paint manufacturers, dry cleaners, and gasoline stations—collectively make a major contribution. The automobile stubbornly remains a chronic polluter despite the advent of efficient emission-control technologies. One reason is that pre-1970 vehicles, the worst auto polluters because they lack emission controls, are not being replaced as quickly as predicted. In addition, an ever-growing fleet of new, highly polluting light trucks and other sports vehicles continues to capture a large proportion of the domestic new-vehicle market. Many state and local governments also have failed to enforce their own implementation plans, especially requirements for annual auto emission inspections, proposals to limit auto access to urban areas, and other arrangements annoying to the public and costly to businesses. Even the best available technologies may be insufficient to control adequately all important emissions. Emission controls now remove 96 percent of the pollutants emitted before controls were instituted in 1972.[13] Many experts believe existing auto emission controls have reached "the knife edge of technological feasibility"[14] and that additional emission reductions are unlikely unless a great many states require motorists to switch from conventional to new, more-expensive, reformulated fuels or hybrid motor vehicles.

In a forceful, politically risky move to reduce urban air pollution further, the EPA in 1997 promulgated new ambient air-quality standards for ozone and particulates, two primary causes of smog, but it did so only after a ferocious political fight that laid bare the tensions between state and federal governments inherent in regulatory federalism. The EPA's review of these standards had been long overdue, according to the requirements of the CAA, and was compelled only through a lawsuit sponsored by the American Lung Association. The new standards, finally proposed in early 1996, were considerably tougher than the existing ones. Experts predicted that the new regulations would increase the number of counties (virtually all urban) out of compliance with particulate standards from 41 to 150 and those violating the ozone standard from 189 to 332—in short, a huge increase in the number, and thus the political weight, of the counties affected. Massive opposition from organized business developed quickly.

The EPA defended its decision by citing strong support from its own scientific advisory panels and by asserting that the new rules would avert 15,000 premature deaths, 350,000 cases of aggravated asthma, and 1 million cases of decreased lung function in children.

Congress—the second front in all political battles between the states—was immediately embroiled in the affair. Eleven different congressional committees collectively held more than a month of hearings on the revised standards. More than 250 senators and representatives wrote to the EPA and congressional committees about the matter. Congressional alignments generally reflected the ongoing battle over smog between the northeastern and midwestern states. Northeastern states believed the new regulations would diminish cross-border air pollution originating in the Midwest and would compel Midwestern utilities to assume more responsibility for reducing those emissions. The midwestern states, generally in compliance with existing air-quality standards, anticipated having to enact economically costly, politically distasteful new air-emission controls, especially on utilities, some of which would have to reduce existing emissions by 85 percent. Bill Clinton's administration wavered for months; the president's own congressional party was deeply divided on the matter. Finally, in July 1997, President Clinton approved the regulations. Several months later, even as the EPA proposed stringent, new emission controls on utilities to implement the new air-quality standards, the northeastern states renewed the geographical struggle. They sued the EPA for failing to order emission reductions in 40 Midwestern power plants in accordance with other provisions of the CAA. When the EPA did finally release its final version of the regulations, the regulated utilities promptly, and unsuccessfully, sued the agency in an effort to prevent the implementation of the new standards.

The advent of the George W. Bush administration provoked additional confrontations between the EPA and the northeastern states. Complaining that Midwestern air pollution made the Northeast "the tailpipe of America," nine northeastern states sued the EPA in 2002 to prevent the enactment of new rules delaying the installation of new pollution-control technologies on older Midwestern utilities (see the section "Politics and Regulatory Change: New Source Review" later in the chapter). The Northeast's sustained legal and political pressure on the EPA produced a truce of sorts by 2007. The battle over New Source Review had stalled in the courts, and the Bush administration announced in 2005 a new Clean Air Interstate Rule (CAIR) that was intended to reduce power plant emissions of nitrogen and sulfur oxides by more than 60 percent within a decade. The EPA estimated that the CAIR, the centerpiece of the Bush administration's air pollution policies, would prevent 17,000 deaths annually by 2015 and appeared to be another regulatory pathway to cleaner Northeastern air that environmentalists generally supported.

Like virtually all major environmental regulations, however, the CAIR was also quickly embattled in the federal courts. Dissatisfied environmentalists, state officials, and some regulated industries launched the CAIR on a convoluted judicial journey that appeared to end in July 2008, when the federal district court, supporting environmentalist critics of CAIR, declared that CAIR was "contrary to law and unsupported adequately by reasoned decision-making" and ordered the EPA to reconsider the regulation's new emission standards. But, it was soon apparent that the court's ruling assured a regulatory muddle that all contending factions wished to avoid. "In anticipation of CAIR's adoption, some utility companies have already invested significantly in pollution controls for their power plants that might be too costly to operate if the tighter policies do not end up taking effect," explains one analyst. Moreover,

> state officials are also in a bind. They face deadlines for other longstanding air quality standards. . . . Without the now-vacated Bush policies, the affected states probably won't hit their deadlines, and could face penalties as a result. The Bush rules would have given power plants a financial incentive to reduce pollution. With those incentives off the table, plants may back out of contracts for new pollution control equipment or run the equipment less.[15]

In December 2008, federal judges, responding to further initiatives from virtually all major interests involved in the CAIR, reversed themselves and agreed to permit the EPA to enforce the CAIR rules temporarily, thus assuring sufficient predictability of the new regulations while the Obama administration considered further rule revisions. When the Obama administration did propose a new version of its proposed CAIR in 2012, however, critics of the new version again took the issue to court and won a temporary victory when a federal district court ruled that the EPA's newest proposal included provisions that exceeded EPA's authority. And so, the proposed regulations were once again sent back to the EPA for yet another rewriting.[16] Such a tooth-and-claw sectional brawl is unlikely to end quickly, no matter how the EPA writes its next proposed regulation because the conflict feeds on deeply nested political tensions in the federalist system: sectional competition for political and economic power, conflict over interpretation of the Constitution's federalist language, pluralistic private and public interests, congressional advocacy of state and regional viewpoints, scientific contention about environmental standards, judicial intervention in regulation, the resort to litigation as a political weapon, and much more that is fundamental to U.S. environmental policy making.

Science and Regulatory Change: Small Particulates. Regulation strives for predictability, consistency in interpreting and applying the law, and stability in established norms for decision making. Science breeds discovery, embraces change, promotes experimentation, and challenges tradition. Science is a troubler to regulatory order. Since 1970, the CAA has regulated airborne particulates as one of the original criteria pollutants. But, the continuing enrichment of scientific data since 1970 is forcing a change in the understanding of which substances should be regulated and which levels can be tolerated. New scientific evidence poses for the EPA difficult and disruptive new choices about particulate regulation.

In 1971, the EPA issued air-quality standards for particulates without distinction regarding size. Particulates (extremely small, solid particles of matter found in the air and produced by dust, smoke, fuel combustion, agriculture, and forest cultivation, among other sources) have been known for many decades to pose health hazards. Initially, however, the EPA's standards on particulates assumed that size was not a significant factor in the health risks posed. By 1987, accumulating scientific research had demonstrated conclusively that small particulates, those smaller than 10 microns (1 micron, or micrometer, equals 1/25,000 inch), are especially hazardous to humans because they can be inhaled into lung tissue, unlike larger particulates, which are caught in the air passages to the lungs.[17] These smaller particulates are commonly found in cigarette smoke, diesel engine emissions, windblown dust, and many other sources. They are also dangerous because they can carry carcinogenic chemicals into the lungs. In 1987, the EPA issued new air-quality standards for small particulates. However, existing emission controls for particulates were not designed specifically to control small particulates, and many sources of small particulates were not regulated at all.

About 250 air-quality control regions failed the new ambient air-quality standards for fine particulates. In the West, a major problem was windblown dust, not easily controlled by any existing technology. The EPA established tailpipe standards for emissions from diesel trucks and buses, beginning with the 1988 model year, that became increasingly stringent for models beginning in 1991. But, monitoring data about the origin and distribution of fine particulates was inadequate, and states were slow to identify the magnitude of their problems and the sources to be regulated. Control technologies for stationary sources of small particulates were not well tested, and the control costs were not accurately known. In effect, small particulates had become a separate emission-control problem, and the states spent much of the 1990s acquiring a capability to regulate them. The EPA's most recent particulate standards, enacted concurrently with the 1997 revised smog rules, created new regulations specifically for particulates smaller than 2.5 microns because scientific research had demonstrated that these posed a distinct human health risk. Automobile manufacturers, fossil-fuel-burning facilities, and the trucking industry were predictably concerned about the additional compliance costs to meet the proposed standards. And, they were angered by this "regulatory ratcheting"—the appearance of new, progressively more stringent regulatory rules with which they must comply—creating the third different particulate standard within a decade. Proponents of the new standards argued that they were protecting the elderly, children, and people with chronic lung disease from a new, scientifically verified health risk. For regulated interests, the real problem seemed to be the potent, economically disruptive impact of regulatory science on their existing environmental control strategies.

Predictably, the disaffected truckers, utilities, and other regulated industries took their case to court—all the way to the Supreme Court—challenging the EPA's authority to promulgate the new regulatory rules in what turned out to be perhaps the most significant environmental regulatory cases since the 1970s. Essentially, the dissidents challenged the EPA's discretionary authority, granted by Congress in the CAA, to set ambient air-quality standards solely on the basis of public health considerations. The EPA, they argued, had interpreted this authority too broadly, and Congress had been negligent in permitting the agency too much discretion in interpreting such authority. Had the Supreme Court agreed with this argument, the logic could well have overturned a huge array of other environmental regulations across the whole domain of federal environmental regulation and left a chaos of regulatory confusion. The Supreme Court, however, rejected the assault on the EPA's congressionally delegated authority and in a landmark ruling (*Whitman v. American Trucking Associations*, 531 U.S. 457) affirmed in 2001 both the delegated authority and the EPA's latitude in interpreting that authority.

What followed was a splendid example of EPA decision making driven by the judicial lash. With Supreme Court approval, the EPA began to issue regulations in 2002 to implement its small particulate standards. But, the agency was sued again in 2002, this time by environmental groups for failing to review its standards for small and large particulates by a 2002 deadline set by the CAA (which required an EPA review of all air-quality standards every five years). After further negotiation, the EPA reached a settlement with the environmental groups in which it agreed to review again its particulate standards. In 2006, the EPA decided to implement its new small particulate standard and also to abandon its earlier standard for large particulates—another instance of regulatory ratcheting driven by ongoing scientific research. Meanwhile, the EPA estimated in 2005 that at least 129 counties with more than 68 million people appeared to exceed the standard for small particulates established in 1997 and that almost 400 additional counties with a population exceeding 91 million people had provided insufficient data to even determine whether they had met particulate standards.[18] Thus, a substantial proportion of the national population, most of them urban dwellers, appeared to be living in areas that might be subjected in the near future to increasingly stringent air pollution controls that could significantly affect economic development.

Critics of the new standard accused OIRA, the White House entity so often censured for improper intervention in the EPA's regulation writing (see Chapter 5), of more interference in EPA rule making by pressuring the EPA to ignore the advice of its scientific advisers, who had recommended an even lower standard than was proposed.[19] In November 2009, EPA administrator Lisa Jackson announced that the EPA would begin reviewing, and if necessary revising, existing standards for particulates and all criteria pollutants regulated by the CAA. But, the EPA was too slow to satisfy 11 states who joined health and environmental groups in suing the agency for its delay. Finally, in June 2012, the EPA proposed revised regulations that would reduce the amount of fine particulates in the air by 17 percent below currently permitted levels. The EPA was required to issue its final version of the new regulations by December 2012, thus leaving the next White House occupant another inheritance of ongoing contention over CAA regulations.[20]

Politics and Regulatory Change: New Source Review. In mid-2002, the EPA brought to a full boil a controversy simmering since the CAA's creation in 1970. By then, the conflict had escalated into a major confrontation between the George W. Bush administration and environmentalists. All this resulted from a volatile combination of circumstances that repeatedly transformed environmental rule making into partisan political warfare: large regulatory costs and environmental risks, a major economic sector, vague legislation, and (especially in this instance) a new presidency. The outcome, moreover, was likely to profoundly affect air quality for a generation or more.

The controversy began with an arcane section of the CAA concerned with "new source performance standards." The original CAA of 1970 required all major stationary sources of air pollution built after 1975 to install pollution control technologies but exempted existing pollution sources. Many of these existing operations, especially major pollution sources, such as coal-burning electric-power plants, continued to operate older facilities with occasional modification instead of building new plants with the required expensive pollution control technologies. This situation, in effect, perpetuated thousands of major air-polluting facilities well beyond their normal lifetimes and prompted Congress to amend the law.

The Clean Air Act Amendments of 1977 added to the original legislation a new source review (NSR) provision that required older air-polluting facilities to install the best available control technologies whenever they underwent "major modification," a strategy meant to discourage the continued existence of the older pollution sources. At the same time, however, the act still permitted companies to carry out "routine maintenance" of existing facilities without replacing them. Thus, a crucial issue arose: When did "routine maintenance" become a "major modification"? As one legal analyst explained,

> The wording of the NSR was vague enough to allow companies to fight regulators over the definition of major modification. . . . [The companies] could try to define almost all construction on existing plants as minor or routine. The grandfather clause exempting old plants, combined with uncertainty about what, exactly, was routine maintenance, permitted companies not only to keep old, heavily polluting plants running, but to use those plants to boost output in a way that escaped Clean Air Act emission requirements.[21]

Companies—especially the electricity utilities—fought the EPA over the NSR standards. Throughout the 1980s and most of the 1990s, the federal and state governments struggled with the definition of *major modification,* and few companies were compelled to upgrade their existing facilities by the NSR provisions.

This stalemate ended in the late 1990s. New York, on behalf of other Northeastern states downwind of air pollution originating from Midwestern power plants, sued several large Midwestern utilities in 1999 for failure to comply with the NSR standards that required new pollution controls. The Clinton administration also sued 51 large, coal-fired electricity utilities for similar reasons. The stakes were enormous. The court rulings would affect 17,000 power plants nationally, involve several billion dollars in potential new pollution control costs for the utilities, and possibly determine the breadth and quality of national air pollution control for decades. The new litigation was vigorously opposed by the coal-fired electricity utilities and their trade associations, the petroleum and mining industries, major manufacturing corporations, and virtually every other economic interest at risk if the NSR provisions were aggressively enforced as interpreted by the Clinton administration's EPA. Corporations with facilities at risk argued that the EPA's standards for defining *major modification* were unclear and that, in any case, there were more economically and technically efficient ways of achieving the purposes of the NSR than an inflexible requirement that new facilities must install the best new pollution controls.

This litigation was still before the courts when the 2000 presidential elections brought a sea change to environmental regulation in Washington. The new Bush administration strongly identified with the nation's energy producers and their regulatory viewpoint while opposing the EPA's general command-and-control approach to air pollution regulation during the Clinton era. In addition, the first National Energy Plan proposed by the Bush administration tilted heavily in the direction of new energy production and called for, among other increased production measures, the building of 1,300 to 1,900 new electric-power plants by 2020. Bush preferred to terminate the Clinton administration's lawsuits against the electricity utilities and, instead, to encourage expansion of the electric-power industry by relaxing the NSR standards and creating a market for emissions trading as an alternative to technological controls for all new electric-power plants. Congressional Democrats generally regarded the Bush proposals as a reincarnation of Reagan's antienvironmentalism, and debate over reforming the NSR tended to divide along party lines. In late 2003, the EPA proposed revising the NSR regulations by generously increasing the opportunities for companies to enlarge their existing pollution sources without installing the pollution control technologies that the NSR seemed to require.[22] A coalition of environmental, public health, and state regulatory agencies promptly initiated a lawsuit challenging the EPA's new proposal. The coalition charged that the proposal would drastically increase the volume of future air pollution and further discourage the replacement of older, polluting facilities with newer, environmentally cleaner ones, and a federal court agreed.[23]

The EPA was now under court order to rewrite its NSR standard again. In late 2005, the EPA proposed—to the satisfaction of most environmental groups—a new NSR standard creating nationwide consistency in how states implemented the program for electricity-generating units. The proposed changes would standardize the emissions tests used in NSR to determine whether a physical or operational change at a power plant would cause an emission increase that would require the plant to install additional pollution controls. By the end of 2006, a series of additional federal court decisions had largely eliminated the NSR standards supported by the Bush administration. The new, tougher NSR standards were, for the moment, in place and would, if implemented, affect 800 electric-power plants and 17,000 factories nationally. The EPA, however, initiated no new enforcement actions until the Obama administration took office; then, as major electricity utilities expected (and regretted), the EPA declared its intention to enforce aggressively the new NSR standards.

Urban smog, airborne toxics, and small particulates are a few among many ambient air problems challenging the nation's ability to realize the ambitious goals set by the CAA in 1970. These problems test the nation's technological skill and economic resiliency. They will challenge the political determination of its officials and the public's commitment to the environmental protection that the majority professes to support. These problems are also reminders of how incrementally slow the implementation and how modest the achievements of the CAA have been. The nation's experience with regulating water pollution has been much the same.

Regulating Water Quality

The nation's aquatic inheritance is not just water but different water systems, each essential to modern U.S. society and each currently threatened, or already severely polluted, by different combinations of pollutants.

Surface Water

The nation's surface waters—streams, rivers, lakes, wetlands, and coastal areas—are the nation's most visible water resources. Almost 99 percent of the population lives within 50 miles of a publicly owned lake. Streams, rivers, and lakes account for a high proportion of all recreational activities, commercial fishing grounds, and industrial water resources. Because surface waters are so intensively used and so highly visible, their rapidly accelerating degradation became the most immediate cause for congressional action in the 1960s and 1970s; arresting water pollution and restoring the nation's once high water quality became a focal point for environmental legislation. In 1972, Congress enacted the nation's most important water pollution control legislation, the Federal Water Pollution Control Act, also called the Clean Water Act. The legislation created a national water pollution regulatory program intended to achieve "zero discharge of pollutants into waters of the United States by 1985" and "fishable and swimmable waters" by 1983. These ambitious goals were more inspirational than achievable, but they did signal the onset of a determined federal and state government initiative to reclaim degraded waters, protect endangered watersheds, and preserve pristine rivers, streams, and lakes.

Most of the fragmentary data available on national water quality since 1970 has come from monitoring surface-water conditions. Surprisingly little reliable information exists about the quality of most U.S. surface waters Even after the turn of the 21st century, estimates of surface-water quality continue to be ambiguous and uncertain, largely because comprehensive, reliable monitoring data remain unavailable. Federal agencies such as the EPA and the CEQ have traditionally based their surface-water-quality indexes on only six pollutants, excluding common sources of water degradation such as heavy metals, synthetic organic compounds, and dissolved solids. In general, surface-water quality seems, despite some spectacular achievements, to have remained in about the same condition since the late 1980s. It is often difficult, in any case, to know what significance to impute to available statistics because EPA assessments cover only about one third of all U.S. surface-water area. This translates into an assessment of approximately 19 percent of river miles, 43 percent of lake acres, and 36 percent of estuary square miles. Wetlands are still largely terra incognita; little more than 8 percent of wetlands acreage has been evaluated for water quality.

The states' haphazard water-quality monitoring creates massive information deficiencies that frustrate accurate national assessment. Just how problematic is state monitoring is suggested by a GAO description of the evaluated data used by many states. "Evaluated data," explains the GAO report, "include site-specific monitoring data more than 5 years old and information that serves as an indicator of water quality conditions, such as anecdotal evidence or reports on wildlife or habitat conditions"[24]—in short, sophisticated guesswork.

Considering the nation's population growth and economic expansion since 1980, the stability of water quality must be considered an achievement of sorts—it could have been much worse. Nevertheless, the quality of the nation's surface water apparently is not greatly improved. The goals of the FWPCA more than four decades after its enactment, still seem decades from achievement. Equally important, available and reliable water-quality information remains inadequate. And so, things will remain as long as the dull but essential task of data collection remains politically unattractive and underfunded.

The leading causes of surface-water pollution, along with the data limitations, can be identified readily (see Figure 6–2). By far, the largest contributors to this pollution are agricultural runoff, urban runoff, and other sources of nonpoint pollution (i.e., pollution arising from diffuse, multiple sources rather than from a pipe or other point source); these are the most technologically and politically formidable pollutants yet to be controlled.

Figure 6–2 Major Sources of Impairment in Assessed Rivers and Streams

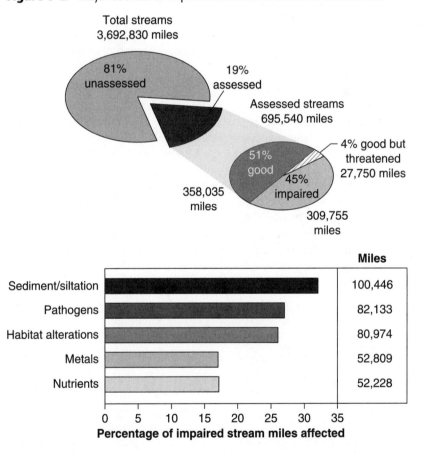

Source: U.S. EPA, Office of Water, "National Water Quality Inventory and Report to Congress, 2002 Reporting Cycle," Report no. EPA-841-R-07–001, Washington, DC, 2007, 8.

Note: Percentages do not add to 100 percent because more than one cause or source may impair a water body.

The Federal Water Pollution Control Amendments. The 1972 amendments to the Clean Water Act completely changed the substance of the earlier legislation and established the regulatory framework that now prevails. The most important provisions include the following:

1. *Goals.* The amendments established two broad goals whose achievement, if possible, assumed an unprecedented regulatory structure and unusually rapid technological innovation:

   a. That "the discharge of pollutants into navigable waters of the United States be eliminated by 1985."
   b. That "wherever attainable, an interim goal of water quality which provides for the protection and propagation of fish, shellfish and wildlife and provides for recreation in and on the water be achieved by 1 July 1983."

2. *Regulating existing dischargers.* The legislation required that all direct dischargers into navigable waterways satisfy two different standards: one relating to water quality and the other to effluent limits. The water-quality standards, established by the states according to guidelines issued by the EPA, were to identify the use for a body of water into which a polluter was discharging (such as recreation, fishing, boating, waste disposal, or irrigation) and to establish limits on discharges to ensure that use. Effluent standards, established by the EPA, were to identify what technologies any discharger had to use to control its effluents. In meeting these dual requirements, the polluter was required to achieve whichever standard was stricter. A different set of standards was established for municipal wastewater treatment facilities.

   a. *Effluent limits for existing nonmunicipal sources.* Except for city waste treatment plants, all existing dischargers were required to have technological controls prescribed by the EPA:

      i. The "best practicable control technology currently available" by July 1, 1979.
      ii. The "best available technology economically achievable" by July 1983.

   b. *Effluent limits for municipal treatment plants.* All treatment plants in existence on July 1, 1977, were required to have "secondary-treatment" levels. All facilities, regardless of age, were required to have "the best practicable treatment technology" by July 1, 1983.

   c. *Effluent limits for new nonmunicipal sources.* All new sources of discharge, except municipal treatment plants, were required to use

control technologies based on "the best available demonstrated control technology, operating methods or other alternatives."

   d. *Toxic effluent standards.* The EPA was required to establish special standards for any discharge determined to be toxic.

3. *Regulating indirect dischargers.* Many pollutants, including chemical toxics, are released into municipal wastewater systems by industrial and commercial sources and later enter waterways through city sewage-treatment plants that are unable to eliminate them. The law required the EPA to establish pretreatment standards, which were to prevent the discharge of any pollutant through a public sewer that "interferes with, passes through or otherwise is incompatible with such works."

4. *Federal and state enforcement.* The EPA was authorized to delegate responsibility for enforcing most regulatory provisions to qualified states, which would issue permits to all polluters specifying the conditions for their effluent discharges.

5. *Waste treatment grants.* The act authorized the expenditure of $18 billion between 1973 and 1975 to assist local communities in building necessary wastewater treatment facilities. The federal government assumed 75 percent of the capital cost for constructing the facilities.

6. *Nonpoint pollution regulation.* Amendments added in 1987 required each state to have a plan approved by the EPA for controlling pollution from nonpoint sources. Such plans must include "best management practices," but states are permitted to decide whether to require owners and managers to use such practices or to make their use voluntary.

The 1972 legislation was also intended to be technology forcing, in effect, compelling the nation to create new technologies, if necessary, to meet is ambitious pollution control standards.

Even the most ardent advocates of the legislation, however, recognized that the rigorous compliance deadlines for effluent treatment and wastewater facility construction would not be attained. They were convinced that pressing technology ultimately worked—eliminating all pollutants from the nation's waters hardly seemed impossible to a people who could launch a satellite carrying their language a billion light-years into space. Acknowledging the likelihood of short-term failures, advocates of the legislation were nonetheless convinced that only by pressing technology relentlessly for rapid compliance with regulations could they sustain the sense of urgency and bring sufficient weight of federal authority to bear on polluters to obtain their long-term objectives.

The Political Setting. The political struggle over implementation of the FWPCAA has been shaped by several factors. First, the implementation of the legislation is federalized. The 1972 law permitted the states to decide on the designated use for a body of water. In general, state regulatory agencies are more vulnerable than is Washington, DC, to pressure from local water polluters to designate uses for bodies of water that will permit moderate to heavy pollution. This propensity of local regulatory agencies to accommodate regulated interests also extends to enforcement of designated water uses and the associated emission controls. Regulated interests often are likely to press vigorously for a major state role in the administration and enforcement of water-quality standards, believing that this works to their advantage more than implementation through the EPA's regional and national offices. State enforcement of pollution controls on major dischargers has improved significantly since 1972, but many violators still go undetected or unpunished.

Thirty-five states have assumed major implementation responsibilities, such as issuing and enforcing permits for effluent dischargers, initiating requests for federal grants to build new local waste treatment facilities, and supervising the administration of the grant programs in their jurisdictions. The states thus exercise considerable influence on program implementation directly through their own participation—and the pursuit of their own interests in the program—and through their congressional delegations, which remain ever vigilant in protecting the interests of the folks back home. Moreover, conflict arising from differing state and federal viewpoints on program implementation becomes interjected immediately into the daily administrative implementation of the law. Control standards vary greatly among the states for the same pollutant, often provoking states with strict standards to complain that more lenient states enjoy an unfair advantage in the competition for new business. Among six major states, for instance, the same five toxic pollutants were treated very differently:

> In some states, the permitting authorities consistently established numeric limits on the discharges, while in other states, the authorities consistently required monitoring. In some states, no controls were imposed. In addition, the numeric discharge limits for specific pollutants differed from state to state and even within the same state for facilities of similar capacity.[25]

The political character of the program also depends on the enormous administrative discretion left to the EPA in prescribing the multitude of technologies that must be used by effluent dischargers to meet the many different standards established in the law. In 1972, when the Clean Water Act was amended, for instance, about 20,000 industrial dischargers were

pouring pollutants into more than 2,500 municipal waste treatment facilities. The EPA was charged with identifying the pretreatment standards to be used by each major class of industrial discharger. This might eventually require standards for several hundred different classes and modified standards for subclasses. The final standards issued by the EPA in 1976 for industries producing "canned and preserved fruits and vegetables" alone contained specifications for 51 subcategories. Administrators also are limited by the state of the art in treatment technologies and by dependence on the regulated interests for information concerning the character of the discharger's production processes and technical capacities. We already have noted that administrative discretion invites political pressure and conflict. The technical determinations required in setting effluent standards also invite controversy and litigation.

Finally, the program's implementation has been affected continually by the active, if not always welcome, intervention of the White House, Congress, and the federal courts in the program's development. Federal and state regulatory agencies have had to conduct the program in a highly political environment, in which all major actions have been subject to continual scrutiny, debate, and assessment by elective public officials and judges. This is hardly surprising for a program involving so many billions of dollars and so many politically and economically sensitive interests. But, as we observe later in this chapter, the economic and environmental costs of such politicized administration are high.

A Stubborn Problem: Nonpoint Pollution. The most common source of surface-water pollution remains virtually uncontrolled in every state since the 1972 passage of the FWPCAA. Nonpoint pollution is estimated to be the major cause of pollution in 65 percent of the stream-miles not meeting state standards for their designated use.[26] Overall, more than one third of the stream-miles in the United States appear to be affected by nonpoint pollution. Nonpoint pollution also affects groundwater quality. Earlier, we noted that nonpoint pollution is the leading cause of water-quality impairment. Figure 6–3, which portrays the proportion of nitrogen in major streams across the United States originating from nonpoint sources, illustrates the geographical breadth of nonpoint pollution.

This pollution is especially troublesome for several reasons. Its origin is often elusive. Almost all states lack enough information to identify most of the nonpoint sources polluting their surface waters.[27] It is not easily controlled technically or economically. Many different sources require many different control strategies. The largest source of nonpoint pollution is agriculture; croplands, pasture, and rangelands together pollute about one third of the nation's stream-miles with metabolic wastes from animals, sediment, fertilizers, pesticides, dissolved solids, and other materials.

Figure 6–3   Point and Nonpoint Sources of Nitrogen in Watersheds of the
Continental United States

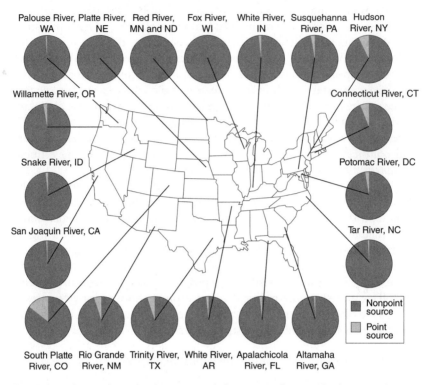

*Proportions of nonpoint and point sources of nitrogen vary in watersheds across the
continental United States. Commercial fertilizer and manure typically constitute the
major sources of nitrogen to the first NAWQA study units. Atmospheric nitrogen is
significant in most study units except in the far West and the Northern Great Plains.
Point sources are an important source of nutrients to watersheds near large urban
areas, such as Denver in the South Platte River Basin and Hartford in the Connecticut,
Housatonic, and Thames River Basins.*

Source: U.S. Department of the Interior, U.S. Geological Survey, "The Quality of Our
Nation's Water—Nutrients and Pesticides," Circular No. 1225 (November 2000), 29.

Agricultural runoff and urban storm water runoff are the major causes of
the eutrophication of lakes, whereby dissolved organic substances create
such a high level of oxygen demand in the waters that higher forms of
plants and animals die from oxygen deprivation. Eutrophication eventually
leaves most lakes lifeless.

Reducing agricultural pollution requires several difficult strategies
because technological solutions are rarely available. Most often, production

practices must be altered. Farmers might be encouraged, or required, to reduce the volume of fertilizer, pesticides, and other chemicals used in crop production. Animal populations might be limited or dispersed. New crop and land management techniques might reduce soil runoff. In many instances, land-use planning might be used to prevent, or reduce, agricultural activities. But, powerful agricultural groups and members of Congress for whom they are a major constituency believe such strategies will have adverse economic impacts and have opposed most measures intended to reduce agricultural runoff by most of these methods. Many state governments, fearful of damaging a major component of the state economy, are reluctant to do more than encourage farmers to voluntarily seek ways to limit their pollution runoff.

The current strategy for controlling nonpoint pollution has set regulators on a collision course not only with agricultural organizations but also with the commercial timber industry, the commercial and residential construction industry, meat packers and shippers, coal-mining firms, and a multitude of trades and professions associated with each. Since the early 1990s, the EPA has required states to identify all their waters that fail water-quality standards and, for each impaired water, to identify the amount by which each nonpoint pollutant must be reduced to meet these water-quality standards. Specifically, each state is required to specify for each nonpoint pollutant a total maximum daily load (TMDL), that is, the maximum amount of each pollutant permitted in each water body over a 24-hour period. This calculation has proved to be enormously difficult and controversial. The scale of the undertaking is staggering. The National Academy of Sciences reported in 2000 that

> Given the most recent lists of impaired waters submitted by EPA, there are about 21,000 polluted river segments, lakes, and estuaries making up over 300,000 river and shore miles and 5 million lake acres. The number of TMDLs required for these impaired waters is greater than 40,000 [and] most states are required to meet an 8- to 13-year deadline for completion of the TMDLs.[28]

Nonetheless, most states have created some TMDLs or have attempted to do so. Perhaps the most nationally visible conflict over these calculations has arisen from efforts by the state of Florida and the federal government to create TMDLs for dissolved phosphorous in runoff degrading the Everglades from the vast sugar-growing region north of Lake Okachobee. In this instance, as in most others involving the creation of TMDLs, scientific and legal controversy abounds and litigation proliferates. The TMDL calculation remains inherently problematic, and state regulators complain that the process is so adversarial that TMDL should mean "too many damn lawyers."

"This State's Gone Hog Wild": The Battle over Concentrated Animal Farms. In mid-1997, corporate animal farms first made national news—and in the worst possible way. In eastern North Carolina, one corporate hog farm, home to 12,000 pigs, was flooded by runoff from heavy rain. The swirling runoff flushed 25 million gallons of feces and urine from the farm's 8-acre waste lagoon into a knee-deep tide that inundated surrounding cotton and tobacco fields and then poured into the New River. The spill killed 10 million fish along a 17-mile stretch of the river between Richlands and Jacksonville, closed 364,000 acres of wetlands to shell fishing for months, and prompted Rep. Charlie Rose, D-NC, to demand that the EPA declare a moratorium on new factory farms until their environmental contamination could be controlled. The following year, North Carolina's largely corporate hog farms produced more than 16 million hogs—the nation's second-largest state hog production. "This state's gone hog wild," Rose complained. "We have a wonderful quality of life here, but a greedy, unregulated hog industry will ruin it overnight if we're not careful."[29]

The North Carolina spectacle was among the first of an increasing number of highly publicized incidents to thrust the problem of concentrated animal farming into national visibility and frame an ongoing political struggle in almost every agricultural state. Concentrated animal feeding operations (CAFOs) are a textbook example of the vexing regulatory challenge posed by a rapidly evolving environmental problem accompanied by meager relevant information and fragmented regulatory laws. CAFOs are the collision point between the rapidly accelerating vertical integration in U.S. food production and the tired pace of regulatory reform—another instance of regulation racing to catch up with economic and technological innovation. Moreover, the issue is a tangle of surface water, groundwater, and drinking water regulatory problems falling between the margins of state and federal water pollution laws and provoking the jurisdictional problems common to regulatory federalism.

CAFOs are quickly transforming virtually all sectors of major animal production in the United States—cattle, hogs, poultry, turkeys, and dairy. The EPA describes these farms as

> facilities that confine animal feeding activities, thereby concentrating animal populations, animal manure, and animal mortality. AFO [animal feeding operation] activities can cause a range of environmental and public health problems, including oxygen depletion and disease transmission in surface water, pathogens and nutrient contamination in surface and ground water, methane emissions to the air, and excessive buildup of toxins, metals, and nutrients in soil.[30]

CAFO farming has expanded rapidly until, currently, more than 77 percent of the beef cattle and 72 percent of hogs and (egg-)layers in the United States are raised and managed on large farms. CAFOs also produce prodigious quantities of waste that must be managed. A large farm with 800,000 hogs, for example, produces more than 1.6 million tons of manure per year, which is one and a half times more than the annual sanitary waste produced by the city of Philadelphia, Pennsylvania (about 1 million tons), with a population of almost 1.5 million people.[31] The production of small, family-owned AFOs is diminishing rapidly in the wake of increasing CAFOs. Here are two examples:

- "The structure of the pork industry has also changed dramatically during the past three decades. The number of hog producers in the United States was more than 1 million in the 1960s but fell to about 67,000 by 2005. . . . Although the total inventory of hogs has changed little over the years, the structural shift toward concentration has been dramatic with the 110 largest hog operations in the country, each of which has over 50,000 hogs, now constituting 55% of the total national inventory (USDA 2005)."[32]
- "The number of farms in Iowa raising hogs decreased from 64,000 in 1980 to 10,500 in 2000—an 84% decrease—while the average number of hogs per farm increased from 250 to 1,430 over this same period. . . . Farms with more than 500 hogs now account for 65% of the statewide inventory and 75% of the U.S. inventory."[33]

More than 7,000 very large CAFOs currently operate in the United States, most owned by large food production corporations and housing from 1,000 to more than 100,000 animals each. Currently, 10 corporations produce 92 percent of all domestic poultry, and 50 pork farms account for almost half the nation's pork production.

In Oklahoma, North Carolina, Missouri, Georgia, Colorado, Texas, and Utah—to cite but a few examples—corporate animal production has become a major agricultural industry and the provocation for bitter political conflict. The EPA estimates that groundwater in 17 states has been impaired by fecal streptococci and fecal coliform bacteria originating on animal feedlots. In these states, CAFOs are more than an environmentalist matter; they set smaller family farmers against corporate farms, rural legislators against urban ones, and economic boomers against proponents of slow growth.

At least four major laws, including the Clean Water Act and the CAA, provide the EPA with authority to regulate some aspects of CAFO waste, but no single federal law currently creates an integrated regulatory approach.[34] The states vary enormously in the extent to which their existing water pollution laws control CAFOs. Intense disputes have become common concerning how strictly CAFOs should be regulated and whether their continued proliferation should be encouraged. Congressional members from every state experiencing a growth surge in large CAFOs have introduced legislation calling for a comprehensive federal regulatory program affecting all states and thereby eliminating the possibility that some states might create so-called pollution havens for large CAFOs. Although President Clinton called for newer, more stringent regulations in his 1998 Clean Water Action Plan, neither Congress nor the responsible federal regulatory agencies initiated tougher comprehensive measures, an impasse due largely to conflicts between Washington and the states over their respective roles in a new regulatory regime and to disagreement among major corporate animal producers over acceptable regulations.

By 2008, CAFOs so dominated commercial animal production that the EPA, despite growing state action, initiated a needed national regulatory strategy to address the environmental issues. From its inception, the initiative has been limited by the EPA's lack of relevant data and limited resources for implementation. As a 2008 GAO report noted,

> For example, with regard to water quality, EPA officials acknowledged that the potential human health and environmental impacts of some CAFO water pollutants, such as nitrogen, phosphorus, and pathogens, are well known. However, they also stated that EPA does not have data on the number and location of CAFOs nationwide and the amount of discharges from these operations. Without this information and data on how pollutant concentrations vary by type of operation, it is difficult to estimate the actual discharges occurring and to assess the extent to which CAFOs may be contributing to water pollution.[35]

The EPA expects to have relevant data available in about 2013. The CAFO wastes also create a variety of potentially hazardous and unregulated air emissions because the human and environmental health effects have not been characterized sufficiently to determine their relevance to the CAA. Among these emissions are methane, nitrous oxide, hydrogen sulfide, ammonia, and possibly the products from decomposition of animal manure and urea, as well as particulate matter from dry manure, bedding and feed materials, biological matter (animal dander and feathers), and unpaved dirt lots.[36]

Groundwater

During the 1980s, the nation's groundwater became a major concern. Lying below Earth's upper porous surface and a lower layer of impermeable rock, groundwater percolates through the upper layer and collects until it eventually saturates subsurface soil and rock. Much of this water flows slowly to the sea through permeable layers of sand or gravel called aquifers. These aquifers sustain the life and vitality of communities throughout much of the United States. Groundwater is as essential as surface water to the nation's existence, and it is far more abundant—the annual flow of groundwater is 50 times the volume of surface flows, and most lies within a half mile of Earth's surface. Almost 50 percent of the U.S. population and 95 percent of its rural residents depend on groundwater for domestic uses. More than 40 percent of all agricultural irrigation originates from groundwater. Perhaps most importantly, more than 105 million Americans receive their drinking water from public water systems whose source is groundwater.[37] Because groundwater filters slowly through many levels of fine soil as it percolates downward and flows onward through the aquifers, it traditionally has been virtually free of harmful pollutants. Today, however, groundwater is seriously degraded in many areas of the United States.

Although groundwater monitoring has improved since Earth Day 1970, the complexity of groundwater systems and the expense of monitoring have convinced the EPA that "we may never have a complete picture of the nature and extent of the problem."[38] But, the EPA has identified an enormous number of actual or potential sources of groundwater contamination:

- About 13,000 hazardous waste sites that are now potential candidates for the Superfund National Priority List (an inventory of the most dangerous sites)
- Millions of septic systems
- More than 180,000 surface impoundments, such as pits, ponds, and lagoons
- An estimated 500 hazardous-waste land disposal facilities and about 16,000 municipal and other landfills
- Millions of underground storage tanks (USTs)
- Thousands of underground injection wells, used to dispose of hazardous and solid wastes by flushing them into deep aquifers
- Millions of tons of pesticides and fertilizers spread on the ground, mostly in rural areas

Many Programs, Many Governments, Many Agencies. The 1977 discovery of massive groundwater contamination caused by the abandoned hazardous waste site at New York's Love Canal became the nation's first groundwater crisis. Groundwater contamination has been a crisis-driven issue, thrust on governmental agendas by waves of public apprehension following revelations of widespread groundwater contamination from hazardous waste dumps, agricultural chemicals, and industrial and governmental chemical accidents. Improved monitoring also has added urgency to the groundwater issue by revealing previously unknown chemical contamination (although often in only trace amounts). But, monitoring has just begun, and the quality of most underground waters remains unknown.

Traditionally, groundwater management has been considered a state and local governmental responsibility. Although the federal government has no comprehensive groundwater management program, approximately 45 different federal programs affect groundwater in some manner.[39] The primary federal responsibility for implementing many of the major programs affecting groundwater rests with the EPA. In addition to the FWPCAA, other important legislation affecting groundwater quality includes the Marine Protection, Research and Sanctuaries Act (1972); the Safe Drinking Water Act (SDWA; 1974) and its 1986 amendments; the RCRA (1976); and the Superfund legislation (1980) together with its 1984 amendments. However, many other agencies and programs are also involved. The mélange of federal agencies and programs involved in groundwater management ensure incoherence, inconsistency, and competing authority in the federal government's approach to groundwater problems.

The states' considerable responsibility for groundwater management has been acquired through federal legislation and their own initiative. Forty-one states currently have their own groundwater-quality standards, although little consistency exists among them. The number of groundwater contaminants regulated varies from 14 in one state to 190 in another. In addition, almost all states have assumed responsibility for implementing federal drinking water standards established under the SDWA.

Controlling subsurface pollution is troublesome because groundwater filters very slowly as it flows. An aquifer may move no more than 10 to 100 feet annually. In any case, many toxic contaminants are not captured or neutralized by filtering. Moreover, the extent of groundwater pollution may be impossible to estimate adequately because the pollution plume radiating outward through an aquifer from a pollution source can take a number of unpredictable directions. Often, plumes will contaminate millions or billions of gallons of water.

Moreover, many sources of groundwater contamination are still being identified. The nation's estimated 1.2 million abandoned oil and gas wells, of which perhaps 200,000 are not properly plugged, are examples. Abandoned wells, often drilled to a depth of more than 1 mile, can contaminate groundwater with brine, which is four times more saline than seawater and contains heavy metals, radioactivity, and other possible toxic substances (toxics). In Texas, perhaps 40,000 to 50,000 abandoned wells may still pose pollution problems, and an estimated 386,000 wells have never been registered. A Texas health official observed, "We've found leaking wells from the old days that were rock-plugged, bucket-plugged, tree-stump plugged and even one plugged with nothing more than a glass jug." In Louisiana, almost 1,500 unplugged wells are uncontrolled because money is lacking.[40]

Continuing Chemical Contamination. The many substances known or suspected to contaminate groundwater defy concise enumeration. One survey indicated that the states collectively have set standards for approximately 35 inorganic compounds, 39 volatile organic compounds, 125 nonvolatile organic compounds, and 56 pesticides, among other substances.[41] These chemicals represent only a small portion of those used in the U.S. economy and found in groundwater. These contaminants originate from many sources. The states are just beginning to regulate many of these sources, such as USTs, underground injection wells, and abandoned waste sites. Although most states have at least some standards for groundwater quality, it is unclear how well the standards are enforced. Among groundwater contaminants, synthetic chemicals and nutrients, particularly nitrates and phosphates, remain especially difficult to regulate because of their great number and wide diffusion in the ecosystem. Most states set standards for and monitor only a fraction of the chemicals likely to be present in groundwater. Almost all states identify toxics as a major source of water-quality problems. These toxics can originate in thousands of abandoned and poorly regulated hazardous waste sites or from agricultural activity, injection wells, municipal landfills, and sludges. Sludges (the semisolid wastes produced in many air and water pollution control activities) often contain many hazardous or toxic chemicals.

During the 1990s, federal and state regulators made three chemical groundwater contaminants a priority: nutrients, pesticides, and USTs. Nutrients, such as nitrates, are found most often in groundwater affected by agricultural production, including both crops and livestock. Nitrate infiltration is not now considered a major national problem, but pesticides and USTs are more troublesome. In the 1990s, at least 143 pesticides and 21 of their transformation products were detected in the groundwater of 43 states. These pesticide concentrations usually do not exceed state water-quality standards for agricultural areas. However, pesticides may be a more serious problem in nonagricultural areas, particularly around golf courses, commercial and residential areas, rights-of-way, timber production and processing areas, and public gardens. In any case, pesticides are ubiquitous in all U.S. waters. The U.S. Geological Survey reported that more than 90 percent of the water and fish samples from all streams contained one or several pesticides, and half the wells sampled contained pesticides—all evidence that pesticides have seriously infiltrated U.S. groundwater.

A major concern is the limited information available about the health effects associated with exposure to most pesticides, even in trace amounts. Federal groundwater standards, called maximum contaminant limits (MCLs), have yet to be established for most of these pesticides. Existing MCLs are often based on incomplete information. The U.S. Geological Survey has cautioned that

> Existing criteria may be revised as more is learned about the toxicity of these compounds. . . . MCLs and other criteria are currently based on individual pesticides and do not account for possible cumulative effects if several different pesticides are present in the same well. Finally, many pesticides and most transformation products have not been widely sampled for in ground water and very little sampling has been done in urban and suburban areas, where pesticide use is often high.[42]

Governmental concern about USTs grew steadily through the 1990s with the increasing number of discovered sites. Five to six million tanks, most used for retail gasoline or petroleum storage, are buried throughout the United States. Of the 1.7 million USTs currently regulated, perhaps as many as 20 percent are estimated to be leaking. These leaks contaminate the groundwater, damage sewer lines and buried cables, poison crops, and ignite fires and explosions. More than 80 percent of the tanks in use were constructed of bare steel, are easily corroded, and had to be replaced or severely modified to meet new federal standards mandated in the mid-1990s. Unfortunately, many of these USTs have been abandoned and long forgotten. Often located under active or abandoned gasoline stations, airports, large trucking firms, farms, golf courses, and manufacturing plants, many leaking sites may never be discovered.

Federal law required all known USTs to comply with stringent new control standards by December 1998. As a result, 1.3 million substandard USTs have been closed, and about 760,500 have been registered under the new standards with regulators. However, discovering and controlling the remaining USTs will be a formidable matter. Among those yet to be controlled, half of the abandoned USTs known to regulators have been orphaned (that is, no identifiable owner can be found), and perhaps as many as half of the remaining abandoned USTs (an estimated 76,000) may never be located.[43]

Drinking Water

We need look no further than the kitchen tap for an emerging groundwater concern. All ecosystems are intricately and subtly interrelated. The negligent dumping of contaminants into surface water and groundwater eventually follows a circle of causality, delivering the danger back to its source. So it is in the United States.

The average American uses 100 gallons of water daily (most of it to water lawns and wash motor vehicles). More than 80 percent of the nation's community water systems depend on groundwater for domestic use, and the remainder use surface water to provide Americans with the 1 billion glasses of drinking water consumed daily. Recognizing that community drinking water was threatened by the rising volume of pollutants entering surface and groundwater, Congress passed the SDWA in 1974 to ensure that public water supplies achieved minimum health standards. In 1977, the EPA, following the SDWA's mandate, began to set national primary drinking water standards that established maximum levels in drinking water for microbiological contaminants, turbidity, and chemical agents, and by 1985, standards existed for approximately 30 substances. Standard setting lagged badly at the EPA, however, and in another demonstration of excessive congressional control, the 1986 amendments to the SDWA required the EPA to adopt standards for 61 more contaminants by mid-1989, create 25 more standards from a new list by 1991, and set standards for 25 additional chemicals every three years thereafter. Once standards are established, the states are given primary responsibility for enforcing them, and other provisions of the act, on more than 79,000 public water systems. Since the 1986 amendments were written, the number of regulated contaminants has expanded to 72 and reached 288 by 2013.[44]

By 1996, it was apparent that this excursion into legislative micromanagement was ill-conceived, and in an enlightened moment rare to its oversight of the EPA, Congress relaxed its grip on the EPA's regulatory process with the 1996 amendments to the SDWA. The amendments instructed the EPA to focus its efforts on the highest-risk drinking water contaminants, with special attention to those particularly dangerous to the elderly and children—a more manageable and productive task. Equally important, the 1996 amendments contained right-to-know provisions that required all community drinking water systems to provide consumers with periodic information about the quality of their drinking water, about compliance with existing federal and state quality controls, and about opportunities for public involvement in local drinking water regulation. The states welcomed other provisions of the amendments that offered federal financial assistance to upgrade local water systems because a great many states lacked the financial, technical, and staff resources to enforce even the SDWA's minimum standards, and many small and large water systems were virtually ignored.

In many respects, the SDWA has been a success. By the end of the 2011, about 90 percent of the U.S. population was served by community water systems with no reported violations of existing health-based standards, and almost 100 contaminants were regulated under the act.[45] Unfortunately, many water systems, including some of the largest, are still infiltrated by dangerous concentrations of chemical and biological contaminants—many of which have no set standards and, as a consequence, have no regulatory controls. For example, as Map 6–1 illustrates, a very substantial proportion of the sources for public water supply sampled by the United States Geological Survey in 2010 revealed evidence of at least one pollutant exceeding safe levels for public health. In many cases, existing treatment technologies cannot fully remove many microbial and chemical contaminants, including synthetic organic compounds and pesticides.

Injection wells continue to be a major significant of drinking water contamination. More than 253,000 active or abandoned injection wells exist in the United States. About one half of all liquid hazardous waste generated in the United States is pumped into these injection wells, the largest portion from oil and gas production and refining facilities. Although liquid hazardous wastes are subject to federal regulation, no detailed national standards exist for the solid waste eliminated through the injection wells. Rural water supplies seem especially vulnerable to contamination from injection wells and

Map 6–1   Quality of Water from Public Wells in the United States

- One or more contaminants at concentrations greater than human-health benchmarks (206 wells)
- One or more contaminants at concentrations greater than one tenth of benchmarks, but less than benchmarks (539 wells)
- No contaminants at concentrations greater than one tenth of benchmarks, or no contaminants detected (187 wells)

Source: Patricia L. Toccalino and Jessica A. Hopple, "Quality of Water from Public-Supply Wells in the United States, 1993–2007: Overview of Major Findings," Circular 1346, U.S. Department of the Interior, U.S. Geological Survey, 20, available at pubs.usgs.gov/circ/1346/pdf/circ1346.pdf.

abandoned hazardous waste sites. A 1984 EPA assessment of rural water quality reported unsafe levels of cadmium in about one sixth of the nation's rural wells, mercury concentrations above safe levels in about one quarter of the wells, and lead at dangerous levels in one tenth of these wells.

Conclusion

Air and water are the primary issues on the environmental agenda. They are the first, most essential, most politically visible, and most important tasks of environmental restoration and regulation. The condition of the nation's air and water has been examined in considerable detail in this chapter to emphasize the daunting scope and complexity of the challenge of ecological restoration and to illustrate how short a distance the United States has traveled toward that goal since environmentalism emerged as a major political force in the country in the 1970s.

This chapter illustrates that the difficulties encountered in cleaning up the nation's air and water cannot be blamed solely on political incompetence, policy deficiencies, administrative failures, or scientific bungling. Rather, scientific and technological development continually poses new challenges to regulation by creating new chemicals and new technologies with unanticipated environmental effects. In addition, scientific research continually redefines and elaborates the nature of environmental degradation and its consequences—as shown in the study of airborne particulates and toxics, for instance—forcing continual rethinking of and change in regulatory strategies. And, even so unexciting and obscure an activity as environmental monitoring leads to new definitions of environmental degradation, as the study of groundwater contamination reveals. The United States, as with all other nations now committed to environmental restoration, must suffer a learning curve. It must acquire experience in a policy domain with which no government on Earth was involved a scant few decades ago. Those who govern can learn, but it takes time.

This review of the nation's current air and water pollution control programs is a sobering reminder that it will take a very long time, and require an enormous amount of money, scientific resources, and administrative skill, to give us back the healthful air and water we once had and hope to have again. So formidable a goal will not be easily realized. It may not happen in the lifetime of any American living today.

Suggested Readings

Bryner, Gary C. *Blue Skies, Green Politics: The Clean Air Act and Its Implementation.* 2nd ed. Washington, DC: CQ Press, 1995.

Cohen, Richard E. *Washington at Work: Back Rooms and Clean Air.* New York: Macmillan, 1992.

Morag-Levine, Noga. *Chasing the Wind: Regulating Air Pollution in the Common Law State*. Princeton, NJ: Princeton University Press, 2003.

Rogers, Peter. *America's Water: Federal Role and Responsibilities*. Cambridge, MA: MIT Press, 1999.

Sharpstein, Bill. *Dirty Water: One Man's Fight to Clean Up One of the World's Most Polluted Bays*. Berkeley: University of California Press, 2010.

Thornton, Joe. *Pandora's Poison: Chlorine, Health, and a New Environmental Strategy*. Cambridge, MA: MIT Press, 2000.

Notes

1. Industry estimates based on U.S. Department of Commerce, *Pollution Abatement Costs and Expenditures, 2005* (Washington, DC: Government Printing Office, 2008), v; and Robert Esworthy, "Federal Pollution Control Laws: How Are They Enforced?," *Congressional Research Service Report to Congress* (Washington, DC: Congressional Research Service, 2012, Summary, available at www.fas.org/sgp/crs/misc/RL34384.pdf (accessed September 5, 2012); public spending estimated from EOP, OMB "Outlays Function and Subfunction: 1962–2113, The Budget for Fiscal Year 2009, Historical Tables," Table 3.2, available at http://www.gpo.gov/fdsys/browse/collection.action?collectionCode=BUDGET&browsePath=Fiscal+Year+2 009&searchPath=Fiscal+Year+2009&leafLevelBrowse=false&isCollapsed=false&isOpen=true&packageid=BUDGET-2009-TAB&ycord=397 (accessed September 10, 2012).

2. U.S. EPA, Office of Air Quality, Planning, and Standards, Our Nation's Air: Status and Trends Through 2010, Report No. EPA-454/R-12-01 (Washington. DC: Author, February 2012), 1, available at http://www.epa.gov/airtrends/2010/ (accessed February 21, 2013).

3. U.S. GAO, "EPA: Major Performance and Accountability Challenges," Report no. GAO-01–257, Washington, DC, January 2001, 16.

4. EPA, Office of Water, "Water Quality Conditions in the United States: A Profile from the 1998 National Water Quality Inventory Report to Congress," Report no. EPA-841-F-00–006, Washington, DC, June 2000, 1.

5. Francis E. Rourke, *Bureaucracy, Politics, and Public Policy* (Boston: Little, Brown, 1969), 103.

6. Paul B. Downing and James N. Kimball, "Enforcing Pollution Laws in the U.S.," *Policy Studies Journal* 11 (September 1982): 55–65.

7. GAO, "EPA Cannot Ensure the Accuracy of Self-Reported Compliance Monitoring Data," Report no. GAO/RCED 93–21, Washington, DC, March 1993, 4; GAO, "Air Pollution: Difficulties in Implementing a National Air Permit Program," Report no. GAO/RCED 93–59, Washington, DC, February 1993, 2.

8. GAO, "Clean Water Act: Longstanding Issues Impact EPA's and States' Enforcement Efforts," Report no. GAO 10–165T, Washington, DC, October 15, 2009.

9. GAO, "Environmental Protection Agency: Major Management Challenges," Report no. GAO 09–434, Washington, DC, March 4, 2009.

10. EPA, "Climate Change-Greenhouse Gas Emissions," March 12, 2007, available at www.epa.gov/climatechange/emissions/index.html#proj (accessed August 14, 2009), based on data from U.S. Department of State, "U.S. Climate Action Report—2002," Washington, DC, 2002. For other U.S. projections, see EPA, "Inventory of U.S. Greenhouse Gas Emissions and Sinks: 1990–2004," Report no. USEPA-430-R-06–002, Washington, DC, April 2006; Juliet Eilperin, "Ex-EPA Chiefs Agree on Greenhouse Gas Lid," *Washington Post*, January 19, 2006, A04.

11. These summaries are adapted from Gary C. Bryner, *Blue Skies, Green Politics: The Clean Air Act of 1990 and Its Implementation*, 2nd ed. (Washington, DC: CQ Press, 1995), chap. 4.

12. Ibid., 126.
13. *New York Times,* March 29, 1989.
14. Allan R. Gold, "Shift in Fight on Air Rules," *New York Times*, October 5, 1989, B1.
15. Rebecca Adams, "Clean Air Policy Gets a Little Murkey," *CQ Weekly—In Focus,* August 4, 2008, available at http://www.cqpolitics.com/wmspage.cfm?docID=weekly report-000002933551&cpage=1 (accessed May 4, 2010).
16. Jeremy P. Jacobs, "In Blow to Obama Administration, Court Sends EPA Back to Drawing Board on Cross State Rule," *Greenwire*, August 21, 2012, available at www .eenews.net/public/Greenwire/2012/08/21/1 (accessed September 5, 2012).
17. EPA, Office of Air and Radiation, "1995 National Air Quality Trends Brochure: Particulate Matter (PM-10)," Washington, DC, 1997.
18. EPA, "Air Trends," available at www.epa.gov/air/airtrends/sixpoll.html (accessed March 1, 2007).
19. "EPA to Overhaul Air Pollution Standards," OMB Watch, November 10, 2009, available at http://www.ombwatch.org/node/10550 (accessed January 25, 2010).
20. Lesline Kaufman, "Pressured, E.P.A. Proposes Soot Limit," *New York Times,* June 15, 2012, A29.
21. Environmental Literacy Council, "New Clean Air Regulations," May 5, 2003, available at www.enviroliteracy.org/article.php/537.html (accessed March 20, 2004).
22. The details of this controversy are described by Katherine Q. Seelye, "Regulators Urge Easing U.S. Rules on Air Pollution," *New York Times,* January 8, 2002, A10; Christopher Drew and Richard Oppel, Jr., "Remaking Energy Policy: How Power Lobby Won Battle of Pollution Control at E.P.A.," *New York Times,* March 6, 2004, A10.
23. For details, see "Lawsuit Challenges Gutting of Crucial Clean Air Act Program," Earth Justice, October 27, 2003, available at www.earthjustice.org/news/print.html?ID=705 (accessed March 20, 2004).
24. GAO, "Water Quality: Identification and Remediation of Polluted Waters Impeded by Data Gaps," Report no. GAO/T-RCED 00–88, Washington, DC, February 2000, 5. See also GAO, "The Nation's Waters: Key Unanswered Questions About the Quality of Rivers and Streams," Report no. GAO/PEMD 86–6, Washington, DC, September 1986, 3.
25. GAO, "Drinking Water Quality," Report no. GAO/RCED 97–123, Washington, DC, July 29, 1997, 3–4.
26. EPA, "Environmental Progress and Challenges: EPA's Update," Washington, DC, 1996, 49.
27. GAO, "National Water Quality Inventory Does Not Accurately Represent Water Quality Conditions Nationwide," Report no. GAO/RCED 00–54, Washington, DC, March 22, 2000, 27.
28. National Academy of Sciences, Commission on Geosciences, Environment and Resources, *Assessing the TMDL Approach to Water Quality Management: Executive Summary* (Washington, DC: National Academies Press, 2000), 2.
29. Quoted in Michael Satchell, "Hog Heaven—and Hell," *U.S. News & World Report,* January 22, 1996, 55, 57–59. See also Natural Resources Defense Council, "America's Animal Factories: How States Fail to Prevent Pollution From Livestock Waste," December 1998, available at www.nrdc.org/water/pollution/factor/aafinx.asp (accessed March 30, 2004).
30. EPA, "Concentrated Animal Feeding Operations (CAFO)-Final Rule," available at http:// cfpub.epa.gov/npdes/afo/cafofinalrule.cfm?program_id=7 (accessed February 6, 2007).
31. GAO, "Concentrated Animal Feeding Operations: EPA Needs More Information and a Clearly Defined Strategy to More Effectively Protect Air and Water Quality," Report no. GAO 08–1177T, Washington, DC, September 24, 2008, 14.
32. Kelley J. Donham, Steven Wing, David Osterberg, Jan L. Flora, Carol Hodne, Kendall M. Thul, and Peter S. Thorne, "Community Health and Socioeconomic Issues Surrounding Concentrated Animal Feeding Operations," *Environmental Health Perspectives* (November 14, 2006), 1.

33. Peter S. Thorne, "Environmental Health Impacts of Concentrated Animal Feeding Operations: Anticipating Hazards—Searching for Solutions," *Environmental Health Perspectives*, 115, no. 2 (2007): 297, available at http://www.ncbi.nlm.nih.gov/pmc/articles/PMC1817701/ (accessed February 22, 2013).

34. Ibid., "Summary."

35. GAO, *Concentrated Animal Feeding Operations: EPA Needs More Information and a Clearly Defined Strategy to Protect Air and Water*, "Highlights," Publication GAO-08-944 (September 2008), available at http://www.gao.gov/assets/290/280238.html (accessed February 22, 2013).

36. National Academy of Sciences, "Air Emissions from Animal Feeding Operations: Current Knowledge, Future Need," Washington, DC, 2003.

37. Peakwater, "Quality of Water From Public-Supply Wells in the United States," available at http://peakwater.org/2010/05/quality-of-water-from-public-supply-wells-in-the-united-states (accessed September 10, 2012).

38. EPA, "Environmental Progress and Challenges," 52.

39. GAO, "Groundwater Quality: State Activities to Guard against Contaminants," Report no. GAO/PEMD 88–5, Washington, DC, February 1988, 13.

40. Thomas C. Hayes, "Making a Difference; Taking on Big Oil," *New York Times,* April 12, 1992, 3, 14.

41. GAO, "Groundwater Quality," 38–39.

42. U.S. Geological Survey, "Pesticides in Ground Water," USGS Fact Sheet FS-255–95, Washington, DC, 1995.

43. EPA, Office of Underground Storage Tanks, "The UST Corrective Action Program," Washington, DC, 1997. See also EPA, Office of Underground Storage Tanks, "Report to Congress on a Compliance Plan for the Underground Storage Tank Program," Report no. EPA-510-R-00-001, Washington, DC, June 2000.

44. EPA, Office of Water, *2012 Edition of the Drinking Water Standards and Health Advisories,* available at water.epa.gov/action/advisories/drinking/.../dwstandards2012.pdf (accessed September 30, 2012).

45. EPA, Office of Water, "Drinking Water: Past, Present, and Future," Report no. EPA-816-F-00-002, Washington, DC, February 2000.

Chapter 7

A Regulatory Thicket
Toxic and Hazardous Substances

National Journal: Dioxin, a chemical that EPA has recognized as a likely human carcinogen, has been in the assessment process for almost two decades. Why is it taking so long to assess dioxin?

Stephenson: It's hard to tell. You've got to think the end result of these assessments is that someone's going to have to do something, going to clean it up, and it's going to cost a lot of money. So there's a lot of care and attention being given to just how risky is this chemical; what would we need if we put a chemical control designation on it; what would it cost to clean it up? The Department of Defense uses many of these chemicals, and so they would be tasked with cleaning up. Should there be a standard or regulation for a chemical? And there's a legitimate concern about the scientific research. There's generally research that's contradicting on both sides of the argument. And they have to sift through all that research.

—John Stephenson, director,
Natural Resources Division, U.S. GAO, 2009[1]

If legal historians should choose a top ten in toxic litigation, a place surely will be reserved for the small community of Glen Avon, California. There, in early 1993, a legal spectacle began that demanded superlatives. "It's got to be among the top five civil cases in the history of American jurisprudence," one defense lawyer burbled as the proceedings began. Indeed, everything seemed dramatically oversized, like a production from some Hollywood of hazardous waste.[2] After eight years of planning and the screening of 2,000 jurors, the trial began with 3,700 plaintiffs (all Glen Avon residents); 13 defendants, including the state of California and major corporations such as Rockwell International, Northrop, McDonnell Douglas, and Montrose Chemicals; and injury claims exceeding $800 million.

241

At issue was liability for injuries alleged to have been inflicted on Glen Avon residents from exposure to more than 200 chemicals in 34 million gallons of waste dumped into the Stringfellow Canyon between 1956 and 1972. The legal battle over financial responsibility for the Stringfellow disaster ended—or seemed to end—in late 2012, almost two decades after litigation began.

At the time the trial began, Glen Avon residents had already received more than $50 million in damages from 100 companies that had used the site for dumping, but $22 million had been spent to initiate the new trial. The 30 lawyers and 24 jurors would eventually review more than 300,000 pages of court documents and 13,000 defense and 3,600 plaintiff exhibits for the initial proceeding. By then, the Stringfellow site had graduated from top billing on the EPA National Priority List (NPL) of the nation's worst abandoned waste sites to "one of the most contaminated sites on the planet."[3]

The trial has been held in installments. The first trial, involving 17 plaintiffs, ended on September 17, 1993, when the jury found the state of California responsible for allowing toxic releases from the Stringfellow site but awarded the plaintiffs only $159,000 of the $3.1 million they had claimed in damages. The second trial, which began in September 1994, involved plaintiffs claiming much more serious injuries. In 1994, most of the plaintiffs settled out of court and the number of plaintiffs was reduced to only 763. The next year, the federal court ruled that the state of California was liable for all the site cleanup costs. After three more years of litigation, California agreed to assume the cleanup costs if 17 private plaintiffs dropped their demands for $90 million in reimbursement for their own cleanup costs.

In early 2000, another federal judge determined that only 135 of the 763 remaining plaintiffs still had standing-to-sue status (see Chapter 3). At that time, estimates suggested that the site may require 400 years of remediation at a cost of $740 million. In 2000, California also initiated lawsuits against 35 of its own insurers for refusing to compensate the state for the Stringfellow cleanup costs. In early 2005, 16 insurers finally settled with the state for $93 million in cleanup costs (which made the list of "The 100 Top Insurance Verdicts of 2005" in one legal publication).[4] Trials began in 2006 for the first of the remaining 19 insurers who claimed that they were not compelled to pay the full amount of all the policies they had issued to California for the Stringfellow property; meanwhile, California was spending more than $10 million annually to clean up and monitor the waste site. Finally (perhaps), in August 2012, the California courts ruled that the state's insurers would have to pay the full amount on all the policies they had each issued for the waste site.[5] The box score: more than 40 years from site closure to last litigation, $180 million spent on cleanup, $100 million in current settlement costs, 17 acres of contaminated ground, and 34 million gallons of toxic waste for which to account.[6] Considering the magnitude of the site contamination and the cleanup so far accomplished, the EPA in 2004 impetuously claimed Stringfellow a "success story."[7] But, new pollution still appears. In 2002, plumes of the chemical perchlorate were discovered contaminating drinking water wells near the site. After an EPA investigation revealed perchlorate diffusion into the site itself, a remedial study was initiated in December 2008 and the EPA, collaborating with state environmental agencies, will be conducting pilot tests as part of the design of a new pretreatment plant to be constructed and operational by 2013.

It may also take decades to dissipate the emotional pain associated from Glen Avon's civic life. The local school board voted in 2003 to name a new $60 million school Glen Avon High School only after months of bitter contention within the community. Opponents of the new name contended that it perpetuated the Stringfellow stigma. "Glen Avon," explained one civic activist, suggests to many people a community that is "nothing but white trash, toxic waste and toothless women."[8]

The Stringfellow Canyon site is considered among the worst toxic site cleanups ever attempted. Even so, many legal experts believe that the Stringfellow litigation is a signpost along a sprawling road of ever more expansive and expensive future litigation as hazardous waste regulations multiply and government seeks more aggressively to satisfy public apprehension about toxic and hazardous substances. An ironic counterpoint to this growing litigation with its burgeoning liability awards has been the mounting disagreement among scientific experts about the extent of public risk from exposure to manufactured, stored, and abandoned chemical substances. Indeed, in no other area of environmental regulation has scientific uncertainty about the extent of the risk and identity of hazardous substances been greater or more public. This chapter is about the ambitious and extraordinarily difficult task of regulating the creation, use, and disposal of the nation's hazardous and toxic wastes. Currently, more than 24 federal laws and a dozen federal agencies are concerned with regulating the manufacture, distribution, and disposal of carcinogenic substances and other toxic or hazardous chemicals. The chapter focuses upon the EPA's implementation of five of these laws concerned with chemical risks to public health. Congress once predicted that three of these laws—the TSCA (1976), the RCRA (1976), and the Comprehensive Environmental Response, Cleanup and Liability Act (known as "Superfund"; 1980)—would amount to *cradle-to-grave regulation* of toxic and hazardous substances. The fourth law, the Emergency Planning and Community Right-to-Know Act (EPCRA; 1988) created perhaps the most widely publicized of all toxic chemical laws, the TRI. The final law, the Food

Quality Protection Act (1996), is an effort to improve regulation as a result of new concerns about public exposure to hazardous and toxic substances arising since the earlier laws were enacted. Implementing these laws has proved enormously challenging not only because the scope and expense of regulation were vastly underestimated but also because new scientific controversies arise concerning the extent to which existing hazardous and toxic substances—or others continually being created—constitute significant risks to humans or to the environment. To illustrate why these conflicts defy satisfactory resolution, the chapter describes the ongoing scientific and political controversies associated with continuing efforts to clean up the most famous of all existing abandoned waste sites at Love Canal, New York, and the challenges involved in proving that a group of recently identified chemicals, called *endocrine disruptors,* are a public health menace requiring regulation and not, as critics claim, a political and scientific fiction . . . that should be regulated.

These and other federal regulatory programs have significantly reduced public exposures to numerous chemical hazards. Still, after many decades of massive public investment in a multitude of regulatory programs aimed at almost every aspect of toxic and hazardous substances, accomplishments seldom satisfy either program proponents or critics—even though (or maybe because) the EPA must enforce altogether 13 major laws affecting hazardous substance use and disposal in the United States

An Ambiguous Inheritance

The environmentalists' hell is a firmament of compacted pesticide awash in toxic sludge. Environmentalists are not alone in attributing to chemicals a special malevolence. Most Americans apparently believe that the air, water, and earth are suffused with real or potential toxic menaces. The Gallup Organization polled a sample of Americans in mid-2012 concerning environmental risks about which they "worried a great deal" and discovered that Americans worried most about (1) soil and water contaminated by toxic waste; (2) polluted drinking water; (3) polluted rivers, lakes, and streams, and (4) air pollution—all more or less associated with chemical substances.[9] Americans are often misinformed about the extent of environmental risks and frequently exaggerate the danger from the environmental pollutants they most fear. But, widespread media coverage of hazardous chemical spills, newly discovered abandoned toxic waste sites, and other real or alleged chemical crises have forced attention on toxic and hazardous substances and imparted a sense of urgency to resolving the problems. Toxic and hazardous substances have progressed rapidly from secondary importance in the environmental agenda in the early 1970s to a primary concern in the early years of the 21st century.

Chemicals

Most toxic and hazardous substances are an inheritance of the world-wide chemical revolution following World War II. The creation of synthetic chemicals continued at such a prolific pace after 1945 that, by the mid-1960s, the American Chemical Society had registered more than 4 million chemicals, an increasing proportion of which were synthetics created by U.S. chemists since 1945. Today, more than 84,000 chemicals are used daily in U.S. industry; between 500 and 1,000 new chemicals are created annually. Currently, the EPA has more than 10,000 new chemicals pending review, as required by TSCA.[10]

About 98 percent of chemical substances used commercially in the United States are considered harmless to humans and the ecosystem. However, more than 120,000 establishments in the United States create and distribute chemicals, and the industry's capacity to produce and distribute still more new substances is growing. TSCA does not require chemical companies to test the approximately 700 new chemicals now annually introduced into commerce for toxicity, and companies generally do not voluntarily perform such testing.[11]

Toxic and Hazardous Chemicals

Many chemicals have been tested to determine their hazardousness—it is often relatively easy to decide if a chemical is corrosive, ignitable, or otherwise clearly dangerous when handled or abandoned in the environment—but few have been tested rigorously to determine their toxicity or risk to human or environmental health. Testing is particularly difficult and expensive when the long-term effects of a chemical are being investigated. Studies may require decades. The EPA has struggled diligently to reduce the time and complexity involved in its chemical risk assessments, but as Table 7–1 suggests, the agency's evaluation of potentially dangerous chemicals can consume many years and sometimes more than a decade.[12]

Cancer is the gravest and most widely feared of all toxic impacts from chemical exposures. By 2010, perhaps 1,500 to 2,000 of all chemical substances, a small proportion of all suspected carcinogenic chemicals produced in the United States, had been tested sufficiently by federal agencies to determine their carcinogenicity. Among those tested, more than 300 showed substantial evidence of carcinogenicity.[13]

In recent years, the EPA has improved the speed and efficiency of its own risk assessments. But, the EPA's risk assessing is hobbled by an inadequate budget, limited staff, a huge burden of different regulatory programs, and the constant tide of newly manufactured chemicals added to

Table 7–1   *Completed EPA Chemical Risk Assessments from 2009 through 2011*

IRS assessment	Level of complexity[a]	Assessment completion date	Length of time to complete assessment
Trichloroacetic acid	Moderately complex	Sept. 30, 2011	7 years, 9 months
Trichloroethylene (TCE)	Exceptionally complex	Sept. 28, 2011	13 years, 9 months
Hexachloroethane	Standard	Sept. 23, 2011	6 years
Urea	Standard	July 13, 2011	3 years, 6 months
Chloroprene	Moderately complex	Sept. 30, 2010	11 years, 10 months
Dichloroethylene-1,2-Cis-	Standard	Sept. 30, 2010	6 years, 8 months
Dichloroethylene-1,2-Trans-	Standard	Sept. 30, 2010	6 years, 8 months
Pentachlorophenol	Moderately complex	Sept. 30, 2010	12 years, 9 months
Tetrachloroethane-1,1,2,2	Standard	Sept. 30, 2010	5 years
Hydrogen cyanide	Standard	Sept. 28, 2010	7 years, 6 months
Dioxane-1,4-(oral route)	Moderately complex	Aug. 11, 2010	6 years, 6 months
Carbon tetrachloride	Moderately complex	Mar. 31, 2010	10 years, 3 months
Ethylene glycol monobutyl ether (EGBE)	Moderately complex	Mar. 31, 2010	6 years, 2 months
Acrylamide	Exceptionally complex	Mar. 22, 2010	9 years, 1 month
Bromobenzene	Standard	Sept. 30, 2009	6 years, 8 months
Thallium	Standard	Sept. 30, 2009	7 years, 9 months
Trichloropropane-1,2,3 (TCP)	Moderately complex	Sept. 30, 2009	6 years, 5 months
Cerium oxide	Standard	Sept. 29, 2009	4 years, 3 months
Hexanone-2	Standard	Sept. 25, 2009	4 years, 8 months
Chlordecone (kepone)	Standard	Sept. 22, 2009	6 years, 8 months
Average time to complete			**7 years, 6 months**

Source: GAO, *Chemical Assessments: Challenges Remain with EPA's Integrated Risk Information System Program*, GAO-12-41, December 2011, 14, available at htttp://www.gao.gov/assets/590/586620.pdf.

a catalog of many thousand existing and newly manufactured chemicals. Thus, TSCA requires the EPA to demonstrate that certain chemicals may constitute a potential health risk before it can require industrial manufacturers or users to test such chemicals, but the EPA examines only a very small portion of chemicals currently used or newly manufactured for their possible health risks.[14] Persuasive scientific evidence that environmental chemicals, such as pesticides and toxic industrial air emissions, are causing widespread cancer is quite often insufficient or nonexistent. Such environmental chemicals have frequently been suspected of creating cancer epidemics, but the National Cancer Institute and the U.S. Centers for Disease Control and Prevention have usually reported a lack of confirmed evidence to support these accusations.

Pesticides are a substantial component of proven or suspected toxic chemicals and chemical wastes. Pesticides are so widely and routinely used in U.S. agriculture that many farmers believe productivity cannot be sustained without them. Common foods, such as vegetables and fruits, are treated with dozens of possible carcinogens among the 20,700 pesticides currently available in the United States. More than 3 billion pounds of these pesticides are annually applied in agriculture production. These products contain more than 890 active ingredients.[15] Most of the pesticide products used in the United States since 1947 were registered before their long-term effects were understood. Federal legislation in 1972 required the EPA to reevaluate all existing pesticides in light of new information about their effects on humans and the environment. The EPA has prohibited, or limited severely, the use of many pesticides, including DDT, aldrin, dieldrin, toxaphene, and ethylene dibromide, and as a result, the levels of persistent pesticides in human fatty tissue had declined from about 8 parts per million in 1970 to slightly more than 2 parts per million today.

Even if a chemical product is restricted or prohibited, the EPA often lacks the resources to implement controls quickly. One striking example is that the EPA estimated before 1980 that more than half a million office buildings, apartment houses, stores, and other public or commercial buildings contained potentially dangerous loose asbestos, but the agency decided by 1988 to take no action because the federal government, the states, and the private sector lacked the money and personnel to remove safely the deteriorating asbestos.[16]

Toxic Chemicals and Risk Assessment

Because most federal regulations restricting the use or manufacture of toxic chemicals will involve testing for their risk to human health or the environment, the regulatory risk assessment discussed in Chapter 4 arises continually with toxics management. Chemical testing of any sort is time-consuming and costly, but when the long-term effects of a chemical are involved, studies may require decades. Moreover, substances currently suspected of having toxic effects often have not existed long enough for long-term impacts to be apparent. If testing deals with chronic effects of exposure to small quantities of chemicals—doses as small as parts per billion or trillion—difficulties in identifying the presence of the substance and the rate of exposure among affected populations may be formidable. Even repeated testing and retesting of human exposures to potentially toxic chemicals to establish their magnitudes of risk or the effectiveness of their existing regulation often may not produce conclusive evidence concerning the human health and environmental impact, as exemplified by two continuing toxic chemical controversies. The first, concerning Love Canal, the signature site that dramatized the nation's dangerous abandoned toxic waste problem, illustrates some of the practical challenges in determining when toxic waste is sufficiently regulated. The second matter, the controversy over endocrine disruptors, reveals some common difficulties in proving that a chemical should be a regulated toxic.

Love Canal. Love Canal is now infamous, the chemical dump that produced the Superfund legislation and achieved fame sufficient to have its own webpage on Google Sightseeing. It is also an excellent showcase for some practical challenges involved in deciding how and when to control known toxic wastes in an imperfect regulatory world of limited data, inevitable political controversy, and potentially dangerous public health hazards.[17]

In 1975, federal and state government officials determined that the huge, abandoned industrial chemical dump known as Love Canal, near Niagara Falls, New York, appeared to constitute such a health menace to the surrounding residential communities that hundreds of nearby residents were urged to sell their homes to the federal government and leave the neighborhood. In 1978, President Jimmy Carter ordered 259 families living nearest the site to be evacuated and, subsequently, between 1978 and 1980, a total of more than 950 families were ordered to leave by federal and state agencies. The deserted homes were bordered up and abandoned at a public cost of more than $17 million. Later, in 1982, the EPA and the U.S. Public Health Service released the results of their massive investigation concerning the health effects of the Love Canal site upon the families in the nearby residential community. Contrary to earlier studies by New York State, the EPA asserted that it had found the neighborhood near Love Canal no less safe for residents than any other part of nearby Niagara Falls.

The evidence seemed formidable. More than 6,000 samples of human and environmental materials near the site were collected and subjected to 150,000 analytical measurements to determine what contaminants they contained. This data suggested that only a ring of houses a block from the waste site or closer had been affected significantly. But, the study was challenged immediately because 90 percent of the samples were free of any chemicals. This result, asserted experts, could mean either an absence of chemicals or insufficient sensitivity in the measuring procedures. Other critics changed that the massive evacuation had been politically motivated.[18]

Although New York health officials later testified to congressional committees that they were confident the undetected chemicals could not be present in more than minute quantities, the Environmental Defense Fund's own scientific expert asserted that so much variance existed in the competence of the many laboratories conducting the tests and that so many sources of error could exist in some tests that chemicals could indeed have been present. Officials at the National Bureau of Standards also questioned the sensitivity of the test procedures. That same year, the federal Centers for Disease Control released its own study of former Love Canal area residents, indicating that they were no more likely to suffer chromosomal damage than residents elsewhere in Niagara Falls. Even if such damage were present, noted the study, it was impossible to know if it was linked to the later occurrence of illnesses.[19]

In mid-2004, the EPA appeared to write the last chapter in the Love Canal saga by declaring that the dump, now a Superfund project, was "clean" and, thus, no longer menacing for nearby residents.[20] However, in mid-2012, numerous former students who attended public school near Love Canal when it was discovered now claimed they had experienced serious health problems in later years from exposure to the dump's toxics, asserted that uncontrolled toxic chemical wastes were seeping again from the site, and pledged to revive investigation into the Canal's long-term health impacts.[21]

Endocrine Disruptors. The list of worrisome chemicals lengthened in the latter 1990s when scientific and governmental attention turned suddenly to a potentially huge inventory of chemicals called endocrine disruptors. Scientific research has suggested that certain externally produced chemicals, especially many human-made synthetic compounds, may sometimes mimic naturally produced hormones in humans and animals and may interfere, perhaps disastrously, with the normal functioning of the endocrine system. Many of these disruptors, according to some scientific theories, gain their potency from the bioaccumulation of extremely small doses in human and animal tissue over long periods of time. The possible human health effects could include cancers of the reproductive system, reduced sperm counts in males, abnormalities of fetal development leading to learning and behavioral disorders, and many other pathologies associated with hormonal malfunctions. Some scientists believe that disruptors have been responsible for sexual abnormalities and deformities in gulls, terns, eagles, and fish.[22]

If endocrine disruptors exist, apprehension seems prudent. "The number of substances which have been suggested as possibly contributing to perturbation of the endocrine system . . . is vast," explained one careful study of the issue:

Man-made or generated substances include broad classes of chlorinated and non-chlorinated compounds and heavy metals widely used in industrial and household products such as paints, detergents, lubricants, cosmetics, textiles, pesticides, and plastics, as well as byproducts of sewage treatment and waste incineration and other forms of combustion. Many pharmaceutical products, including contraceptives, have hormonal activity. There are also large amounts of plant hormones (mainly phytoestrogens) commonly ingested in human (and animal) diets—especially vegetarian products. . . . [23]

In short, here is something to unnerve everybody. Yet, the disruptor issue emerges from a fog of enormous uncertainty and scientific controversy. The effect of disruptors on humans and animals, the identity of truly dangerous substances, the results of long- and short-term exposures, the relative dangers to adults and fetuses, and much more are largely unknown. Scientists themselves disagree about the danger. "Even though sound scientific evidence can be found on both sides . . . simple cause and effect data are not available," explained one expert review of the evidence. "But even without certain scientific evidence, the potential health, social and economic effects are forcing government, organizations and the general public to take notice."[24]

The public history of endocrine disruptors is the very model of how environmental issues acquire political clout. Expert meetings held in the United States in 1991 and 1993 first called major scientific attention to the possible danger of endocrine disruptors. However, the issue's political momentum began to mount when, in 1993, the BBC broadcast the documentary *Assault on the Male*, which suggested that human and animal reproductive problems might arise from endocrine disruptors. The issue rose to national attention with the publication in 1996 of *Our Stolen Future*, written by a team of U.S. scientific interpreters, who vividly described the menace presumably posed by disruptors:

> Hormone-disrupting chemicals are not classical poisons or typical carcinogens. They play by different rules. They defy the linear logic of current testing protocols built on the assumption that higher doses do more damage. For this reason, contrary to our long-held assumptions, screening chemicals for cancer risk has not always protected us from other kinds of harm. Some hormonally active chemicals appear to pose little if any risk of cancer. . . . [S]uch chemicals are typically not poisons in the normal sense. Until we recognize this, we will be looking in the wrong places, asking the wrong questions.[25]

This aura of mystery, dread, and imminence proved to be a powerful political catalyst, creating additional media attention, provoking public concern, and compelling a response from government officials. In 1996, Congress passed the Food Quality Protection Act, which amended several major federal environmental and public health laws to require that the EPA create and then implement within three years an endocrine disruptor screening program for chemicals, and—as if to prove beyond refutation its environmental vigilance—Congress further mandated the EPA to add an additional tenfold safety factor to protect infants and children when setting standards for allowable pesticide residues in food, unless reliable data showed that a different factor would be safe. The EPA appointed a scientific advisory committee on endocrine disruptors in 1996, and two years later, it reported that, although the available data were insufficient to verify the magnitude of risk or the variety of chemicals associated with endocrine disruption, enough evidence existed to justify more intensive research and more public information about the potential problems arising from suspected endocrine disruption.

Although Congress mandated that the EPA craft an endocrine disruptor screening program and implement it by 1999, administrative and scientific difficulties have frustrated both objectives—additional testimony to the impotence of congressional micromanagement. Also, preliminary estimates suggest that the necessary testing protocols will probably be extremely expensive, perhaps approaching $1 million for each chemical tested, and that tests would be required for many hundreds of chemicals and their compounds. The chemical industry believes that insufficient evidence exists to justify the imposition of such an expensive testing regimen, and scientists themselves disagree about the magnitude of the endocrine disruptor problem. "Every policy paper, every study gets embroiled in scientific disputes over the EPA's assumptions on everything from children's dietary habits to the amount of roach killer an average family is likely to use," observed one progress report.[26] Although the issue predictably attracts public attention, environmental advocates have yet to discover the political leverage to shake the program from its glacial pace.

Costs and Controversy

It is doubtful that either friend or foe of the federal regulatory programs enacted between 1970 and 1986 realistically understood the enormous expense that would be involved in the new legislation. New regulatory agencies had to be created or existing ones expanded. A small sample of the direct and indirect costs associated with recent hazardous substance legislation can only suggest the scale on which such regulatory programs must operate:

> The average priority abandoned waste site cleaned up by the EPA under Superfund legislation has cost $2.1 million and will cost far more in the future; the aggregate expense for eliminating all the nation's worst abandoned waste sites is expected to be many times the initial Superfund authorization of $1.6 billion.[27]

The EPA's regulations for disposal of hazardous waste on land sites exceeded 500 pages in the Federal Register. EPA officials say the costs of compliance for the affected industries will exceed $1 billion yearly.[28]

When the massive costs are projected against the fragmentary scientific data on the effects of many chemicals and the often tenuous evidence relating chronic impacts to extremely low levels of exposure, arguments over the acceptability of the costs in light of the benefits inevitably arise. Critics of federal environmental programs have asserted that most impose not only unacceptable costs for the regulation of acknowledged hazards but also staggering costs for the stringent control of substances with unproven effects. Numerous critics, including presidents Reagan, George Bush, and George W. Bush, have argued that benefit–cost calculations should become a major consideration, if not a required criteria, when determining whether a substance should be regulated.

Criticism of regulatory costs often feeds on the disparity between the timing and character of the costs and the timing and character of the benefits from regulation. The costs tend to be tangible, immediate, and massive: Dollars must be spent, agencies created, rules promulgated, and other expensive actions initiated. In contrast, years or decades may pass before any apparent benefits accrue. The benefits may be intangibles— deaths and illnesses prevented, public costs of future regulation avoided, or public safety enhanced—that tend to be discounted by those who must pay for regulation in the present. Examples exist, however, that show the future benefits of regulation can be enormous. The number of U.S. deaths from exposure to asbestos as much as 40 years ago will grow to between 8,000 and 10,000 annually. More than 200,000 claims outstanding against major asbestos manufacturers at the beginning of the 21st century must be settled. The current value of these future claims has been estimated conservatively at $40 billion.[29]

Federal Law: Regulation from the Cradle to the Grave?

Among the two dozen federal laws relating to toxic and hazardous substances, five of them, three passed in the 1970s, define the fundamental framework for regulating the disposal of these substances: the TSCA (1976), the RCRA (1976), the Superfund legislation (1980), the EPCRA (1986), and the Food Quality Protection Act (1996). These laws represent a congressional effort to create a comprehensive regulatory program for all chemical substances from their initial development to final disposal— the cradle-to-grave control that seemed essential to achieving, for the first time, the responsible public management of chemical products. Few laws, even by the standard of recent environmental legislation, mandate a more complex and technically formidable administrative process than do these programs. A brief review of their major provisions suggests the immense regulatory tasks involved.

Regulating Chemical Manufacture and Distribution: The Toxic Substances Control Act

The major purpose of TSCA and its 1986 amendments (the Asbestos Hazard Emergency Response Act) is to regulate the creation, manufacture, and distribution of chemical substances so that substances hazardous to humans and the environment can be identified early and then controlled properly before they become fugitive throughout the ecosystem. TSCA and its amendments require the EPA to achieve five broad objectives:

1. *Information gathering.* The EPA is required to issue rules asking chemical manufacturers and processors to submit to the administrator information about their newly developed chemicals. The information is to include the chemical's name, formula, and uses; estimates of production levels; a description of by-products; data on adverse health and environmental effects; and the number of workers exposed to the chemical. In achieving these goals the administrator also is to do the following:
   a. publish a list of all existing chemicals.
   b. see that all people manufacturing, processing, or distributing chemicals in commerce keep records on adverse health reactions, submit to the EPA-required health and safety studies, and report to the EPA information suggesting that a chemical represents a previously undetected significant risk to health or the environment.
2. *Screening of new chemicals.* Manufacturers of new chemicals are to notify the EPA at least 90 days before producing the new chemical commercially. Information similar to that required for existing chemicals is also required for new chemicals. The EPA is allowed to suspend temporarily the manufacture of any new chemical in the absence of adequate information as required under the law and to suspend production of a new chemical permanently if it finds a "reasonable basis to conclude that the chemical presents or will present an unreasonable risk of injury to health or the environment."[30]

3. *Chemical testing.* The EPA is given the authority to require manufacturers or processors of potentially harmful chemicals to test them. The Interagency Testing Committee, composed of representatives from eight federal agencies, was created to recommend to the EPA priorities for chemical testing. As many as 50 chemicals can be recommended for testing within one year.

4. *Control of chemicals.* The EPA is required to take action against chemical substances or mixtures for which a reasonable basis exists to conclude that their manufacture, processing, distribution, use, or disposal presents an unreasonable risk of injury to health or the environment. Permitted actions range from a labeling requirement to a complete ban. The control requirements are not to "place an undue burden on industry," yet at the same time they are to provide an adequate margin of protection against unreasonable risk. TSCA specifically requires the regulation and eventual elimination of PCBs.

5. *Control of asbestos.* The EPA is required to develop a strategy for implementing the congressional mandate that all schools be inspected for asbestos-containing material and to develop and implement plans to control the threat of any asbestos discovered.

How TSCA Regulates. EPA follows a procedure known as IRIS when assessing any chemical that may qualify for its evaluation. While the EPA has considerably improved the speed and efficiency of its IRIS procedure, Figure 7–1 illustrates why IRIS's extensive data and review requirements often move assessments at a glacial pace frustrating for advocates of prompt, economically efficient, effective toxics regulation.

Considering the cumbersome IRIS process, the EPA's record for having so far identified more than 550 chemicals as human health risks among more than 84,000 commercial chemicals now used in the United States should be considered at least an important achievement in light of the public health risks it has reduced or eliminated.[31]

The Regulatory Thicket. One formidable problem posed with TSCA is that it requires the EPA to assume the initiative for creating and interpreting a vast volume of integrated technical information. Obtaining the data often requires that chemical manufacturers, processors, consumers, and waste depositors provide timely, accurate information—information they previously guarded jealously. With this heavy burden of initiative, the agency would have been hard-pressed to meet all its program obligations under TSCA with even the most benevolent funding and generous personnel levels—neither of which it has enjoyed.

Figure 7–1   The Integrated Risk Information System (IRIS)

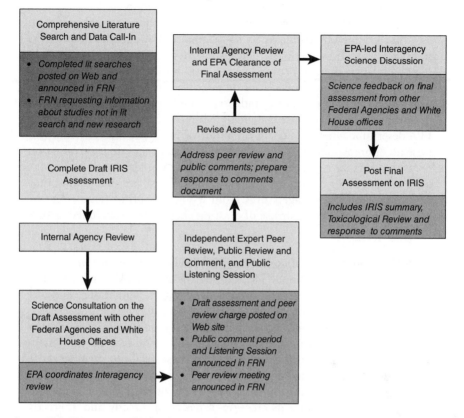

Source: U.S. EPA, *Integrated Risk Information System: IRISTrack,* available at http://cfpub.epa.gov/ncea/iristrac/ (accessed September 20, 2012).

In reality, the EPA has been overwhelmed by TSCA's chemical testing requirements. As a 2009 GAO report concluded,

> EPA lacks adequate scientific information on the toxicity of many chemicals. One major reason is that TSCA generally places the burden of obtaining data about existing chemicals on EPA rather than on chemical companies. For example, the act requires EPA to demonstrate certain health or environmental risks before it can require companies to further test their chemicals. As a result, EPA does not routinely assess the risks of the over 83,000 chemicals already in use.[32]

The prognosis for improvement has been guarded. The GAO concluded that the EPA had significantly improved its risk assessment process, but given the number of obstacles that can impede the progress of IRIS assessments, the viability of this program will depend on effective and sustained management.

By 2009, the EPA had been able to test fewer than 200 of more than 62,000 commercial chemicals on its original TSCA agenda. In an effort to lighten its testing overload, the EPA resorted to an alternative strategy of encouraging chemical companies to voluntarily provide test data on about 2,800 chemicals produced or imported in amounts of 1 million pounds or more. The chemical industry would not agree to provide data on several hundred of these chemicals. Moreover, TSCA requires that the EPA determine whether a chemical about which it has received data will pose an "unreasonable risk" before the EPA can regulate its production or use—a virtual regulatory dead end. "EPA officials say that the act's legal standards for demonstrating unreasonable risk are so high that they have generally discouraged EPA from using its authorities to ban or restrict the manufacture or use of existing chemicals," concluded GAO's investigators.[33]

Publicizing Chemical Releases: The Toxic Release Inventory. The EPCRA created the national TRI, among the most publicized, effective, and publicly accessible of all current federal toxics regulations. The TRI takes chemical regulation a major step beyond TSCA by creating a database containing information collected since 1988 on the disposal or other releases of more than 650 toxic chemicals by thousands of U.S. facilities together with information about how these facilities manage those chemicals through recycling, energy recovery, and treatment. One of TRI's primary purposes is to inform communities about toxic chemical releases to the environment. Since its creation, it has been directly and indirectly responsible for encouraging thousands of organized community and interest group initiatives to identify and regulate exposures to air toxics, many previously unknown.

TRI records a steady decrease in chemical releases since 1988, As Figure 7–2 illustrates, in the decade between 2000 and 2010, total chemical releases decreased about 8 percent. However, embedded in this encouraging long-term trend are several major challenges still posed by toxic releases. First, the TRI throws into sharp relief the enormous importance of the electrical power industry as the source of almost half the total volume of toxic air releases in the United States (see Figure 7–3). As the industry is also the major source of domestic, climate warming chemicals, it is understandable that this industry's environmental performance, especially the extent to which these emissions require further regulation, has become a continuing source of scientific and political contention and a

Figure 7–2 Releases of Toxic Chemicals On- and Off-Site between 2001–2010

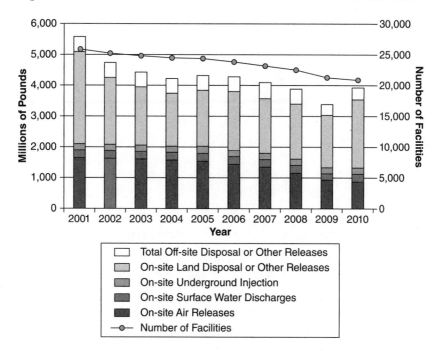

Total Off-site Disposal or Other Releases
On-site Land Disposal or Other Releases
On-site Underground Injection
On-site Surface Water Discharges
On-site Air Releases
—○— Number of Facilities

Source: U.S. EPA, 2010 Toxics Release Inventory: 2010 TRI National Analysis Overview, available at www.epa.gov/tri/tridata/tri10/nationalanalysis/index.htm (accessed September 27, 2012).

crucial issue for environmentalists and public health officials. The TRI also reveals a continuing, substantial, often unregulated discharge of toxic chemicals in the nation's waters. In 2010, the TRI reported that 226 million pounds of toxic chemicals were released into more than 1,400 waterways in all 50 states—the three leading dump sites were the Ohio River, the Mississippi River, and New River in Virginia and North Carolina.[34]

Regulating Solid Waste: The Resource Conservation and Recovery Act

The major purposes of RCRA and its 1980 and 1984 amendments are to control solid waste management practices that could endanger public health or the environment and to promote resource conservation and recovery. Solid wastes are defined in the act to include waste solids, sludges, liquids, and contained gases—all forms in which discarded toxic and

Figure 7-3   Sources of Industrial Air Pollution in the United States, 2011

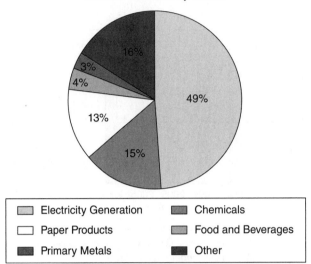

Toxic Air Pollution by Sector

Sector	Toxic Air Pollution (lbs)	% of National Air Pollution
Electricity Generation	381,740,601	49%
Chemicals	112,870,057	15%
Paper Products	103,249,010	13%
Food & Beverages	26,908,977	3%
Primary Metals	24,923,246	3%
Other	121,888,815	16%
Total	771,580,707	100%

Source: Reprinted with permission from the Natural Resources Defense Council. National Resources Defense Council (NRDC), "Curbing Pollution," NRDC Switchboard, available at http://switchboard.nrdc.org/blogs/paltman/the_toxic_20_states_with_the_h.html (accessed October 14 2012).

hazardous substances might be found. In addition to providing federal assistance to state and local governments in developing comprehensive solid waste management programs, RCRA also mandates the following:

1. *Criteria for environmentally safe disposal sites.* The EPA is required to issue regulations defining the minimum criteria for solid waste

disposal sites considered environmentally safe. It is also required to publish an inventory of all U.S. facilities failing to meet these criteria.

2. *Regulation of hazardous waste.* The EPA is required to develop criteria for identifying hazardous waste, to publish the characteristics of hazardous wastes and lists of particular hazardous wastes, and to create a manifest system that tracks hazardous wastes from their points of origin to their final disposal sites. The EPA also is to create a permit system that would require all individuals or industries generating hazardous waste to obtain a permit before managing such waste. Permits would be issued only to waste managers meeting the safe disposal criteria created by the EPA.

3. *Resource recovery and waste reduction.* The act requires the Commerce Department to promote the commercialization of waste recovery, to encourage markets for recovered wastes, and to promote waste recovery technologies and research into waste conservation.

4. *State implementation.* The act provides for state implementation of regulations affecting solid waste management and disposal if state programs meet federal standards. The EPA will enforce these provisions in states that do not, or cannot, comply with federal regulations for the program's enforcement.

5. *Mandated deadlines and waste-by-waste review.* The 1984 RCRA amendments create deadlines for the EPA to set standards for the disposal of specific wastes. If the EPA fails to do so, congressionally mandated standards will be applied. The EPA is also ordered to evaluate 19 specific substances, and deadlines are established for the agency to regulate new kinds of waste disposal activity.

Congress was determined to drive the EPA hard. It instructed the EPA in exquisite detail concerning how to implement virtually every aspect of RCRA, from the allowable permeability of liners for surface impoundments to the concentrations at which many different chemical wastes must be banned from land disposal. Twenty-nine different deadlines for specific program activities were listed, for example, a ban on land disposal of bulk liquid in landfills within 6 months, new regulations for small-quantity waste generators within 17 months, and interim construction standards for underground storage tanks within 4 months.[35]

It is also becoming evident that the number of potential waste storage and treatment facilities in the United States requiring corrective actions under RCRA is likely to exceed vastly the initial estimates. The EPA has estimated that perhaps 3,700 waste treatment and storage facilities will require cleanup under RCRA rules.[36] Moreover, the current list of 20,000 facilities subject to RCRA inspections is likely to grow as more facilities are discovered. If the estimates are accurate, the size and scope of the cleanup program would be as large as the expected Superfund cleanup and may cost more than $22.7 billion. The cleanup of all sites may not be completed until the year 2025.

The impediments to the RCRA program are those common to most federal regulatory efforts: cost and complexity, foot-dragging by regulated waste managers, insufficient money for needed oversight, and wrangling about cleanup terms. "The agency, the states, and companies often disagree on how cleanup should be pursued," explained a GAO report. "These disagreements prolong the cleanup process because more time is needed [to define] the cleanup terms, and companies must sometimes meet the duplicate requirements of both federal and state regulators."[37]

Cleaning Up Abandoned Waste: Superfund

The discovery of Love Canal in 1978 escalated rapidly into a national media event dramatizing to Americans the danger of abandoned toxic wastes within the United States. In the crisis-driven style characteristic of the 1970s, Congress reacted by passing in 1980 the Superfund legislation, which included an appropriation of $1.6 billion to clean up the nation's worst abandoned toxic and hazardous waste sites.

When the first Superfund legislation was enacted, the nation's abandoned and uncontrolled hazardous waste dumps were uncharted territory. Collaboration among the nation's governments seemed essential to identify abandoned sites, assess their health hazards, create standards for cleanup, and if possible, assign to site creators the financial liability for the cleanup. Congress attempted to address these and other major abandoned waste problems through four major Superfund programs:

1. *Information gathering and analysis.* Owners of hazardous waste sites were required to notify the EPA by June 1981 about the character of buried wastes. Using this information, the EPA would create a list of national sites.

2. *Federal response to emergencies.* The act authorized the EPA to respond to hazardous substance emergencies and to clean up leaking chemical dump sites if the responsible parties failed to take appropriate action or could not be located.

3. *The Hazardous Substance Response Fund.* The act created an initial trust fund of $1.6 billion to finance the removal, cleanup, or remedy of hazardous waste sites. About 86 percent of the fund was to be financed from a tax on manufacturers of petrochemical

feedstocks and organic chemicals and on crude oil importers. The remainder was to come from general federal revenues.

4. *Liability for cleanup.* The act placed liability for cleaning up waste sites and for other restitution on those responsible for release of the hazardous substances.

The National Priority List. One important result of this new legislation, which requires the EPA to create a list of the nation's most dangerous hazardous waste sites, called the NPL; to rank the sites according to human health and environmental risks; and to initiate action to clean up the sites according to their ranking. In 2008, the NPL included 1,140 sites in U.S. states and territories (Table 7–2). By 2012, more than 1,100 of the NPL sites had been cleaned up substantially and removed from the NPL list, but new sites are added as these are removed.[38] Moreover, the EPA estimates that there are at least 50,000 eligible sites, and many experts believe the actual number may exceed this estimate by at least 20,000.[39] Thus, even though the pace of Superfund site cleanup has improved

Table 7–2   *Hazardous Waste Sites on the National Priority List by State and Outlying Area, 2008*

State and outlying area	Total sites	Rank	Percentage distribution	Federal	Nonfederal
Alabama	15	26	1.2	3	12
Alaska	5	45	0.4	5	—
Arizona	9	39	0.7	2	7
Arkansas	9	40	0.7	—	9
California	97	2	7.8	24	73
Colorado	20	20	1.6	3	17
Connecticut	15	24	1.2	1	14
Delaware	14	27	1.1	1	13
District of Columbia	1	(X)	0.1	1	—
Florida	52	6	4.2	6	46
Georgia	16	23	1.3	2	14
Hawaii	3	46	0.2	2	1
Idaho	9	41	0.7	2	7
Illinois	49	7	3.9	5	44
Indiana	31	14	2.5	—	31
Iowa	12	33	1.0	1	11
Kansas	12	34	1.0	1	11
Kentucky	14	28	1.1	1	13
Louisiana	13	31	1.0	1	12
Maine	12	35	1.0	3	9

(continued)

Table 7-2 *Hazardous Waste Sites on the National Priority List by State and Outlying Area, 2008 (continued)*

State and outlying area	Total sites	Rank	Percentage distribution	Federal	Nonfederal
Maryland	19	21	1.5	10	9
Massachusetts	32	12	2.6	6	26
Michigan	67	5	5.4	1	66
Minnesota	25	18	2.0	2	23
Mississippi	6	44	0.5	—	6
Missouri	29	16	2.3	3	26
Montana	15	25	1.2	—	15
Nebraska	13	32	1.0	1	12
Nevada	1	49	0.1	—	1
New Hampshire	21	19	1.7	1	20
New Jersey	116	1	9.3	8	108
New Mexico	14	29	1.1	1	13
New York	86	4	6.9	4	82
North Carolina	32	13	2.6	2	30
North Dakota	—	50	0.0	—	—
Ohio	40	10	3.2	5	35
Oklahoma	9	42	0.7	1	8
Oregon	12	36	1.0	2	10
Pennsylvania	96	3	7.7	6	90
Rhode Island	12	37	1.0	2	10
South Carolina	26	17	2.1	2	24
South Dakota	2	47	0.2	1	1
Tennessee	14	30	1.1	4	10
Texas	49	8	3.9	4	45
Utah	19	22	1.5	4	15
Vermont	11	38	0.9	—	11
Virginia	30	15	2.4	11	19
Washington	48	9	3.8	13	35
West Virginia	9	43	0.7	2	7
Wisconsin	38	11	3.0	—	38
Wyoming	2	48	0.2	1	1
Guam	2	(X)	(X)	1	1
Puerto Rico	13	(X)	(X)	1	12
Virgin Islands	2	(X)	(X)	—	2
Total	1,318	(X)	(X)	163	1,155
Total United States	1,301	(X)	(X)	161	1,140

Source: U. S. Department of Commerce, *Statistical Abstract of the United States* (Washington, DC: U.S. Government Printing Office, 2009).

Notes: "—" indicates zero; (X) indicates not applicable. Data are as of December 31, 2008. They include both proposed and final sites listed on the National Priorities List for the Superfund program as authorized by the Comprehensive Environmental Response, Compensation, and Liability Act (CERCLA) of 1980 and the Superfund Amendments and Reauthorization Act (SARA) of 1986.

significantly in recent years, the program still confronts a huge backlog of contaminated sites while contending with massive cost overruns, technical complexities, political squabbles, and endless litigation.

"The Largest, Most Complicated, and Most Disliked." The Superfund program has been a consensus choice as the most controversial, expensive, and problematic of all environmentalism's showcase legislation. By George W. Bush's second term, EPA officials, increasingly testy at the continued criticism of Superfund, were pointing to significant improvements in the speed and economy of site cleanups. By 2007, the EPA claimed to be making "significant progress," and pointed to its substantial accomplishment in cleaning up a total of 1,006 NPL sites.[40]

The EPA's annual Superfund reports remain relentlessly optimistic, but the total Superfund costs cast a more pessimistic aspect. Superfund long ago exhausted its originally authorized funding of $15.4 billion and will greatly exceed the $26.4 billion that the EPA estimated in the early 1990s would be necessary to complete the entire program. Since 1981, Superfund appropriations have totaled more than $32 billion in nominal dollars, or about $1.2 billion annually.[41] Superfund costs during the decade of 2000 to 2010 alone are estimated to have been approximately $14 billion to 16.4 billion.[42]

Completed cleanups have averaged about $2.1 million each, but many troublesome sites are creating enormous cost escalations. One hundred fifty-four Superfund projects costing more than $50 million—such as California's Stringfellow dump—have achieved *megasite* status because of the time, technical complexity, and legal difficulties they entail.[43] About 20 to 33 percent of each Superfund site expenditure has been absorbed in litigation and negotiation, which has become a growth industry for the legal profession. One estimate suggests that approximately 20,000 lawyers are now engaged in Superfund litigation.[44]

The reasons for Superfund's plodding pace and bloated costs are clear. The enormous legal costs generated by Superfund are largely the result of the complexities involved in establishing liability for abandoned hazardous waste dumps and the difficulty in recovering damages from private parties. In 1984, for instance, the EPA placed the Helen Kramer Landfill in Mantua, New Jersey, high on the NPL and awarded $55.7 million for the cleanup contract. To recover these costs through liability claims, the federal government subsequently sued 25 private firms, and the state of New Jersey sued the same firms plus 25 additional ones. A few of these 50 defendants sued 239 other parties who they claimed were responsible for these wastes, including the city of Philadelphia and other municipalities. And, most of these litigants have sued their insurance companies.[45]

The litigation is still active. So far, the EPA has been able to recover only a small fraction of cleanup expenses from parties alleged to be liable for the costs.

Another inducement to delay and expense has been controversy between regulatory officials and communities affected by Superfund over the appropriate amount of cleanup required to make sites safe. Superfund officials predictably endure intense community pressure to achieve the most stringent and costly standards at a site restoration. When officials and communities disagree about the matter, litigation often results even before cleanup begins.

Unquestionable improvements have not pacified program critics, especially congressional Republicans, who seldom find much to like about Superfund. Less partisan experts and even many Superfund proponents, however, also believe additional reforms are imperative. Among the most important, in the opinion of a great many, is the development of a reliable method for ranking all Superfund sites according to the human and environmental health risks and allocating cleanup dollars on the basis of these risk priorities. Many observers believe the EPA needs to recover a much larger share of the site cleanup costs from private parties; the agency has been criticized for failing to recover more than $2 billion in cleanup costs just through careless bookkeeping.[46]

Congress and the White House have been under increasing pressure from insurance companies, private industry, state and local governments—indeed, practically all parties potentially liable to Superfund cleanup claims—to radically simplify the process by which liability for site cleanup is established and to create a cleanup standard that does not require the total elimination of all risk from site wastes.

A Continuing Challenge: Underground Disposal. More than half of the nation's liquid waste is flushed into deep underground cavities or water systems by many industries and municipalities, where it is presumed to disperse too deeply to contaminate water or soil used by humans. Much of this waste is known to contain toxic chemicals. However, such disposal is seldom carefully monitored or regulated. Experts suspect that many hazardous materials buried in this way will migrate through subsurface water flows until they contaminate drinking water wells and aquifers used for irrigation, lakes, rivers, or soil. For these reasons, the National Academy of Sciences has recommended that the federal government promote incineration, chemical processing, or other more modern procedures for waste disposal. Although federal and state water-quality regulators have succeeded in diminishing underground disposal, more than 12 million gallons of waste materials are still injected underground annually.[47]

Chemical Threat or Chemiphobia?

Although experts agree that the public should be concerned about the health risks associated with exposure to chemical substances and chemical wastes, they cannot easily determine which kinds of exposure and how much exposure are unacceptably risky. A related issue is that the elimination of all risk from exposure to toxic and hazardous substances is often impossible or unacceptably expensive, yet federal regulations such as the Superfund legislation do not clearly define how much cleanup is enough. The problem, as two informed critics observed, is "how clean is 'clean,'" and the solution is not apparent. According to political scientists Marc Landy and Mary Hague,

> In principle, one would want to clean until [an abandoned hazardous waste] site is called perfectly "safe." However . . . there is no scientifically identifiable point at which an "unsafe" site becomes "safe." No matter how much cleanup has been performed at a site, it can always be argued that more cleanup would reduce risk even further.[48]

A second issue involves political chemistry. When public fear about hazardous substances blends with official eagerness to appear tough on pollution, the resulting risk-averse political climate often spawns hasty, severe regulatory policies. A political synergy between public fear and governmental overreaction often results, as we have observed previously, in targeting for greatest attention those pollutants exciting the greatest public apprehension rather than those posing the most scientifically documented health risks. Risk-averse regulation can result in a regulatory intolerance for even minimal health risks, mistaken environmental priorities, and excessive regulatory costs.

Finally, regulatory costs have been especially controversial in toxic and hazardous substance regulation because of the rapid and severe escalation in the number of regulations and the growing recognition that future regulations will cost enormously more. Federal regulations, for instance, require all municipal landfills to be built with plastic and clay liners, liquid collectors, and treatment systems to prevent leaking toxic waste. These regulations have drastically raised the cost of opening a new municipal landfill and forced most of the country's existing 6,500 landfills to close when retrofitting became too expensive. And, future landfill costs may be far greater still as the variety of waste-dump toxics and their health risks are better documented.[49]

To many critics, all these problems have produced public chemiphobia while impelling governmental regulators to appease public opinion through excessively harsh chemical controls at enormous economic, scientific, and political cost to the nation. To many conservative critics, these regulations are too often "animated by a quasi-religious mind-set that combines an aversion to even minimal risks with a strong preference for governmental intervention in markets and a fierce hostility toward corporations."[50] Even the many experts who disagree with these conclusions often recognize that toxic and hazardous substance regulation is the most difficult, least satisfactory domain of contemporary environmental policy making. With Superfund and SARA, Congress finished its attempt to craft, within less than a decade, the first truly comprehensive federal regulation of virtually all hazardous or toxic materials in the United States.

The Food Quality Protection Act: Improved Pesticide Regulation

The Food Quality Protection Act is a constructive congressional effort to eliminate the regulatory morass created by 50 years of different statutory standards for pesticide residues on food. The act simplified regulatory standards for an extremely widespread, diverse, and politically contentious group of chemicals. Equally important, it abolished the zero-tolerance provisions for pesticide residues required by the Delaney clause of the Federal Food, Drug and Cosmetic Act (1949), which had become widely regarded as unreasonably stringent scientifically and economically. The most important provisions of the act include the following:

1. *A single, health-based standard.* All pesticide residues must demonstrate "a reasonable certainty of no harm" if they are to be permitted in food products.

2. *Tightened risk standards.* Risk calculations must consider all non-occupational sources of exposure, including drinking water, and exposure to other pesticides with a common mechanism of toxicity when setting tolerances. This provision allows regulators to consider not only the effect of the residue itself but also the impact of other kinds of exposure to the same, or similar pesticides, outside a workplace.

3. *Provisions for children.* This provision requires an explicit determination of safe exposures for children and, if necessary, a tenfold increase in the adult safety standards to be used for children when the relevant children's data are uncertain.

4. *Endocrine testing.* The EPA is required to establish a comprehensive screening program for chemical endocrine effects on humans, to implement the program, and to report on its progress to Congress.

5. *Consumer right to know.* This provision requires distribution of brochures in grocery stores on the health effects of pesticides, how to avoid risks, and which foods have tolerances for pesticide residues based on benefit considerations.

Leading national environmental advocacy groups generally accepted the new legislation warily, recognizing reluctantly that zero tolerance for pesticide residues probably had become an indefensible cancer-exposure standard economically and even scientifically. Still, many environmental leaders feared the new legislation might have breached irreparably a high wall of resistance to cancer risk they had legally erected over 50 years, inviting a flood of other legislation eroding the zero-tolerance standard for other ingredients in food.

The NIMBY Problem

NIMBYs are a common presence at proposed toxic waste and or hazardous facility sites. The NIMBYs (shorthand for not in my back yard) may be white-collar professionals, executives, or articulate, well-educated, and politically sophisticated individuals. They can be housewives, teachers, perhaps salespeople or public officials. They personify members of a well-recognized, potent citizen resistance movement.[51] NIMBY is

> a reaction or attitude towards any project, such as the siting of a hazardous enterprise or affordable housing projects, that is perceived to pose a threat to health or safety, status or reputation of a neighborhood or geographical area. NIMBYism can take the form of a protest against authorities or industry by the formation of action groups comprised by local residents. This response by the local population derives from a variety of reasons, including: a sense that they are being overrun by the authorities or industry to a genuine concern for the health and safety of residents of the community.[52]

NIMBY-ism is all too familiar to federal, state, and local officials attempting to implement state programs for issuing permits for hazardous waste sites as required by RCRA or trying to plan for the designation or cleanup of a Superfund site. It poses a formidable obstacle to waste site management under RCRA and Superfund. It is the environmental movement's problem, too. NIMBY-ism is a dissonance within the environmental ethic—a disturbing contradiction between the movement's commitment to participatory democracy and its insistence on rapid, effective environmental regulation.

NIMBY-ism thrives because of numerous, and still increasing, state and federal laws that empower citizen activism in the implementation of many different environmental laws and regulations. Most states now have legislation in which citizens are given some role in the writing, implementation, and enforcement of environmental laws. Seventeen states require the appropriate agencies to prepare environmental impact statements for their activities and mandate public notice and involvement in the process.[53]

Federal law provides many opportunities for citizen participation in environmental regulation. Major environmental laws, such as the CAA, the Clean Water Act, RCRA, and Superfund grant citizens the standing to sue federal agencies to compel their enforcement of environmental regulations. The Surface Mining Control and Reclamation Act (1977), the 1984 RCRA amendments, and the 1972 Clean Water Act amendments, among many others, require the responsible federal and state agencies to involve the public in writing and implementing regulations. Several federal environmental laws also permit citizens, or citizen organizations, to sue private firms for failure to comply with the terms of their pollution-discharge permits and to recover the costs involved in the suits. Public notice and hearings are routinely required of environmental agencies before major regulations are promulgated or permits are issued for pollution discharges or hazardous waste sites. Behind these generous provisions for citizen participation, legal scholar Michael S. Greve notes, is congressional distrust, a "reflexive suspicion that the executive, if left to itself, would systematically under-enforce the law."[54]

These statutory provisions have set in motion political forces powerfully abetting NIMBY-ism. One such force is the rapid proliferation of national and state organizations specifically committed to educating Americans about hazardous waste and to helping local communities organize politically to deal with local hazardous waste problems. Among the earliest and most visible national organizations is the Citizen's Clearinghouse for Hazardous Waste, created in 1981 by Lois Gibbs, a housewife whose experiences with the Love Canal waste crisis convinced her of a need to educate other communities about hazardous waste. There also has been an explosion of ad hoc state and local groups that have organized to deal with specific hazardous waste issues, ranging from the closing of city waste dumps to state policies for hazardous waste transportation.

Many existing state and national environmental organizations now give major attention to hazardous waste issues and provide technical assistance and education for concerned citizens. These groups believe they are ultimately contributing to better implementation of RCRA and Superfund by ensuring greater citizen understanding and acceptance of waste policy decisions made by government officials. Often, however, this activism arouses or emboldens citizen opposition to providing permits for local hazardous waste sites. Public officials and waste producers commonly complain that organized citizen groups too often agitate rather than educate in community waste issues.

Public resistance to hazardous waste site permits and management plans under RCRA or Superfund is a serious and unsolved political problem afflicting both programs. Coupled with litigation, the many political and administrative strategies available to citizen groups determined to prevent permits for local hazardous waste dumps can delay program implementation for years or decades.

State governments are not innocent of NIMBY-ism. Almost any hazardous waste proposal can arouse it. Public hearings on siting hazardous facilities, as political scientist Michael E. Kraft observed, can become "a perfect forum for elected officials and the general public to give vent to fears and concerns, and to denounce decision making on the siting question. The public hearing procedure . . . facilitated the classic NIMBY response to siting unwanted facilities that impose localized costs and risks while offering diffuse national benefits."[55]

Many administrative strategies have been tried, but none seems to dispel NIMBY-ism. States that financially compensate local governments and citizens for the risks and other problems entailed in accepting a hazardous waste site are no more successful in gaining public approval for the siting than states using only scientific criteria for site selection. Evidence suggests that most citizens who oppose a hazardous waste site will not change their minds under any circumstances.[56] Opponents may occasionally be converted if they are convinced that the local community will have continuing, accurate information about the site status and continuing control over the site's management. But, converts are few. Opponents to hazardous waste sites are numerous, vocal, and unyielding. Moreover, they are apt to win their fights.

NIMBY-ism will continue to be tough, stubborn, and durable, its ranks crowded with well-educated, socially active, organizationally experienced people. NIMBY-ism is rarely routed by better information, more-qualified experts, improved risk communication techniques, and other palliative actions premised on the assumption that the public will be more reasonable about a hazardous facility siting if it is better educated about the issues. All this belies the widespread belief among scientific experts and risk professionals that NIMBY-ism is rooted in the public's scientific illiteracy.[57]

Why is better risk communication not enough? Because NIMBYs usually distrust the source of governmental risk information: public officials and their scientific spokespeople. In addition, the critics of governmental hazardous waste management often have their own experts and information sources. The conflicting sides, notes Harvard physicist and science policy expert Harvey Brooks, tend to become "noncommunicating publics that each rely on different sources and talk to different experts. Thus, many public policy discussions become dialogues of the deaf. . . ."[58] Often, the true wellsprings of public anxiety about waste siting are not understood by technical experts; people worry about "potentially catastrophic effects, lack of familiarity and understanding, involuntariness, scientific uncertainty, lack of personal control by the individuals exposed, risks to future generations," and more.[59]

Critics often hold environmentalists responsible for NIMBY-ism. They assert that the environmentalist rhetoric favored by NIMBYs is little more than deceptive but respectable packaging for middle-class selfishness. In reality, argue the critics, most NIMBYs want somebody else to bear whatever risks are associated with hazardous waste sites, while they continue to benefit from the products and economic activities that produce the waste. Even if NIMBY-ism is well intentioned, critics also note, it fails to solve waste problems. Eventually, waste has to go someplace. It is unfortunate, the critics conclude, that the waste often ends up at whatever sites are the least well defended politically, not at the most appropriate places. Thus, many environmental justice problems (as observed in Chapter 4) and numerous controversies between the states over high-level nuclear waste disposal (see Chapter 8) are created or intensified by NIMBY-ism.

Whatever its merits, the certain continuation of NIMBY-ism poses difficult problems for environmental regulation. Is it possible to secure informed public consent to the siting and management of hazardous waste facilities? If no public involvement techniques or risk communication procedures can produce public consensus or acquiescence to hazardous waste site planning under RCRA and Superfund, must solutions be imposed by judicial, administrative, or political means? Is there danger that continuing the promotion of public involvement in making these decisions will enshrine procedural democracy at the expense of social equity—in effect, will citizen participation gradually result in selectively exposing the least economically and politically advantaged sectors of the public to the most risks from hazardous waste? How much responsibility for the worst impacts of NIMBY-ism rests with the environmental movement? These questions can only grow in importance as the hazardous waste problem magnifies in the 21st century.

Conclusion

In no other major area of environmental policy is progress measured in such small increments as the regulation of toxic and hazardous wastes. The slow pace at which TSCA, RCRA, and Superfund have been implemented so far has produced a quality of regulation so tenuous and variable that a serious question often exists regarding whether regulation in any significant sense has been achieved. Hazardous waste in abandoned or deliberately uncontrolled landfills numbering in the thousands has yet to be controlled properly. Federal and state governments have yet to approve and implement on the appropriate scale the strategies required to ameliorate hazardous waste problems. The risks already associated with hazardous substances, and the many others that will become apparent with continuing research in the 21st century, are unlikely to diminish without a massive and continuing federal commitment of resources to implementing the programs as intended by Congress—a commitment of resources and will on a scale that has been lacking so far.

Even with sufficient resources, the implementation of TSCA, RCRA, and Superfund is likely to be slow because these laws raise technical, legal, and political problems on an order seldom matched in other environmental policy domains. First, no other environmental programs attempt to regulate so many discrete, pervasive substances; we have observed that the hazardous substances that may lie within the scope of these laws number in the tens of thousands. Second, regulation is delayed by the need to acquire technical information never previously obtained by government, to conduct research on the hazardousness of new chemicals, or to secure from corporations highly guarded trade secrets. Third, almost every major regulatory action intended to limit the production, distribution, or disposal of chemical substances deemed toxic or hazardous by government is open to technical controversy, litigation, and other challenges concerning the degree of risk associated with such substances and their suitability for regulation under the laws. Fourth, opponents of regulatory actions under TSCA, RCRA, and Superfund have been able to use to good advantage all the opportunities provided by requirements for administrative due process and the federalized structure of regulation to challenge administrative acts politically and judicially. Fifth, in many instances, the states responsible for implementing the programs have been slow to provide from their own resources the means necessary to ensure proper implementation. None of these problems is unique to hazardous substance regulation, but few other environmental policies raise all these problems persistently and acutely.

From a broader perspective, the enormous difficulties in controlling hazardous substances once they are released into the ecosystem, together with the problems of controlling their disposal, emphasize the crucial role that production controls must play in hazardous substance management. Indeed, it may be that the human and environmental risks from hazardous chemicals may never be constrained satisfactorily once these substances are let loose in the environment. American technology development has proceeded largely with an implicit confidence that whatever human or environmental risks may be engendered in the process can be contained adequately by the same genius that inspired technology's development—a faith, in effect, that science always will cure whatever ills it creates. The risk to humans and the environment from the now-pervasive chemical substances created since World War II ought to prompt thoughtful reservations about the efficacy of technological solutions to technological problems. Toxic and hazardous substances pose for the nation a formidable technological challenge: how to reckon the human and environmental costs of technology development while technologies are yet evolving and, then, how to prudently control dangerous technologies without depriving the nation of their benefits.

Suggested Readings

Foster, Kenneth R., David E. Bernstein, and Peter W. Huber. *Phantom Risk: Scientific Inference and the Law.* Cambridge, MA: MIT Press, 1999.

Gerrard, Michael B. *Whose Backyard, Whose Risk?* Cambridge, MA: MIT Press, 1999.

Rabe, Barry G. *Beyond NIMBY: Hazardous Waste Siting in Canada and the United States.* Washington, DC: Brookings Institution Press, 1994.

Raffensberger, Carolyn, and Joel Tickner, eds. *Protecting Public Health and the Environment.* Washington, DC: Island Press, 1999.

Rahm, Dianne, ed. *Toxic Waste and Environmental Policy in the 21st Century United States.* Jefferson, NC: McFarland, 2002.

Wilson, Duff. *Fateful Harvest: The True Story of a Small Town, a Global Industry, and a Toxic Secret.* New York: Harper Collins, 2002.

Notes

1. From interview in Michelle Williams, "EPA's Chemical Backlog Long and Lingering," *National Journal Insider Interviews,* August 31, 2009, available at http://insiderinterviews.nationaljournal.com/2009/08/epas-chemical-assessment-proce.php (accessed December 20, 2009).
2. Quoted in Nick Madigan, "Largest-Ever Toxic Waste Suit Opens in California," *New York Times,* February 5, 1993, A17.
3. U.S. EPA, "Superfund Success Stories," available at www.epa.gov/superfund/randomize/thumbs3.htm (accessed March 25, 2004).
4. "Top 100 Verdicts of 2005," Verdictsearch, available at www.verdictsearch.com (accessed March 10, 2007).
5. "Insurers Must Pay for Hazardous Waste Site Cleanup, Court Rules," *Los Angeles Times,* August 9, 2012, available at http://latimesblogs.latimes.com/lanow/2012/08/insurance-companies-hazardous-waste-cleanup.html (accessed September 14, 2012).
6. Ibid.
7. EPA, "Superfund Success Stories."
8. Quoted in Will Matthews, "Stringfellow Retains Reputation: 'Glen Avon' Backlash Underscores Lasting Stigma," *Inland Valley Daily Bulletin* (Ontario, CA), January 11, 2003, 1A.
9. Jeffrey M. Jones, "Worry About U.S. Water, Air Pollution at Historic Lows," *Gallup Politics,* April 13, 2012, available at http://www.gallup.com/poll/153875/worry-water-air-pollution-historical-lows.aspx (accessed July 20, 2012).

10. EPA, "Environmental Progress and Challenges: EPA's Update," Washington, DC, August 1988, 126. See also U.S. GAO, "Toxic Substances: Status of EPA's Reviews of Chemicals Under the Chemical Testing Program," Report no. GAO/RCED 92–31FS, Washington, DC, October 1991.

11. GAO, "Observations on Improving the Toxic Substances Control Act: Statement of John Stephenson, Director, National Resources and Environment," Report no. GAO 10–292, Washington, DC, December 2, 2009, "Highlights."

12. GAO, *Chemical Assessments: Challenges Remain with EPA's Integrated Risk Information System Program*, GAO-12-41, December 2011, 14, available at htttp://www.gao .gov/assets/590/586620.pdf.

13. The number of carcinogenic chemicals includes those classified as "known to be a human carcinogen" and those "reasonably anticipated to be a human carcinogen." See U.S. Department of Health and Human Services, Public Health Service, National Toxicology Program, *Report on Carcinogens*, 10th ed. (Washington, DC: National Toxicology Program, 2002).

14. GAO, *Transforming EPA's Process for Assessing and Controlling Toxic Chemicals* (Washington, DC: Author, 2012), available at www.gao.gov/highrisk/risks/safety-security/ epa_and_toxic_chemicals.php#found (accessed August 27, 2012).

15. National Research Council, Committee on the Future Role of Pesticides in U.S. Agriculture, *The Future Role of Pesticides in U.S. Agriculture* (Washington, DC: National Academies Press, 2000), 33.

16. Philip Shabecoff, "EPA Pulls Back on Asbestos Rules," *New York Times,* March 9, 1985, 1, 48.

17. Google Sightseeing, "Why See the World for Real?: Love Canal," available at http:// googlesightseeing.com/2009/05/love-canal/ (accessed October 7, 2012).

18. An accurate and informative summary of the Love Canal issue can be found in Lois Gibbs, "History of Love Canal," The Encyclopedia of the Earth, available at http:// www.eoearth.org/article/History_of_Love_Canal#gen2 (accessed October 10, 2012).

19. U.S. Centers for Disease Control, "Cytogenetic Patterns in Persons Living near Love Canal—New York," May 27, 1983, available at ww.cdc.gov/mmwr/preview/mmwrhtml/ 00000084.htm

20. Anthony dePalma, "Love Canal Declared Clean, Ending Toxic Horror," *New York Times,* March 18, 2004, available at www.nytimes.com/2004/03/18/nyregion/love-canal-declared-clean-ending-toxic-horror.htm (accessed February 26, 2012).

21. Rick Pfeiffer, "Former Love Canal Students Seek Answers," *Niagara-Gazette,* August 21, 2012, available at http://niagara-gazette.com/local/x1088167343/Former-Love-Canal-students-seek-answers (accessed September 5, 2012).

22. Center for Bioenvironmental Research, Tulane and Xavier Universities, "Environmental Estrogens: What Does the Evidence Mean?" New Orleans, LA, 1996; Center for the Study of Environmental Endocrine Disruptors, "Significant Government Policy Developments," Washington, DC, 1996; Center for the Study of Environmental Endocrine Disruptors, "Effects: State of Science Paper," Washington, DC, 1995.

23. Center for the Study of Environmental Endocrine Disruptors, "Effects," 12.

24. Center for the Study of Environmental Endocrine Disruptors, "Significant Government Policy Developments," 17.

25. Theo Colborn, Dianne Dumanoski, and John Peter Meyers, *Our Stolen Future: Are We Threatening Our Fertility, Intelligence, and Survival?* (New York: Penguin, 1996), 7.

26. "Toughest Decisions Still to Come in Pesticide Review," *USA Today,* August 30, 1999, 1A.

27. GAO, "Superfund Estimates of Number of Future Sites Vary," Report no. GAO-/RCED, 95-18.

28. Philip Shabecoff, "EPA Streamlines Cleanup Program," *New York Times,* May 14, 1983, 1, 6.

29. Estimates by Paul MacAvoy, *New York Times,* February 14, 1982, B3. See also Library of Congress, Congressional Research Service, "Six Case Studies of Compensation for Toxic Substances Pollution," report to the Committee on Environment and Public Works, U.S. Senate, no. 96–13, Washington, DC, 1980.

30. Linda Schierow, "Summaries of Environmental Laws Administered by the EPA: The Toxic Substances Control Act," Congressional Research Service Report no. RL30022, Washington, DC, 2006, 2.

31. National Research Council, Committee on Improving Risk Analysis Approaches Used by the U.S. EPA, Science and Decisions: Advancing Risk Assessment, "Summary," (Washington, DC: National Academies Press, 2009). See also GAO, *Chemical Assessments: Challenges Remain With EPA's Integrated Risk Information System Program,* "Highlights," GAO-12-41, December 2011.

32. GAO, "Observations," "Highlights."

33. GAO, "Chemical Regulation: Actions Are Needed to Improve the Effectiveness of EPA's Chemical Review Program," Report no. GAO-06–1032T, Washington, DC, August 2, 2006, 1; see also Mary Cole, "When Superfund Expenses Go Mega," *Los Angeles Times,* January 26, 2007, 1A.

34. Environment America Research and Policy Center, Wasting Our Waterways 2012, "Executive Summary," available at http://www.environmentamerica.org/reports/ame/wasting-our-waterways-2012 (accessed October 20, 2012).

35. Ibid., 90–91.

36. GAO, "RCRA Corrective Action Program," Report no. GAO/RCED 97–3, Washington, DC, 1997; GAO, "Hazardous Waste: EPA Has Removed Some Barriers to Cleanups," Report no. GAO/RCED 00–2000, Washington, DC, August 2000, 10–11. See also EPA, Office of Solid Waste, Economics, Methods, and Risk Analysis Division, "A Study of the Implementation of the RCRA Corrective Action Program," September 25, 2000, available at www.coxcolvin.com/newsletter/CAImplemstudy.pdf (accessed May 15, 2002).

37. GAO, "RCRA Corrective Action Program," 2.

38. EPA, Office of Solid Waste and Environmental Remediation, "Treatment Projects Applied to 62 Percent of Superfund Sites," March 10, 2004, available at www.epa.gov/superfund (accessed March 26, 2004).

39. GAO, "Superfund: Estimates of Number of Future Sites Vary," Report no. GAO/RCED 95–18, Washington, DC, November 1994, 14. See also CEQ, *Environmental Quality, 1992* (Washington, DC: U.S. Government Printing Office, 1993), 127.

40. EPA, Region Six, "Superfund Success: EPA Continuing Cleanup Progress at Hazardous Waste Sites," December 2006, available at www.epa.gov/Region6/6xa/superfundjump .htm (accessed March 30, 2007).

41. GAO, "Superfund Funding and Cost," Report no. GAO-08–841R, Washington, DC, July 18, 2008, 4.

42. Robert Hersh, Michael B. Batz, and Katherine D. Walker, *Superfund's Future: What Will It Cost?* (Washington, DC: Resources for the Future), 131.

43. GAO, "Superfund Program: Current Superfund Program and Future Challenges," Report No. GAO-04–475R, Washington, DC, February 18, 2004.

44. Landy and Hague, "Coalition for Waste." On the general problems with Superfund, see, for example, Steven Cohen and Sheldon Kamieniecki, *Environmental Regulation Through Strategic Planning* (Boulder, CO: Westview Press, 1991); Daniel Mazmanian and David Morell, *Beyond Superfailure: America's Toxics Policy for the 1990s* (Boulder, CO: Westview Press, 1992).

45. Barnaby J. Feder, "In the Clutches of the Superfund Mess," *New York Times,* June 16, 1991, 3, 1.
46. Ibid.
47. EPA, "2007 Toxics Release Inventory (TRI), Public Data Release Reports," Report No. EPA 260-R-09-001, Washington, DC, April 2009, 6.
48. Marc Landy and Mary Hague, "The Coalition for Waste: Private Interests and Superfund," in *Environmental Politics: Public Costs, Private Rewards,* eds. Michael S. Greve and Fred L. Smith (New York: Praeger, 1992), 70.
49. Keith Schneider, "Rule Forcing Towns to Pick Big New Dumps or Big Costs," *New York Times,* January 6, 1992, A1.
50. Michael S. Greve, "Introduction," in *Environmental Politics: Public Costs, Private Rewards,* eds. Michael S. Greve and Fred L. Smith (New York: Praeger, 1992), 5–6.
51. On the sources and impact of NIMBY-ism generally, see Luther J. Carter, *Nuclear Imperatives and Public Trust: Dealing with Radioactive Waste* (Washington, DC: Resources for the Future, 1987); Clarence Davies, Vincent T. Covello, and Frederick W. Allen, eds., *Risk Communication* (Washington, DC: Conservation Foundation, 1987); Roger E. Kasperson, "Six Propositions on Public Participation and Their Relevance for Risk Communication," *Risk Analysis,* 6 (September 1986): 275–281; Patrick G. Marshall, "Not in My Backyard," *CQ Editorial Research Reports,* June 1989, 311.
52. Olurominiyi Ibitayo and Misse Herber, "NIMBYism," *The Encyclopedia of the Earth,* November 18, 2008, available at http://www.eoearth.org/article/NIMBYism (accessed January 5, 2010).
53. Michael S. Greve, "Environmentalism and Bounty Hunting," *Public Interest,* 97 (fall 1989): 15–29.
54. Ibid., 24.
55. Michael E. Kraft, "Managing Technological Risks in a Democratic Polity: Citizen Participation and Nuclear Waste Disposal," paper presented at the national conference of the American Society for Public Administration, Boston, MA, 1987. See also CEQ, EOP, "The National Environmental Policy Act: A Study of Its Effectiveness after Twenty-Five Years," Washington, DC, January 1997.
56. William Lyons, Michael R. Fitzgerald, and Amy McCabe, "Public Opinion and Hazardous Waste," *Forum for Applied Research and Public Policy* 2 (fall 1987): 89–97. See also Michael E. Kraft, "Risk Perception and the Politics of Citizen Participation: The Case of Radioactive Waste Management," in *Advances in Risk Analysis,* vol. 9, ed. Lorraine Abbott (New York: Plenum Press, 1990).
57. Thomas M. Dietz and Robert W. Rycroft, *The Risk Professionals* (New York: Russell Sage Foundation, 1987), 60.
58. Harvey Brooks, "The Resolution of Technically Intensive Public Policy Disputes," *Science, Technology and Human Values* 9 (winter 1984): 48.
59. Kraft, "Risk Perception," 7

Chapter 8

Energy
America's Energy Politics in Transformation

The global energy map is changing, with potentially far-reaching consequences for energy markets and trade. It is being redrawn by the resurgence in oil and gas production in the United States and could be further reshaped by a retreat from nuclear power in some countries, continued rapid growth in the use of wind and solar technologies and by the global spread of unconventional gas production . . .

—International Energy Agency (IEA),
World Energy Outlook, 2012[1]

In late 2012, the IEA released a report that seemed to confirm that something remarkable, almost startling, had happened to the U.S. energy system in fewer than five years. The energy economy was becoming—or had already become—an economy transformed. This was a reality different, sometimes radically remade, from what Barack Obama had confronted upon entering the White House only four years previously. Petroleum imports were falling, domestic production was rising. Experts were anticipating an unprecedented natural gas "boom" that threatened to stifle America's always economically fragile coal industry. The often predicted revival of commercial nuclear power once again seemed an illusion. And in the West, vast wind farms and sprawling, 1,000-acre solar arrays were emerging in grasslands and deserts. There was even serious discussion of a true American energy independence.

The IEA called these changes "profound." The effect of these transformations, concluded the IEA, "will be felt well beyond North America—and the energy sector. . . . The recent rebound in US oil and gas production . . . is spurring economic activity . . . and steadily changing the role of North America in global energy trade. By around 2020, the United States is projected to become the largest global oil producer . . ."[2]

Even if these and related developments fall short of the most optimistic predictions, their powerful impact is already rippling across the U.S. energy sector. Thus, President Barack Obama began his second term, in common with other energy policy makers, confronting an array of new policy options and renewed challenges to established energy policies and institutions.

This chapter explores some of the most important policy issues posed by these emerging changes in the major sectors of the U.S. energy sector. It begins with a discussion the major fossil fuels—petroleum, natural gas, and coal—then turns to important alternative energy options, including nuclear energy and renewable sources (wind and solar). To place these technologies in a policy perspective, the narrative provides a brief overview of each energy sector's importance in U.S. domestic energy production and consumption, then illustrates, often with brief case studies, significant policy issues and institutions currently involved with the various sectors and the implications for the Obama presidency.

The Foundation: A Fossil Fuel Nation

The United States has a ravenous energy appetite, and most of the consumption has been fossil fuel, as Figure 8–1 illustrates. Collectively, Americans constitute approximately 4.5 percent of the world's population and consume about 25 percent of the world's energy production; on average, one American uses more energy in a year than a European, a South American, and an Asian combined.[3] Many of the nation's major pollution problems are caused directly by current methods of producing and consuming this energy. Consider the environmental impact of fossil fuels. About 84 percent of all energy currently consumed in the United States comes from petroleum, natural gas, and coal.[4] The ecological consequences of this combustion are numerous:

- Transportation and other fossil fuel combustion annually produce 34 percent of the VOCs, 78 percent of the carbon monoxide, 85 percent of the sulfur oxides, and 95 percent of the nitrogen oxides emitted into the air.[5]
- The land area disturbed by coal surface mining in the United States now exceeds 5.7 million acres, an area equal in size to the state of New Hampshire. Of this total, more than 3 million acres remains abandoned, creating sterile wastelands.
- During the first decade of this century, an average of more than 9,000 large spills of hazardous substances, mostly petroleum, were reported in U.S. waters yearly. More than 1 million gallons of petroleum and chemicals were spilled annually during the decade.[6]

Figure 8–1   U.S. Energy Consumption by Energy Source, 2011

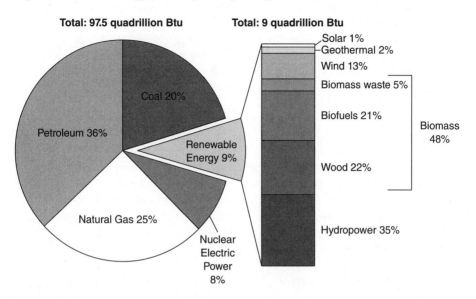

Source: U.S. Energy Information Administration, *Monthly Energy Review*, Table 10.1 (March 2012), preliminary 2011 data.

So intimate is the association between energy and environmental quality—a link revealed again by the emerging problems of global climate warming—that the nation's energy agenda in the second decade of the 21st century will become environmental policy by another name.

In addition to the adverse environmental impact of fossil fuel, particularly coal, America's current energy consumption is doubly precarious. The fossil fuels providing most of the energy that currently drives the national economy come from nonrenewable, and ultimately diminishing, energy stocks that must currently provide more than two thirds of the nation's energy supply well into mid-century. Moreover, about 40 percent of U.S. imported petroleum, a significant portion of all the petroleum that provides a third of national energy consumption flows from insecure, progressively more competitive foreign supplies, primarily in the Middle East, Asia, and Africa. Not surprisingly, Barack Obama has joined every U.S. president since Richard Nixon in his preoccupation with reducing national dependence on imported petroleum and mitigating the environmental impact of other fossil fuels.

Petroleum: A Revived Economy?

While the United States in 2012 still depended upon imported oil for more than 40 percent of its domestic consumption, one of the most important emerging transformations in the American energy economy has been the decline of imported petroleum beginning in 2010: At the beginning of the second Obama administration, imports had decreased from almost 55 percent of total consumption in 2008 to 42 percent in 2012, a declining trend predicted to prevail well into the decade (see Figure 8–2). The growing American oil production is primarily the result of the improvement and rapid national dispersion of fracking, the technology introduced in Chapter 1 and further explored when natural gas is next considered.

The World's Leading Oil Exporter—Perhaps

The rapid reversal of American imported oil consumption has been accompanied by an equally significant increase in domestic petroleum refining, again reversing a trend of declining domestic oil production that prevailed since the early 1970s. Together, these dual transitions have rapidly created a new petroleum market quite unlike that which prevailed as late as 2009. If these trends continue, as many experts now predict, the United States would replace Saudi Arabia as the world's leading oil producer in less than a decade.

At the same time, the IEA also cautions, the United States is not an "energy island"' invulnerable to the global energy economy and its

Figure 8–2   U.S. Dependence on Imported Oil Declining

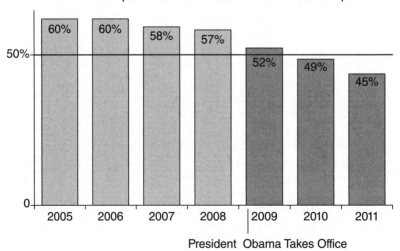

Net imports of oil as a share of domestic consumption

President Obama Takes Office

Source: U.S. Energy Information Administration, http://energy.gov/science-innovation/ energy-sources/fossil.

environmental implications. For example, the IEA predicts that mainland China's rapid economic growth will increase its dependence on imported petroleum from 22 percent of its annual petroleum consumption in 2000 to 77 percent by 2020, and that, during the same period, European dependence on imported oil will rise from 52 to 79 percent of annual demand.[7] Thus, there will likely be growing competition for the global oil supply upon which the U.S. must depend for a significant amount of imported oil it will still consume in the future. This is an important reason many energy experts join environmentalists in advocating increased domestic energy conservation as a national security issue to protect against future imported oil blockades.

Oil, the Outer Continental Shelf, and the Environment

While a revival of domestic petroleum production and exports has an almost irresistible economic and political allure for American policy makers, it is also loaded with long-standing, controversial environmental issues as well as new ones, such as fracking technology. The history of petroleum production since Earth Day is inseparable from environmental conflicts incited by the political and economic pressure to expand traditional production from existing petroleum reserves despite the environmental risks.

Petroleum production from oil reserves on federal lands has been one traditional source of impassioned conflict between proponents of accelerated petroleum production and environmentalists. The long and fierce conflict over petroleum drilling on the huge continental area constituting the Alaskan National Wildlife Refuge introduces the next chapter concerning public lands. Another major flashpoint for these controversies in recent years has been the ecological impact of oil production from submerged public lands on the Outer Continental Shelf (OCS).

The OCS consists of the submerged between a continent and the deep ocean. America's OCS encompasses 1.76 billion acres of submerged, taxpayer-owned lands. Generally, the OCS begins 3 to 9 nautical miles from shore (depending on the state) and extends 200 nautical miles outward, or farther if the continental shelf extends beyond that limit. The federal government administers the submerged lands, subsoil, and seabed of the OCS. Jurisdiction over OCS lands is divided between the coastal states, whose authority extends three miles from their ocean borders (except for Texas and the west coast of Florida, where state jurisdiction extends to 9 nautical miles) and the federal government, which controls OCS lands for 200 miles beyond the state 3-mile limit. Altogether, production from existing state and federal energy leases accounts for about 30 percent of domestic petroleum production and 25 percent of natural gas.

The DOI has estimated that federally controlled OCS lands contain reserves of 8.5 billion barrels of oil and 29.3 trillion cubic feet (tcf) of natural gas (the United States consumes about 19 million barrels of petroleum and 1.6 million tcf of natural gas daily).[8] The DOI regulates energy exploration in the OCS by determining the location of OCS land open to exploration, issuing permits for exploration, and enforcing safety and environmental regulations for energy production from oil and gas wells. Environmentalists have been especially vigilant about federal leasing and supervision of energy production on the OCS. They have persistently criticized federal regulators for insufficient oversight of environmental laws governing OCS energy development and have resisted pressure on the federal government by international energy producers to open vast new OCS tracts to exploration

The ongoing battle over OCS energy development escalated to international attention following the catastrophic incineration and collapse of British Petroleum's *Deepwater Horizon* drilling platform into the Gulf of Mexico in early 2012. The platform's destruction in April 2010 constituted the largest accidental marine oil spill in American history, releasing 4.9 million barrels of crude oil in the gulf and creating the largest oil spill in U.S. history. What followed was an ecological disaster whose long-range environmental impacts will take decades to assess. Environmentalists angrily asserted that the gulf disaster demonstrated both the inherent risks of increased energy exploration in the OCS and the federal government's lax regulatory oversight of OCS petroleum production.

Investigation by the DOI's own inspector general, a bipartisan congressional committee, and numerous other official and unofficial entities between 2010 and 2011 revealed that the Minerals Management Service (MMS) responsible for regulatory supervision of gulf energy production had failed to enforce rigorously its regulatory oversight, which could have prevented the spill. In the aftermath of further DOI and congressional investigations, Secretary of the Interior Kenneth Salazar promised radical reform at the MMS, calling such revelations "deeply disturbing" and "further evidence of the cozy relationship between some elements of the MMS and the oil and gas industry" the department intended to eliminate."[9] The MMS became a classic example of the problem created when federal agencies are responsible for both regulating and promoting the same industry.

Despite the gulf oil spill, the White House and Congress continue to share a keen and increasingly partisan interest in the future of OCS lands. While congressional Republicans have pressed for accelerated OCS energy development and Democrats have usually advocated restraint, political and economic cross-pressures often blur partisan differences, particularly concerning the OCS lands under state jurisdiction. For example, Florida's Senate and House delegations of both parties are usually together in opposing any OCS development likely to create environmental damage to the state's coast. President Obama initially appeared to favor restrained energy development on OCS lands but, even in the aftermath of Deepwater Horizon, was compelled in the presence of the country's persistently deep economic recession to modify his stance and to advocate "safe and responsible" oil production. He went so far as to declare that his administration officials were working to speed up the leasing process for exploration in the already-developed Alaska National Petroleum Reserve, "while also giving oil companies better financial incentives to use and extend certain existing leases in the Gulf of Mexico and elsewhere."[10] The president also indicated his support for accelerated testing of areas off the East Coast for possible future drilling. Numerous Atlantic and Pacific coast states currently receive substantial royalties from energy development on their OCS lands, and as noted earlier, increased leasing is a continual issue among almost all coastal states. The Gulf of Mexico has become a constant battleground between proponents and opponents of exploration on the OCS.

Natural Gas and the Gas "Boom"

Natural gas in its several different forms is often considered the most attractive and versatile of all the fossil fuels in the nation's near future. Natural gas is commercially produced primarily from oil fields and natural gas fields, although the industry is now aggressively extracting natural gas from unconventional sources such as shale gas and coal-bed methane. Traditional *casinghead gas,* principally methane mixed with numerous impurities, is refined into ethane, propane, butanes, pentanes, and other commercial forms, which for convenience are often collectively called *natural gas.* While the largest proven natural gas reserves are located in Russia, Iran, and the Arabian Gulf states, U.S. proven reserves are significant and, as new extraction technologies develop, steadily increasing. To many U.S. energy sectors, natural gas is increasingly important, economically and environmentally, as an alternative to petroleum and coal if the entailed risks of increasing gas production prove acceptable. And, like all projections about future domestic energy use, predictions of future gas supply depend upon numerous assumptions or scenarios—such as continued economic growth and absence of major political crises—that caution against treating predictions as if they are destiny.

Domestic Resources: Increasing Supply and Demand

As Figure 8–3 indicates, natural gas now provides a significant portion of energy to several important U.S. economic sectors.

Figure 8–3 Natural Gas Consumption by Sector, 2010

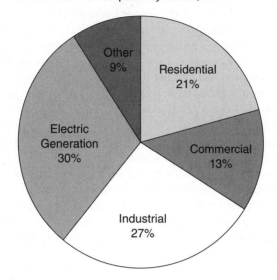

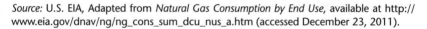

Source: U.S. EIA, Adapted from *Natural Gas Consumption by End Use,* available at http://www.eia.gov/dnav/ng/ng_cons_sum_dcu_nus_a.htm (accessed December 23, 2011).

Proven reserves of domestic onshore and offshore natural gas have grown annually since 1999 as a result of improved technologies and the development of economically practical extraction from shale.[11] According to the EIA, the United States possesses enough natural gas reserves to supply more than 100 years of use at 2010 consumption levels. More than 90 percent of current domestic natural gas originates from onshore sources. Nineteen states are estimated to possess significant natural gas reserves.[12] Domestic production of natural gas is expected to increase significantly in the future, but so is total U.S. energy demand; the EIA has predicted that, by 2030, natural gas will provide about 25 percent of domestic energy consumption—about the proportion of current consumption. However, the predicted change in how natural gas is produced and consumed is important.

Much of the expected change in future natural gas production and consumption is expected to result not only from increased fracking but also from changes in fossil fuel consumption by the electric power and industrial sections, which together consume almost two thirds of current natural production. Both electric utilities and industry have responded to tougher air pollution regulations and the decreasing price of natural gas by substituting gas for coal-fired facilities in existing or planned installations. Progress Energy, for example, one of the nation's largest electric utilities, has announced plans to shut down 11 North Carolina coal plants by 2017 and to substitute natural gas in 2 of them.[13]

Natural gas exploration and production has traditionally entailed environmental hazards. Exploration and drilling for natural gas disturbs surface vegetation and soil as well as subsurface geology; pipelines can pose air and water pollution problems. Natural gas wells and pipelines require infrastructure, such as engines and drilling rigs, also environmentally hazardous when unregulated. Some natural gas, mostly methane, also leaks from drilling sites and pipelines. The oil and gas industry has made an effort to avoid gas leaks, and where natural gas is produced but can't be transported economically, it is *flared,* or burned at well sites. This is considered safer and better than releasing methane into the atmosphere because CO_2 is not as potent a greenhouse gas as methane. The issue that now most conspicuously threatens to dissipate optimism about a coming boom in natural gas production is the environmental risks associated with fracking technology.[14]

Fracking: "Almost a Miracle" or an Environmental Menace?

The rising tide of optimism in the natural gas industry is inspired by fracking technology. At the outset of the Obama administration, the new drilling boom involving fracking seemed to many industry leaders a certain path toward a bright future. "It's almost divine intervention," burbled Aubrey K. McClendon, chairman and chief executive of the Chesapeake Energy Corporation, one of the nation's largest natural gas producers. "Right at the time oil prices are skyrocketing, we're struggling with the economy, we're concerned about global warming, and national security threats remain intense, we wake up and we've got this abundance of natural gas around us."[15] Not all industry experts share this confidence. Still, significantly increased gas production throughout the Obama administration's first term encouraged most energy experts and financial markets to view the industry's future with cautious optimism. Map 8–1 illustrates the most important domestic shale gas deposits.

A Disputed Environmental Impact. Hydrologic fracturing "involves pumping liquids under high pressure into a well to fracture the rock and allow gas to escape from tiny pockets in the rock." Millions of gallons of chemically treated water called *brine* mixed with sand are blasted down a drilling hole to shatter petroleum shale and release the embedded gas. The return water, called *flowback,* is a cocktail of water, chemical toxins and carcinogens, other chemical wastes sometimes including radioactive components, and inert substances that must be purified before the flowback is suitable for other uses. Most of the return water, however, is pumped back underground into shale sites for containment. Almost all natural gas exploration and production from leases on federal lands uses fracking technology regulated by the DOI. The largest private fracking

Map 8–1   Major Oil Shale Deposits in the United States

Source: U.S. Department of Energy, "Modern Shale Gas Development in the United States: A Primer," available at www.netl.doe.gov/technologies/oil-gas/publications/epreports/shale_gas_primer_2009.pdf.

operations are sited on the Barnett Shale formation near Fort Worth and on the vast Marcellus Shale underlying portions of Pennsylvania, New York, West Virginia, and Ohio. Pennsylvania alone has more than 57,000 gas-producing wells. These nonfederal sites are presently regulated by the states.

Chapter 1 illustrated the ambivalence with which environmentalists and many residents near fracking operations regard hydrologic fracturing. Nonetheless, many gas production companies, contending their brine formulas are trade secrets, refuse to publicly disclose their compositions. The industry contends, moreover, that proven technologies are available for distilling an environmentally safe liquid from flowback when needed. The CEO of Halliburton Co., a major energy consulting firm, was so convinced of the safety that he invited an associate to drink some fracking fluid during a meeting of the Colorado Oil and Gas Association, and the media reported that his associate consumed a "bit of the liquid" without harm.

An Uncertain Regulatory Future. Under considerable political pressure from oil shale states, environmentalists, Congress, and communities near fracking operations, the EPA has initiated studies to characterize the content and dispersion of flowback. While the final report is scheduled in 2014, a preliminary study in Wyoming reported in 2011 that the EPA had "found that groundwater in an aquifer around Pavillion, Wyoming, contained compounds likely associated with gas production practices, including hydraulic fracturing." The U.S. Department of Health and Human Services then "advised local residents to use alternative sources of water for drinking and cooking and to use ventilation when showering, in order to air out potentially dangerous chemicals."[17] Whether this early report implies an environmental hazard inherent to fracking technology or describes, instead, a unique local situation remains uncertain, but the implications have prompted the technology's advocates to increase efforts to assure the public and public officials that fracking is essentially safe environmentally.

Coal: The Promise and Perils of Abundance

Every U.S. president from Richard Nixon through George W. Bush has tried, in one way or another, to dam the flow of imported oil into the United States with a wall of coal. Coal is the nation's most plentiful fossil fuel. With reserves sufficient for 250 years at current consumption rates, it is inevitable that federal energy planners should repeatedly attempt to substitute abundant domestic coal for expensive, insecure, imported oil. Economic and environmental problems, however, continue to inhibit a massive national conversion to coal combustion. By 2000, climate warming had become the most recent among many global signatures for coal's environmental risks, another ominous offset to the powerful attractions of coal energy in a nation extravagantly endowed with coal. Barack Obama, lately a U.S. senator from a major coal state, has been walking a political tightrope through the turbulence of coal controversies. His administration has struggled at finding some politically viable equilibrium among its seemingly incompatible commitment to encouraging coal combustion through the rapid development of "clean coal" technologies, actively advocating global climate change emissions control, and aggressively regulating air pollution regulation, all while increasing electric power production—issues with *coal* written all over them.

The Turbulent Economics of Coal. Coal represents about 90 percent of the remaining U.S. hydrocarbon reserves. The coal industry liked to remind Americans during the energy crisis of the 1970s that the nation had the equivalent of Saudi petroleum resources in coal. This coal rests in three geological reserves: Appalachia's wooded hills and hollows sprawling across parts of seven Southeastern states, the Midwestern plains, and the Western plains and grasslands. After years of sluggish growth, regulatory battles, and relentless environmentalist criticism, joined by public health professionals between 1970 and 1990, the coal industry in the mid-1990s began a political and economic revival as a plausible alternative to continued U.S. reliance on imported oil and a dependable answer for rapidly growing demand for electric power.

Currently, coal accounts for about 22 percent of U.S. energy consumption. Electricity utilities, the prime coal consumers, generate more than half their power from coal-fired boilers. Although U.S. coal production reached record levels in the last decade, the industry has been afflicted since the 1950s with declining employment, chronic labor violence, and boom-or-bust economic cycles. The industry's economic fortunes are closely tied to the electric-power and metallurgical industries, which consume 85 and 13 percent of annual coal production, respectively. Because more than 8 of every 10 tons of mined coal are transported by rail, many railroads have become heavily dependent on coal production for revenue. Presidential coal policies have always been rationalized by great expectations. In the midst of the first energy crisis, the coal industry, alert to political opportunity, was quick to proclaim coal the "great black hope of America" and to throw its political weight behind new White House coal initiatives.

The coal industry has become increasingly troubled by the economic impact of fracking's rapid development and the surge of natural gas production it has created. Coal producers have good reason to worry. Sharply rising production has driven down the market price of natural gas to the point where it has become increasingly attractive as an alternative fuel for the electric power industry. Many utilities are now partially substituting natural gas for coal in existing power plants and—more ominous for the coal industry—are switching from coal to natural gas for planned new facilities. The industry has warned the federal government that, unless it does more to reduce the cost and severity of environmental regulations affecting coal production, the industry will be looking over the horizon at an economic depression.

There were several plausible reasons for coal's continuing attraction to energy planners despite related economic and environmental problems. According to some estimates, accelerated coal combustion might displace as much as 2.5 million barrels of imported petroleum consumed by the United States daily. A coal boom might bring 100,000 new workers to Appalachia, reviving its stagnant economy, and perhaps 50,000 more workers to the West; coal-related income in the West and Great Plains might rise by $850 million to $1 billion. Large "mine-mouth" electricity-generating plants, located adjacent to coal seams to reduce transportation costs, could provide dependable, secure electric power for the growing West and Midwest. Coal is secure energy, without menace from Middle Eastern politics and unpredictable world petroleum markets. Because coal combustion produces more than half the nation's electric power, if "clean coal" technology becomes a reality, coal could provide an enormously attractive reserve for the future electric power industry. Coal could glitter as gold if only the new coal boom could be made environmentally and economically tolerable.

The Environmental Legacy of Coal Mining

The most significant adverse environmental impacts associated with coal use are created by surface mining and combustion. Many of these environmental hazards associated with coal combustion were mentioned in the discussion of air pollution in Chapter 4. Coal mining is equally rich with environmental hazards.

Surface Mining. Virtually all coal mined west of the Mississippi River and half the coal produced in Appalachia is surface mined. Surface mining rapidly has replaced underground mining because it is cheaper, more efficient, more profitable, and less labor intensive. Unless rigorously regulated, however, surface mining is environmentally catastrophic. More than 1.5 million acres of American land have been disturbed by coal surface mining; more than a million of these acres remain wrecked and ravaged wastelands, long abandoned by their destroyers. More than 1,000 additional acres are disturbed each week by surface mining, and more than 30 states have been scarred by unreclaimed surface mines.

In Appalachia, surface miners roamed the hills virtually uncontrolled for decades. The evidence is written in the thousands of sterile acres, acidified streams and rivers, decapitated hills, and slopes scarred by abandoned mine highwalls. In the Western prairies and grasslands, unregulated surface mining left thousands of barren, furrowed acres buried under spoil banks so hostile to revegetation that they seem like moonscapes to observers. After decades of resistance, the mining industry has come to recognize the necessity of environmental regulation of surface mining, but vigorous controversy continues over the manner of this regulation and its effectiveness.

President Carter signed the Surface Mining Control and Reclamation Act (SMCRA) of 1977 and thereby created the first federal surface mining regulatory program. The act, strongly promoted by environmentalists against fierce resistance from the mining industry is intended to control the environmental ravages of surface mining by restoring surface-mined land to productivity whenever possible. The act's major features included the following:

- Environmental performance standards with which all surface miners were to comply in order to operate. Standards were to be established for the removal, storage, and redistribution of topsoil; siting and erosion control; drainage and protection of water quality; and many other matters affecting environmental quality.

- Requirements that mined land be returned, insofar as possible, to its original contours and to a use equal or superior to that before mining commenced.
- Protection of land unsuitable for mining from any mine activity.

SMCRA remains a troubled and underfunded program. The Office of Surface Mining Reclamation and Enforcement (OSMRE) and the states confront a hugely expensive and complex problem in protecting public health and safety on America's abandoned coal mine lands. Estimates suggest the total cost of restoring these ravaged and deserted acres is $8.6 billion.[18] Among other tasks, restoration requires the remediation of 9,000 acres of unstable waste piles and embankments, 4 million linear feet of dangerous highwalls, 8,200 acres of subsiding soil, and 23,000 acres of clogged stream lands.[19] A succession of directors continues through the OSMRE's revolving door, and the amount of improvement in program administration remains questionable. The OSMRE struggles to improve its public image (perhaps in desperation, its website now includes a children's link where young viewers can download a coloring book and poster depicting surface mines).[20] It seems apparent, at least, that the OSMRE cannot or will not exercise dependable, vigorous administrative oversight of state enforcement programs.[21] Still, some observers believe that the controversies surrounding SMCRA have had constructive results, including greater sensitivity in Washington, DC, to the needs of the states and greater economic efficiency through more flexibility in program regulations.

Mountaintop Removal. Surface mining along mountaintops has steadily enlarged into a pervasive, bitterly contentions issue as the practice spreads primarily through Appalachia and the Midwest. As science writer David Biello observes,

> The litany of problems—both to the environment and human health—caused by a practice that involves blasting the top off a mountain to get at the coal beneath it more easily [includes] heavy metals, sulfuric acid and other mine contaminants in waterways and drinking-water wells; deformed fish carrying toxic levels of selenium found in 73 of 78 streams affected by mountaintop mining; entire streams filled in by blasted mountain rock; and forests cleared to get at the mountaintop beneath them. Add to that the fact that this form of mining has increased exponentially in the past 30 years, supplying roughly 10 percent of U.S. coal, and you have a recipe for much of the environmental devastation visible across northern Appalachia.[22]

Mining companies argue that it is the only way to get at many coal deposits. "Coal in these areas is found in very narrow seams, and the surrounding rock geology is less stable than in areas of layer seams," explained Carol Raulston, senior vice president of the National Mining Association. "It creates flat terrain on what was the top of the mountain but the mountain is still there."[23] Critics, however, say that the land is devastated, that people, property, and the environment endure severe collateral damage. Predictably, mountaintop mining opponents were critical of the decision by the Obama EPA to permit continued mountaintop removal if the mining is rigorously regulated and monitored. The mountaintop issue seems destined to stalk the White House, EPA, and OSMRE for many years and to assure abrasive confrontations between Obama and his environmentalist constituency.

The Restoration Gamble. One ultimately important test of surface mine regulations is whether they result in an environmentally safer mining industry and a significant restoration of the many thousand orphan mine sites across the United States. The answer to this is elusive, partly because the restoration of surface mine sites is difficult under the best of circumstances, and public resources to underwrite much of the restoration cost remain unpredictable.

Obscured in the controversy over SMCRA's enforcement has been an issue even more important to the future of surface mining: Is restoration of mined lands in the manner contemplated by the act achievable? Technical studies suggest that the capacity of mining companies to restore mined land to conditions equal or superior to their original condition is likely to be site specific, that is, dependent on the particular biological and geological character of each mining site. Western mining sites are often ecologically fragile; relatively limited varieties of sustainable vegetation and scarce rainfall make the ecological regeneration of the land difficult. With only limited experience in the restoration of Western mine sites, most experts are reluctant to predict that mine sites can be restored to ecological vitality even with good intentions, generous funding, and high-quality technical resources.

The prospects for restoration are less forbidding in Appalachia, where an abundance of precipitation, richer soil, and a greater diversity of native flora and fauna are available. Nonetheless, many experts believe that the disruption of subsurface hydrology and the drainage of acids and salts from the mines' spoil heaps may not be controlled easily even when surface revegetation is achieved. Restoration remains a gamble with nature. If restoration proves difficult, confronting public officials with the prospect that a major portion of all surface-mined land may remain virtually sterile for centuries, a further national controversy may erupt over continuing surface mining.

More than three decades' experience with SMCRA leaves only fragmentary evidence of its success. After studying SMCRA's enforcement among many states, for instance, political scientist Uday Desai concluded that the consequences have been mixed at best. Environmentally safe conditions apparently were being maintained at active mine sites in Montana, Pennsylvania, and Wyoming. But, in Kentucky, a major mining state, the law appeared to have had only a "marginal" impact, and in West Virginia, another important coal state, it "had not been thoroughly and rigorously enforced in many areas."[24] Desai's conclusion suggests how far SMCRA's enforcement has yet to go in achieving its purpose:

> It is not possible to make an unqualified overall national assessment, but the evidence . . . indicates that, in most (but by no means all) cases, surface coal mining is being carried out in environmentally less destructive ways than before the Act. However, accomplishment of its ultimate objective has fallen far short of the expectations of many. In addition, there has been a serious deterioration of the situation on the ground in some states such as Kentucky.[25]

Despite the formidable challenges involved, OSMRE resolutely casts restoration in a benign light.

An Emerging Issue: Coal Ash. The regulation of coal-burning emissions, mostly from electric power generation, annually creates 125 million to 130 million tons of toxic ash and sludge, enough to fill a million railcars; more than half this volume resides in ponds and pits, primarily on electricity utility property. This waste was virtually invisible politically until December 22, 2008, when an earthen dam containing a billion gallons of ash waste from the TVA Kingston Fossil power plant, near Kingston, Tennessee, failed. The released slurry erupted through the containment "like a volcano," reported one resident, flooding 300 acres, including Kingston and the nearby Emery River with sludge containing elevated levels of toxic metals (including arsenic, copper, barium, cadmium, chromium, lead, mercury, nickel, and thallium) and other pollutants.[26] Kingston residents claim the residue continues to create serious health problems. A rapid EPA national survey disclosed 431 similar facilities, of which 49 were considered "high hazard" because their failure could endanger human life. These containments are a portion of more than 1,300 sludge and ash pits estimated to exist nationally, most of them unregulated and unmonitored.[27]

Coal ash becomes a problem because it resides in a regulatory twilight zone. Depending on where it appears and what it contains, it can be considered a solid waste, water pollutant, toxic waste, groundwater contaminant, or even an air pollutant, and it is therefore subject to various federal and state regulations—or perhaps to no specific regulation or to conflicting laws. Consequently, although most states regulate some aspects of coal ash deposition, there is little consistency in and considerable ambiguity about how environmental controls are applied and if the most effective management prevails.

The EPA has proposed new comprehensive ash pit regulations, but the EPA and officials in the White House OIRA (see Chapter 5) do not agree on how to proceed. The coal ash pits constitute a major regulatory challenge for the Obama administration that will be closely watched by environmentalists, many critical of what they believe is an irresolute and tardy White House response—in effect, this issue is becoming a test of the administration's political credibility with environmental advocates.

Climate Warming and "Clean Coal" Technology. One of the most unsettled aspects of future CO_2 regulation is the availability of a control technology for the large electrical utilities creating most of the domestic CO_2 emissions. The EPA's anticipated CO_2 regulations are expected to require that new coal-fired plants must use the "best available control technology," although no such commercial technology currently exists for CO_2 emissions. Thus, the coal and electric power industries have been strongly motivated to discover a "clean coal" technique to reduce their air pollution emissions.

In an effort to encourage development of "clean coal" technologies, the Obama administration's massive $775 billion American Recovery and Reinvestment Act (2009) included $3.4 billion in federal support for carbon capture and sequestration (CCS) development. Without the prospect of this substantial federal research and development support, public and private electric power companies were unlikely to invest alone the estimated $1 billion required to create an operational electric power facility equipped with a new and largely unproven CCS technology.[28]

The coal industry's major hope for commercially viable CO_2 emission controls still rests precariously with the experimental CCS technology. In CCS operations, "CO_2 is separated from the fuel and captured either before or after the combustion of coal. It is then compressed to a super critical liquid, transported by pipeline to an injection well and then pumped underground to depths sufficient to maintain critical temperatures and pressures." If the technology works,

> the CO_2 seeps into the pore spaces in the surrounding rock and its escape to the surface is blocked by a caprock, or overlaying impermeable layer. Energy companies boast extensive experience sequestering CO_2 by injecting it into oil fields to enhance oil recovery. Experts are optimistic this practice can be replicated in saline aquifers and other geologic formations that are likely to constitute the main storage reservoirs for CO_2 emitted from coal power plants. Underground storage capacity in the United States is believed to be ample and widespread, and long-term leakage of CO_2 from properly permitted and monitored storage reservoirs is expected to be negligible.[29]

In 2010, with considerable research and development funding by the DOE, the American Electric Power Co. began site experiments at its Mountaineer power plant near New Haven, West Virginia, with the earliest pilot CCS project.[30] An enormous weight of political and economic expectations had been loaded onto the Mountaineer project, and the company's decision to cancel Mountineer less than a year later was a severe setback to the coal and electric power industries. Significantly, even though the DOE was willing to invest more than $300 million in Mountineer, American Power was reluctant to invest further until the murky future of national CO_2 emissions regulation is clarified.[31]

CCS and Coal Combustion's Murky Future. The fate of the Mountaineer projects suggests a few of the formidable and unresolved issues impeding the development of a commercially practical CCS technology. The uncertainties crowding the future of CCS, moreover, are a microcosm of the disarray permeating federal climate policy and, with it, the future of domestic coal combustion. Barack Obama has inherited a daunting challenge in defining a politically and economically viable climate policy and in resolving implications for the future of coal combustion in his second term.

CCS itself remains a primitive technology. Assuming an optimistic scenario, the time required from initiation of a successful pilot project to the construction of a commercially viable facility is estimated to require perhaps two decades and an investment of several billion dollars. If federal CO_2 regulations are enacted, a significant reduction in electric power emissions will require CCS installation or retrofitting in perhaps hundreds of facilities; many electric power industry experts believe the federal government must commit much more to CCS development than the present $3.4 billion available from the American Recovery and Investment Act. In an obituary for the failed Future Gen, the principle research engineer for MIT's CCS program warned about government failure to understand the magnitude of the CCS challenge. "How can we do hundreds of these plants by 2050—and that's what we'll need" he commented, "if we can't even do one?"[32] Environmentalists have largely opposed any version of CCS because they assert CCS power plants will be too costly to build and maintain in comparison to their economic or environmental benefits and will divert investment from more productive, renewable energy technologies. Additionally, they cite substantial and often unknown environmental risks inherent to CCS.

Fossil Fuel Alternatives: Nuclear Power and Renewable Energy

The environmental hazards and security problems inseparable from fossil fuel combustion have inspired both the federal government and the private sector to invest in the creation and commercialization of alternative energy technologies, which are asserted to be more environmentally benign and more robust because they do depend less, if at all, on insecure or exhaustible fuels. Three of these technologies—nuclear power, wind power, and solar energy—dominate current national energy discourse and debate.

The Fading Renaissance

The catastrophic tsunami that ravaged Japan's northeast coast on March 11, 2011, left in its wake a disastrous succession of unprecedented emergency nuclear equipment failures, several reactor meltdowns, and significant radioactive emissions. It also devastated far more than the Fukushima Daiichi commercial nuclear power facility. It may have shattered the American nuclear industry's cherished vision of a "nuclear renaissance." The Japanese disaster became the latest dramatic episode in the contentious development of the American commercial nuclear power industry and another chapter in the crisis-driven history of the domestic nuclear power policy.

The Elusive Revival

After decades of economic stagnation, the domestic nuclear power industry seemed, in 2010, about to revive. In 2000, statistics about commercial nuclear power read like the industry's obituary. Since 1980, the nuclear dream—the vision of almost unlimited, cheap electricity generated by hundreds of nuclear reactors—had been dying. The commercial nuclear power industry was failing under a burden of economic and technological misfortunes, an increasingly hostile political climate, inept public relations, persistent environmental risks, and mounting regulatory pressures.

By late 2010, however, industry leaders and supporters were speaking confidently about a "nuclear renaissance."[33] One potent source of this optimism might be called the "other greenhouse effect." Capitalizing on growing national and international attention to global climate warming, in the 1990s, the industry initiated an aggressive campaign to promote commercial nuclear power as the most desirable economic and environmental alternative to the greenhouse gas emissions associated with fossil fuel combustion to generate electric power. Another powerful stimulus was the federal government's vigorous political and economic initiatives since the George W. Bush administration.

In 2004, the George W. Bush administration, acting through the DOE, proposed building 50 new power plants and prolonging the operating life of numerous existing facilities to the year 2020. Additionally, the Energy Policy Act (EPAct), sponsored by the Bush administration, promised a very substantial commitment to nuclear power development and seemed to the industry's advocates a confirmation that industry was, at last, truly reviving. In keeping with a half-century tradition of massive federal governmental subsidies, research grants, and other economic patronage, EPAct provided financial incentives for the construction of advanced nuclear plants amounting to $18.5 billion, which the industry requested be increased to $100 billion. Barack Obama added additional momentum to the nuclear resurgence when, much to the disappointment of environmentalists, his campaign platform endorsed the continued development of commercial nuclear power, a commitment reinforced when his 2010 State of the Union speech advocated "a new generation of safe, clean nuclear power plants" and proposed to triple public financing for nuclear power.[34]

Underlying these decisions, and doubtless encouraging them, had been rising public approval for commercial nuclear power to the point where, in mid-2009, the Gallup Poll reported "new high levels of support," with 59 percent of Americans favoring domestic nuclear energy.[35] Added good news was an anticipated 30 percent escalation of the U.S. demand for electric power, a very substantial increase in nuclear output capacity, and the absence of a high-visibility facility accident or security lapse. The industry also anticipated that a planned new generation of reactor technologies (Generation III) would be considerably more efficient, safer, and economical than present operating models. As if to challenge history, moreover, the U.S. Nuclear Regulatory Commission—less than a year after the Fukushima disaster—approved construction of the first new commercial nuclear reactor since 1978 in Georgia.[36]

Fukushima Daiichi, however, shattered visions of a bright commercial nuclear future. The Japanese tragedy—considered by the International Nuclear and Radiological Event Scale (INES) as comparable to the world's worst reactor accident at Chernobyl—seemed to dramatize globally the ominous predictions about commercial nuclear electric power so long voiced by its domestic critics. The domestic future of commercial nuclear power seemed blighted anew. Public support for commercial nuclear energy fell on a typical national poll from 71 to 50 percent.[37] The disaster "shook confidence in nuclear power around the world," reported one contemporary survey.[38] Concerned about the vulnerability of U.S. commercial reactors to severe earthquakes akin to cause of the Japanese accident, the U.S. NRC rapidly initiated a safety survey of U.S. commercial nuclear reactors and concluded that, while domestic reactors were generally safe, they could be better prepared for a kind of damage inflicted by the Japanese tsunami.[39] "All of the nation's 104 nuclear reactors will need to undergo analysis using cutting-edge technology and the most recent data to assess how well they can withstand earthquakes," the NRC also warned.[40] Plant operators will be required to study the safety of their facilities using a new seismic risk model created by the NRC, Electric Power Research Institute (EPRI), and U.S. Geological Survey, which should be available in 2013. "We want to be able to manage the situation in which you lose all electric power and to maintain safety systems and instrumentation and control systems for a much longer period of time than what our plants are designed for right now," concluded NRC chairman Gregory Jaczko.[41] The sudden reversal of fortune after Fukushima Daiichi confronted the Obama administration with a dilemma. The Obama administration had expressed support for limited new commercial reactor development albeit at a slower pace and scale than Bush program. Now, the Obama administration reluctantly confronted a newly revived, malignant image of nuclear power. So, the issue relentlessly facing every presidency since Jimmy Carter arrived again at the White House door: What is to be done about commercial nuclear power? The issue is the more politically tangled because the federal government has been deeply implicated in commercial nuclear power development for more than a half century.

The Federal Patron

Washington is largely responsible for the development of the nation's commercial nuclear power; federal policy has sustained the industry since its inception in the early 1950s, with aggressive promotion, benign regulation, and massive financial infusions of subsidies, development grants, and research promotion.

The industry prospered in its first several decades due to this benevolent regulation, generous federal funding, public and political favor, and unique governmental concessions never given its competitors, such as the Price-Anderson Act (renewed in 2005), which limited a nuclear industry's total insurance liability to $12.6 billion, thus ensuring that the industry would obtain the necessary insurance coverage. Until the 1970s, all but a handful of scientists, economists, and public officials associated with the new technology seemed, according to economists Irvin C. Bupp and Jean-Claude Derian, so "intoxicated" by the enterprise that they largely ignored grave technical and economic problems already apparent to a few critical observers.[42] When problems could not be ignored, they usually were hidden from public view; when critics arose, they were discredited by Washington's aggressive defense of the industry.

Despite the troubled history of the industry after the 1970s, by the beginning of the Obama presidency, the industry had received by conservative estimate more than $100 billion in federal subsidies—approximately 60 percent of the total federal energy research expenditures and far exceeding Washington's support for any other energy.[43] Critics have argued that, without these direct and indirect subsidies, the industry was unlikely to have been competitive in any market. "The nuclear power industry has benefited—and continues to benefit—from a vast array of preferential government subsidies," asserted the Union of Concerned Scientists (UCS). "Indeed . . . subsidies to the nuclear fuel cycle have often exceeded the value of the power produced. This means that buying power on the open market and giving it away for free would have been less costly than subsidizing the construction and operation of nuclear power plants. Subsidies to new reactors are on a similar path.[44]

Along with the Price-Anderson Act, federal financial backing is still the most potent driver of the nuclear industry's hope for a "renaissance" because this aid addresses the industry's chronically unsettled economic prospects. The largest current federal incentives for construction of new commercial nuclear facilities are provided by EPAct's loan guarantees for new plant construction debt covering as much as 80 percent of construction cost and additional production tax credits.[45] Given the considerable economic risk involved in new plant construction, federal support is a crucial incentive for the construction of several first-starter facilities proving the commercial success of the new reactor generation; otherwise, the industry has scant motivation to plan future facilities.[46]

The Nuclear Industry Today

In 2013, there were 104 operating nuclear reactors licensed to U.S. electrical utilities, down from a peak of 112 in 1990. Most reactors are located along the East Coast, in the Southeast, and in the Midwest (see Map 8–2). These reactors currently represent about 21 percent of U.S. net electricity-generating capacity. Under their original schedule, the licenses for these reactors were issued for 40 years, and half of the reactors would have ended their legal operating lives between 2005 and 2015; the remainder would have shut down before 2075. In short, commercial nuclear power would disappear within a few generations unless the present facility licenses were extended and new reactors were constructed because U.S. utilities had ordered no new reactors since 1979 and simultaneously had cut back sharply on planned construction. In 2000, however, the NRC began to renew utility licenses through a prolonged process involving extensive NRC safety reviews, public meetings, and state consultation. By mid-2009, the NRC had extended the licenses of 54 reactors and anticipated an additional 31 applications by 2013.[47]

Despite notable improvements in the industry's safety procedures, technology, and operating efficiency since Three Mile Island, its troubles remain substantial, including economic and technical difficulties, unsolved waste management problems, and a regulatory regime uneasy about the possibility of terrorist attacks on nuclear facilities.

Map 8–2   Commercial U.S. Nuclear Power Reactors, Location and Age, 2012

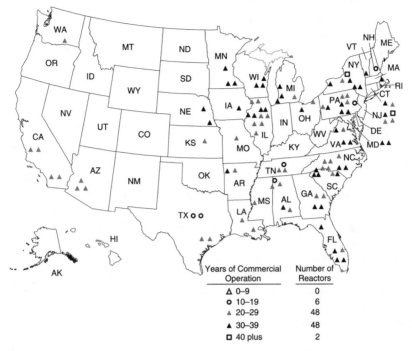

Years of Commercial Operation	Number of Reactors
▲ 0–9	0
○ 10–19	6
▴ 20–29	48
▲ 30–39	48
□ 40 plus	2

Source: U.S. Nuclear Regulatory Commission, www.nrc.gov/reading-rm/doc-collections/nuregs/staff/sr1542/v15/.

Note: There are no commercial reactors in Alaska or Hawaii.

The Problematic Economics of Nuclear Power. The gloss applied to the industry's public image by partisans of a nuclear "renaissance" cannot quite conceal some problematic economics. The cost of constructing and maintaining commercial nuclear power plants climbed so steeply between 1980 and 2006 that private capital became increasingly scarce and costly. Even when an industry recovery seemed plausible after 2000, the managing director of a major national investment firm was warning that the "challenge of new construction is very difficult . . . Project sponsors must spend large amounts of capital for long lead-time procurement before the project has been licensed by the NRC and before the construction schedule is set. As a result, the project cost estimates have risen dramatically in the past year and are expected to continue rising. In the eyes of lenders and investors, these projects will face the potential risk of serious delay and cost overruns."[48] Private investment is likely to be even more elusive in the aftermath of the 2007 economic recession and the bloating estimates for new plant construction. Early in 2008, the *Wall Street Journal* and several other publications carried headline news stories about the skyrocketing cost projections for new nuclear facilities, indicating that it might cost $9 billion to $12 billion to build a single new nuclear power plant. Florida Power and Light's first estimate for a large new plant off the Florida Keys reached $12 billion to $18 billion. Progress Energy's proposed plan for a similar Florida plant was predicted to cost $17 billion, triple the previous year's estimate.[49]

Thus, the economic viability of commercial nuclear power continues to be one of the industry's most chronically unsettled and vexing issues despite the proposed federal largesse in loan guarantees and tax credits. Problematic construction costs are particularly unsettling. The industry's history abounds with instances of huge construction cost overruns, low operating capacity, and failed market competitiveness. The Congressional Budget Office estimated, for example, that the average cost overrun for new nuclear plants in the 1970s and 1980s was about 200 percent.[50] Estimates of new plant construction costs are extremely tentative because the U.S. has had no experience in nuclear facility construction for 30 years. These construction costs are driven primarily by the expense of reactors. "The fuel and operating costs of existing nuclear reactors are usually lower than those of other conventional technologies for producing electricity; construction costs—coupled with long construction periods and associated financing costs—have been and continue to be the economic Achilles' heel of the nuclear industry."[51] Among the critical, often unpredictable determinants of new facility economics are the comparative costs of alternative natural gas and coal and the impact of existing or future competition from other utilities in a specific market. (The EIA has estimated that, nationally, nuclear electricity averages about $114 per megawatt compared to $66 for natural gas and $95 for coal.)[52] Nuclear power is competitive with other fuels for electric generation, particularly in the northeastern and southern United States, where the domestic cost of competing fuels is highest.

Facility Safety Issues. The NRC's public admission in the aftermath of the 2011 Fukushima Daiichi disaster that the NRC lacked adequate information about the vulnerability of U.S. commercial reactors to severe seismic shocks was a reminder that the national debate about reactor safety remains alive and vigorous. A major reason—often *the* reason—for the cost escalation of new plant construction is concern about public safety and environmental protection. The time required to secure the many governmental licenses that ensure a facility will meet safety and environmental standards steadily lengthened after 1970. Despite more recent efforts to streamline the review process, surmounting the regulatory hurdles still requires four to eight years and may involve almost 100 different federal, state, and local governmental permits. Industry officials also complain about the costs imposed during plant construction through regulatory ratcheting by the NRC (its habit of requiring facilities to make new safety modifications or other expensive design changes many years after plant construction). Additional costs have also been imposed on many utilities by protracted litigation involving environmental groups and others challenging various aspects of plant design and safety. [53] And, serious, expensive technical problems continue to beset the industry.

Proponents of nuclear power argue correctly that its safety record, notwithstanding the accident at Three Mile Island, is excellent and that critics have exaggerated its technical problems. However, continuing revelations of technical difficulties suggest serious deficiencies in the basic design and operation of the plants and frequent carelessness or incompetence in plant management.[54] Whatever their real significance, these problems have worked against the industry politically. Continuing admissions of safety risks and technical difficulties at a time of growing public apprehension about nuclear terrorism continue to inspire the opposition.

Several technical problems have been especially damaging to the industry. Materials and design standards for many plants currently have failed essential safety requirements. Reactor parts, for instance, have aged much faster than anticipated. Steam generators meant to last a plant's lifetime—approximately 50 years—are wearing out much sooner than expected; this is a particularly serious problem in New York, Florida, Virginia, Wisconsin, and South Carolina.[55] Mistakes have been made in plant specifications or construction. Pipes have cracked and *wasted* (the walls becoming thinner) from extended exposure to radiation. As early as 1988, the GAO recommended a mandatory inspection of all plants for pipe deterioration after finding that nearly one third of the plants it surveyed did indeed have pipe deterioration. Finally, continuing revelations of plant mismanagement, administrative bungling, and secrecy raise serious questions about the competence of plant managers and technicians. The industry must still contend with disclosures such as the NRC's announcement in early 2007 that it had downgraded the safety rating of the nation's largest nuclear plant. As the Associated Press reported in 2007,

> The NRC's announcement ended three years of problems in various safety systems at the Palo Verde nuclear plant west of Phoenix. Inspectors in September found that one of its emergency diesel generators had been broken for 18 days. Emergency generators are critically important at nuclear reactors, providing electricity to pumps, valves and control rooms if the main electrical supply fails. Only FirstEnergy Corp.'s Perry nuclear plant in Ohio has a safety rating as bad as Palo Verde's, NRC spokesman Victor Dricks said.[56]

Industry officials insist that critics have misrepresented the safety record of commercial nuclear utilities by seizing on these disclosures as if they characterized the entire industry. Indeed, many utilities have a virtually uninterrupted record of safe operations and skilled management. Still, after more than 30 years of operation, the industry continues to experience serious design, management, and engineering failures. The UCS's verdict seems fair:

> Is nuclear power in the United States safe enough today just because a reactor has not experienced a meltdown since 1979? The answer is a resounding no. In the 27 years since the TMI [Three Mile Island] meltdown, 38 U.S. nuclear power reactors had to be shut down for at least one year while safety margins were restored to minimally acceptable levels. Seven of these reactors experienced two-year-plus outages. Though these reactors were shut down before they experienced a major accident, we cannot assume we will continue to be so lucky. The number and length of these shutdowns testify to how serious and widespread the problem is.[57]

The Continuing Challenge of Nuclear Waste. Controversy about the safe disposal of radioactive reactor waste has become, like unsettled economics, an intractable problem blighting the nuclear industry's visions of an imminent revival.

The waste problem was never anticipated when the federal government first promoted commercial nuclear power in the 1950s. To encourage the nation's public and private utilities to build nuclear power plants, Washington had assured the industry that the federal government would provide a "reprocessing" technology for the radioactive wastes contained in the spent nuclear fuel rods used to generate reactor power. Thus, existing and planned commercial facilities were designed to store temporarily no more than three years of accumulated spent fuel rods in cooling ponds. Excess fuel assemblies were to be removed from temporary onsite storage, reusable radioactive materials extracted, and the waste safely isolated elsewhere. However, the anticipated reprocessing proved an economic and technical failure.[58] Since the early 1970s virtually all commercial spent fuel has remained in the onsite cooling ponds.[59] Until 1982, no comprehensive federal plan existed for the "permanent" storage of these nuclear wastes. Instead, federal and state governments had wrangled acrimoniously for more than a decade over the design and location of a permanent waste depository that no state wanted.

The Battle of Yucca Mountain. In 1982, Congress finally passed the Nuclear Waste Policy Act (NWPA), intended to create a process for designating and constructing the first permanent nuclear waste repository. The legislation assigned the site-selection task to the DOE and created what appeared to be a meticulously detailed, impartial, and open process by which all possible sites would be studied and reduced to a few from which the president would eventually select two for "permanent" repositories.

However, the political leadership in every eligible state fought vehemently in Congress and the courts to prevent its designation as an eligible waste site. Rather than abide the continuing controversy, Congress found a simple solution. In December 1987, Congress suddenly renounced NWPA procedures, summarily designated Yucca Mountain, Nevada, to be the first permanent depository site, and assured the nuclear power industry that Nevada would be ready by 1998 to accept delivery of the spent fuel rods cooling at reactor sites.

Nevada residents and political leaders have been outraged. Nevada continues an unremitting resistance to the uncompleted Yucca Mountain facility with every available political and legal resource. This trench warfare, accompanied by fierce scientific controversy concerning Yucca Mountain's geologic safety has slowed the facility's construction to a crawl.[60] The DOE abandoned its initial repository plan in 1989 because it lacked confidence in the technical quality of the proposal and predicted that the repository would be delayed until at least 2010 even though commercial utilities had already paid $3 billion in taxes to use the repository.[61] By 2007, it was evident that the DOE was unprepared to receive wastes at even a temporary repository and that a "permanent" site was still speculative. Frustrated by these continuing delays, the Bush administration in 2002 promised to open the site by 2010, requested a large budget increase to underwrite accelerated site construction, and was promptly sued by the state of Nevada and numerous other plaintiffs, thereby relegating the Yucca Mountain facility to a judicial limbo and an uncertain future while controversy continued over the facility's safety. In an effort to settle the matter, in 2010, Secretary of Energy Steven Chu recommended to President Obama that the facility be terminated. But, the repository's destiny was further muddled when Obama pledged to eliminate its federal funding while simultaneously continuing its operation until the complex legal path to its termination is completed.

A Possible Alternative Plan. The prospective close of the Yucca Mountain facility would require that some alternative storage space be available to accommodate the continuing increment of new waste at reactor sites. Any near-term solution must necessarily be temporary, pending the outcome of federal–state negotiations over the final deposition of commercial nuclear waste or a judicial order. The most plausible solution for on-site and off-site temporary containment of the high-level wastes utilities may no longer be able to accommodate at their existing on-site cooling ponds is *dry cask* storage.

"Dry cask storage," explains the NRC, "allows spent fuel that has already been cooled in the spent fuel pool for at least one year to be surrounded by inert gas inside a container called a cask. The casks are typically steel cylinders that are either welded or bolted closed. The steel cylinder provides a leak-tight containment of the spent fuel. Each cylinder is surrounded by additional steel, concrete, or other material to provide radiation shielding to workers and members of the public. Some of the cask designs can be used for both storage and transportation." Dry-cask storage is already utilized in several states for high-level and low-level commercial waste. Debate lingers about the reliability of dry-cask waste sequestration and cask vulnerability to terrorism. However, dry casks have been approved for waste storage by the NRC, the DOE, and an expert panel of the National Academy of Science.[62]

A number of states with commercial nuclear reactors, already uneasy about the safety of existing fuel rods that may remain in cooling ponds for at least several more decades, were further disconcerted when, in December 2010, the NRC modified its rules for on-site radioactive waste storage to double the storage time to 60 years after a facility goes out of service. The attorneys general of New York, Vermont, and Connecticut, expected to be the forerunners of future similar lawsuits by other states, have demanded that the NRC require commercial power companies to file environmental impact statements for the cooling ponds.[63] Thus, the contentious federalism that has characterized commercial nuclear power regulation for many decades seems destined to continue until, and if, the federal government can create a "permanent" nuclear waste depository.

Decommissioning. Once a civilian nuclear facility has finished its useful life, the NRC and the DOE require that the owners decommission the facility by removing from the site the radioactive materials, including land, groundwater, buildings, contents, and equipment, and by reducing residual radioactivity to a level permitting the property to be used for any other purpose. Before a nuclear power plant begins operations, the licensee must establish or obtain a financial mechanism—such as a trust fund or a guarantee from its parent company—to ensure that there will be sufficient money to pay for the ultimate decommissioning of the facility.[64] Because a commercial reactor's life span was originally expected to be 50 years, an increasing number of the nation's reactors had to be decommissioned beginning in the 1990s. In 2012, 12 commercial nuclear power reactors were being decommissioned. At the end of 2012, 10 commercial reactors were completely decommissioned and 13 others were in earlier stages of dismantling.[65] The 10 fully decommissioned sites are considered safe enough to be reclaimed for any purpose including agriculture, housing, or green space. Among the remaining reactors, six will be wholly decontaminated and six will be placed in SAFSTOR status, where they will be sequestered until future full contamination.

"According to Paul Genoa, director of policy development of the Nuclear Energy Institute, a trade group for the nuclear power industry, decommissioning costs typically run at $500 million per unit. But actual costs vary based on the plant's size and design, and some have reached over $1 billion—between 10 percent and 25 percent of the cost of constructing a nuclear reactor today."[66] Although the NRC requires utilities to set aside funds during the operating life of a reactor in anticipation of future decommissioning costs, many utilities may be inadequately preparing for these costs. In 2009, the NRC notified about a quarter of the operating utilities that they may be not be setting aside sufficient funds for decommissioning.[67]

The Nuclear Regulatory Commission

The NRC, whose regulatory responsibilities for commercial nuclear power reactors was described in Chapter 3, has found no relief during the Obama administration from contention over the management of an ever-growing volume of commercial nuclear waste accumulating at commercial reactor sites and the continual appearance of new facility safety issues. Defenders of the NRC assert that many of these continuing regulatory lapses and unresolved issues result from the NRC's chronic understaffing and underfunding and from the regulatory changes required by the NRC, which often take years for utilities to accomplish. Some observers argue that the NRC must be doing its job reasonably well because it is such a frequent target of criticism from the nuclear power industry itself. The most publicly and politically contentious issues on the NRC' agenda during the second Obama administration continue to be the challenge to find a scientifically and publicly acceptable method for removal and safe storage of the reactor wastes now cooling at commercial nuclear sites and the emerging problems posed by the Japanese nuclear disaster. The Fukushima meltdown loosened not only a political backlash against the commercial nuclear power industry but forced upon the NRC multitude of sudden, unanticipated new regulatory issues involved with assessing and assuring the seismic safety or all existing commercial facilities. And, lingering over all else is the transcendent political question of whether the NRC and the Obama administration are presiding, however reluctantly, over the gradual extinction of the nuclear dream.

The Revival of Renewable Energy

Barack Obama's first election campaign had been rich in environmentalist substance and symbolism. Obama had committed early and often to an ambitious, new, environmentally attractive energy agenda. The campaign platform had promised "an American clean energy industry," petroleum policies that "will curb our dependence on fossil fuels and make America energy independent," air pollution measures that "after decades of inaction . . . will finally close the carbon pollution loophole by limiting the amount of carbon polluters are allowed to pump into the atmosphere," and much more.[73]

All this was a prelude to what Obama had promised would become the policy pathway toward "a new energy future . . . embracing alternative and renewable energy, ending our addiction to foreign oil, addressing the global climate crisis and creating millions of new jobs that can't be shipped overseas."[74] This vision of a "new energy future," like virtually all public policy proposals to release America from a fossil fuels dependency, has been inspired by a common reliance on wind and solar energy as a technological foundation. Despite the powerful appeal of wind and solar technologies for energy conservation, events soon demonstrated to the Obama administration what all recent presidents have discovered—that the practical politics of transforming a new energy era from vision into policy and the stubborn realities embedded in the American energy economy pose inevitable, often daunting challenges inherent to American public policy making.

A Risky New Agenda

When the Bush administration needed $135,000 to print copies of its 2001 energy plan, the money came from the DOE's solar and renewable energy conservation funds.[75] This was a bleak preview of the apathy toward renewable energy and, especially, energy conservation that customarily prevailed throughout most of George Bush's administration from 2001 to 2008. At Barack Obama's inauguration in 2008, all forms of renewable energy provided only 7 percent of the nation's total energy consumption. Although national renewable energy consumption had risen by modest increments since 1970, the White House, Congress, and the public had feebly and inconstantly embraced renewable energy and conservation compared to the national investment in fossil fuels.

By George Bush's second term, the adverse impacts associated with the continued national dependence on imported oil and fossil fuels hastened passage of EPAct, Bush's most substantial commitment to promoting renewable energy and conservation. Aside from its promotion of nuclear energy, EPAct created numerous federal subsidies, tax incentives, and research support for the development of new, energy-efficient technologies and improved energy conservation practices in the domestic economy. The important energy conservation and efficiency features included $4.19 billion in tax credits for the production of renewable energy (biomass, wind, solar, thermal, and hydroelectric) and increased energy efficiency in existing homes, new energy standards for a large variety of appliances, tax credits for hybrid vehicle purchases, and increased federal spending and tax incentives for production and blending of biofuels in domestic motor vehicles.

Although the Bush-era programs seem unambitious compared to the Obama agenda, they constitute a foundation on which the Obama administration has mounted its vastly more expansive and expensive energy renewal and conservation efforts.

The Obama Agenda

The policy foundation for the Obama administration includes an authorization in the American Recovery and Reinvestment Act (ARRA) of 2009 for more than $80 billion in the development of clean energy technologies and jobs. Included in this $80 billion is $36.7 billion to the DOE to support loans and subsidies for the manufacture and commercial distribution of advanced solar and wind technologies. The White House has created an enormous political investment in the success of these renewable technologies freighted with formidable political risks, not least of which is the economic gamble in expensive, often unproven new technologies in the shadow of the nation's most severe economic recession since the end of World War II, huge federal budget deficits, and congressional Republican distaste for massive new renewable technology spending.

Renewable Energy's Rewards and Risks

"Every gallon of oil each one of us saves," remarked Jimmy Carter in the aftermath of the nation's first, nationally disruptive energy crisis during the 1970s, "is a new form of production." Similar affirmations have become ritual in every subsequent American presidency. Still, the virtues of renewable energy are bundled with problematic trade-offs and risks that policy makers cannot avoid.

The Good News. The energy saving potential of wind and solar technologies is substantial and widely advertised. Predictions about the beneficial impact of solar and wind technologies on the national energy economy have been impressive:

- A quarter of the U.S. land area has winds strong enough to generate electricity at the same price as natural gas and coal.
- Seven states in the Southwest have the potential to provide ten times the current electric-generating capacity through solar power.
- Renewable energy sources could provide about an additional 500 TWh (trillion kilowatt-hours) of electricity per year by 2020 and

perhaps an additional 1,100 TWh per year by 2035 through new deployments in favorable resource locations (total U.S. electricity consumption at present is about 4,000 TWh per year).[76]

- Based on the average U.S. electricity fuel mix, 1 MWh (million kilowatt-hours) of wind energy displaces about 1,200 tons of CO_2. U.S. wind capacity installed through 2008 will reduce CO_2 by about 44 million tons annually.[77]
- The total amount of electricity that could potentially be generated from wind in the United States has been estimated at 10,777 billion kilowatts annually—more than twice the electricity generated in the United States today.

Renewable energy can also generate employment. The Solar Energy Industries Association, which estimates that the domestic solar industry created almost 20,000 new jobs across the United States in 2009, predicts that as many as 45,000 new jobs could be created in a year with the proper federal tax and grant incentives. Given favorable sites and economic incentives, national corporations have been alert to the advantages of renewable energy.

- FedEx Corp will install solar panels covering about three acres and capable of generating 2.42 megawatts of electricity atop its distribution hub in Woodbridge, New Jersey; when completed, it is expected to be the largest rooftop solar facility in the United States, producing about 30 percent of the facility's electricity needs.
- Wal-Mart, whose ultimate goal is to produce 100 percent of its power with renewable energy, is installing solar panels on 10 to 20 stores and distribution centers in California by 2011; the company has already installed solar panels on 18 Wal-Mart and Sam's Club stores in California and Hawaii, where each solar project will create enough energy to power the equivalent of 2,600 homes.

While the federal government's commitment to renewable energy waivered throughout the Bush administration, the states seized the initiative to create some of the most convincing demonstrations of public-sector confidence in renewable's potential. By 2010, 27 states had adopted Renewable Portfolio Standards (RPS) requiring utilities to obtain a percentage of their electric power, varying among the states from 4 to 30 percent, from renewable energy, especially wind and solar technologies. California, often a leader in environmental innovation, enacted legislation requiring (perhaps too optimistically) that 20 percent of its electric power be obtained from renewable energy by 2010.

Renewable energy also poses economic and environmental risks, and sometimes difficult trade-offs, to policy makers. One major concern is that renewable energy and its technologies are highly vulnerable to the vicissitudes of the marketplace. Changes in the price of competing fuels, unanticipated international trade events, the cost of technology development, and much else can produce chronic or sudden economic difficulties. For example, "[p]rices for turbines and solar panels, which soared when the boom began a few years ago, are falling," reported the *New York Times* in early 2009. "Communities that were patting themselves on the back just last year for attracting a wind or solar plant are now coping with cutbacks."[78] The onset of the severe economic recession in 2007 created a credit crisis for the industry—the 18 large banks and financial institutions extending credit to underwrite wind turbines and solar arrays shrank to four lenders within two years.

The renewables industry also depends heavily on federal government patronage to provide economic incentives in the form of subsidies, research and development grants, and tax breaks that stimulate production and consumer interest. Federal and state regulations are another constant concern. Regulatory restrictions on carbon dioxide emissions prompted by global climate change, for instance, will probably raise electric power prices and perhaps make the additional costs entailed in adding renewable energy to the mix unwelcome for consumers (some estimates suggest that the cost of wind power may be more than 50 percent higher per kilowatt than conventional electricity produced by coal).

Another persistent trade-off entailed by renewable energy technology development—and to environmentalists the most vexing—is the potential adverse environmental risks to be balanced against the attractions of renewables. The implications can pit environmental advocates against each other and arouse accusations of NIMBY-ism from one side or another. Here are some examples:

- "By 2030, environmental and lobby groups are pushing for the U.S. to be producing 20% of its electricity from wind. Meeting that goal, according to the Department of Energy, will require the U.S. to have about 300,000 megawatts of wind capacity, a 12-fold increase over 2008 levels. If that target is achieved, we can expect some 300,000 birds, at the least, to be killed by wind turbines each year."[79]
- The planned development of solar-panel farms covering thousands of desert acres in California, Arizona, Utah and other western states has frequently been vigorously opposed by coalitions of environmentalists and local residents intent on preventing the intrusion into their lifestyles, the risk to endangered species, and the possible disruption of the native ecosystems.

- The manufacture and distribution of solar and wind technologies generates significant quantities of climate-warming CO_2 and related air emissions.

Many of these problematic aspects are likely to become increasingly evident and publicly contentious as the Obama administration attempts to implement its ambitious renewable energy programs.

Conclusion

The implications of current energy policy for the future are environmentally profound, creating compelling and difficult policy imperatives for American policy makers. First, the United States today still depends primarily upon nonrenewable fossil fuels for most of its energy with the environmental hazards entailed; policy makers are challenged to find a sure and plausible path to a rapid increase in renewable energy as a substitute for fossil fuels. While the Obama administration has greatly accelerated and enlarged the federal government's commitment to financing the development of new, efficient renewable energy sources such as wind and solar power, fossil fuels are certain to remain the nation's primary energy resource well beyond 2050.

Second, the rapid improvement and proliferation of fracking technology has initiated what is predicted to be a new natural gas "boom" that is gradually reducing the market price of natural gas and stimulating its increasing use, especially in the electric power industry. Although this apparent boom is anticipated to make the U.S. the world's leading exporter of petroleum by mid-century and to enhance American energy security from foreign petroleum blockades, it will also encourage continued dependency upon fossil fuels as the foundation of the domestic energy economy.

Third, the well-known, severe adverse environmental impact of coal mining and combustion, now compounded by the recognition that coal combustion is the principle source of domestic climate warming gases, creates a major challenge for U.S. policy makers because there is no readily available, inexpensive substitute for coal as a primary energy source for the next several decades. Moreover, the prospects for a rapidly available "clean coal" technology to diminish coal's environmental hazards seem bleak. While proponents of commercial nuclear power have promoted the technology as an environmentally attractive alternative to coal for power generation because nuclear energy creates no climate-warming emissions, the Japanese nuclear disaster at Fukushima Daiichi and the continuing problem of nuclear waste storage appear to have shattered any vision of a nuclear revival.

Finally, given the reality that no quick fix is politically or economically feasible to diminish rapidly U.S. dependence on fossil fuels, a continuing aggressive, and perhaps more stringent, federal and state regulation of fossil fuel production and combustion is essential. The implementation of rigorous, and perhaps new, environmental controls of fossil fuel utilization will be a formidable political challenge to policy makers who will encounter persistent pressure from petroleum, coal, and natural gas producers to increase production as a strategy to combat the continuing adverse impact of the severe economic recession beginning in 2008. No energy sector now appears more vulnerable to an economic recession than the coal industry, and no industry poses a greater political challenge to federal and state policy makers to find a way to effectively balance new, imperative environmental regulations with the protection of coal mining's economic stability.

Suggested Readings

Duffy, Robert J. *Nuclear Politics in America.* Lawrence: University Press of Kansas, 1997.

Flynn, James, James Chalmers, Doug Easterling, Roger Kasperson, Howard Kunreuther, C. K. Mertz, Alvin Mushkatel, K. David Pijawka, Paul Slovic, and Lydia Dotto. *One Hundred Centuries of Solitude: Redirecting America's High-Level Nuclear Waste Policy.* Boulder, CO: Westview Press, 1995.

Freese, Barbara. *Coal: A Human History.* New York: Perseus, 2003.

Nye, David E. *Consuming Power: A Social History of American Energies.* Cambridge, MA: MIT Press, 1997.

Notes

1. International Energy Agency, *World Energy Outlook 2012: Executive Summary* (Paris, France: International Energy Agency, 2012), 1, 2. Also available at www.worldenergy outlook.org

2. Ibid.

3. U.S. Department of Commerce, Bureau of the Census, *Statistical Abstract of the United States, 2000* (Washington, DC: U.S. Government Printing Office, 2001), 584.

4. U.S. Energy Information Administration (EIA), "Energy Basics 101," available at www .eia.doe.gov/basics/energybasics101.html (accessed January 3, 2009).

5. CEQ, *Environmental Quality, 1992* (Washington, DC: U.S. Government Printing Office, 1993), 331.

6. U.S. Department of Commerce, Bureau of the Census, *Statistical Abstract of the United States, 1997* (Washington, DC: U.S. Government Printing Office, 1998), 273.

7. IEA, *World Energy Outlook, 2002* (Paris, France: Author, 2002), 90, Table 3.1.

8. Marc Humphries, Document RL 33493, "Summary," in *Outer Continental Shelf: Debate Over Oil and Gas Leasing and Revenue Sharing* (Washington, DC: Congressional Reference Service, 2008). Another 86 billion barrels of oil and 420 tcf of natural gas are classified as undiscovered resources.

9. Ibid.

10. Ted Barrett and Alan Silverleib, "Senate Rejects GOP Oil Drilling Plan," *CNN*, May 18, 2011, at http://articles.cnn.com/2011–05–18/politics/senate.oil.drilling_1_drilling-moratorium-oil-gas-prices/2?_s=PM:POLITICS (accessed July 16, 2010).

11. Proven reserves of natural gas are estimated quantities that analyses of geological and engineering data have demonstrated to be economically recoverable in future years from known reservoirs.

12. EIA, *Annual Energy Outlook, 2011with Projections to 2035,* available at http://www.eia.gov/forecasts/aeo/source_natural_gas.cfm (accessed July 23, 2011).

13. Rebecca Smith, "Progress to Shutter 11 Plants Using Coal," *Wall Street Journal,* December 2, 2009, B4

14. Natural gas is made up mostly of methane, which is a very potent greenhouse gas. Some methane leaks into the atmosphere from coal mines, oil and gas wells, natural gas storage tanks, pipelines, and processing plants. These leaks are the source of about 25 percent of total U.S. methane emissions but only about 3 percent of total U.S. greenhouse gas emissions.

15. Clifford Krauss, "Drilling Boom Revives Hopes for Natural Gas," *New York Times* (late ed., East Coast), August 25, 2008, A.1.

16. A comprehensive discussion of the environmental issues associated with fracking can be found in U.S. Government, EPA, U.S. Geological Survey, *Risks and Rewards: The Controversy About Shale Gas Production and Hydraulic Fracturing, Ground Water Pollution, Toxic and Carcinogenic Chemical Dangers, Marcellus Shale, Hydrofrac and Fracking* (Progressive Management Publications, 2011), Amazon Digital Service.

17. James O'Toole *CNN Money,* December 9, 2011, available at http://money.cnn.com/2011/12/09/news/economy/epa_fracking_wyoming/index.htm?hpt=hp_t2 (accessed December 7, 2011).

18. U.S. DOI, OSMRE, "Abandoned Mine Land Reclamation: Update on the Reclamation of Abandoned Mine Land Affected by Mining That Took Place Before the Surface Mining Law Was Passed in 1977," Washington, DC, 2003, 20, available at http://www.osmre.gov/aml/remain/zintroun.htm

19. Ibid.

20. U.S. DOI, OSMRE, "Mining and Reclamation Coloring Book," January 23, 2002, available at www.osmre.gov/coloring.htm (accessed April 7, 2004); U.S. DOI, OSMRE, "Mining and Reclamation Poster," February 28, 2002, available at www.osmre.gov/poster.htm (accessed April 7, 2004).

21. GAO, "Surface Mining: Interior Department and States Could Improve Inspection Programs," Report no. GAO/RCED 87–40, Washington, DC, December 1986, 3. See also Richard Miller, "Implementing a Program of Cooperative Federalism in Surface Mining Policy," *Policy Studies Review* 9 (autumn 1989): 79–87; Richard Harris, "Federal-State Relations in the Implementation of Surface Mining Policy," *Policy Studies Review* 9 (autumn 1989): 69–78.

22. David Biello, "Mountaintop Removal Mining: EPA Says Yes, Scientists Say No," *Scientific American Observations,* January 8, 2010, available at http://www.scienti ficam erican.com/blog/post.cfm?id=mountaintop-removal-mining-epa-says-2010–01–08. See also Margaret A. Palmer, E. S. Bernhardt, W. H. Schlesinger, K. N. Eshleman, E. Foufoula-Georgiou, M. S. Hendryx, A. D. Lemly, G. E. Likens, O. L. Loucks, M. E. Power, P. S. White, and P. R. Wilcock, "Mountaintop Mining Consequences," *Science* 327 (January 8, 2010): 148–149.

23. Jennifer Weeks, "Coal's Comeback," *CQ Researcher,* October 5, 2007, 825.

24. Uday Desai, "Assessing the Impacts of the Surface Mining Control and Reclamation Act," *Policy Studies Review* 9 (autumn 1989): 104–105.

25. Ibid., 105.

26. David A. Fahrenthold, "Still Unresolved, Tennessee Coal-Ash Spill Only One EPA Hurdle," *Washington Post,* December 22, 2009, A1.

27. Shaila Dewan, "Huge Coal Ash Spills Contaminating U.S. Water," *New York Times,* January 7, 2009, available at www.nytimes.com/2009/01/07/world/americas/07iht-sludge.4.19164565.html (accessed September 5, 2009).

28. In 2009, for example, Summit Power Company's contemplated Odessa power plant with CCS would have cost an estimated $1.6 billion, or about 10 times as much as a modern gas-fired power plant. (Rebecca Smith, "U.S. News: States Vie for Share of Clean-Coal Cash," *Wall Street Journal* [Eastern ed.], Mar 23, 2009, A3.)

29. Center for American Progress, *Coal Capture and Sequestration, 101,* available at www .americanprogress.org/issues/2009/03/ccs_101.html (accessed June 18, 2011).

30. Mountineer was to employ so-called chilled ammonia technology, which relies on ammonium carbonate chemistry to pull CO_2 out of the exhaust gases. . . . Mountaineer takes the captured CO_2 and compresses it to at least 2,000 pounds per square inch, liquefying it and pumping it roughly 8,000 feet down into the ground. That deep, the liquid CO_2 flows through the porous rock formations, adhering to the tiny spaces, slowly spreading out over time and, ultimately, chemically reacting with rock or brine (David Biello, "Burying Climate Change: Efforts Begin to Sequester Carbon Dioxide From Power Plants," *Scientific American,* September 22, 2009, available at www.scientific american.com/article.cfm?id=burying-climate-change#comments).

31. David Biello, "Advanced CO_2 Capture Project Abandoned Due to 'Uncertain' U.S. Climate Policy, *Scientific American,* July 14, 2011, at http://blogs.scientificamerican. com/observations/2011/07/14/advanced-c02-capture-project-abandoned-due-to-uncertain-u-s-climate-policy/ (accessed January 11, 2012).

32. Rebecca Smith and Stephen Power, "After Washington Pulls the Plug on Future Gen, Clean Coal Hopes Flicker," *Wall Street Journal,* February 2, 2008, A7.

33. See, for example: Matthew W. Wald, "After 35-Year Lull, Nuclear Power May Be in Early Stages of a Revival," *New York Times* (late ed., East Coast), October 24, 2008, B3; Mark Williams, "The Renaissance of Nuclear Power Appears Inevitable: Nuclear Power Renaissance Faces Serious Obstacles," *Huffpost Green,* February 2, 2010, www .huffingtonpost.com/2010/02/26/nuclear-power-renaissance_n_477934.html; Sally Adee and Erico Guizzo, "Nuclear Reactor Renaissance," August 2010, http://spectrum .ieee.org/energy/nuclear/nuclear-reactor-renaissance.

34. World Nuclear Power Association, "Nuclear Power in the USA."

35. Jeffrey M. Jones, "Support for Nuclear Energy Inches Up to New High, Majority Believes Nuclear Power Plants Are Safe," Gallup, March 20, 2009, available at http:[www.gallup .com/poll/117025/support-nuclear-energy-inches-new-high.aspx] (accessed June 14, 2009).

36. Stephen Mufson, "NRC Approves Construction of First New Reactors Since 1978," *Washington Post,* February 9, 2012, available at www.washingtonpost.com/business/ economy/nrc-approves-construction-of-new-nuclear-power-reactors-in-georgia/2012/02/09/ gIQA36wv1Q_story.html (accessed June 20, 2012).

37. Marcia Clemmitt, "Nuclear Power: Can Nuclear Energy Answer Global Power Needs?," *CQ Researcher,* vol. 21, no. 2, 507, available at www.cqresearcher.com (accessed December 12, 2011).

38. Christopher Joyce, "Commission: U.S. Must Make Nuclear Plants Safer," *NPR,* August 19, 2011, available at www.npr.org/2011/07/19/138513212/commission-u-s-must-redefine-nuclear-plant-safety.

39. Near-Term Task Force Review of Insights From the Fukushima Dai-Ichi Accident, *Recommendations for Enhancing Reactor Safety in the 21st Century* (Washington, DC: Nuclear Regulatory Commission, 2011).

40. U.S. NRC, *Briefing on NRC Response to Recent Nuclear Events in Japan,* March 21, 2011, available at www.nrc.gov/reading-rm/doc-collections/ . . . /tr/ . . . /20110321.pdf (accessed October 8, 2011).

41. Christopher Joyce, op cit.

42. Irvin C. Bupp and Jean-Claude Derian, *The Failed Promise of Nuclear Power* (New York: Basic Books, 1978), chap. 5.

43. Estimates of federal nuclear power subsidies vary greatly because of different methods of calculation. The conservative estimate is based upon Doug Kaplow, "Nuclear Power

in the US: Still Not Viable Without Subsidy," Earth Track, Inc (Cambridge, MA: Earth Track, Inc., 2005); see also Marshall Goldberg, "Federal Energy Subsidies: Not All Technologies Are Created Equal," Renewable Energy Policy Project Research Report No. 11 (Washington DC: Renewable Energy Policy Project, 2000). See also Doug Koplow, *Nuclear Power: Still Not Viable Without Subsidies* (Washington, DC: UCS, 2011).

44. Doug Koplow, *Nuclear Power*, op cit, 1.

45. Congressional Budget Office, *Nuclear Power's Role in Generating Electricity* (Washington, DC: Congressional Budget Office, May 2008), Publication No. 2986.

46. Notes the NRC of the National Academy of Sciences: "The handful of plants that could be built in the United States before 2020, given the long time needed for licensing and construction, would need to overcome several hurdles, including high construction costs, which have been rising rapidly across the energy sector in the last few years, and public concern about the long-term issues of storage and disposal of highly radioactive waste. If these hurdles are overcome, if the first new plants are constructed on budget and on schedule, and if the generated electricity is competitive in the marketplace, the committee judges that it is likely that many more plants could follow these first plants. Otherwise, few new plants are likely to follow" (p. 447); see also UCS, *Nuclear Power: A Resurgence We Can't Afford.*

47. World Nuclear Power Association, "Nuclear Power in the USA."

48. John Gilbertson, Managing Director, Goldman Sacs. "Statement of John Gilbertson." Hearing of the Clean Air and Nuclear Safety Subcommittee of the Senate Environment and Public Works Committee. Subject: Nuclear Regulatory Commission's Licensing and Relicensing Processes for Nuclear Plants. Available from www.neinuclearnotes .blogspot.com/2008_07_01_archive.html.

49. Rebecca Smith, "New Wave of Nuclear Plants Faces High Costs," *Wall Street Journal*, May 12, 2008, 1; Michael Grunwald, "Nuclear's Comeback: Still No Energy Panacea," *Time,* December 31, 2008, available at http://www.time.com/time/magazine/article/ 0,9171,1869203-1,00.html

50. Cited in UCS, *Nuclear Power*, 2.

51. Ibid.

52. EIA, *Annual Energy Outlook for 2011* (Washington, DC: Author, 2010), 75.

53. EIA, *Annual Energy Review 2002* (Washington, DC: U.S. Government Printing Office, 2002), 254. See also Max Schulz, "Nuclear Power Is the Future," *Wilson Quarterly* (autumn 2006): 98–107.

54. A concise, comprehensive discussion of reactor safety and related issues is found in Marcia Clemmitt, "Nuclear Power: Can Nuclear Energy Answer Global Power Needs?," *CQ Researcher*, vol. 21, no. 2, available at www.cqresearcher.com (accessed December 12, 2011). See also David Lochbaum, *The NRC and Nuclear Power Plant Safety in 2010: A Brighter Spotlight Needed,* UCS, March, 2011, available at www .ucsusa.org/assets/documents;nuclear_power/nrc-2010-full-report.pdf

55. Matthew L. Wald, "As Nuclear Reactors Show Age, Owners Seek to Add to Usable Life," *New York Times,* June 22, 1989, A1.

56. "Safety Rating for Nation's Biggest Nuclear Plant Lowered," Associated Press, February 22, 2007, available at www.cnn.com/Nuke%20Safety%20Problem07.html

57. David Lochbaum, *Nuclear Tightrope: Unlearned Lessons of Year-plus Reactor Outages* (Washington, DC: UCS, 2006), 1.

58. The federal government, in fact, gave surprisingly little attention to the whole problem of reactor waste disposal. See Robert J. Duffy, *Nuclear Politics in America* (Lawrence: University of Kansas Press, 1997), 184–189.

59. www.reuters.com/article/2011/06/13/idUS178883596820110613.

60. Among the major Yucca Mountain problems: the uranium in the fuel waste "in SNF is not stable under the oxidizing conditions in Yucca Mountain and would convert rather rapidly to more soluble higher oxides. Substantial amounts of water exist in the pores and fractures

of the volcanic tuff. The geologic complexity of the Yucca Mountain site, including seismicity and relatively recent volcanism, and the proposed reliance on engineered barriers, notably titanium drip shields to protect the casks from water, make the safety analysis complicated and less than convincing." (Rodney C. Ewing and Frank N. Von Hippel, "Nuclear Waste Management in the United States—Starting Over," *Science,* July 10, 2009, 151, available at www.sciencemag.org/content/325/5937/151 [accessed May 18, 2011].)

61. NRC, *Fact Sheet on Decommissioning Nuclear Power Plant,* available at www.nrc.gov/reading-rm/doc-collections/fact-sheets/decommissioning.html (accessed July 10, 2012).

62. U.S. NRC, *Fact Sheet on Dry Cask Storage of Spent Nuclear Fuel,* 2009, Available at http://www.nrc.gov/reading-rm/doc-collections/fact-sheets/dry-cask-storage.html, accessed June 20, 2010; see also National Academy of Sciences, Committee on the Safety and Security of Commercial Spent Nuclear Fuel Storage, National Research Council, *Safety and Security of Commercial Spent Nuclear: Fuel Storage: Public Report (2006),* available at www.nap.edu/catalog/11263.html (accessed January 14, 2010).

63. Abby Luby, "As U.S. Moves Ahead with Nuclear Power, No Solution for Radioactive Waste," *Inside Climate News,* March 3, 2011, available at http://insideclimatenews.org/news/20110302/us-nuclear-power-energy-radioactive-waste-storage-yucca-mountain (accessed December 18, 2011).

64. NRC, Office of Public Affairs, *Fact Sheet on Decommissioning Nuclear Power Plants* (Washington, DC: Author, 2011).

65. Lisa Song, "Decommissioning a Nuclear Plant Can Cost $1 Billion and Take Decades," *Reuters,* June 13, 2011, available at http://www.reuters.com/article/2011/06/13/idUS 178883596820110613 (accessed December 12, 2011).

66. Ibid.

67. Doug Koplow, *Nuclear Power,* 93.

68. U.S. NRC, "The Commission," available at http://www.nrc.gov/about-nrc/organization/commfuncdesc.html (accessed March 5, 20111).

69. Robert J. Duffy, *Nuclear Politics in America,* 171.

70. GAO, *NRC Has Made Progress in Implementing Its Reactor Oversight and Licensing Processes but Continues to Face Challenges* (Washington, DC: GAO, 2007), Report No. GAO-08–114T, "Summary."

71. Stephen Tetreault, "NRC Staff Blasts Bid to Shutter Yucca Project," *Las Vegas Review Journal,* June 24, 2011, available at http://www.lvrj.com/news/nrc-staff-criticizes-jaczko-over-yucca-124522529.html (accessed July 15, 2011).

72. On continuing concerns about oversight of existing commercial reactors, see: "Near-Term Task Force Review of Insights From the Fukushima Dai-Ichi Accident," in *Recommendations for Enhancing Reactor Safety in the 21st Century* (Washington, DC: NRC, 2011) vi, vii.

73. White House, "Energy and Environment," March 2009, available at http://www.white house.gov/issues/energy-and-environment (accessed November 23, 2009).

74. Ibid.

75. Thomas Doggett, "Bush Tapped Solar Energy Funds to Print Energy Plan." *Reuters News Service,* March 29, 2002, available at www.solar-energy.net/bushtappedsolar energyfunds.htm

76. Committee on America's Energy Future; National Academy of Sciences; National Academy of Engineering; National Research Council, *America's Energy Future: Technology and Transformation: Summary Edition 2009* (Washington, DC: National Academy Press, 2009), 2.

77. Center for Sustainable Systems, *U.S. Renewable Energy* (Ann Arbor, MI: Center for Sustainable Systems, 2011).

78. Kate Galbreth, "Dark Days for Green Energy," *New York Times,* February 4, 2009, B1.

79. Robert Bryce, "Windmills Are Killing Our Birds," *Wall Street Journal,* September 8, 2009, A19.

Chapter 9

635 Million Acres of Politics
The Battle for Public Lands

> *For many westerners, particularly those in the Rocky Mountain states, the sport appeals to the urge for unfettered—and fast—exploration of large swaths of terrain. But environmentalists say the snowmobile's continued presence [in Yellowstone Park] represents the triumph of commercial interests over conservation.*
>
> *Representatives of both camps were standing within 50 feet of each other on Tuesday afternoon as Old Faithful spewed velvety veils of water into the cold, sunny air. O'Neal Browder, 63, an accountant from Birmingham, Ala., who has snowmobiled into the park half a dozen times in the past 25 years, called those who would ban the machines "a bunch of elitists." Nearby, Norman Ashcraft, a former Manhattanite now living in Connecticut, rested on his ski poles. Told that [Secretary of the Interior] Norton was nearby, he grimaced and said, "She's the enemy."*
>
> *—New York Times, February 17, 2005*[1]

The year was 2001. Buried toward the back of the 200-page-thick national energy plan conceived by the George W. Bush administration was a proposal guaranteed to embroil the White House, Congress, energy developers, and environmental advocates in a national controversy already smoldering for more than a decade and involving energy buried beneath millions of acres of land most Americans would never see and could not locate on a map. Seven years later, the controversy over the Arctic National Wildlife Refuge (ANWR) was very much alive when presidential candidate Barack Obama pledged to restrict oil and gas exploration in ANWR; three years later, he expected finally to settle the affair by reaffirming that promise. He was wrong. ANWR had become a political cauldron fueled by a history of powerful economic, political, and regional conflicts inseparable from the management of the nation's public lands. It was one more chapter in an historic struggle that no president or congress can put to rest.

The ANWR conflict swirls about 19.6 million acres of pristine polar wilderness in the remote northeastern corner of Alaska, among the wildest and most inaccessible of U.S. public lands (see Map 9–1). ANWR is huge and resplendently wild, a sprawling panorama of tundra marshes

Map 9–1   Arctic National Wildlife Refuge

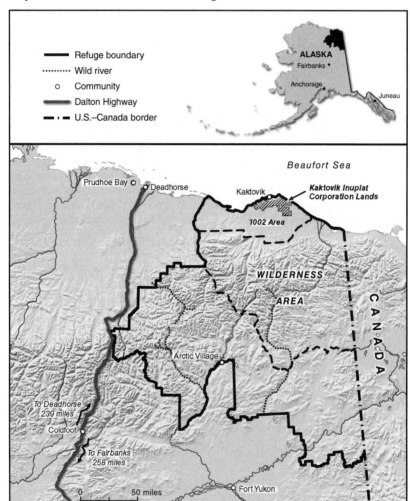

Source: U.S. Fish and Wildlife Service, http//arctic.fws.gov/shade.htm (accessed November 1, 2011). Map reproduced by International Mapping Associates.

and lagoons, interlaced with glacier-fed rivers and lodged between the foothills of the soaring Brooks Range and the expansive, frigid Beaufort Sea. All parties to the conflict agree—it is stunningly beautiful. They agree on little else.

Political conflicts over access to the nation's public land have flared repeatedly throughout U.S. history. In many ways, ANWR is a microcosm of the larger political forces, actors, and institutions historically drawn into these unrelenting conflicts over the use of vast natural resources held in trust by the federal government for the people of the United States. Beginning with a brief description of the actors and issues involved in the Alaskan dispute, this chapter explains why the nation's public lands have always been a battleground between advocates of contending, and often sharply conflicting, uses for the natural resources involved. The explanation involves the ambiguous, and often confusing, congressional legislation intended to determine which interests shall have access to these resources; the impact of the environmental movement on public land politics; and the constantly embattled federal agencies, especially the U.S. DOI and the U.S. Forest Service (part of the U.S. Department of Agriculture), which are responsible for the politically arduous job of simultaneously preserving these lands, promoting use of their resources, and protecting their most valuable ecological functions. Using the national forests and wilderness areas as examples, the narrative illuminates currently significant public lands controversies.

The Arctic National Wildlife Refuge: Public Land Politics at a Boil

The Bush national energy plan recommended that the "President direct the Secretary of the Interior to work with Congress to authorize exploration and, if resources are discovered, development of the 1002 area of ANWR."[2] But, Congress should "also require the use of the best available technologies and should require that activities will result in no significant adverse impact to the surrounding environment." To the U.S. energy production industries and their allies, this proposal seemed reasonable and plausible, a long overdue, practical remedy to the nation's dangerously growing dependence on imported oil. The proposal infuriated environmentalists, conservationists, and their allies. Environmentalists frequently characterized ANWR as "the crown jewel of America's refuge system" and predicted that further energy exploration there would result in catastrophic air pollution, habitat destruction, wildlife decimation, and ecological degradation. Arrayed among these colliding forces were a multitude of other interests that, in differing combination, are commonly drawn into disputes over the use of the public lands.[3]

"The Biological Heart" of a Wilderness

As with most public lands owned by the federal government, ANWR's size and purpose are defined by Congress, and the responsibility for its oversight is vested in the DOI. ANWR was created in 1980 from federal lands within Alaska for the purposes of wildlife conservation, habitat preservation, wilderness protection, promotion of recreation, and energy exploration—an example of a multiple-use designation that almost ensures a constant battle among the contenders for different uses. Much of ANWR's 19.6 million acres has been opened to oil and natural gas exploration. The Trans-Alaskan pipeline, created in 1971, has been producing almost 1 million barrels of petroleum daily from Prudhoe Bay on Alaska's North Slope, and 90 percent of the adjacent coastal lands remain open for gas and oil leasing. However, about 1.5 million acres of the coastal plain, considered to be the most biologically rich and vulnerable within ANWR, has been restricted from energy exploration unless such activity is specifically authorized by Congress. This region, often called the 1002 Area, in reference to its authorizing legislation, is the epicenter of the political conflict over ANWR.

The ecological riches of the 1002 Area are undisputed. This natural endowment includes 160 bird species; the most important onshore denning area in the United States for polar bears; the principal calving ground for 130,000 migratory porcupine caribou; habitat for grizzly bears, arctic foxes, wolves, wolverine, and numerous whales; and many endangered plant and animal species. Ruggedly beautiful wilderness and vast Arctic panoramas invite recreation and tourism. This language of ecological values, biological conservation, and environmental aesthetics resonates powerfully among environmentalists. Much of this, they believe, would be sacrificed to produce exaggerated quantities of petroleum unlikely to alleviate significantly the nation's energy problems.[4]

At Stake: America's Energy Security?

Proponents of energy exploration in the 1002 Area speak primarily about national security, energy supply, and coexistence between energy production and environmental protection. They assert, for instance, that drilling in the area could yield as much as 16 billion barrels of oil, an amount equal to 30 years of oil imports from Saudi Arabia. They also assert that newer, more efficient energy production technologies will limit the amount of land that would be disturbed by energy production to a few thousand acres and, in any case, that the ecological disruption involved is vastly exaggerated by environmental opponents. Most important, proponents of further energy production argue that the reserves now untapped under the 1002 Area will significantly improve U.S. security by decreasing dependence on imported oil, which threatens to increase in the future. All these arguments speak to the nation's sensitivity to its petroleum dependency, rising energy needs, and domestic security awakened in the aftermath of the September 11, 2001, terrorist attacks.[5]

The Play of Politics

Since 1980, the DOI has been ready to sell energy exploration leases on the 1002 Area, but because Congress must first agree, the political battle over exploration has been waged largely within Congress and the White House. In 1996, President Bill Clinton vetoed congressional authorization to permit the leasing. Since then, similar legislation has been approved in the House of Representatives 17 times and then defeated, usually in the Senate.[6] In July 2003, the Senate unexpectedly rejected an ANWR leasing proposal vigorously promoted by the Bush administration. Still, the White House ANWR campaign persisted with dependable support from the entire Alaskan congressional delegation and from the DOI (whose ANWR website, for instance, pointedly includes a "How Long Would Your State Run on ANWR Oil?" chart to demonstrate the value of ANWR to each state).[7] Although the Bush administration's FY 2008 budget had assumed that legislation would be approved to open the ANWR to energy exploration, Congress took no further action, leaving the decision to the Obama White House. Barack Obama had repeatedly voted in the Senate against ANWR exploration and drilling and again declared his opposition during his presidential campaign. Obama's secretary of the Interior Salazar also emphasized that the Obama administration would stand firm that the Alaska refuge "is a very special place" that must be protected and that he is not yet convinced that directional drilling would meet that test, thus leaving the fate of the 1002 Area insecure and destined for continual contention among a multitude of political and economic interests.

The stakeholders in ANWR's resources include local, state, and federal governments; the federal bureaucracies administering the public lands; the economic interests seeking to exploit resources and the interests determined to protect them; and foreign governments, including Japan and China, that might become large consumers of the petroleum produced from the 1002 Area. In brief, ANWR epitomizes the pluralistic political struggles over natural resources in the public domain that have erupted continually throughout U.S. history.

Some of the stakeholders in the ANWR conflict have been highly visible; Congress, the White House, the DOI, environmental advocates, and energy industries rarely escape national attention. Congressional Republicans and Democrats have been divided over ANWR for two decades. Another important stakeholder is the state of Alaska. Many states benefit from economic royalties received from resource exploitation on public lands in their jurisdiction, but Alaska's situation is unique. Royalties from energy production are the state's economic foundation. Every Alaskan resident—man, woman, and child—is reminded about this economic dependence by an annual check (currently about $1,100) representing his or her share of more than $660 million in annual dividends from state oil royalties.[8] Alaskans largely support energy exploration in the 1002 Area, believing energy production and environmental protection are compatible. Many resent what they consider interference by Washington, DC, and other interests, including environmentalists, in what they believe should be Alaska's own affair. Not surprisingly, Alaska's Republican governor Frank Murkowski complained about "America's extreme environmental community" after the Senate's rejection of ANWR energy leasing in 2003 and promised that he would open as much as a million acres of state-owned offshore waters to energy exploration.[9] Many of Alaska's Native Americans, however, were unlikely to cheer. The Inupiat Eskimos and the Gwich'in Indians, an indigenous subsistence culture, are among the native tribes heavily dependent on the 1002 Area's continued ecological vitality for food and fuel. The state's commercial fishing interests were also disturbed by the possible degradation of their offshore stocks.

In late 2012, the Obama administration took a further step toward protecting ANWR when the DOI's Fish and Wildlife Service proposed to Congress that the 1002 Area be designed a *wilderness area,* which would protect it from any form of energy exploration. Environmentalists and conservationists were delighted, and Congressional Republicans—long intense proponents of federally permitted gas and petroleum exploration on ANWR—were predictably angered. ANWR's designation as a wilderness area, however, requires Congressional approval that the Republican majority in the House is virtually certain to prevent. Following the Republican majority's, 17th unsuccessful proposal to open ANWR to energy exploration in 2012, the struggle was destined to the grind ahead into yet another appearance during Obama's second administration.

A History of Contested Access

The controversy over ANWR renews an environmental struggle begun long before the concept of environmentalism was imagined. Fierce political contention over the use of the public domain runs like a dark and tangled thread throughout the fabric of U.S. history, reaching to the republic's inception. During the first century of American independence, the conflict was largely between the states and private economic interests to obtain as much public land as possible for their own advantage. Only in 1976, in fact, did the government of the United States officially end its policy of conveying huge expanses of public lands to private control. By then, more than 1.1 billion acres of land, an expanse larger than Western Europe, had been surrendered to the states, farmers and trappers, railroads, veterans, loggers and miners, and canal builders—in other words, to any interest with the political strength to make a persuasive claim to Congress. Land shaped the American character more decisively than did any other aspect of the nation's environment. With the mobilization of the conservation movement in the early 20th century, the federal government began to restrict private control of the public domain in the interest of the American people. Although vastly reduced, the public domain remains an enormous physical expanse embracing within its continental sprawl, often accidentally, some of the nation's most economically and ecologically significant resources, a biological and physical reserve still largely unexploited. The struggle to determine how this last great legacy shall be used constitutes, in large part, the substance of the political struggle over public lands.

At one time, most of the land in the United States was public domain. Over the past two centuries, the federal government has owned almost four of every five acres on the continental United States. This land, held in trust for the people of the nation, is governed by Congress, in whom the Constitution vests the power to "dispose and make all needful Rules and Regulations respecting the Territory or other Property belonging to the United States."[10] Until the beginning of the 20th century, Congress had been concerned primarily with rapidly divesting itself of the lands, turning them over to the states or to private interests in huge grants at bargain-basement prices. Only belatedly did Congress, powerfully pressured by the new American conservation movement, awaken to the necessity of preserving the remaining natural resources in the public domain before they were wholly lost. By this time, most of the remaining public lands lay west of the Mississippi River; much was wilderness too remote and inaccessible to be exploited easily or was grasslands and rangelands seemingly devoid of economic attraction.

The Public Domain

Today, the federal government owns approximately 635 million acres of land, about 28 percent of the total U.S. land area (Map 9-2). Many western states are largely public domain; more than half of Alaska, Idaho, Nevada, Oregon, Utah, and Wyoming are federally owned, and public lands constitute more than one third of Arizona, California, Colorado, and New Mexico. Much of this land, originally ceded to the western states when they joined the Union, was rejected by the states as useless for timbering, grazing, or farming; some was held in trust for Native American tribes by the federal government. Only later, well into the 20th century, did exploration reveal that vast energy and mineral resources might reside under the tribal reservations, wilderness, timberland, and grasslands remaining in the public domain. The economic value of public lands increased greatly in 1953, when the United States joined other nations in redefining the limits of national authority over offshore waters. Before 1953, the traditional standard had limited national sovereignty to three miles offshore. In 1953, Congress passed the Outer Continental Shelf Lands Act despite the vigorous opposition of coastal states such as Florida and California. The act declared federal government ownership of OCS lands extending as far as 200 miles offshore. The legislation, ratifying an international treaty negotiated by the State Department, ended a long-standing dispute between the federal and state governments over control of offshore energy resources by immediately vesting in the federal government control over almost all of the 1.1 billion acres of submerged continental shelf land. By accident and design, that third of the nation, together with its spacious offshore lands, now controlled by the federal government, has become a public trust of potentially huge economic value. And, the land is a moneymaker. In recent years, for example, federal collections from user fees, mineral and fossil fuel

Map 9-2   Federal Land as a Percentage of Total State Land Area (excluding trust properties)

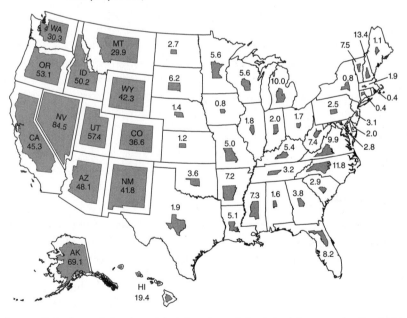

Source: U.S. General Services Administration, *Federal Real Property Profile,* 2004, available at http://www.gsa.gov/Portal/gsa/ep/contentView.do?noc=T&contentType=GSA_DOCUMENT&contentId=13586 (accessed March 17, 2006).

extraction, land sales, timber production, and other economic activities added more than $1 billion annually to federal government income.

An Unanticipated Bounty

The magnitude of mineral, timber, and energy reserves in the public domain remains uncertain. Many areas, including much of the gigantic Alaskan wilderness, have yet to be inventoried fully. Estimates of the resources on more accessible lands also can be controversial. However, commonly cited figures concerning estimated resources on public land suggest the reasons why public lands have assumed such importance to major economic interests in the United States[11]:

- 35 percent of U.S. petroleum
- 39 percent of U.S. natural gas
- 42 percent of U.S. coal
- 17 percent of hydropower
- 50 percent of geothermal energy
- 30 percent of untimbered forests

Beyond those resources on which a price can be placed, the public domain contains both incalculable natural treasures whose worth has become evident to generations—Yosemite, Yellowstone, the Grand Canyon, and the other national parks—and nameless wild and free places, the wilderness that the naturalist Aldo Leopold has called "the raw material out of which man has hammered the artifact called civilization" and to which, he reminds us, we need often return, in fact and imagination, as to a sanctuary.[12] Indeed, much of what remains undisturbed on the American earth, still available to this generation in something like its original condition, can be found only in federal wilderness areas. Whether wilderness is or should be a thing beyond price and beyond exploitation remains among the most bitterly controversial of all environmental issues.

Diversity within the Public Domain

The public domain has been divided by Congress into different units committed to different uses and administered by different executive agencies. The most important of these uses are these[13]:

- *National Wilderness Preservation System.* Created by Congress in 1964, the system currently comprises 105.8 million acres of land, including more than 50 million acres of Alaskan wilderness added in 1979. By legislative mandate, wilderness lands are to be set aside forever as undeveloped areas.

- *National Park System.* Created in 1872 with the designation of Yellowstone National Park, the system currently constitutes 66 national parks and 388 national monuments, historic sites, recreational areas, near-wilderness areas, seashores, and lakeshores, altogether embracing more than 83 million acres. Closed to mining, timbering, grazing, and most other economic uses, the system is to be available to the public for recreational purposes.
- *National Wildlife Refuge System.* The system currently includes more than 96 million acres, two thirds in Alaska but also distributed among all 50 states. The more than 500 refuges are to provide habitat for migratory waterfowl and mammals, fish and waterfowl hatcheries, research stations, and related facilities.
- *National Forests.* Since 1897, Congress has reserved large forested areas of the public domain and has authorized the purchase of additional timberlands to create a forest reserve, to furnish continuous timber supplies for the nation, and to protect mountain watersheds. Forest lands are to be managed by a multiple-use formula that requires a balance of recreation, timber, grazing, and conservation activities. Currently exceeding 190 million acres, national forests are found principally in the far western states, the Southeast, and Alaska.
- *National Rangelands.* The largest portion of the public domain, located primarily in the West and Alaska, is made up of grassland and prairie land, desert, scrub forest, and other open spaces collectively known as rangelands. Although often barren, a substantial portion of the 404.7 million acres of rangeland is suitable for grazing. Federal agencies issue permits to ranchers for this purpose.

Such a classification implies an orderly definition of the uses for the public domain and a supporting political consensus that do not exist. Behind the facade of congressionally assigned uses stretches a political terrain strewn with conflicts of historical proportions over which lands should be placed in different categories, which uses should prevail among competing demands on the land, how much economic exploitation should be permitted in the public domain, and how large the public domain should be.

Since 1970, two national public land policies have provoked the most significant of these conflicts: (1) the congressionally mandated practices of multiple use, or balanced use, for much of the public domain and (2) the creation of vast tracts of highly restricted wilderness areas and roadless areas precluding all or almost all human development. This chapter examines the ecological and political context in which multiple-use and wilderness conflicts arise and the participants that are drawn into the struggles. These conflicts characteristically pit federal resource management agencies, state and local governments, commodity producers and users, and environmentalists against one another over issues that long predate the first Earth Day.

Conflicts over Multiple Use

Disputes over multiple use of the public domain customarily evolve in roughly similar political settings. Conflict focuses on land administered by one of the federal resource agencies, usually the DOI's Bureau of Land Management (BLM) or the Department of Agriculture's Forest Service, that are charged with the stewardship of millions of acres of the public domain under a multiple-use mandate.

Struggling to interpret an ambiguous congressional mandate for land management, the resource agency will commonly find several parties in conflict over the interpretation of *multiple use*. These parties include the states within whose jurisdictions the land resides, the various private economic interests with a stake in the decision, congressional committees with jurisdiction over the agency's programs, and perhaps the White House. Especially since 1980, environmental interests have been important and predictable participants. Sometimes, the issues are resolved— that is, if they are resolved—only by congressional reformulation of land-use policy.

The Land-Use Agencies

Management of the public domain is vested principally in four federal agencies whose collective jurisdiction, more than a million square miles, exceeds the size of Mexico. The Forest Service, the National Park Service, the BLM, and the Fish and Wildlife Service control about 90 percent of all the land currently in the public domain. The Forest Service and the BLM control by far the largest portion of this collective jurisdiction. Unlike the National Park Service and the Fish and Wildlife Service, the Forest Service and the BLM are required by Congress to administer their huge public trusts under the doctrine of multiple use. The two agencies come to this task with strikingly different political histories and territorial responsibilities.

The Forest Service. Created as part of the Department of Agriculture in 1905, the Forest Service is one of the proudest and most enduring monuments to America's first important conservation movement. Founded by Gifford Pinchot, one of the nation's greatest conservationists, the service has a long and distinguished history of forest management. Widely recognized and publicly respected, the service has been adept at cultivating vigorous congressional support and a favorable public image—who is not familiar with Smokey the Bear and other service symbols of forest preservation? The service's jurisdiction covers 191 million acres of the land, including some grasslands, within the U.S. forest system. With more than 38,000 employees and a budget exceeding $2.0 billion, the Forest Service historically has possessed a strong sense of mission and high professional standards. "While the Forest Service has frequently been at the center of political maelstroms," political scientist Paul J. Culhane writes, "it has also been regarded as one of the most professional, best managed agencies in the federal government."[14] Operating through a highly decentralized system of forest administration, local forest rangers are vested with great discretion in interpreting how multiple-use principles will apply to specific forests within their jurisdictions.

The Bureau of Land Management. The BLM manages more than 264 million acres of public domain and leases another 200 million acres in national forests and private lands, but the bureau remains obscure outside the West. The BLM's massive presence throughout the West is suggested by Map 9–3, which identifies the proportion of state lands currently managed by the agency and suggests, as well, why western political interests have been so deeply implicated in the BLM's political history. The BLM has struggled to establish standards of professionalism and conservation that would free it from its own long history of indifference to conservation values and from unflattering comparisons with the Forest Service.

The BLM was created in 1946, when President Harry S. Truman combined the DOI's old Grazing Service and General Land Office to form the new bureau with the largest land jurisdiction of any federal agency. Starting with responsibility for managing federal grasslands and grazing lands, the BLM gradually added to its jurisdiction other lands with mineral resources and, more recently, 78 million acres of Alaskan lands, including many large wilderness areas. The BLM has inherited a great diversity of lands with different dominant uses: the Alaskan wilderness, more than 2.5 million acres of prime Douglas fir timber in western Oregon, and 146.9 million acres of grazing lands. The BLM also is responsible for arranging the leases for mineral exploration on all public domain lands and on the OCS.

Lacking the prestige of the Forest Service and burdened with a long history of deference to the ranching and mining interests that form a major portion of its constituency, the BLM has struggled to achieve greater professionalism, more sensitivity to conservation, and more aggressive enforcement of land-use regulations within its jurisdiction. Throughout its history, it has suffered from chronic understaffing and underfunding—its budget and staff are less than one third of that of the

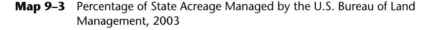

Map 9–3 Percentage of State Acreage Managed by the U.S. Bureau of Land Management, 2003

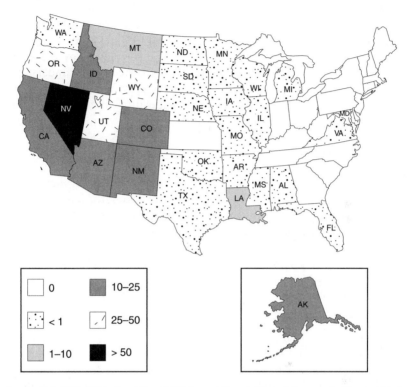

Source: U.S. DOI, BLM, *Fiscal Year 2003 Annual Report: Shared Community Stewardship for America's Public Lands* (Washington, DC: U.S. Government Printing Office, 2003), 73.

Forest Service despite its greater jurisdiction. And, the BLM has never enjoyed the relative insulation from top departmental management that the Forest Service has experienced. This, to many environmentalists, is one of its chronic problems. According to resource expert James Baker, "The multiple-use concept suffers at the BLM because management decisions are influenced by top policy personnel appointed by the administration in power, who inherently focus on one single use, such as mining, and ignore or give short shrift to such other legitimate uses as wildlife and recreation."[15]

The BLM and the Forest Service work in a political milieu whose character is shaped by the ambiguous, and sometimes inconsistent, requirements of multiple-use land management; by pressures from the private interests seeking access to resources on land within agency jurisdictions; by conflicts with environmentalists over the appropriate balance between environmental protection and resource use, both of which the agencies are expected to promote; by frequent conflicts between the president and Congress over their respective authority over the agencies; and by state governments, particularly in the West, determined to press their claims for preference in policy making on the agencies, Congress, and the White House. All these conflicts were exacerbated in the 1980s by the White House's determination to force major changes in the existing understandings about such issues and in the 1990s by the growing political strength of the wise use movement that arose in opposition to environmentalist pressures on federal land management agencies.

An Ambiguous Mandate

In carrying out their assigned tasks, managers in these agencies often must walk an administrative tightrope fashioned from the inconsistencies and vagaries of their legislatively defined missions. Three different federal statutes charge the BLM and the Forest Service with administering the lands in their trust according to multiple-use principles. The most elaborate definition of the doctrine, ripe with the ambiguities that create so many problems in its implementation, is found in section 530 of the Multiple Use–Sustained Yield Act (1960):

> "Multiple use" means: the management of all the various renewable surface resources of the national forest so that they are utilized in the combination that will best meet the needs of the American people; making the most judicious use of the land for some or all of these resources or related services over areas large enough to provide sufficient latitude for periodic adjustments in use to conform to changing needs and conditions; that some land will be used for less than all of the resources; and harmonious and coordinated management of the various resources, each with the other, without impairment of the productivity of the land, with consideration being given to the relative values of the various resources, and not necessarily the combination of uses that will give the greatest dollar return or the greatest unit output.[16]

The intent of this complicated mandate is to make sure that, in land management "any use should be carried out to minimize interference with other uses of the same area and, if possible, to complement those other uses."[17] But, it provides to agency managers scant information concerning how these differing values are to be defined and balanced when differing claims on land use must be resolved. Such problems are commonplace because almost 60 percent of all public lands are held by federal agencies under some form of multiple-use law, and conflict over their resolution is predictable. The BLM, for instance, has wrestled for years with managing desert areas east and north of Los Angeles to the satisfaction of both conservationists and vehicle-racing enthusiasts. Each year, the BLM processes more than 100 applications for motorcycle races, some annual events with as many as 3,000 competitors. Conservationists have argued that the races permanently scar the land, alter native ecological balances, and create noise and other disruptions for other recreationists.[18] In trying to reduce the impact of such racing, the BLM must determine the proper balance between recreation and conservation values in terms of these specific desert lands. Any decision becomes controversial.

The agencies frequently discover that multiple use also leads to a conflicting mandate. The Forest Service is expected to protect the national forests from excessive timbering but at the same time assist state and private forest owners in obtaining access to federal forests. Wildlife refuges are supposed to protect and preserve the ecologically viable habitat for endangered species but also provide grazing, hunting, and perhaps mining opportunities to private interests.

But, the multiple-use doctrine also gives both agencies, and particularly the local resource managers who must often translate the doctrine into operational terms, a means of managing the conflicting interest pressures on the land. Multiple use requires a balancing of uses, and concern for a variety of claims, without ensuring that any one is dominant. This formula leaves resource managers with the opportunity to balance and negotiate among interests claiming the use of public resources. It also promises constant pressure on the agencies to create or alter interpretations of multiple use by whatever interests feel that existing interpretations discriminate against their claims on the land.

The Pluralistic Politics of the Public Lands

Multiple-use legislation is a mirror to U.S. resource politics, capturing the continual competition between a multitude of public and private interests for access to the public domain. The balance of forces changes over time, as we will continually observe, but the conflict plays out across lines of political cleavage created by federalism, the separation of powers, and interest group liberalism so deeply embedded in U.S. political culture.

State, Regional, and Private Interests

State governments, particularly in the West, historically have been deeply concerned with federal land-use policies and, for more than a century, have pressed Washington, DC, for greater control over the public lands within their boundaries. Because the public domain constitutes so large a portion of many western states, decisions made at the federal level affecting land use can have an enormous economic, political, and social impact on the western governments. The states have a direct economic stake in multiple-use management. Approximately 20 percent of Forest Service receipts for timber sales are returned to local governments in lieu of property taxes on federal lands. More than one third of the BLM's annual receipts for mining royalties and other uses of its land is returned to the states.

The Sagebrush Rebels. Regional politics is also deeply implicated in resource controversies. In general, the western states have long believed that they have been denied a properly influential voice in decisions affecting their lands. They often perceive themselves to be governed by a remote and unresponsive bureaucracy insensitive to their special concerns. In particular, the western states want a louder voice in determining grazing rights, in setting conditions for mineral exploration, in establishing timbering quotas, and in deciding how revenues from resource use in the public domain will be allocated. The conflict between the West and Washington over the public lands prevails no matter which party controls the White House or Congress or what the issue might be. "I'd love to say that this is a partisan issue and that if this [Obama] administration changes, it's going to be all sweetness and light," observed the head of the New Mexico Cattle Growers Association concerning its ongoing battle with Washington over grazing rights to the public lands. "But I have 22 years experience telling me otherwise. It's not a partisan issue . . . People in Washington just don't understand the West. They don't understand the wide open spaces and how we live and how we manage the land."[19]

Many states, such as Utah, have insisted that the federal government ought to divest itself of much of the land within the state borders, turning the land and all its resources over to the states. By the 1980s, the western determination to assert greater state and regional control over federal lands had assumed a political identity known as the Sagebrush Rebellion. The rebellion found powerful spokesmen in President Ronald Reagan, a former California governor, and James Watt, his combative secretary of the interior, who promised—but eventually could not deliver—the liberation from Washington's public land controls so long coveted in the West.

President Clinton reignited the volatile mix of political resentments that had fueled the earlier western Sagebrush Rebellion by his decision, without congressional cooperation, to designate 43 million acres of western national forest lands as roadless areas, thereby virtually precluding any form of economic development. Western political interests again found a presidential champion in newly elected George W. Bush, himself a westerner, an oil man deeply committed to domestic energy development and a political conservative unsympathetic to the Clinton administration's restrictive public lands policies. Bush left no doubts about his political inclination by appointing Gale Norton as secretary of the interior. Norton was another westerner with a political pedigree strongly reminiscent of Watt's, the *beau ideal* of the Sagebrush Rebels. Congressional conservatives, especially Republicans, were strongly encouraged by these congenial presidential signals to mount an aggressive legislative assault on the roadless-area designations and related Clinton land-use regulations. The situation foreshadowed numerous, early, barbed confrontations between the new Bush administration and environmentalist interests that were a prelude to Bush's turbulent relationship with environmentalism following his inauguration.

This persistently combative environment, prevailing throughout the Bush administration, was expected to turn considerably more benign with the advent of the Obama presidency and the appointment of Ken Salazar as secretary of the interior. Optimistic expectations, however, often prove fragile in the volatile policy conflicts that sooner or later erupt between public land policy makers and environmentalists—often divided among themselves—during any presidency. It wasn't long before Obama was criticized for doing too little to protect the public lands when he approved limited oil and gas exploration in the Gulf of Mexico and opened new western public lands to more petroleum production in the West during his first administration. Even the suggestion by any presidential administration that it might consider more energy exploration on public lands detonated an immediate and intense reaction among environmentalists and conservationists who suspected a needless raid on public resources.

Energy Conflicts. Given the conflict over ANWR described at the chapter's outset, it is understandable that the concepts of energy and energy crisis evoke particularly intense political emotions among environmentalists concerned with public lands. A long historical shadow reaching back to the 1980s falls over any current discussions of either issue. Because an estimated 62 percent of the estimated oil and 41 percent of the estimated natural gas in the public domain is located on land presently classified as *inaccessible* for drilling and development, conflict over access to these vast energy reserves is inevitable.

The 1980s were characterized by unusually open and bitter conflicts over the management of the public domain, particularly energy resources, triggered by the Reagan administration's vigorous attempts to change land policies in a manner that angered conservationist and environmental groups throughout the United States while attracting support from many western states. The protracted controversy profoundly alarmed environmentalists and many of the more traditional conservationists. It left the environmental movement with a lingering suspicion about Republican energy policies, a lingering paranoia about western political intentions, and a deeply embedded antipathy toward any individuals or political impulses even faintly reminiscent of resource politics during the Reagan years.

Energy development has been historically inseparable from the politics of U.S. public lands since the beginning of the 20th century. Energy exploration and production have been powerful justifications for the development of public lands, and the related array of organized economic interests embraces many of the nation's largest and most powerful corporations and politically potent state and regional political coalitions, especially those historically identified with the Midwestern and Western "oil patch." Between 1981 and 1988, the Reagan administration and its opponents waged a conflict of historic proportions over the fate of energy and related resources on public lands. The administration began the 1980s with a determination to open public lands to energy and mineral exploration and to transfer tracts of public lands to state and private control on a scale unmatched by any other administration in the 20th century. These grand designs for resource development were frustrated by resistance from moderates of both congressional parties, a fierce opposition campaign by environmentalists and their conservationist allies, and inept political promotion by Reagan administration spokespeople. Perhaps most important, domestic energy supplies recovered rapidly with the collapse of the OPEC oil embargo; petroleum prices fell, and public concern for an energy crisis evaporated. Reagan's Republican successor, George Bush, largely avoided confrontations with the environmental community over resource management.

Clinton, in contrast to Reagan and Bush, deliberately and repeatedly frustrated efforts by energy developers to expand their access to fossil fuel resources on continental public lands and on the OCS. Clinton's sweeping designation of new roadless areas and other restrictions on public land development during his final years in office, described earlier, especially antagonized domestic energy producers, who looked to George W. Bush for redress.

And so it was left for Bush to propose aggressive, new energy development in his national energy plan and thereby demonstrate how close to the surface of American life the political tensions of the Reagan years remained. When Bush announced within a few weeks of assuming the presidency that the nation faced another energy crisis, it was inevitable that environmentalists would respond as if another Republican-led assault on public lands was forthcoming, particularly because energy interests had contributed substantially to Bush's presidential campaign. Moreover, Bush was also a westerner, and his energy policies tilted strongly toward the interests of western states. The Bush national energy plan, and its subsequent legislative proposals, seemed to confirm environmentalist suspicions that Bush was enthusiastically resurrecting Reagan's public lands policies with further embellishments. Environmentalists pointed to initiatives such as the acceleration of oil and gas exploration permits on public lands, a drastic slowdown in the designation of new wilderness areas, the relaxation of environmental restrictions on mineral mining on federal land, and a revocation of limits on off-highway recreation vehicles on public lands to demonstrate that Bush "threatens to do more damage to our environmental protections than any other [president] in U.S. history."[20] Although environmentalists and their allies were able to defeat some of these initiatives in Congress, many other administration initiatives were accomplished because they could be implemented entirely by the White House or bureaucratic agencies.

Barack Obama had aroused vigorous support from conservationists and environmentalists during his 2008 presidential campaign by a commitment to an expansive program of renewable energy development on the public lands and to ending the Bush administration's aggressive effort to open vast tracts of public land for oil and gas exploration. Obama, however, had inherited a severe economic recession, public resentment at rising prices at the gas pump, an imperative to stimulate employment, and a Congress deeply divided over energy policy—all of which compelled him to strike a difficult balance between energy conservation and energy production sure to disappoint proponents of a radical shift away from new energy production on the public lands. "The reality is that this president has had challenges on his plate that no modern president has had to deal with, ending two wars, saving the economy. This has been a very time-consuming four years," Interior secretary Ken Salazar said in an interview.[21]

Criticism that conservation had become a non-priority persisted throughout Obama's first administration from conservationists and environmentalists. The complaints intensified whenever Obama made what appeared to be necessary concessions to congressional Republicans and other proponents of accelerated energy development on public land. However, in the latter years of its first term, several Obama administration initiatives were clearly intended to also reduce or remove other vast areas of public land from fossil fuel exploration. These initiatives included a decision by the Interior department in 2010 to protect several million acres of pristine western public land by classifying them as having *wilderness characteristics*—a decision that might protect much land from energy exploration and that did set up "a howl of protest" from the Republican congressional delegation.[22] Another initiative involved the creation in 2010 by the BLM of a draft plan to reduce the amount of land available in Colorado, Wyoming, and Utah for oil and oil shale development. This would reduce the amount of public land in these states available for development from 2 million to about 500,000 acres. It might also prevent access to a large portion of the estimated 1.5 trillion barrels of potentially recoverable shale oil laying beneath the western states in the Green River Formation.[23]

The Ambivalent States. Despite Sagebrush Rebellion rhetoric, the states are often guilty of doublethink about resources in the public domain. Eager to reap the economic advantages of greater resource use on lands within their domain—more royalties, more severance taxes, and greater industrial development—the states were equally determined not to pay calamitous ecological and economic costs for rapid resource exploitation. The federal government's new public lands policies often aroused not enthusiasm but hostility among the western states. These states wanted resource development and environmental protection.

Conflict between the federal government and the states was focused most sharply on the federal government's proposal for accelerated leasing of exploration rights to oil and gas on the OCS. In 1978, Congress had passed the Outer Continental Shelf Lands Act Amendments to increase greatly the environmental safeguards required for OCS exploration. To this end, extensive federal consultation with the states was required prior to any lease sales off their shores. The federal government's announced intention to sell 32 oil lease tracts off the central California coast sent California to the federal courts seeking an injunction to prevent the leasing. Citing federal failure to consult with the state under terms of the 1978 legislation, the court issued the injunction, and the DOI subsequently withdrew most of the disputed tracts from auction.

Responding to pressure from California state officials, including the new Republican governor, most environmental groups, and most of the state's congressional delegation, Congress in 1982 and 1983 further restricted lease sales off the northern and central California coast by denying appropriations to implement the leasing. In 1984, Congress banned leasing in several OCS basins off Florida and Massachusetts. Often, states have taken unilateral action to impede or prevent the development of OCS lands. Even Bush family values could not prevail against state interests on energy matters when, in mid-2002, Governor Jeb Bush of Florida successfully opposed federal efforts to commence oil exploration in Florida OCS waters, which his brother, the president, had supported. Thus, the OCS states have largely succeeded in substantially reducing, at least temporarily, the scope of offshore energy exploration through a combination of legal and political strategies. Environmentalists, however, remain uneasy about the future because substantial OCS leasing is still permitted.[24] As if to confirm the worst environmentalist suspicions, Congress passed new legislation in late 2006 opening about 8.3 million acres of OCS to exploration in the eastern Gulf of Mexico and rewarding Louisiana, Mississippi, Alabama, and Texas with 37.5 percent of all new energy production revenues.

Resource conflicts at the boundaries between federal and state power are inevitable, grounded in the bedrock of the U.S. constitutional system itself. As long as the federal government continues to push aggressively for greater energy exploration and production on public lands or asserts its regulatory control over the public domain, the states will continue to press with equal determination for greater influence, if not control, over decisions about such activities within their own borders.

Private Resource Users

Interests using resources in the public domain, or ambitious to be among the elect, are important participants in the process of making public land-use policy. Each of the major federal land-use agencies has its "clientele," that coalition of organized groups with a major economic or ideological stake in the agency's programs. In general, resource users want to expand their access to resources in the public domain, to use the resources as cheaply as possible, to protect the continuing availability of renewable resources, and to maintain or enhance their influence within the agencies making decisions about resources strategic to them. For example, sheep and cattle ranchers customarily participate actively in the political struggles over BLM rangeland regulations; individual timber companies, such as Weyerhaeuser and Crown Zellerbach, and timber trade associations, such as the National Forest Products Association, are involved in Forest Service determinations about allowable timber harvests; and Peabody Coal and Climax Coal, two of the largest coal-mining companies in the United States, are found with the spokesperson for the National Coal Association actively attempting to influence the BLM or the Fish and Wildlife Service in writing regulations for coal leasing on land within their agency jurisdictions.

This intimate and historical involvement of clientele in land agency politics often has been criticized sharply, first by the earlier conservation movement and currently by environmentalists. Critics have asserted that agencies are easily "captured" by the clientele, who then promote resource exploitation at the sacrifice of balanced use and, particularly, with little regard for environmental values. Conservationists once dismissed the BLM as the "Bureau of Livestock and Mining." Similarly, environmentalists routinely sued the BLM in the 1980s for allegedly failing to enforce surface mining regulations on coal lessees in New Mexico and Wyoming. The Forest Service's exemplary reputation has been no shield from accusations that it sanctions clear-cutting and other timber practices abhorrent to environmentalists because the service allegedly has come to define its mission largely as timber production in response to commercial timber company demands. Agency administrators, however, often have a legislative mandate to promote resource use within their jurisdictions, and as a consequence, some community of interest with resource users is inevitable. As we have often observed, the right of access by affected private groups to those administrators making decisions affecting such groups is regarded as a fundamental principle in U.S. politics. Both tradition and law make the continued involvement of resource users in agency decisions inevitable and their self-interested pressures on the agencies a continual threat to the concept of balanced use. Often, environmental and conservation groups constitute practically the only politically active and effective force for balanced use within the private pressure group system.

Congress and the Public Domain

Congress ultimately decides how the public domain will be used. Although it cautiously shares some of this authority with the president, Congress traditionally has been a jealous and vigilant guardian of its prerogatives to decide finally how the states, federal land management agencies, private resource users, and others shall use the lands it holds in trust for the people of the United States. This authority flows from Article IV of the Constitution and from numerous Supreme Court decisions affirming the primacy of legislative authority in determining the character of the federal lands. Recent Supreme Court decisions have compelled Congress to share with the president the power to withdraw public lands from private use, but Congress has been quick to challenge presidents and their executive agencies when it has felt they were usurping a legislative prerogative in land management.

As in other policy areas, congressional control over the public domain is exercised through the committees and subcommittees in each chamber with jurisdiction over federal land management agencies. Although Congress vigorously defends its authority to define agency programs, it has also left the agencies with enormous discretion in deciding how lands within their jurisdictions will be used; the many multiple-use laws enacted in the past several decades leave to local land managers great latitude in establishing the character of specific land uses. These agencies, as a result, operate in a politically risky milieu, in which discretion is always subject to congressional challenge. When the presidency and Congress are controlled by the same party, conflicts between the two branches over agency decisions are seldom prolonged or serious. But, the situation becomes ripe for conflict when different parties control the White House and one, or both, congressional chamber. Then, agency managers, exercising what they believe to be their discretionary authority on behalf of the president's program, may find themselves and their agencies under congressional attack. Many of the most publicized conflicts over the Reagan administration's land-use policies erupted as battles between the secretary of the interior and Democratic-controlled House committees with jurisdiction over the department's land programs. During the Clinton presidency, the situation was reversed, with a Democratic president and secretary of the interior usually defending the administration public lands policies against a largely critical Republican majority in both congressional chambers. Feeding the conflict were partisan disagreements over which programs the department should implement and traditional disputes over the limits of executive discretion.

George W. Bush's two presidential terms were crowded with clashes between congressional Democrats, the Republican president, and his Republican supporters in Congress. As the two congressional parties increasingly polarized over conservation and environmental policy, disagreements progressively hardened into deadlock and impasse over important policy issues, which persisted throughout Barack Obama's first presidential term. The most successful and important energy initiative of Bush's presidency, a rare example of bipartisan collaboration between White House and Congress, was the Energy Policy Act of 2005 (Pub.L. 109–58), the most significant omnibus energy legislation in a decade. Its provisions, estimated to cost $14.5 billion, included tax incentives for domestic energy production and energy efficiency, a mandate to double the nation's use of biofuels, repeal of restrictions on interstate utility holding companies, faster procedures for energy production on federal lands, and authorization of numerous federal energy research and development programs. With a Republican majority in the House and a Senate majority of Democrats, however, the Bush years typically involved repeated Democratic efforts to thwart Bush's proposals to reduce federal regulatory enforcement to accelerate fossil fuel exploration and production and to open more public land to private use.

Barack Obama began his initial term with a Democratic majority in the Senate and a fragile majority in the House. However, with the exception of the huge ARRA of 2009, a $773.5 billion economic recovery measure creating massive spending to promote renewable energy on public lands, and to provide generous federal research and development for new, efficient energy technologies, White House public land initiatives were soon mired in continuing policy deadlock afflicting congress. Obama's most important environmental policy initiative, the 2009 legislative proposal for a national cap-and-trade program to control domestic climate warming emissions, failed despite Democratic majorities in both legislative chambers. The return of a Republican majority to the House in 2010 assured a renewed congressional deadlock and wrote an obituary for any ambitious new Obama public land legislative initiatives during the remainder of his first term.

The Environmental Movement and Public Lands

Environmentalists always have given the management of public lands a high priority. Both the National Park Service and the Forest Service were created near the beginning of the 20th century in response to vigorous promotion by the great American conservation movement, the ideological and political predecessor of the existing environmental movement. Historical legal and political battles had been waged by the Sierra Club, the Audubon Society, and other environmental groups against ecologically reckless projects promoted by federal water resource agencies long before the environmental era was named. In the 1970s, environmentalists achieved a number of legislative and judicial victories that vastly expanded their influence in federal land management activities and compelled even the ecologically primitive BLM to develop, at least fitfully, an environmental conscience.

Among the most important of these achievements was passage of NEPA. As defined by the CEQ, which is responsible for its implementation, NEPA required that environmental impact statements (EISs) be prepared by federal land management agencies for major land-use decisions affecting the environment—in effect, for most major land management planning. Draft statements had to be circulated for public review and comment prior to completion, and agency officials were obligated to give the statements careful consideration in all relevant decisions.

In practical terms, the EISs became an early warning system for environmental groups, alerting them to the implications of numerous agency policies whose importance might otherwise have gone unnoticed. Environmentalists had the opportunity to organize a political strategy for influencing land management decisions. Further, the statements often forced agencies, such as the BLM, to give greater attention to the ecological impacts of their management practices. Not least important, the EIS was a legally enforceable procedure; environmental groups skillfully exploited many opportunities to use the federal courts to delay or frustrate agency decisions they opposed by challenging the adequacy of impact statements.

Federal courts, often with the explicit approval of Congress, greatly expanded the environmentalists' standing to sue federal agencies for alleged failures to give environmental values sufficient attention in land-use planning. This greatly liberalized standing often enabled environmental interests to compel federal agencies to give them a voice in agency proceedings. Critics charged, sometimes justifiably, that environmentalists were seizing on these new strategies primarily to disrupt administrative procedures and thereby to harass their opponents even when their case lacked merit. But, the environmental activities inspired by the enhanced standing, as well as the impact statement procedures, quite often resulted in valuable ecological improvements in federal land management and greater federal attention to the balanced use of land, to which many agency managers previously had given little more than lip service.

Finally, congressional attempts to encourage greater public involvement in the making of land management decisions by the Forest Service, the National Park Service, and the BLM also provided environmentalists with effective strategies for influencing federal policies, particularly at the local level at which so many land-use decisions were made. Indeed, environmental groups have perceived correctly that generous provision for public involvement in federal land-use planning has been among the most effective structural means of giving them access and influence in the administrative process generally. For this reason, they have been acutely concerned about the enforcement of these participation provisions in federal land law and convinced that any attempts to narrow such opportunities, by law or administrative manipulation, were covert attacks on their political bases.

In many respects, the 96 million acres of pristine federal land now congressionally protected from development under the Wilderness Act are a monument to environmentalist activism and to the laws and administrative regulations that enormously enlarged the environmentalists' administrative and congressional influence. As political scientist Craig W. Allin observed, provisions for public involvement in federal land-use planning at the local level provided wilderness advocates with the incentive and resources to expand their power at the congressional grassroots:

> Wilderness advocates quickly overcame their initial organizational disadvantage in local areas. Grassroots organizations sprang up, meeting the demands for public participation and pressing for inclusions of favored areas [in the National Wilderness Preservation System]. National conservation organizations assisted through local chapters and by publishing information about successful tactics.[25]

In a political system in which localism dominates congressional life, this ascent of environmentalist power from the grassroots was an instance of capturing the political base from the opposition.

The Wise Use Movement Emerged, Submerged, and Revived

Out of the political turbulence inspired by the Reagan administration's aggressive attempt to promote greater private access to public lands, the wise use movement emerged in 1988. The movement is a loose alliance of public lands user groups: resource developers seeking more public resources such as timber and fossil fuels; grazing and ranching interests opposed to increased user fees on public lands; and a multitude of other economic, regional, and political interests whose assorted agendas share a desire to diminish severely the federal government's restrictions on access to the public domain. Under the wise use banner march groups that are in other respects very dissimilar, such as the National Inholders Association (private property owners within public lands), the National Farm Bureau Federation, the Western Cattlemen's Association, the American Freedom Coalition (a part of the Reverend Sun Myung Moon's Unification Church), the Blue Ribbon Coalition (off-road vehicle manufacturers), off-road vehicle owners, timber interests, and petroleum companies. It is not, however, simply another incarnation of the Sagebrush Rebellion. The idea of property rights as a legal and philosophical basis for action—a strategy that greatly expanded the movement's political appeal beyond the West—has given the wise use movement a national reach and an intellectual depth. As political scientist Sandra K. Davis explains,

> The idea of protection of property rights was borrowed from the property rights movement, which originated in eastern states, and derived its basic concept from the libertarian party. It has been nurtured by intellectual leaders such as Richard Epstein, a law professor at the University of Chicago, and Roger Pilon of the Cato Institute. The Wise Use Movement's adoption of the property rights issue has facilitated its appeals for political support and its likelihood of succeeding in legal cases.[26]

The ideological underpinning of the movement is provided by various economic theories and theorists who argue that the private use of many presently protected natural resources—timber, fossil fuels, and grazing lands especially—would constitute a more economically efficient and nationally beneficial policy (or wise use) than the present restrictions on public resource exploitation. In this respect, wise use is in many ways a modern reprise of the progressive movement's conviction that the "highest and best use" of the public domain often implied its economic development. By grounding its arguments in economic theory, moreover, the movement gains a measure of intellectual respectability and a breadth of appeal to political and economic conservatives that is lacking in arguments based solely on often-arcane disputes over specific resource economics. The movement also shares a hearty dislike for environmentalists that occasionally erupts into vitriol, such as one leader's assertion that the movement intended "to destroy the environmental movement once and for all."[27]

The wise use movement packed a potentially powerful appeal but lacked a charismatic national political leader and proven political impact at the polls. It also lost much of the financial support provided by large resource-dependent corporations, such as Boise Cascade, Coors, and Weyerhaeuser, which were disappointed by the movement's feeble political impact and overheated rhetoric. Instead, corporate promoters of wise use have turned increasingly to think tanks such as the Cato Institute, the Heritage Foundation, and the Heartland Institute, which appeal to a much broader intellectual and social constituency while offering a greater promise of political return on their investments. Nonetheless, the environmental movement regards the wise use idea with considerable apprehension. Many environmentalists believe that wise use ideas, if not the name, were revived in the land use philosophy of important Bush administration land managers such as former secretary of the Interior Gale Norton, former secretary of agriculture Ann Veneman (whose political background and land use philosophy closely resembled Norton's), and many of their subordinate administrative appointees.[28]

The Department in the Middle

The DOI is inevitably the focus of controversy over energy exploration in the public domain. More than 200 billion tons of coal, perhaps one fourth of the nation's coal reserves, lie below western lands under the DOI's jurisdiction. Since passage of the Mineral Leasing Act of 1920, the secretary of the interior has had the discretionary authority to sell leases and to establish conditions for private mineral and energy exploration on public lands. Such leases, to be sold at "fair market value," must be "diligently developed" into mining operations within a decade; both federal and state governments charge royalties for coal production within their boundaries. Until the 1980s, however, the department promoted coal and other resource exploration on its lands rather indifferently, and during the 1970s, leasing was virtually suspended while the DOI, Congress, and the White House struggled to fashion a comprehensive leasing program. One finally emerged in the late 1970s, but it soon was challenged by the Reagan administration's new coal programs.

The change in coal-leasing philosophy under the Reagan administration was immediate and dramatic. In 1981 alone, the DOI leased more than 400 times the acreage for coal exploration than it had the previous year. Proponents of a greatly accelerated leasing program asserted that the nation needed the energy resources lying unused in the public domain, that federal regulations could protect the lands from the ravages of surface mining, and that the economic productivity created by private use of the energy resources would generate more jobs and greater prosperity. Many of those within the DOI's political leadership would have said a hearty, if perhaps private, "amen" to the summary conclusion on the subject by the president of the American Mining Congress: "Our society is built on the stuff that comes out of the hole in the ground and if we don't unplug the red tape stuffing the hole, this country is going to be in one hell of a mess."[29]

The DOI's announced intentions to accelerate the sale of leases for oil and gas exploration on the OCS and its interest in leasing when legally possible even wilderness areas for exploration convinced environmental groups and congressional opponents of the Reagan programs that a massive public campaign to counteract the new policies was imperative. Congress became the institutional weapon.

The Politics of Presidential Leadership

The balance of political party strength in Congress may affect the environmentalists' agenda for good or ill, but the presidency is also a repository of formidable independent constitutional and political resources to promote or frustrate that agenda. The presidency offers opportunities for policy initiatives, for dramatizing and popularizing issues, and for invoking the constitutional prerogatives of the chief executive and his administrative authority in ways enabling the president—or his administrative appointees—often to achieve the president's environmental goals with little, if any, congressional collaboration. Presidential history from Reagan to Barack Obama amply illustrates the impact of this executive presence on public lands management.

The fierce struggle between the Reagan administration and Congressional Democrats over development of the public lands demonstrated that a resolute president could use his existing budgetary authority, his discretionary authority, and the powers of his sectary of the interior, to make numerous small revisions in administrative procedures that can advance federal policy strongly toward more resource development on public lands. George Bush's administration (1988–1992) began on a more conciliatory note, with the president committing himself to an active environmental agenda and implicitly distancing himself from Reagan's public lands policies. But, the environmental community was not pleased with the administration's new secretary of the interior. The president's choice, Manuel Lujan, Jr., a former congressional representative from New Mexico, had been identified closely with mining, timber, and other corporate resource users during his legislative tenure. He was widely perceived within the environmental community as more antagonist than ally. Lujan's early pronouncements, including his advocacy of greater energy exploration on OCS lands, did little to dissipate this image or abate congressional Democratic suspicion of Bush's intentions to invoke his executive authority to bypass Congress to achieve greater energy and commercial development on western public lands.

The Clinton administration (1992–2000) arrived in Washington freighted with environmentalist expectations of a major reversal in public lands policies that never occurred. Despite the appointment of Bruce Babbitt, an environmentalist paragon, as secretary of the interior and his outspoken commitment to turning away from the pro-development policies of the Reagan and Bush administrations, the White House seemed indecisive and uncertain in its land-use policies. As a result, Babbitt was frequently left without the president's apparent support in major clashes with Congress over forest management, energy exploration licenses, and grazing fees on public lands—all major concerns to public lands activists of all political persuasions. Furthermore, Babbitt's, and Clinton's, environmentalist reputation was progressively deflated. However, Clinton's performance during his final months in office proved immensely gratifying to environmentalists and, in his final days, a spectacular demonstration of presidential authority over the public lands.

In December 2000, Clinton declared formally the creation of the largest nature preserve in U.S. history and thereby achieved a record unique to U.S. politics. With the addition of the new Northwestern Hawaiian Islands Coral Reef Ecosystem Reserve—a huge South Pacific expanse as large as Florida and Georgia combined and containing more than 70 percent of the nation's existing coral reefs—Clinton's administration had created more public lands for recreational and conservation purposes than any other presidency in U.S. history. The Hawaiian designation was the final flourish to an ongoing presidential performance that had been moving at breakneck speed through the final year of the administration in Clinton's determination to leave Americans what he called his land legacy. Altogether, Clinton's land legacy would be more than 50 million acres of new or newly protected public domain and the designation of 65 million acres of existing public forest land in Washington, Oregon, Idaho, and Montana as roadless areas, thereafter off limits to commercial timbering.

Clinton's action left behind a lingering, bitter controversy. Wherever commercial access to natural or biological resources was prohibited, and that was virtually everywhere, the resource developers—timber companies, petroleum and natural gas corporations, ranchers, coal and mineral miners, and commercial fishermen among them—complained of national assets being locked up. Many members of Congress, and Republicans especially, were infuriated because Clinton's land-use decisions, especially during that last frantic year, were frequently made without congressional approval through authority granted unilaterally to the president by the American Antiquities Act of 1906. Moreover, Clinton was quick to blame Congress for its inaction. "Where Congress has been unable or unwilling to act," his spokesperson pointedly noted about the Hawaiian preserve, "this administration had not hesitated to use its full Executive authority to protect public health and the environment."[30]

Many western political leaders found additional reason to complain, particularly about the new roadless areas. Clinton's designation, for instance, had removed almost 20 percent of Idaho's land area from commercial timbering. "I think we Pacific Northwesterners," went one characteristic complaint, "ought to tell them Easterners to get the hell out of our area. Clinton, Gore, and whoever else is managing things back there: leave us alone!"[31] The U.S. Forest Service found the reaction of western resource developers so hostile that the service's website summarized the response as "Roadless Rage." Hawaiian commercial fishermen protested about the prohibition on their activity in the new ocean reserve. "The President's order," went one sarcasm, "gives the Great White Father in Washington control of Hawaiian resources."[32]

George W. Bush demonstrated the ability of skillful presidents to use the vast authority over public lands granted them by legislation and the inherent constitutional powers of the president as chief executive to overcome the failure of White House congressional initiatives. Despite vehement congressional Democratic opposition, Bush was able to prevent the DOI from temporarily protecting public land with wilderness characteristics. The president, acting through his secretary of the interior, opened large tracts of undeveloped public land for oil and gas exploration and logging. The DOI's Fish and Wildlife Service, again led by White House appointees, significantly reduced its enforcement of the Endangered Species Act, a favorite target of Republican and Democratic criticism but strongly supported by President Clinton and his secretary of the interior.

Barack Obama proved again during his first term that presidential resort to executive authority is a successful bipartisan skill—at least sometimes—when the White House is determined to find a way to bypass, or overcome, congressional opposition to White House public lands policy. For example, using existing authority vested in the president and the DOI, Obama late in his first administration provided conservationists with some welcome White House initiatives affecting the Western public lands:

- DOI established 19 million acres—nearly 30,000 square miles—of so-called variance zones that will allow developers to propose solar projects in those areas. Environmental and other review of projects proposed in variance zones would be handled on a case-by-case basis.
- The government authorized 17 new solar energy zones on 285,000 acres in six states: California, Nevada, Arizona, Utah, Colorado, and New Mexico. More than half of the land—153,627 acres—is in Southern California.

- The Obama administration authorized 10,000 megawatts of solar, wind, and geothermal projects that, when built, would provide enough energy to power more than 3.5 million homes.[33]

The Fate of the Forests

More than 1 in every 10 acres in the public domain could be used for commercial timber production. This land, about 89 million acres, lies mostly within the jurisdiction of the Department of Agriculture's Forest Service. Since the end of World War II, pressure has been unremitting on the Forest Service to increase the size of the annual timber harvest from the national forests to satisfy the nation's growing demand for wood products. Recently, there has been increased pressure to open many undisturbed old-growth timber stands and wilderness areas to commercial logging. Against this economic pressure, the Forest Service is required not only to enforce the doctrine of multiple use, which forbids the service from allowing timber cutting that will preclude other forest uses, but also to manage timber cutting to ensure a sustained yield from any forest reserve used for commercial timbering. Congress has left to the Forest Service the difficult and politically contentious responsibility of defining how much timber cutting is compatible with multiple use and sustained yield.

The struggle over competing timber uses is fought in the arcane language of forest economics—*nondeclining, even-flow* formulas, *allowable cuts,* and *allowable-cut effects*—but the larger interests and issues at stake are apparent. The struggle represents a collision between preservationist and developmental priorities for timber, between competing definitions of the nation's economic needs, and between differing definitions of the Forest Service's mission. It is a struggle likely to intensify well into the future.

A Disputed Treasure in Timber

About half of the nation's softwood sawtimber reserves and a substantial portion of its remaining hardwoods grow today in the national forests. The Pacific Coast region, particularly the timbered hills and lowlands of the Pacific Northwest, contains the largest of these timber stands within the public domain; the area contains almost half the pine, spruce, fir, and other softwoods in the national forests. These timber reserves, more than three times the size of all the private commercial forests in the United States and currently worth more than $20 billion, will increase in value.

Although timber cutting was permitted in the national forests from their inception, the demand for commercial timber in the forests assumed major proportions only after World War II. In the early 1940s, the Forest Service sold about 1.5 billion board-feet of timber per year; by 1973, the cut exceeded 12.3 billion board feet. Driven by the nation's ravenous postwar desire for new housing, the demand for wood products rose steadily in the three decades following 1945. Private timber companies, approaching the limits of their own production, began to look increasingly to the national forests as an untapped timber reserve. This demand, if wholly satisfied, would probably result in a doubling of the annual timber harvest from the national forests, in keeping with the industry's estimates that the U.S. demand for wood products would double by the early 21st century.

Pressure to expand the allowable timber cut has been particularly intense in the Pacific Northwest. Many of the Douglas fir forests in Oregon and Washington are old-growth stands, virgin forests never touched by a logger's saw, growing in a continuity of development many centuries old. These forests are among the most ecologically diverse and historically unique of all timber stands in North America, reminders of a continent once largely timbered with a profusion of species greater than all of Europe's. Many virgin forests, together with other less spectacular timberlands, are on Forest Service lands that are still classified, or eligible for classification, as wilderness. To many environmentalists and to organized preservation groups such as the Sierra Club and the Wilderness Society, these lands are the living expression of the preservationist ethic, the values of the movement made visible. They are, in political terms, *gut issues.*

The Greening of Forest Policy

The environmental movement has profoundly changed forest management policies since 1970 by altering its political underpinnings. Before the 1970s, as political scientist George Hoberg observed, "the forest policy regime was characterized by a dominant administrative agency, a strong orientation toward the development of timber resources, and little input from the public."[34] By the early 1970s, the organized environmental movement had acquired political muscle and, together with its political allies, had promoted new environmental laws and new federal agencies to implement them. Environmentalists aggressively used their newly expanded judicial access to fashion litigation into a potent political weapon. New statutory and administrative provisions for public involvement in the implementation of forest policy and greater congressional oversight of Forest Service policies expanded environmentalist influence in day-to-day forest management. These changes meant a new pluralism in forest management politics in which resource developers no longer dominated and in which environmentalists had become major players whose interests had to be acknowledged, along with their allies, in policy making at all governmental levels.

Once again, as in other aspects of environmental policy, environmental organizations found the courts during the 1970s and early 1980s to be an effective ally. Especially important was the growing trend among federal courts to scrutinize carefully the Forest Service's management decisions to ensure they were compatible with newly enacted environmental laws rather than to defer, as the courts had done traditionally, to the Forest Service's professional expertise in cases in which the service's decisions were challenged. It was its success in overturning the historic Forest Service practice of clear-cutting in the early 1970s, observed Hoberg, that demonstrated what this shift in judicial attitudes meant for environmentalists:

> Conservationists found an obscure provision of the original authorizing statute of the Forest Service . . . requiring that harvested trees had to be "dead or matured" and that they had to be marked before being cut. Although these requirements were legislated even before the development of the forestry profession in the United States, the court refused to defer to the Forest Service's interpretation of the statute's meaning and enjoined clear-cutting in the Monongahela National Forest in West Virginia and the Tongass National Forest in Alaska. By outlawing the most common method for harvesting timber, these rules created a crisis of timber management. Congress was forced to rewrite management laws.[35]

The Forest Service did not respond warmly to most of these early provocations. Professional foresters and the Forest Service's rank and file often resented the challenge to their professional judgment and the environmentalist insinuations that they were ecologically unenlightened. The rise of politically organized and powerful environmentalism, moreover, spelled the end of the Forest Service's administrative autonomy, especially the customary judicial deference and the congenial congressional oversight it had come to expect. When Congress passed the National Forest Management Act (NFMA) in 1976, it compelled the Forest Service to open its forest management planning process from the lowest levels to environmentalist involvement and to set new standards for multiple-use decisions in which ecological values had to be given major consideration. Gradually, however, the Forest Service adapted to the new environmental realities, with the considerable assistance of progressive leaders within professional forestry itself. The academic training and recruitment of Forest Service professionals was transformed to include a much greater emphasis on environmental values and ecologically supportive practices

in job preparation. The Forest Service adjusted its organizational structure and decision-making procedures to the new requirements of NEPA,
NFMA, and other judicial and congressional mandates to better incorporate environmental values in its policy making.

Still, the Forest Service, like other federal land management agencies,
must live with the multiple-use laws as the fundamental calculus for its
land-use decision making, environmentalism notwithstanding. Thus, forest managers are never free of conflicting forces and values pressing constantly on them whenever major forest management policy must be
formulated or implemented. Indeed, multiple-use legislation creates the
fundamental political order out of which all forest management decisions
must ultimately arise.

Multiple Use and Sustained Yield

Because Congress has chosen not to specify how it expects foresters
to define *multiple use* or *sustained yield* in specific jurisdictions, the Forest Service has been left with enormous discretion in translating these
formulas into practice. As with the multiple-use doctrine, the congressional definition of *sustained yield* is open to diverse interpretations; as
section 531 of the Multiple Use–Sustained Yield Act suggests, "Sustained
yield . . . means the achievement and maintenance in perpetuity of a
high-level annual or regular periodic output of the various renewable
resources of the national forests without impairment of the productivity
of the land."[36]

Conflict over the interpretation of multiple-use mandates has been
intensified by requirements in the Resource Planning Act of 1974, as
amended by NFMA, that the Forest Service prepare comprehensive
development and management plans for each of the more than 120 management units it operates. The Forest Service began this process in the late
1970s and still has not adopted final plans for all its management units.
These management plans often become a catalyst for controversy among
interests with competing demands on particular planning units. Moreover, the final adoption of a management plan does not necessarily end
the controversy because arguments often continue over whether the plan
is being implemented properly. The Forest Service often finds itself in the
middle of a continuing, and often unresolvable, conflict over which pattern of multiple use is, or should be, implemented in a given forest tract.

Both the sustained-yield and multiple-use doctrines are important to
the commercial timber industry because they provide the basis for the
Forest Service's determination of the allowable cut in a given *timber
reserve,* the amount of timber that can be removed from a particular
resource area in a given period. The Forest Service has interpreted

sustained yield to require a nondeclining, even-flow policy, which limits the timber cut in a given area to a constant or increasing rate—but never a declining one. In effect, this has limited severely the cutting of old-growth forests, particularly in the Pacific Northwest, to the ire of the timber industry, local communities, and those economists who believe a larger cut of old-growth timber is more economically efficient and compatible with the multiple-use doctrine. Environmentalists generally support the protection of old-growth forests and advocate further reductions on the allowable cut elsewhere.[37]

In response to pressure from the timber industry and the Reagan administration's own preferences, the Forest Service began to increase the timber harvest substantially in the mid-1980s and to plan for increasing harvests through the 1990s. Between 1982 and 1989, the total timber cut in the national forests grew from 6.7 million to 12.7 million board feet.[38] Forest Service professionals contend that this expansion is consistent with the statutory mandate to maintain a sustained yield. But, the timber industry wants more production. With its own reserves being depleted rapidly, the industry contends that only a timber harvest from the national forests significantly above the currently projected levels will provide enough wood for the U.S. economy in the next several decades.

Jimmy Carter's administration, responding to the rising cost of new housing, had ordered the Forest Service to depart "in a limited and temporary way" from its general sustained-yield principles and to open up some wilderness areas not specifically included in the National Wilderness Preservation System for timber harvesting. The Reagan administration, more sympathetic to the viewpoint of the National Forest Products Association, advocated that the Forest Service permanently modify its sustained-yield practices to permit greater timber cuts without violating the balanced-use principle. In keeping with this production bias, the Reagan administration's budgets substantially increased spending for Forest Service activities closely associated with timber production, such as new forest road construction.

The Forest Service asserted that it could meet the higher timber production levels demanded by the Reagan administration only by cutting deeply into the Pacific Northwest old-growth timber, including many of the nation's remaining virgin forests. Although towering stands of old Douglas fir and associated species within these forests provide incomparable vistas and sustain a great variety of plant and animal life, they are not particularly productive from an economic viewpoint. About one quarter of the trees will rot once they mature. Most of these forests have already matured, and most of the timber has ceased to grow. In addition, the trees cover highly productive land on which second- and third-growth timber could flourish, producing much greater income during the 21st century than could be realized from its current use. Professional foresters associated with the commercial timber industry have asserted that protecting most of the old-growth forests from commercial cutting largely prevents decaying old forests from being converted to more productive young stands. Moreover, the Forest Service's critics note, higher timber cuts do not mean an end to all, or even most, of the old-growth stands but a selective cutting of some and the conversion of others to second-growth production.

Environmentalists have long opposed the logging of old-growth forests, citing the soil destabilization and ecosystem disruption they assert are almost inevitable. Nor do they find the economic arguments persuasive. The battles tend to be fought on a forest-by-forest basis as the Forest Service proposes the required long-range plans for each forest and then files the necessary EISs. Environmentalists often challenge the overall adequacy of the impact statements and the specific timber production goals. The struggle over timber use spills into the related issue of wilderness designation, where the Forest Service also exercises discretionary authority. George Bush's administration inherited one of these struggles, an especially emotional and public dispute provoked by Forest Service plans to permit greatly expanded timber cutting in old-growth Northwestern forests. The plan might have succeeded, except for ecological serendipity in the form of the northern spotted owl.

The Northern Spotted Owl versus the Timber Industry

The spotted owl is now an icon of American resource politics, a symbol of the clash between competing approaches to valuing natural resources. In the mid-1980s the Forest Service had planned to permit commercial timber companies to make substantial cuts in the old-growth Oregon forests, whose 2.3 million acres represent the last 1 percent of the nation's original forest cover. In 1985, biologists in the DOI's Fish and Wildlife Service reported to the departmental leadership that the northern spotted owl, whose habitat was almost exclusively northwestern old-growth forests, was fast disappearing and should be designated an endangered species. Estimates indicated that about 1,500 nesting pairs of owls remained, all in the first-growth stands. One consequence of this designation would be to protect this habitat, if geographically unique, from almost all forms of development. The DOI's leadership initially overruled this recommendation under considerable pressure from the timber industry and a variety of local Oregon and Washington interests, including timber mills, community leaders, unions, local congressional representatives, and timber industry workers.

Spokespeople for these interests argued that designating the northern spotted owl an endangered species would virtually end logging on 1.5 million acres of old-growth timber in Oregon and Washington. The federal government estimated that between 4,500 and 9,500 jobs would be lost, but the timber industry asserted that the actual figure was 10 times that amount. "You're talking about complete devastation of communities," protested then-Senator Slade Gorton, R-WA. The president of the Northwest Forestry Association, a trade group, repeated a familiar refrain among local economic interests in Washington and Oregon: "To devastate a regional economy over the spotted owl seems absurd. You're talking about affecting half our industry."[39] The timber industry's outrage was exacerbated further because much of the old-growth softwood timber was exported, primarily to Japan, where it could command several times the domestic price.

Environmentalists had opposed commercial logging in old-growth forests long before the specific tracts in Oregon and Washington had entered the dispute. Environmentalists have argued that intensive logging in old-growth forests, with the building of logging roads and disruptive soil practices sure to attend it, will greatly reduce the forest's ability to conserve water and to prevent soil erosion, thus violating the principle of balanced use. Spokespeople for environmental organizations also contend that much of the old-growth timber is found in poor soil—at high elevations and on steep slopes—and exposure to weathering will cause rapid erosion after logging begins. Moreover, they assert, these forests support a unique ecosystem with a great variety of important and irreplaceable flora and fauna. Finally, environmentalists challenge the presumption that a major increase in the timber harvest would significantly decrease housing costs. In any case, many acceptable substitutes for wood exist in the U.S. economy that can be had without sacrificing virgin forests, they note.

Except for the northern spotted owl, these arguments might have succumbed to the political weight of the local, regional, and national interests defending commercial access to first-growth timber. In fall 1988, environmental organizations obtained a federal court order that instructed the secretary of the interior to list the northern spotted owl as endangered, and in mid-1989, the DOI complied with the court's demand. The designation appeared almost to end commercial logging in Northwestern first-growth forests, but it did nothing to diminish the rancor, or the economic stakes, involved in the continuing controversy over the appropriate use of the national forests.

Timber Sales Reform

George Bush's administration came into office committed to an active environmental agenda, explicitly distancing itself from the Reagan–Watt era in its goals for public lands. Although the environmental community had been displeased with the administration's choice of Lujan as the new secretary of the interior, it was considerably more receptive to the administration's proposal in early 1990 to reduce timber sales substantially in 12 national forests. The new proposal seemed to repudiate the previous administration's resource policies and to signal a major effort to reform traditional Forest Service sales practices, which had long been criticized by environmentalists.

The sales-below-cost controversy—political dynamite in the western states—seemed to set the new administration's public lands policy on a collision course with vast segments of the Forest Service's constituency. The controversy had been simmering for decades. As the Conservation Foundation notes,

> The Forest Service typically constructs the roads and assumes other management and administrative responsibilities that allow private companies to harvest [public forest timber] economically. . . . However, several studies have alleged that the nation actually loses money (as well as valuable wilderness and wildlife habitat) in many cases, particularly in the Rocky Mountain region, because the Forest Service must spend more to allow the harvesting to occur than it receives from the harvests. The Forest Service denies that the economics of sales such as those in the Rocky Mountains and the Northwest are as unfavorable as many critics claim.[40]

Environmentalists, as well as critics within the Forest Service, had long asserted that this practice amounted to public subsidies for the commercial timber industry and a sacrifice of all other multiple-use values, such as recreation or wildlife habitat, to timber sales. "We think the Forest Service overestimates what is sustainable," argued a spokesperson for the National Wildlife Federation. "They overestimate how much timber a given area can produce, they overestimate the potential for the lands to be reforested and they underestimate the impacts on fish and wildlife. The bottom line is they are timber-dominated."[41]

When the Forest Service initiated a new bookkeeping system in 1987, the system appeared to demonstrate that the service was losing money on about two thirds of its timber sales.[42] Critics cited Alaska's Tongass National Forest as an example of the losses disclosed by the new bookkeeping; the Forest Service had spent about $50 million annually to finance the cutting of 450 million board-feet of timber that brought less than $1 million to the government in revenue.[43] Nonetheless, the new proposal had many formidable opponents, including loggers, timber companies, state and congressional political spokespeople for the affected areas, and the Forest Service itself. Because much of the Forest Service budget was spent on preparing and auctioning acreage for commercial logging, a reduction in these sales would mean a substantial budget reduction for the service. In effect, the administration's plan represented the first major assault on a forest management practice that had endured for more than a half century, fortified by a powerful coalition of political and economic interests and defended by one of the federal government's most successful and respected public agencies.

The Clinton administration used the new bookkeeping system to considerable advantage in its efforts to restrain continuing efforts by the commercial timber industry and western state governors to expand allowable timber cuts in the national forests. The new system also worked to the advantage of conservation elements within the Forest Service who had been pressing for greater timber conservation for many decades. It was now possible to demonstrate not only that federal timber sales were not the financial asset they had been asserted to be but also that increased road building and logging in the national forests often increased the federal timbering deficit.

How Much Wilderness Is Enough?

A substantial portion of the 65 million undeveloped acres under the jurisdiction of the Forest Service—the roadless regions—could become part of the National Wilderness Preservation System and thereby be forever excluded from timbering. A large portion of this roadless area is eligible for assignment to timber production. Timber producers, environmentalists, the Forest Service, and Congress have disagreed since the 1980s over how much of this roadless area should be designated for multiple use—in other words, how much of the area should be open to timbering, mineral exploration, and other nonrecreational and nonconservation uses. Perhaps as much as a third of the whole national forest system, including many old-growth stands, is in these roadless areas.

Environmentalists have been apprehensive that any multiple-use designation for large, undeveloped tracts will be an invitation not only to aggressive timbering but also to oil, natural gas, and coal exploration. They predict that energy industries, on locating energy reserves, will seek exceptions to environmental regulations. Air pollution from electric power plants and energy refining operations adjacent to public lands with energy reserves will result, and the quality of the lands will be degraded irreversibly. They would prefer that most of the roadless areas under the Forest Service's jurisdiction be included in the National Wilderness Preservation System.

With some justification, environmentalists also allege that the Forest Service's strong commitment to its traditional multiple-use doctrine makes it reluctant to turn large tracts of roadless areas over to a single dominant use such as wilderness preservation. This conviction led environmentalists to criticize the manner in which the Forest Service conducted its first major inventory of roadless areas within its jurisdiction in the early 1970s.

Nonetheless, the Multiple Use–Sustained Yield Act requires the Forest Service to include wilderness protection among other multiple uses of land within its jurisdiction. The NFMA also requires the Forest Service to draw up a master plan for the use of land under its jurisdiction that includes the consideration of wilderness designation. Thus, the Forest Service was given both ample authority and explicit responsibility to recommend to Congress additional roadless areas for inclusion in the National Wilderness Preservation System. Although Congress alone possesses the authority to assign land to the system formally, the Forest Service's recommendations frequently influence the decisions. The White House, however, often has proposed its own plans for the roadless areas, sometimes at variance with Forest Service initiatives.

The Carter and Reagan administrations offered proposals to Congress for allocating the roadless areas between wilderness and multiple-use categories; both proposals departed in significant ways from the Forest Service's own proposals. The Carter administration's plan, the more conservative of the two, would have allocated about 10 million acres to wilderness and reserved another 10 million for further study. The Reagan administration, committed to increasing the size of territory open to timbering and energy exploration, rejected the Carter proposal. Congress, as it has often done, chose to follow its own agenda for wilderness preservation. After the Reagan administration, relatively few new areas were designated for wilderness because Congress and the White House could reach no agreement on priorities until the Clinton administration's controversial last-minute designation of more than 50 million acres of new or newly protected public domain

As the renewed flaring of the wilderness issue during Clinton's late presidency illustrates, these controversies stalk almost any administration's public lands vision and no administration avoids them totally. George W. Bush, already deeply suspect among conservationists before he took office, earned their further animosity but also the enthusiastic approval of traditional exponents of public land development, from his administration's "no more wilderness" policy. The policy resulted in 2003 from federal court case involving the DOI. That litigation resulted in the DOI agreeing that the BLM would make no further inventory of possible wilderness areas within all the 256 million acres of federal public lands until Congress decided whether to create additional wilderness areas—an unlikely event in the politically polarized Congress. The Obama administration, however, determined to reverse this policy and, aided by Democratic majorities in both congressional chambers, signed in 2009 a legislative bill designating 2 million additional acres of public and as wilderness areas—just in time, from the viewpoint of conservationists, since Republicans regained control of the House of Representatives in 2010, making any further congressional approval of new wilderness designations unlikely for some time.

Conclusion

The struggles over energy exploration, mining, and timbering on public lands reveal a durable structure underlying the political conflicts over the use of public resources in the United States. The pattern tends to be repeated because it grows from political realities inherent in the U.S. governmental system.

At the center of the conflict is a federal executive agency guarding the resource as a public trust and wrestling with an ambiguous mandate for its management. Most often, this agency will be part of the DOI or the Forest Service. The mandates will be vague because Congress must rely on a professional administrator to make expert resource decisions—hence the generality of the mandates—and ambiguous because Congress often shrinks from choosing between conflicting claims on resources. Thus, multiple-use prescriptions for forest or range management appear to offer something to recreationists, conservationists, and resource developers without really settling the competing claims. The administrative managers for the public resource inevitably will find their professional decisions politicized as conflicting interests seek to influence technical decisions to their advantage. Technical decisions themselves can often be made and justified in different, scientifically defensible ways. All this means that resource administrators sometimes can exercise their professional judgment in the service of their own group and political loyalties. In all these ways, the resource management agency finds itself at the center of a political conflict over the public domain.

Further, both the White House and Congress will become partisan advocates of resource management policy, attempting to influence administrative decisions relevant to resource management and responding to pressure from organized interests with a stake in resource management. As we have observed in timber, wilderness, and energy development policies, Congress has the predictable tendency to intervene in administrative management to protect interests important to the legislators. So, too, Presidents Carter, Reagan, Bush, Clinton, George W. Bush, and indeed every president before them for a half century, have directed the DOI and the Forest Service to pursue specific objectives in resource management compatible with their ideological biases and political commitments. Indeed, Congress and the White House often compete in attempting to influence administrative determinations affecting the public domain. The president, despite the illusory title of chief executive, has no guarantee of success in the struggle.

The plurality of organized interests involved in resource decisions means that Congress, the White House, and the administrative agencies are enmeshed in a process of coalition building with organized groups during resource policy making. These organized interests, moreover, involve not only private interests but also the states within which the public domain resides and for which the use of the domain's resources have significant political and economic consequences.

Finally, policy struggles quite often are waged in the technical language of resource economics and scientific management. Perhaps more than most environmental issues, public resource management is an arcane business to most Americans, particularly those living where few public lands exist. In such circumstances, specialized private groups, such as environmentalists and resource users, tend to operate almost invisibly to the public. The outcome of the policy struggles depends particularly on the groups' organizational resources, technical expertise, and political adeptness in the administrative infighting and legal wrangling that often characterize resource policy making. It is a political arena, more particularly, in which organized environmental groups often constitute practically the only expression of viewpoints not associated with resource users or administrators.

Suggested Readings

Clark, Jeanne N., and Daniel McCool. *Staking Out the Terrain: Power Differentials among Natural Resource Management Agencies.* 2nd ed. Albany, NY: SUNY Press, 2000.

Lowry, William R. *Dam Politics: Restoring America's Rivers.* Washington, DC: Georgetown University Press, 2003.

Nie, Martin A. *The Governance of Western Public Lands: Mapping Its Present and Future.* Lawrence: University of Kansas Press, 2009.

Reisner, Marc. *Cadillac Desert.* Rev. ed. New York: Penguin, 2001.

Vaughn, Jacqueline, and Hanna Cortner. *George W. Bush's Healthy Forests: Reframing the Environmental Debate.* Boulder: University Press of Colorado, 2005.

Notes

1. Felicity Barringer, "Secretary Tours Yellowstone on Snowmobile," *New York Times,* February 17, 2005, A18.
2. National Energy Policy Group, *National Energy Policy* (Washington, DC: EOP, 2001), 5–9.
3. For a legislative history of the ANWR, see M. Lynne Corn, Michael Ratner and Kristina Alexander, *Arctic National Wildlife Refuge (ANSR): A Primer for the 112th Congress,* February 14, 2012 (Washington DC: Congressional Research Service, 2012), Document RL33872, available at www.fas.org/sgp/crs/misc/RL33872.pdf (accessed November14,2012).
4. Defenders of Wildlife, "Arctic National Wildlife Refuge," available at http: www .savearcticrefuge.org (accessed May 1, 2007).

5. Charli Coon, "Tapping Oil Reserves in a Small Part of the ANWR: Environmentally Sound, Energy Wise," August 1, 2001, available at www.heritage.org/research/energyand environment/em763.cfm (accessed April 14, 2004).

6. For a legislative history of ANWR, see M. Lynne Corn and Bernard A. Gelb, "Arctic National Wildlife Refuge (ANWR): Controversies for the 108th Congress," Report no. 1B10111, Congressional Research Service, Washington, DC, 2003.

7. U.S. DOI, "Environmentally Responsible Energy Production in Alaska's Arctic National Wildlife Refuge (ANWR)," July 21, 2003, available at www.doi.gov/anwr/index.html (accessed April 15, 2007).

8. Rachael D'Oro, "Alaska Environment, Development Co-Exist," November 17, 2003, available at www.lists.envirolink.org/pipermail/ar-news/Week-of-Mon-20031117/010930.html (accessed May 1, 2007).

9. Mike Chambers, "Alaska Governor Invites U.S. Oil Drilling," *AP Online,* April 1, 2004, www.highbeam.com/library/doc3.asp?DOCID=1P1:929982 (accessed April 6, 2004).

10. Article IV, section 3, clause 2.

11. Tom Arrandale, *The Battle for Natural Resources* (Washington, DC: Congressional Quarterly, 1983), chap. 1; U.S. DOI, "About the Department of the Interior: Quick Facts," available at http://www.doi.gov/facts.html (accessed January 23, 2010).

12. Aldo Leopold, *A Sand County Almanac* (New York: Oxford University Press, 1949), 222.

13. A useful survey of public lands can be found in U.S. DOI, Bureau of Land Management, *Managing the Nation's Public Lands* (Washington, DC: U.S. Government Printing Office, 1983).

14. Paul J. Culhane, *Public Lands Politics* (Baltimore: Johns Hopkins University Press, 1981), 60.

15. James Baker, "The Frustrations of FLPMA," *Wilderness,* 47 (winter 1983): 11. See also Jeanne N. Clarke and Daniel McCool, *Staking Out the Terrain: Power Differentials Among Natural Resource Agencies* (Albany, NY: SUNY Press, 1985), chaps. 4–5.

16. 16 U.S.C. § 530, 74 Stat. 215 (1960). On the impact of sustained use on the Forest Service, see Culhane, *Public Lands Politics,* chap. 2.

17. 16 U.S.C. § 530, 74 Stat. 215 (1960).

18. CEQ, *Environmental Quality, 1979* (Washington, DC: U.S. Government Printing Office, 1980), 309.

19. Ann O'Neill, "Spotted Owl Could Be a Game-Changer in Tombstone Water War," *CNN News,* June 9, 2012, available at www.cnn.com/2012/06/09/us/tombstone-shovel-brigade/index.html (accessed August 10, 2012).

20. Natural Resources Defense Council, "The Bush Record," available at http://www.nrdc.org/ bushrecord/default.asp (accessed May 15, 2008).

21. Juliet Eilperin,"Obama's Wilderness Legacy Remains Uncertain," *Washington* Post, June 10, 2012, available at www.washingtonpost.com/national/health-science/obamas-wilderness-legacy-remains-uncertain/2012/06/10/gJQAOlCLTV_story_2.html (accessed August 24, 2012).

22. Scott Straeter, "'Wild Lands' Policy Stokes Flames of Dissent in Utah County," *New York Times,* January 6, 2011, available at www.nytimes.com/gwire/2011/01/06/06 greenwire-wild-lands-policy-stokes-flames-of-dissent-in-92049.html?pagewanted=all (accessed September 25, 2012)

23. Stephanie Simon, "Western Policy Sparks Western Ire," *Wall Street Journal,* December 30, 2010, available at http://online.wsj.com/article/SB10001424052748704543004576051981953491522.html (accessed February 5, 2011).

24. On the history of recent federal OCS legislation, see Marc Humphries, "Outer Continental Shelf: Debate Over Oil and Gas Leasing," Congressional Research Service Report to Congress, Washington, DC, August 14, 2006.

25. Craig W. Allin, "Wilderness Policy," in *Western Public Lands and Environmental Politics,* ed. Charles Davis (Boulder, CO: Westview Press, 1997), 179.

26. Sandra K. Davis, "Fighting over Public Lands: Interest Groups, States, and the Federal Government," in *Western Public Lands and Environmental Politics,* ed. Charles Davis, (Boulder, CO: Westview Press, 1997), 23.

27. Quoted in World Resources Institute, *The 1994 Information Please Environmental Almanac* (New York: Houghton Mifflin, 1993), 159.

28. Sheldon Rampton, "Fish out of Water: Behind the Wise Use Movement's Victory at Klamath," *PR Watch* 10 (April–June 2003): 117–126.

29. Philip Shabecoff, "Debate Over Wilderness Area Leasing Intensifies," *New York Times,* February 15, 1982, D6.

30. Quoted in Douglas Jehl, "In Idaho a Howl Against Roadless Forests," *New York Times,* July 5, 2000, A10.

31. Quoted in ibid.

32. Jesse T. Holland, "Clinton Creates Largest U.S. Nature Preserve," *New York Times,* December 5, 2000, 1A.

33. GOPUSA, "Obama Administration Sets Aside Large Public Land Tracts to Develop Solar Power Plants," available at www.gopusa.com/news/2012/10/13/obama-admin-sets-aside-large-public-land-tracts-to-develop-solar-power-plants/ (accessed 11/2/2012).

34. George Hoberg, "From Localism to Legalism," in *Western Public Lands and Environmental Politics,* ed. Charles Davis (Boulder, CO: Westview Press, 1997), 48.

35. Ibid., 53.

36. 16 U.S.C. § 530, 74 Stat. 215 (1960).

37. Culhane, *Public Lands Politics,* chap. 2.

38. U.S. Department of Commerce, Bureau of the Census, *Statistical Abstract of the United States, 1989* (Washington, DC: U.S. Government Printing Office, 1990), 656.

39. Timothy Egan, "U.S. Stand on Owl Seen Saving Trees in West," *New York Times,* April 27, 1989, A18.

40. Conservation Foundation, *State of the Environment: A View Toward the Nineties* (Washington, DC: Conservation Foundation, 1987), 220.

41. Margaret E. Kriz, "Last Stand on Timber," *National Journal,* March 3, 1990, 509.

42. Philip Shabecoff, "Aid Is Asked on Recreation in Forests," *New York Times,* February 17, 1988, B5.

43. Timothy Egan, "Logging in Lush Alaskan Forest Profits Companies and Costs U.S.," *New York Times,* May 29, 1989, sec. 1, 1.

Chapter 10

Climate Change, Domestic Politics, and the Challenge of Global Policy Making

Managers of zoos and aquariums are wrestling with how to educate visitors about the dangers of climate change while keeping attendance numbers high in an era of polarized views on global warming. Their organizations are regarded with trust, putting them in an ideal position to teach, especially as their ties to conservation groups increase. But exhibits that focus on damaged coral reefs and dying trees could scare off visitors, prompting some zoos and aquariums to keep the topic of climate change limited to, say, a sign about Arctic melting in the polar bear exhibit.

"You don't want them walking away saying, 'I paid to get in, I bought my kid a hot dog, I just want to show my kid a fish—and you are making me feel bad about climate change,'" said Paul Boyle, the senior vice president for conservation and education at the Association of Zoos and Aquariums.

—Greenwire, August 27, 2012[1]

Twenty years ago when we started worrying about global warming, we thought we'd have a generation to pay those bills off. But we were wrong—the planet was more finely balanced than we'd realized. The melting Arctic is the call from the repo man.

—Bill McKibben, American
environmental scholar and activist[2]

On December 9, 2009, at the very beginning of his first term, President Barack Obama was preparing for a journey to Copenhagen to join other world leaders and several thousand delegates gathered at the United Nations Climate Change Conference (COP 15; the 15th Conference of the Parties to the UN Framework Convention on Climate Change). He

361

was shadowed by a large polar bear. The bear arrived first. Alongside the cavernous conference hall, the United States had erected a handsome pavilion visited daily by crowds drawn from more than 40,000 participants and delegates attending this most important global climate change conference in a decade. Inside the hall, Secretary of the Interior Ken Salazar's press conference was underway. Visitors watched a video of the president's Nobel Prize address on a wall screen. Many, however, were more attentive to the sociable bear on his hind legs, animatedly describing his species' threatened extinction from the effects of global climate change, paws waving and wagging at the video, warning Obama to return from Copenhagen with a viable global climate change agreement.[3]

The polar bear was a temporary alter ego for the public lands director of the Center for Biological Diversity (CBD) who, uncomfortably encased within his costume, represented one of the environmental advocacy groups that successfully used litigation to force the U.S. DOI to list the bears as an endangered species. The bear, perhaps the most recognizable icon for global climate change, could as easily symbolize the most daunting environmental challenge confronting the White House—the bear's sojourn to Copenhagen a political metaphor for an issue destined to stalk Obama's administration—as it has done with a growing presence in every presidency since Ronald Reagan and continued to do throughout Obama's first term.

The way to a global climate treaty had become a tortuous path leading from Kyoto in 1998 through the inhospitable Bush administration and culminating with COP 18 in November 2012. Nationally, the journey has become a tangle of obstruction and delay compounded of the Bush White House opposition to an international treaty or comprehensive federal legislation controlling greenhouse gas (GHG) emissions and congressional deadlock over domestic GHG regulatory legislation. Meanwhile, 16 states have seized the initiative and created, or tried to create, their own state and regional GHG regulatory programs. Environmentalists and other treaty advocates, frustrated with a decade of Washington inertia, enthusiastically anticipated Barack Obama's election as a breakthrough for domestic and international GHG regulation. Obama had made a "green economy" and renewed federal and international action on a global climate treaty the centerpiece of his environmental platform. However, the lethal partisan polarization within Congress over climate policy defeated in 2010 Obama's ambitious, politically risky legislative initiative for a new GHG regulatory program. The issue was extinguished for the remainder of Obama's first term.

The climate change issue is evidence that the distinction between domestic and international environmental policy is rapidly eroding as both science and diplomacy force the recognition of their increasing interdependence.

Climate change is one of numerous global environmental issues, such as acid precipitation and stratospheric ozone depletion that now routinely compel attention on the White House domestic policy agenda. Climate change seems to be an especially formidable issue for policy makers even though the military has accepted both its reality and its serious implications for national security. For example, the "May 2010 version of the National Security Strategy repeatedly groups together violent extremism, nuclear weapons, climate change, pandemic disease, and economic instability as security threats that require strength at home and international cooperation to address adequately," reports one survey. Moreover, the "February 2010 Quadrennial Defense Review links climate change to future conflict and identifies it as one of four issues in which reform is 'imperative' to ensure national security."[4] Nonetheless, public officials at all government levels continue to disagree over the credibility of the scientific data and the scientists supporting the climate warming issue.

Unlike acid precipitation, there are no stunted and withered forests to dramatize the problem, no sprawling ozone hole visible with satellite imagery to translate stratospheric ozone depletion into immediately recognizable public form—in short, there is little readily understandable, unambiguous evidence that domestic policy makers can summon effectively to frame the issue. Moreover, many of the most ominous global consequences predicted from climate warming—for example, the northern migration of the global temperate zone or the extinction of an indigenous species—may be diffused and attenuated over decades or centuries, thereby easily inhibiting a sense of urgency and relevance among the public and its officials. Because climate warming is conceived globally on a scale never historically experienced by humans, public opinion studies often suggest that the average American can feel intimidated and personally helpless to do much about it. In addition, the potential domestic and international economic cost and worldwide scale of political action essential to mitigating climate change or adapting to it require international diplomatic and economic collaboration that is difficult to achieve. Above all, the primal vortex about which the domestic policy debate over climate change swirls, the most powerful engine driving the nationwide political conflict over the climate change issue, is contested science.

The Contested Science of Atmospheric Warming

The catalyst to the ongoing controversy over the scientific validity of global climate change predictions has been the Intergovernmental Panel on Climate Change (IPCC), established in 1988 under the auspices of the United Nations Environment Programme and the World Meteorological Organization for the purpose of assessing "the scientific, technical and socioeconomic information relevant for the understanding of the risk of human-induced climate change."[5] The IPCC reports have each engaged more than 2,400 scientists across the globe in a continuing process of collecting, integrating, and evaluating the vast diversity of scientific research on virtually every aspect of climate change. The IPCC "does not carry out new research nor does it monitor climate-related data. It bases its assessment mainly on published and peer reviewed scientific technical literature."[6] The goal of these assessments is to inform international policy and negotiations on climate-related issues. The IPCC has become the most globally visible and consistently controversial of the scientific institutions associated with climate change research. Although the IPCC periodic reports are as close to Holy Writ as exists within the scientific community associated with climate change advocacy, the IPCC has been consistently diligent to acknowledge explicitly the limitations that may be inherent to their assessment's data or conclusions, lest the reports lose their credibility.

The Four Intergovernmental Panel on Climate Change Assessments.
The First Assessment Report of the IPCC (1990), as well as a supplemental report prepared in 1992, supported the establishment of the United Nations Framework Convention on Climate Change (UNFCCC) at the United Nations Conference on Environment and Development (UNCED, commonly known as "The Earth Summit") held in Rio de Janeiro, Brazil, in 1992. The UNFCCC treaty, which the United States has signed, serves as the foundation of international political efforts to combat global warming.

The IPCC's reports were also influential at the first COP to the UNFCCC, held in Berlin, Germany, in 1995. COP conferences, at different national locations, have subsequently been held at regular intervals, the last (COP 15) in Copenhagen in December 2009. The first COP delegates produced the Berlin Mandate, setting out the terms for a negotiation process that would produce binding commitments by the industrial countries to reduce their heat-trapping emissions after the year 2000.

The significantly strengthened IPCC Second Assessment Report (SAR; 1996) provided key input to the negotiations that led to the adoption of the Kyoto Protocol at the UNFCCC in 1997. The Kyoto Protocol is an international agreement that established binding targets for reducing the heat-trapping emissions of developed countries. After the SAR was published, a number of technical papers and special reports were prepared on the impact of aircraft, land use, technology, and changing emission levels on global warming. The IPCC Third Assessment Report (TAR; 2001) concluded that temperature increases over the 21st century could be significantly larger than previously thought and that the evidence for human influence on climate change is stronger than ever. The level of acceptance of this assessment within the extensive community of IPCC scientists was quite remarkable. The Fourth Assessment Report (FAR; 2007) has become the most internationally influential scientific document currently involved with climate change research, representing what most atmospheric scientists and related professionals consider to be a thorough, carefully explained view of the state of climate change science in 2001. The FAR

> provides the strongest statement to date on the extent and causes of climate change. This report expresses much greater confidence than past assessments that most of the observed warming over the past half-century is caused by human activities (greater than 90% certainty). It notes that the rates of warming and sea level rise accelerated during the 20th century, the latter representing a major new finding. It also notes other important changes such as more intense precipitation, drought, and to some extent tropical cyclones.[7]

Changes of the magnitude predicted by the FAR and without mitigation would profoundly, and possibly catastrophically, affect much of the world. Low-lying areas, including many economically underdeveloped countries in Africa and Asia as well as island nations, would be inundated by seawater, their economic and ecological sustainability severely jeopardized. Economically and technologically advanced nations with exposed seacoasts or levee-protected lowlands would also confront formidable economic, engineering, and logistical problems in adjusting to rising sea levels. Generally, the world's temperate zones would probably shift further north, accelerating the desertification and deforestation of many continental areas in Asia, Africa, Europe, and North America, while transforming agricultural production in many others. Along with these transformations would come shifts in regional ecology and a multitude of other natural changes that are difficult to predict precisely. Not all the predicted changes would necessarily be adverse. Some experts have also predicted longer and more productive growing seasons for many crops as a result of increased ambient carbon dioxide, the transformation of some northern latitudes into new agricultural breadbaskets, and other benign consequences. In any event, the profound global alterations attending significant climate warming, however characterized, would apparently create a relatively swift, pervasive transformation of human societies and world ecosystems unprecedented in modern human history.

The FAR also doubled the top end of possible climate warming globally to 11°F over the coming century and predicted an acceleration of the trends causing concern earlier. According to the report, the 20th century was the warmest in the past thousand years. During that period, the sea level rose 10 times faster than the average rate over the past 3,000 years.

While continuing to acknowledge the tentativeness of many of its conclusions, the FAR seemed to confirm a growing scientific consensus about the imminence of climate warming and to strengthen political pressure for international governmental responses. Since the first IPCC assessment report, numerous public and private institutions have also conducted extensive research to characterize the global and domestic implications of the assessments. If the FAR is substantially accurate in its conclusions, the consequences are expected to profoundly alter almost every aspect of U.S. domestic life, a transformation on an ecological, economic, and social scale without historical precedent, as the predictions in Box 10–1 suggest.

Box 10–1   *Global Climate Change Impacts in the United States: Key Findings*

---

1. Global warming is unequivocal and primarily human-induced.
Global temperature has increased over the past fifty years. This observed increase is due primarily to human-induced emissions of heat-trapping gases.

2. Climate changes are underway in the United States and are projected to grow.
Climate-related changes are already observed in the United States and its coastal waters. These include increases in heavy downpours, rising temperature and sea level, rapidly retreating glaciers, thawing permafrost, lengthening growing seasons, lengthening ice-free seasons in the ocean and on lakes and rivers, earlier snowmelt, and alterations in river flows. These changes are projected to grow.

3. Widespread climate-related impacts are occurring now and are expected to increase.
Climate changes are already affecting water, energy, transportation, agriculture, ecosystems, and health. These impacts are different from region to region and will grow under projected climate change.

4. Climate change will stress water resources.
Water is an issue in every region, but the nature of the potential impacts varies. Drought, related to reduced precipitation, increased evaporation, and increased water loss from plants, is an important issue in many regions, especially in the West. Floods and water quality problems are likely to be amplified by climate changes in most regions. Declines in mountain snowpack are important in the West and Alaska, where snowpack provides vital natural water storage.

5. Crop and livestock production will be increasingly challenged.
Agriculture is considered one of the sectors most adaptable to changes in climate. However, increased heat, pests, water stress, diseases, and weather extremes will pose adaptation challenges for crop and livestock production.

6. Coastal areas are at increasing risk from sea-level rise and storm surge.
Sea-level rise and storm surge place many U.S. coastal areas at increasing risk of erosion and flooding, especially along the Atlantic and Gulf Coasts, Pacific Islands, and parts of Alaska. Energy and transportation infrastructure and other property in coastal areas are very likely to be adversely affected.

7. Threats to human health will increase.
Health impacts of climate change are related to heat stress, waterborne diseases, poor air quality, extreme weather events, and diseases transmitted by insects and rodents. Robust public health infrastructure can reduce the potential for negative impacts.

8. Climate change will interact with many social and environmental stresses.
Climate change will combine with pollution; population growth; overuse of resources; urbanization; and other social, economic, and environmental stresses to create larger impacts than from any of these factors alone.

9. Thresholds will be crossed, leading to changes in climate and ecosystems.
There are a variety of thresholds in the climate system and ecosystems. These thresholds determine, for example, the presence of sea ice and permafrost and the survival of species, from fish to insect pests, with implications for society. With further climate change, the cross of additional thresholds is expected.

10. Future climate change and its impacts depend on choices made today.
The amount and rate of future climate change depend primarily on current and future human-caused emissions of heat-trapping gases and airborne particles. Responses involve reducing emissions to limit future warming and adapting to the changes that are unavoidable.

Source: U.S. Global Climate Change Research Project, "Executive Summary," *Global Climate Change Impacts of the United States* (New York: Cambridge University Press, 2009), 12.

Dissent. Although the IPCC reports and related research appear to represent what has been called a consensus among climate scientists, the IPCC data and conceptual models constituting the foundation for its predictions about the magnitude of global climate change and its implications have been contested from the inception of international discussion about global climate change. As the IPCC has become increasingly assertive in its major conclusions, the scientific debate has become increasingly strident; this has occasionally escalated into venomous exchanges within the scientific community. But, more often, these exchanges have taken place within the political arena, where the issue has transmuted into a polarizing partisan confrontation between contending factions promoting competing claims concerning the scientific validity and political acceptability of the proposed solutions. IPCC dissenters not only have contested the IPCC's major scientific conclusions and supporting research but, in some instances, also accused various scientific proponents and organizations of willfully conspiring to suppress and falsify scientific data inconsistent with the major premises of climate change.

Climate change dissenters (sometimes anointed *contrarians*) range across a broad, extremely diverse social and scientific spectrum: scientists engaged in climate research and related fields, other scientific professionals, political partisans ideologically hostile to the proposed social or

economic solutions for climate change, and corporations vulnerable to
the regulatory controls required to control climate warming emissions.
Proponents of the IPCC's conclusions and related initiatives to regulate
climate-warming emissions have been especially vehement in asserting
that many of the individuals and institutions opposing the IPCC's conclusions are proxies for the global petroleum corporation Exxon-Mobil,
which has spent millions of dollars on its own corporate media campaign
attacking the credibility of the IPCC and its allies. Moreover, Exxon-
Mobil has a considerable number of corporate allies in the business of
underwriting opposition to the IPCC, including numerous other corporations and advocacy groups associated with fossil fuel mining and combustion and with petroleum distillation and distribution.

The ongoing scientific debate swirls around a multitude of complex
technical issues certain to confuse the public. The critics' favorite target
has been the computer models used to generate climate warming predictions, which have been assailed continually for faulty assumptions and
inadequate data about current climate trends. Some experts have asserted
that many computer models are based on inaccurate measurements of
historical temperature change, that climate warming models fail to
describe the long-range physics of climate change, that other historical
climate data are misconstrued or misapplied in climate modeling, and
much more. Some experts cite other causes, such as solar activity and ter-
restrial volcanoes, to explain climate warming. Others rely on different
models suggesting that the greenhouse effect is not inevitable. Still others
do not believe sufficient evidence exists to make any responsible judgment
about future climate warming.

The already fierce contention over climate change science was further
exacerbated, and the critics enormously inspired, by the emergence of
what has been called the *climategate* affair in November 2009, with its
serious political repercussions. Hackers captured more than 1,000
e-mails from scientists at the Climate Research Unit (CRU) at Great
Britain's University of East Anglia, a major global climate change
research center supporting the IPCC reports, and publicized the pur-
loined e-mails internationally.[8] Climate critics asserted that the e-mails
revealed (as they had always suspected) evidence of a conspiracy among
global climate scientists to fabricate data supporting climate warming
while suppressing contrary evidence. Coming less than a month before
the COP 15, the revelation could not have been better timed to further
confound the already difficult negotiations anticipated at Copenhagen.
Climate critics asserted that the messages, covering a period of 13 years,
constituted an arsenal of "smoking guns" destroying the credibility of
the IPCC FAR. Despite evidence that the scientists were sometimes rude,

dismissive of critics, and intensely partisan to their own research, the e-mails did not seem to vindicate the climate critics' worst allegations—that fundamental climate data was counterfeit.[9] Nevertheless, the whole affair, however, was politically damaging regardless of the ultimate credibility of the CRU critics. The CRU e-mails had seized global media attention, throwing climate proponents on the defensive and prompting numerous investigations.

The Public and Climate Change. In the United States, the CRU affair appeared, at least temporarily, to erode the already receding domestic political support for American participation in a global agreement limiting climate warming emissions—this at a time when the embattled president was already in Copenhagen, struggling to salvage at least a symbolic triumph from the contentious deliberations.

However, public opinion, reacting to the continuing public debate about climate science and to events that seemed to verify or to contradict climate warming, has been on a roller-coaster ride between belief and disbelief since 2000, as Figure 10–1 illustrates. By the end of 2012, the public mood seemed to be moving toward a growing acceptance of the climate warming argument, which could prove politically productive for a new Obama regulatory initiative—if that mood prevails. In 2012, in any event, climate

Figure 10–1   Public Response to Statement "Yes, Solid Evidence Exists that the Earth Is Warming," 2006–2012

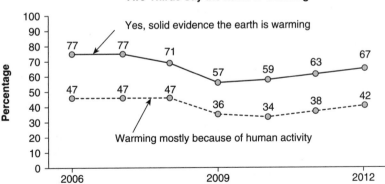

Source: Pew Center for People and the Press, "More Say There Is Solid Evidence of Global Warming," October 15, 2012, available at /www.people-press.org/2012/10/15/more-say-there-is-solid-evidence-of-global-warming/ (accessed November 16, 2012).

warming was still not among the most important environmental issues concerning the public and seldom rose from the lower depths of most opinion surveys reporting the matters most concerning the American public. Moreover, a deep and persistent disagreement not conducive to a consensus on climate warming regulation continues to divide Republicans and Democrats in Congress and the nation, as illustrated by Figure 10–2.

The domestic debate about the evidence for climate warming and the policy implications also unfolds within a broader world arena shaping the political contours of the domestic issue in important ways. This creates the setting for what has been called the transboundry politics of environmental policy making so characteristic of the climate issue.

The Domestic Setting of Climate Change Politics

The United States is second only to China in the volume of its global GHG emissions (see Figure 10–3), and the magnitude of these emissions has risen steadily throughout the last several decades. Until the late 1980s, however, the nation's emission of these climate-warming gases was largely a concern of scientists, a matter virtually unknown and, in any case, uninteresting to the public.

Figure 10–2   Partisan Differences among the Public Concerning Evidence of Climate Warming, 2006–2012

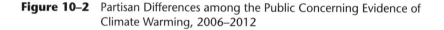

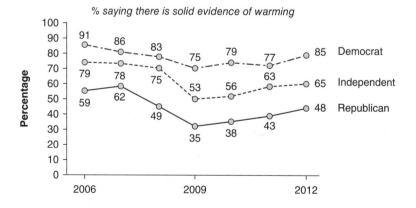

Source: Pew Center for People and the Press, "More Say There Is Solid Evidence of Global Warming," October 15, 2012, available at /www.people-press.org/2012/10/15/more-say-there-is-solid-evidence-of-global-warming/ (accessed November 16, 2012).

Figure 10–3   National Global Emissions of Climate Warming Chemicals, 2010

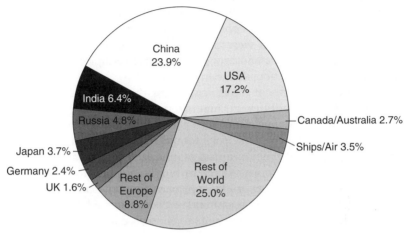

2010 Annual Emissions

Source: http://transitionvoice.com/2010/12/china-can-slow-global-warming-if-the-us-wont/ (accessed January 20, 2013).

In mid-1988, James E. Hansen, director of the NASA Goddard Institute for Space Studies, testified before the members of the Senate Energy and Natural Resources Committee that it was "99 percent certain" that the unusually hot summer of 1988 was evidence that a global climate warming was underway.[10] That remark instantly caught the attention of Congress and the media. Suddenly, global warming, often called the *greenhouse effect,* bore the imprimatur of NASA science; it was speculation no more. Hansen had accomplished what the environmental movement could not despite many years of labor. Global warming had acquired political credibility.

In fact, the scientific evidence was less than compelling at the time, but global climate warming had arrived politically on a wave of international scientific advocacy, and presidents were compelled to act as if it were imminent. The U.S. involvement in global climate warming diplomacy was inevitable. Both the George Bush and Clinton administrations, uneasy with the science and politics of climate warming, initiated measures, albeit irresolutely, to mitigate the impact of global warming.

A great diversity of domestic political interests are caught up in the regulatory battle over GHG emissions, including electrical utilities, which account for 80 percent of all domestic coal combustion; automobile manufacturers and petroleum producers, whose products create significant carbon emissions; agricultural crop and livestock producers; and almost any other fossil-fuel-consuming industries. Throughout the 1990s, the domestic campaign for national and international controls on GHG emissions was led primarily by scientists, environmentalists, and segments of the national media. They were strongly supported by most European nations and Japan, which were prepared to negotiate a tough climate treaty by the early 1990s and brought considerable diplomatic pressure on the United States to act similarly.

Most of the segments of the U.S. economy that potentially would be regulated, led by the utilities, car manufacturers, and petroleum producers, were joined by organized labor in early opposition to any domestic or international agreements setting compulsory timetables and targets for cutbacks in fossil fuel emissions associated with climate warming. This domestic opposition was joined by most of the developing nations, which collectively account for 30 to 40 percent of current global GHG emissions. Some developing countries believed that the largely Western scientific community advocating climate controls could not speak to the interests of the developing world. Some poorer nations, for instance, resented calculations produced by the IPCC indicating that deforestation and livestock in developing nations contributed to global climate warming. From the perspective of developing countries, this unfairly stigmatized their difficult economic circumstances. In their view, "deforestation is a matter of desperation, not choice, and subsistence animals who provide a variety of useful functions cannot be compared with surplus, overfed stock in rich countries."[11] Developing countries also asserted that GHG abatement should be the industrialized nations' responsibility because developing nations needed all their resources for survival. "How can we devote our precious resources toward reducing emissions," asked Malawi's minister of Forestry, Fisheries and Environmental Affairs at the Kyoto conference, "when we are struggling every day just to feed, clothe and house our citizens?"[12] Nor did the developing countries find most economists helpful. Economists who asserted that developing countries could abate their fossil fuel emissions far more cheaply than could developed ones seemed to be feeding the appetites of the privileged nations while thrusting the abatement burden as much as possible onto others.

In any event, the estimated costs to the United States alone to reduce its carbon dioxide emissions would be enormous. The cost of abating carbon dioxide emissions in the United States would fall heavily on coal users and producers, particularly the electrical utilities, and on the auto industry. The capital cost of installing control technologies for carbon dioxide emissions—and no commercially proven technology yet exists—is estimated to be 70 to 150 percent of the entire cost of a new electricity-generating facility. This cost could raise the average American's electric bill by 75 percent.[13] Every American would feel some impact of the abatement policies on his or her lifestyle and pocketbook.

Until the early 1990s, scientific disagreement and public passivity forced policy makers to become scientific judges and scientists to become salespeople in the struggle to determine whose data would govern policy decisions. By the end of George Bush's administration in 1992, however, the combined scientific and diplomatic pressures, together with gradually emerging public concern about climate warming, forced the White House to confront the greenhouse effect diplomatically. At the 1992 Rio conference, the U.S. delegation reluctantly agreed to reduce voluntarily U.S. GHG emissions to 1990 levels by the year 2000. It was evident two years later that neither the United States nor several other industrialized nations would meet their voluntary emission abatement targets. President Clinton later agreed to negotiate a binding treaty at the 1997 Kyoto conference, convened at the initiative of the parties to the UNFCCC. Thus, the United States for the first time was apparently committed to a compulsory target-and-timetable agreement. But, no consensus on the need for such a treaty existed within either congressional party or among the public as the negotiations began, leaving the outcome very much in doubt. Soon, Bill Clinton was absorbed in an epic impeachment struggle, and the Senate, as expected, overwhelmingly rejected the agreement. The subsequent presidential election of George W. Bush in 2000 virtually ended active U.S. domestic or international initiatives for comprehensive regulation of climate change emissions until Barack Obama's administration.

The failure of the Senate in 1998 to ratify the Kyoto Protocol, compounded by the subsequent election of a Republican majority in both congressional chambers and George W. Bush's presence in the White House, forestalled any further U.S. international initiatives on global climate warming until the Obama presidency. However, the states became so active in the absence of federal action that they had become the domestic leaders in climate change legislation at the conclusion of the Bush administration.

The States Take the Lead. By the time the Obama administration was inaugurated, 16 states had adopted GHG emissions reduction targets, 39 states had joined the multistate Climate Registry to monitor and report their GHG emissions, and state partnerships had formed three regional cap-and-trade programs: the eastern RGGI, the Western Climate Initiative, and the Midwestern Climate Initiative.[14] In addition, California had enacted a regulatory program that exceeded federal standards for GHG emissions from the transportation sector, and 12 other states proposed the adoption of the standards as well. The state programs involve a mix of different provisions, which usually include the following[15]:

- *State climate change commissions.* Executive or legislative commissions that examine the possible consequences of climate change for a state and the costs and benefits associated with addressing them and that then develop recommendations for appropriate policies.
- *Climate action plans.* State-designed climate action plans to meet individual state conditions.
- *GHG reporting.* Mandatory or voluntary reporting of GHG emissions from major sources in many states, such as California, Wisconsin, West Virginia, and Hawaii. Most of these states also joined the national Climate Registry, a nonprofit organization measuring and reporting publicly GHG emissions through a consistently common, accurate, and transparent process across industry sectors and borders.
- *Economy-wide GHG reductions.* Emissions goals (usually voluntary rather than compulsory) for all major emission sources within the state.
- *GHG performance standards for electric power.* A requirement that all electric power generated within the state meet a common standard for GHG emissions. Most of the performance programs create a Renewable Portfolio Standard (RPS) requiring that electrical utilities obtain a fixed percentage of their generated power from renewable sources such as wind, solar, biomass, and geothermal.
- *GHG performance standards for vehicles.* Federal law requires states to follow federal emissions standards for cars and light trucks or to follow California's higher standard. Eleven states had adopted, or planned to adopt, the California standard following a Supreme Court ruling in 2007 that the EPA had authority under the federal Clean Air Act to regulate CO_2, the principal GHG.

Belated Federal Action. The pall of inertia enveloping the White House during the Bush administration dissipated only in Bush's last year when the federal courts compelled the federal government to act on the climate issue. In 2006, Stephen Johnson, Bush's EPA administrator, against the advice of his own staff ruled that CO_2 was not a pollutant that EPA was compelled to regulate under the CAA. Later, again contrary to staff advice, Johnson decided that EPA would not issue a waiver allowing California to enact stronger automobile emissions standards than the federal government (the proposed California standards were intended, among other objectives, to reduce auto emissions of GHG). This waiver was permitted by the CAA and had customarily been granted to California when the state requested the authority to enforce other air pollution regulations that were more stringent than the federal standards. Moreover, 11 other states were prepared to adopt the California standards, as the CAA also permitted.

A coalition of states, asserting that the CAA did compel EPA to regulate CO_2, immediately challenged the EPA's contrary interpretation in the federal courts. In a landmark decision, the Supreme Court ruled in *Massachusetts v. Environmental Protection Agency* (2007) that CO_2 could potentially endanger human health or the environment as defined by the CAA. The Court then instructed the EPA to determine whether CO_2 was, in fact, a threat to humans or the environment (the *endangerment finding*) and, if so, to write appropriate regulations to control domestic CO_2 emissions. The Court's decision accelerated a cascade of climate-warming bills, resolutions, and amendments already emerging from Congress—235 proposals in the 110th Congress (2007–2008) following the 106 from the previous session. Congress, however, was more preoccupied with other matters and never came close to enacting climate legislation before the end of Bush's second term.

Washington Revives: The Obama Administration. In keeping with his campaign commitment to reinvigorate federal climate change policy, one of Obama's first acts as president was to order his new EPA administrator, Lisa Jackson, to review the EPA's prior refusal of the California waiver, with the expectation that the EPA would now approve the state's request. At the same time, the president urged Congress to enact legislation creating a comprehensive domestic GHG regulatory regime.

With the advent of Democratic majorities in both congressional chambers and the Obama presidency following the 2008 elections, environmentalists had expected a renewed congressional effort to enact the comprehensive climate bill so long delayed. Throughout 2008 and early 2009, Congress ponderously struggled to produce a climate bill, but it was not until early 2009 that comprehensive climate legislation finally emerged from either congressional chamber. In June 2009, the House of Representatives, after an exhausting struggle and continual White House pressure, enacted the American Clean Energy and Security Act (ACES) by a vote of 219–212, sending it to the Senate, where its arrival late in the congressional session amid a multitude of other urgent issues precluded any Senate progress on ACES or an alternative.

The gargantuan ACES legislation, consuming more than 800 pages, would have been one of the longest, most complex congressional enactments ever written. Although Congress had to renew its effort to produce a major climate bill in 2010, ACES was a prototype in important respects for any future congressional climate legislation. Among the ACES provisions likely to reappear in future legislation was a cap-and-trade strategy for controlling GHG emissions. A version of cap-and-trade already existed in the CAA for the domestic regulation of SO_2 and NO_x, the major emissions from coal-burning electrical utilities. In addition, cap-and-trade had become a commonly proposed regulatory model for a global climate treaty.

Cap-and-Trade. At the time Congress began to consider climate warming legislation promoted by the Obama administration, several variations of cap-and-trade had already been created by American states as the framework for three regional GHG emissions control agreements: the eastern RGGI, the Western Climate Initiative, and the Midwestern Climate Initiative. The essence of a cap-and-trade program, the Pew Center explains, is that

> the government determines which facilities or emissions are covered by the program and sets an overall emission target, or "cap," for covered entities. This cap is the sum of all allowed emissions from all included facilities. Once the cap has been set and covered entities specified, tradable emissions allowances (rights to emit) are distributed (either auctioned, or freely allocated, or some combination of these). Each allowance authorizes the release of a specified amount of greenhouse gas emissions, generally one ton of carbon dioxide equivalent (CO_2e). The total number of allowances is equivalent to the overall emissions cap (e.g., if a cap of one million tons of emissions is set, one million one-ton allowances will be issued). Covered entities must submit allowances equivalent to the level of emissions for which they are responsible at the end of each of the program's compliance periods.[16]

Allowance trading occurs among regulated facilities because

> firms face different costs for reducing emissions. For some emitters, implementing new, low-emitting technologies may be relatively inexpensive. Those firms will either buy fewer allowances or sell their surplus allowances to firms that face higher emission control costs. Since a ton of carbon dioxide (CO_2) emitted from one source has the same warming effect as a ton emitted from any other, the location of a given emissions reduction does not matter. By giving firms a financial incentive to control emissions and the flexibility to determine how and when emissions will be reduced, the capped level of emissions is achieved in a manner that minimizes overall program costs.[17]

Proponents of cap-and-trade assert that it has numerous advantages as a domestic, regional, or international GHG regulatory regime:

- It provides a continuing incentive for firms to create new methods of emissions control because such innovation can significantly reduce regulatory compliance costs.

- It allows regulated firms to "bank" excess emissions credits to be later used or sold on the emissions market to other firms needing emission credits.
- It creates strict limits on emissions that can produce large pollution reductions.
- It promotes high compliance levels, transparency, and accountability.
- It is compatible with existing local, state, and regional emissions reduction programs.
- It is an economically efficient use of government resources.
- It is estimated to provide more benefits at less cost to regulated firms.[18]

The Search for a "Clean Coal" Technology. A cap-and-trade regulatory strategy comes equipped with some problematic elements, in part because local, state, and federal governments have had little experience with it. One of the most unsettled aspects of cap-and-trade concerns the availability of emissions control technology for the large electrical utilities that are the primary source of GHG emissions. Currently, no proven technically or economically feasible emissions control technology exists for these sources. In 2010, the federal government had hoped to begin experiments at the Mountaineer power plant near New Haven, West Virginia, with a "clean coal" technology called CCS, the primary method now proposed for GHG regulation domestically. The CCS project would have taken captured CO_2 emissions, compressed and liquefied them, and pumped them about 8,000 feet into deep, porous rock formations, where it would be sequestered indefinitely. [19] In 2011, however, the power plant's owner, American Electric Power, suspended the project because of uncertainties concerning future federal climate warming policy and a weak economy.

An enormous weight of expectations, political and economic, had been loaded on this and other "clean coal" technologies currently under domestic development. In effect, Mountineer's suspension still leaves unresolved whether CCS is a gateway or a blind alley to the near future of domestic GHG regulation

Transboundary Environmental Politics

Since the 1990s, three global issues—acid precipitation, stratospheric ozone depletion, and global climate warming—have dominated the nation's international ecological agenda and increasingly affected its domestic environmental policies. The United States has been a party to international environmental agreements since 1921, but the scope and pace of this global ecological involvement have increased significantly since the 1960s.[20] Before the 1980s, most of these ecological agreements, like the UN Law of the Sea Convention signed in 1984, dealt with protection and preservation of the marine environment and fisheries or, like agreements relating to Antarctica and outer space, with freedom of access to common global resources. Transboundary air and water pollution, and especially human-induced (anthropogenic) changes in global climate, received little, if any, diplomatic attention. The rapid rise after the 1970s of scientific concern about cross-national pollution and human-induced climate change, together with a growing volume of information, increasingly sophisticated global environmental monitoring, and the mounting political strength of global environmental organizations, encouraged increased worldwide governmental attention to transboundary pollution problems. As the geographical and climatological scale of scientific analysis expanded, the politics of international environmentalism was transformed. By the mid-1980s, the cross-national transport of pollutants and its global impact had become a major distinctive issue.

Historic Markers: Stockholm, Rio, and Kyoto

The rapid growth of U.S. involvement in global environmental diplomacy, and especially the nation's increasing engagement in problems of transboundary pollution, can be documented by three historic markers—the Stockholm, Rio, and Kyoto environmental conferences—spanning the years between 1972 and 1997. Growing U.S. activism began with the 1972 Conference on the Human Environment in Stockholm, Sweden, the first truly international conference devoted exclusively to environmental issues; it was attended by 113 states and representatives from 19 international organizations. The theme "Only One Earth" dramatized internationally for the first time the growing gravity and scale of global environmental problems ranging from population growth to outer-space pollution. Among the other significant accomplishments of the Stockholm meeting were the creation of the UN Environmental Program, initially supported vigorously by the United States, and the enactment of many other, largely symbolic measures that committed the United States to a major role in future international environmental activities.[21]

The second major international meeting, the 1992 Conference on Environment and Development (The Earth Summit) was held in Rio de Janeiro; it was attended by an even larger international delegation of representatives from 179 countries, including 116 heads of state. The new conference theme, "Our Last Chance to Save the Earth," invoked the growing sense of urgency about global environmental degradation that characterized the meeting, which focused special attention on the environmental concerns of developing countries. The Rio Declaration on Environment and Development, probably the most widely known of all the conference statements, proclaimed 28 guiding principles to strengthen global environmental governance. Although U.S. delegates attended the conference and actively participated in almost all its proceedings, the official U.S. delegation, representing the viewpoint of President George Bush and his Republican administration, was widely and severely criticized for its reluctance to lead in conference policy making and, in particular, for its refusal to join other industrial nations in agreeing to timetables and reduction goals for the GHG emissions that were assumed to be responsible for global climate warming.

Although environmentalists were deeply disappointed in the U.S. delegation's lackluster performance in Rio, the Earth Summit unleashed powerful domestic and international political pressures on the United States that resulted in the Clinton administration's commitments to the timetables and emission targets for the GHG reduction incorporated into the 1997 Kyoto Protocol.

By the time of the Kyoto meeting, the United States had also signed the 1987 Montreal Protocol on Substances That Deplete the Ozone Layer, limiting domestic production and consumption of CFCs and related chemicals that are destroying the global stratospheric ozone layer; it had resumed financial support for the UN Fund for Population Activities, earlier halted by the Reagan and Bush administrations; and it had ratified the Biodiversity Treaty and the UN Law of the Sea Convention, again reversing Reagan–Bush presidential policies. Although the United States seemed unlikely to sign the original Kyoto agreement in light of George W. Bush's outspoken opposition and the continued Senate disagreement over its details, worldwide diplomatic pressure virtually compelled the United States to remain involved in global climate-warming treaty negotiations. Thus, the U.S. diplomatic trajectory from Stockholm to Kyoto had led the country steadily, if unevenly, toward a broadening and deepening commitment to international environmental governance.

Environmental Diplomacy: Incentives and Disincentives

A multitude of events in the last quarter of the 20th century, such as the development of satellite Earth-monitoring computer technology, new environmental sciences, and especially, the growth of an international scientific community deeply engaged in ecological research, have all compelled national governments to recognize the reality of transboundary pollution while raising a new global consciousness of its scope and impact. Transboundary pollution eludes the jurisdiction of any national government. Its management—for example, combating pollution of the Mediterranean Sea—often requires local or regional collaboration among governments. But, as science becomes more sophisticated in its ability to monitor and to understand pollution processes, it increasingly frames transboundary environmental problems in terms of complex, intricately related, virtually global causes and effects. This impulse toward comprehensive conceptions of international pollution also animates modern science, however unintentionally, to continually push prospective solutions up the scale of international management.

State Sovereignty Versus Ecological Stewardship. All international diplomacy occurs in a global setting that is frequently considered anarchic in the sense that there is no sovereign political regime—no determinate governmental institutions, laws, processes, or principles—to which national governments give dependable allegiance. In this sovereignless political arena, national relations are governed at different times and places by many principles in various combinations—political or economic power, cultural affinities, historical antagonisms, a regional or global superpower, technological and geographical resources, the rule of law, and much else—the nature of which is a source of unending preoccupation for diplomats and scholars. It is no surprise that the political foundation on which modern nations are expected to ground their international environmental diplomacy is at best precarious, a structure currently designed to satisfy two dissonant principles: national sovereignty over indigenous resources and national responsibility for environmental stewardship. Hence, it is inherently insecure.

Embedded in modern environmental diplomacy, therefore, is the fundamental tension between these two principles. Today, the United States and other nations recognize both principles as stated in Article 21 of the Stockholm Declaration (1972) and later reaffirmed by the Rio Declaration:

> States have in accordance with the Charter of the United Nations and the principles of international law, the sovereign right to exploit their own resources pursuant to their own environmental policies, and the responsibility to insure that activities within their jurisdiction or control do not cause damage to the environment of other states or of areas beyond the limits of national jurisdiction.

Article 21 prudently recognizes the reality of state sovereignty and self-interest and implicitly recognizes its primacy in international politics. Virtually all national policy makers, in any case, act as if state sovereignty and self-interest were higher principles, even while genuflecting in the direction of environmental responsibility toward their neighbors. In effect, the United States conducts its international environmental diplomacy in a global political arena where its own self-interest and sovereignty, and those of every other nation with which it negotiates, are always at risk of conflict with U.S. environmental goals or with the global policies deemed essential to resolve satisfactorily an international environmental problem. Moreover, the U.S. government, superpower or not, cannot routinely or legally assert its sovereign will over other nations in environmental matters as it can often do in domestic political dealings with the states and other domestic political institutions.

National Costs and Benefits. Transboundary environmental issues, like domestic ones, involve an uneven distribution of costs and benefits, ones calculated in regional, international, and global metrics that involve money, sovereignty, national prestige, and historical experience. Virtually all transboundary problems, such as acid deposition, entail upstream–downstream relations in which one nation, or a group of nations, disproportionately bears the impact of pollution migration while the polluter is likely to reap the benefits, or to believe it does. This upstream–downstream disjunction is rich in political, social, and economic cleavages sure to erupt whenever issues of pollution management arise.[22] The United States plays both roles in international politics. It is a major source of GHG emissions associated with global climate warming and of the airborne chemicals responsible for stratospheric ozone depletion, but it also shares the ecological and human health risks from both problems along with other nations. The United States is also producer and recipient of transboundary acid deposition. International environmental issues are typically first raised, often exclusively, by the downstream pollution recipients, as happened in the case of acid deposition.[23]

Many international environmental problems—such as climate change or the depletion of commercial fishing species—also involve significant cross-generational costs. The cost of this generation's failure to abate the rising depletion of commercial ocean species will be fully experienced by another, later generation that may be unable to earn a living at all from the once-thriving Atlantic tuna or cod fisheries. Rising global sea levels, shifting temperate climate zones, and other major impacts predicted by climate-warming studies may not create significant human problems for several decades or for a single generation. As with domestic issues, observes political scientist Lynton Caldwell, "policies are made or affirmed and implemented by people accountable to the present, not to the future generations. Therefore, the urgency of an issue as an object of policymaking is not necessarily a measure of its ultimate significance."[24] In the case of international issues, the problem of cross-generational impacts is further complicated because many of the most severe cross-generational consequences will be experienced by the world's smaller, or most economically or culturally disadvantaged, nations—those that can exert comparatively meager political leverage on international affairs and that are least able to mitigate or adapt to prospective ecological change.

Moreover, the so-called developing or underdeveloped nations habitually view international ecological issues through the lens of their political history, infusing their environmental diplomacy with ideologies, passions, and assumptions drawn from their colonial experience or from past diplomatic, political, or economic associations with Western and industrialized countries. The United States invariably wears distinctive mantles in the perceptions of such nations engaged in environmental diplomacy. It is *Western, colonial,* or *capitalist;* a *superpower, Northern,* or *white*—all perceptions, along with many others similarly derived, that inevitably affect the conduct of any ecological negotiations involving not only the United States but also other Western and industrialized nations. Postcolonial and other developing nations are likely to suspect initially that U.S. or other Western diplomatic initiatives concerning the environment are covert attempts at exploitation or subjugation. Latin American nations may suspect that U.S. environmental initiatives are a newer version of the deeply resented "big stick" diplomacy that the United States employed toward its southern neighbors earlier in the 20th century. Nonetheless, people in developing societies are increasingly aware of and concerned about environmental problems.

Even if history casts no long shadow over environmental diplomacy, the natural rivalries and tensions among sovereign states and the omnipresent impulse to national power and sovereignty always threaten to create a chokehold on national environmental sensibilities; all nations appraise prospective environmental policy first by its apparent impact on their own sovereignty and power. The surest poison for any international environmental agreement is a conviction held by a national leadership that its country's sovereignty will be compromised. Thus, opponents launching an early attack on a possible U.S. agreement in Kyoto to limits on U.S. domestic GHG emissions were quick to conjure images of imperiled national autonomy. "We are taking national sovereignty away from every nation that signs this treaty," charged Senator Chuck Hagel, R-NE. "Would [a binding treaty] mean a United Nations multinational bureaucracy could come in and close down industry in the United States?" he queried, adding meddling bureaucrats to the menace.[25]

Almost as potent in shaping environmental diplomacy is national prestige and image; leaders recoil from negotiations that imply national responsibility for an environmental offense or that attack the legitimacy of domestic environmental practices. "Any attempt by states or international bodies to alter national [policy] regimes immediately brings into play questions of sovereignty and the competence of a national bureaucracy. Once allegations are made against countries or their subjects, powerful defensive impulses from those identified as polluters may be expected," notes European scholars Sonja Boehmer-Christansen and Jim

Skea.[26] Negotiations get prickly when issues, or apparently impartial scientific data, are construed in a good guy–bad guy style that appears to create national villains and victims. As a cautionary tale, political scientist Marc Levy describes the result of this strategy during the 1993 negotiations among European countries over a treaty to reduce acid-rain-producing emissions. Using environmental monitoring data, "Swedish and Norwegian officials branded the United Kingdom an irresponsible renegade guilty of damaging Scandinavian resources. In one heated moment, Norwegian environment minister Thorbjorn Berntsen publicly called his British counterpart, John Gummer, a shitbag."[27] Negotiations will be far less impassioned, and usually more productive, when issues and technical data are constructively interpreted to emphasize a problem's solutions and alternative strategies.

Given the many risks and costs perceived in international environmental diplomacy, national governments are strongly motivated to assume a wait-and-see attitude toward environmental initiatives generated elsewhere, especially if they can become free riders to multilateral agreements made by other countries, in which—as in the case of climate change—benefits cannot be reserved only for those countries signing the treaty. International environmental agreements often require some sort of new implementation structure, perhaps a regional or global monitoring system for a pollutant, and this may also be an inducement for a government to stay on the diplomatic sidelines. This is particularly likely when the scientific evidence supporting action is not compelling. Even so, hundreds of environmental treaties exist, and more are being negotiated despite the disincentives. In addition, a large and complex array of international institutions functions to implement these agreements. Clearly, powerful incentives compel nations to participate in international environmental diplomacy.

Incentives to Cooperation. Perhaps the most compelling and common incentive for nations to negotiate environmental agreements is the recognition of a shared problem or the possibility of mutual advantage. The Montreal Protocol, the 1987 agreement in which 47 nations, including the United States, pledged themselves to specific targets and timetables for reducing their production and use of ozone-destroying CFCs, was driven largely by persuasive scientific evidence of a large hole in the ozone layer above the Antarctic and predictions of a disastrous depletion of atmospheric ozone in less than a century. Significantly, the original signatories negotiated further agreements in 1990 and 1992 to accelerate the pace and scale of CFC reductions when additional scientific data indicated that global ozone depletion was even more serious than originally assumed. These agreements were greatly facilitated by a broad scientific consensus on the problem, by the appearance of a vivid, visible ozone hole, and by the recognition that the serious human health and ecological risks of continued stratospheric ozone depletion would be shared globally. Nonetheless, developing nations such as China, India, and the African states were initially reluctant to join the Montreal accords. They were persuaded by a ten-year extension of their compliance deadline and an assurance of financial assistance in finding CFC substitutes through a special multilateral fund established for that purpose. This instance of side payments (incentives designed to encourage reluctant nations to join in multilateral agreements) illustrates a strategy often used in environmental, as well as other, international agreements.[28]

Like expediency, prestige also works to the advantage of environmental diplomacy. Nations often join international agreements—especially when the apparent costs are minimal—when the perceived gain is prestige, improved national image, or political advantage. France, Belgium, and Italy, for example, signed the 1979 Convention on Long Range Transboundary Air Pollution not only to wear the halo of a good environmental citizen in Europe but also because they anticipated that the national emissions reduction goals to which they agreed would be achieved even without the agreement.[29] In a similar vein, the Clinton administration agreed in 1992 to stabilize GHG emissions at 1990 levels by the year 2000, thereby reversing the Bush administration's policy, a decision that won environmentalist approval and obscured much of the international censure of the United States for its opposition at the Rio conference to such goals. However, the administration's implementation plan relied largely on voluntary compliance and other nonregulatory strategies, which many domestic critics charged were relatively costless economically or politically and were ultimately ineffective.

National security and other military considerations can become potent incentives for international environmental cooperation. The United States, like almost all other nuclear powers, has entered into a variety of international weapons management and disarmament agreements, such as limits on the above-ground testing of atomic weapons and the global dispersion of nuclear weapons and materials. In a broader perspective, the growing evidence of global environmental degradation and the concurrent recognition of the mounting capability of technologies to profoundly alter the physical and biological bases of all global life—indeed, to eliminate it in some instances—are promoting a growing perception among policy makers that national security and environmental protection are becoming inextricably linked for virtually all nations.

Political and economic power, often wielded not so subtly, are also common weapons in environmental diplomacy. With its huge presence in the global economy, for instance, the United States can use access to its domestic market as a potent inducement for agricultural exporting nations to accept U.S.-promoted controls on pesticides and other potentially toxic chemicals on commodities shipped abroad. Nor has the United States been reluctant to use foreign aid or the promise of other kinds of economic or technical assistance to facilitate environmental agreements on climate diplomacy, hazardous waste management, the protection of Antarctica, and many other diverse matters.

The Crucial Role of Science. Scientists and science have assumed an important and sometimes (in the case of current global climate issues) decisive role in promoting environmental issues to international significance. The relatively recent ascent of environmental science as a crucial force in setting the international environmental agenda has many explanations: the proliferation of and collaboration among scientific organizations at all international levels; the growing technical capability and sophistication of the physical and biological sciences, abetted by increasing national investments in environmental research among the technologically advanced countries; the rapid elaboration of highly efficient global communications systems; and the exponential growth of global environmental monitoring and assessment data.[30]

A striking aspect of contemporary science is not only its capacity to compel international attention to environmental issues but also its success in doing so on the basis of predictions, computer models, and other extrapolations. The effect has been to project politics and policy issues far into the future, thereby linking present-day decision making in concrete and explicable ways to what has been traditionally treated as a remote, and quite frequently irrelevant, social world. This amounts to a subtle but ongoing and pervasive redefinition of political time and space for the world's key policy makers; a lengthening of the conceptual horizons in policy thinking; and frequently a forced, and not necessarily welcome, confrontation with the long-term consequences of today's decisions defined in the more or less authoritative language of science.

The resources and authority of modern environmental science originate primarily among the world's technologically advanced and largely Western societies, especially in the United States, Western Europe, and Japan. Because of its enormous scientific infrastructure, American science frequently assumes a major, often dominating role in Western scientific undertakings. Although the environmental science driving global ecological concerns draws considerable strength from its pervasive American and Western character, this becomes an impediment to global environmental diplomacy when non-Western and developing nations suspect, as they often do, that Western science is manipulated to serve Western political and economic interests.

Global Politics Is Different

Even a brief depiction of the global political arena illuminates its vast differences from the domestic setting of U.S. environmental politics. Unlike the constitutionally sorted and ordered division of U.S. domestic governmental power, no sovereign authority—no widely understood, accepted, or explicit apportionment of power—predictably directs international affairs. Rather, it is a world of competing national sovereignties where power in all forms is customarily the real legitimating and coercive force in international agreements. It is a world of highly pluralized political interests that become yet more fragmented as traditional nation states are increasingly forced to accommodate, and often compete with, nongovernmental organizations, multinational corporations, regional and international governmental bodies, and other entities for diplomatic influence. It is also a world as yet untouched by the moderating influence of a liberal democratic civic culture or of any common cultural grounding at all. It is a world of dangerous ideological and cultural cleavages, where the hold of environmental governance is still tenuous. In this setting, environmental diplomacy has only just begun to temper the force of power and sovereignty, and a global environmental consciousness is but recently emergent.

From Kyoto to Qatar

By the time the Kyoto conference convened in December 1997, national opinion polls indicated strong public support for U.S. action to limit climate warming, even unilaterally if necessary, and the IPCC report released that year added further impetus for action.[31] Nonetheless, the Clinton administration, facing an unsympathetic Republican congressional majority and continued domestic opposition from almost all the prospective regulated interests, seemed irresolute and confused, leading environmentalists and their allies to doubt that the United States would agree to tough GHG emissions controls despite previous promises. Because any agreement signed at Kyoto would require Senate approval, the congressional mood constantly preoccupied the U.S. negotiators. The Senate characteristically viewed the proceedings through political bifocals, continually scrutinizing the international implications for U.S. sovereignty and then the likely domestic economic impacts, particularly in home states. With Senate Republicans generally skeptical and Democrats divided on the treaty's merits, the U.S. delegation knew that eventual Senate approval of any agreement would be problematic.

With 120 nations attending and worldwide media coverage, Kyoto became one of the century's historic international environmental conferences. To the considerable surprise of environmentalists and others expecting an indecisive performance, the U.S. delegation eventually committed to what many observers considered a rigorous schedule of emissions reductions.

In the United States, however, the Kyoto Treaty was doomed before the negotiations had even begun. There was virtually no enthusiasm for the agreement in the Senate, whose approval is mandatory for any international treaty. The most vociferous Senate criticism focused on the failure of China, India, and other rapidly industrializing nations to accept compulsory GHG emissions limits, but numerous other treaty provisions evoked disapproval on both sides of the partisan divide in Congress. Moreover, the president was embroiled in his impeachment battle and had neither time nor resources to invest in international climate diplomacy.

After the change of administration, George W. Bush's early opposition to the agreement seemed additional assurance—if more were needed—that the protocol would never survive Congress in its original form. Moreover, public concern about climate warming, although still rising, lacked the intensity to elevate the matter to a high priority among the nation's most important public issues, even though it was increasingly identified as a major environmental problem. The Gallup Poll reported in mid-2004, for instance, that the proportion of the public that reported worrying about climate warming "a great deal or a fair amount" had declined from 72 percent in mid-2000 to 51 percent by Earth Day 2004.[32] On Earth Day 2007, Gallup noted that "overall, Americans' concern about global warming has not generally shown much fluctuation since Gallup first asked the question in 1989."[33] Numerous members of both parties have pledged their opposition unless the developing nations also agree to mandatory domestic emissions cutbacks, which they have so far vigorously rejected. Other major senatorial concerns involve fears of lost sovereignty and adverse domestic economic impacts. Somewhat unexpectedly, tentative support for the agreement emerged among some segments of the automobile manufacturing, petroleum, and electrical utility industries, but powerful opposition remains. Further, many scientists believe that the Kyoto Protocol is at best a first step toward what must be a greatly accelerated timetable, with much greater emissions reductions among all major industrial nations if the worst impacts of a future climate warming are to be averted.

Ambiguity and Impasse at Copenhagen

However, by the time the president joined the Copenhagen Conference in December 2009, the national political mood was considerably less benign about a climate treaty. In the aftermath of climategate, a major national poll reported that public approval of the president's management of the climate issue had fallen from 65 percent in early 2009 to 45 percent in December 2009 and that 40 percent of the respondents had responded that they trusted "not at all" what "scientists had to say about the environment."[34]

By the time Obama arrived in Copenhagen, the meeting had become the most important international climate change conference in more than a decade, attended by 190 nations, more than 8,000 delegates, more than 500 nongovernmental organizations, and 40,000 other participants. To the dismay of climate treaty advocates, the already fragile prospects for a meaningful treaty seemed to evaporate as Copenhagen evolved into an international spectacle of angry national conflicts, hardening disagreement between regional blocs of nations, and rapidly darkening prospects for compromise or conciliation between the large developed nations and the smaller underdeveloped ones. Obama's dramatic intervention in the conference's closing hours to broker a compromise among the major developing nations produced what became the Copenhagen Accord, the most important, and highly controversial, agreement that could be salvaged from the conference. Obama was careful to acknowledge the substantial limitations of the accord. "Today we made a meaningful and unprecedented breakthrough here at Copenhagen," he announced. "But it is going to be very hard, and it is going to take some time to get a legally binding treaty." Such a treaty, he concluded "was not achievable at this conference."[35]

In the aftermath of Copenhagen, the accord's ambiguities and contingencies created a legacy of continuing disagreement about its achievements and importance to the United States, sharply dividing environmentalists over the document's ultimate value. "The Copenhagen Accord is clearly a work in progress," concluded a carefully balanced assessment by the UCS, a major environmentalist organization, "with key details such as the emission reduction targets for industrialized countries and emission mitigation actions of developing countries to be filled in later." Then, noting a primary source of conflict about the agreement, the UCS adds, "It is also a voluntary framework, with negotiations to continue in 2010 towards a legal binding instrument that would either accompany or supersede the Kyoto Protocol."[36]

The Copenhagen Accord was, at best, highly limited and often ambiguous in its implications, with many widely recognized deficiencies even amongst its most ardent environmental proponents, including the following[37]:

• *Level of ambition.* Assuming that industrialized and major developing countries put forward only their current offers on emissions targets and actions, the collective level of effort will not put the world on a track to stay below the 2°C temperature limitation goal that the accord endorses. The accord was largely negotiated among three countries—the

United States, China, and India—that have resisted calls from others to put forward a greater level of ambition in limiting their emissions; this has led many to wonder whether the accord will prove adequate to the task, or as some fear, represents a "coalition of the unwilling."

- *A move away from legally binding.* The accord, with its voluntary framework on emissions limitations, its lack of any compliance provisions, and its open-ended review in 2015, does little to calm concerns about enforcement. Without the creation of a legally binding framework for the United States, it is clear that Japan, Russia, and Canada will refuse to accept deeper reduction targets for the next commitment period of the Kyoto Protocol; thus, that instrument will wither away after 2012—and with it, the whole framework of meaningful, legally binding, international commitments on climate change.

- *The negotiations process.* The way the accord was hammered out, in a process starting with just 28 countries in the room and ultimately being decided after President Obama walked in, uninvited, to a coordination meeting of Brazil, China, India, and South Africa, raises questions about the continued relevance of the whole United Nations negotiating process. Although the UN process leaves much to be desired and can allow small groups of countries—or even individual negotiators—to hold the process hostage for a time, it is not clear that replacing it with a less transparent process of deal making among a handful of powerful countries will produce superior results either in terms of overall ambition or equity.

Where Do We Go from Here?

The formal negotiations continued with session in Bonn, Germany, in June 2010 and the COP 16 held in Mexico November 29 to December 10, 2010. Like the previous Copenhagen conference, the Cancun meeting produced a limited new set of agreements that nudged progress forward toward a truly effective global climate warming treaty. The important decisions at Cancun included agreement on the details of an international system for reporting national climate warming emissions, a procedure for assuring transparency and accuracy in the reporting process, and an arrangement for continuing global consultation on emissions measurement, reporting, and verification. The succeeding COP 17 meeting in Durban, South Africa, again moving incrementally ahead, produced several important documents. The Durban Platform for Enhanced Action a "non-binding agreement that calls for a new climate treaty to be reached by 2015 that brings all countries under the same legal regime by 2020. Because this agreement departs from the long-standing UNFCCC division of the world's countries into those with serious emissions-reduction responsibilities (the Annex I countries) and those with no responsibilities whatsoever, it opens up the negotiation process to new thinking about international climate policy architecture."[38] Another agreement created a second period for commitment to the Kyoto Protocol by most of the nations signing the original protocol, thus keeping alive at least to 2017 all the arrangements for international consultation and information exchange in the original agreement. The most recent meeting, COP 18, was held in Doha, Qatar, between November 26 and December 7, 2012.

Following the 2012 elections, the Obama administration faces continuing partisan polarization within Congress and a still-fragile economy, which portend ill for a successful legislative initiative creating a cap-and-trade regulatory program to control domestic climate warming emissions—or for virtually any other kind of comprehensive congressionally produced climate regulation. Obama, however, has pressed ahead with an alternative regulatory strategy based upon the CAA. Using the Supreme Court's earlier discussed 2007 endangerment finding that supported the authority of EPA to regulate CO_2 emissions under the CAA, the EPA has initiated four new regulations to control CO_2 emissions from new sources—actions supported by the federal courts again in 2012. These regulations established three important regulatory principles, which accomplished the following:

- Set new CO_2 emission standards for cars and light trucks (the Tailpipe Rule)
- Determined that CO_2 emissions regulations applied to major stationary sources such as power plants and cement factories
- Decided to tailor its regulations to different types of emission sources, beginning with the largest power plant emissions sources, rather than pass a blanket rule applied to all sources

The auto industry generally supported EPA's decision to create nationally uniform tailpipe emissions standards, which avoided the prospect of many different, and economically burdensome, state auto standards. Unlike the automakers, many other large industry groups, including electric utilities, coal mining, and petroleum refiners joined with major commercial trade associations such as the National Chambers of Commerce in continued opposition to the EPA's aggressive approach to new climate emissions regulations. Joined by several states, including Texas and Arizona, this broad, politically potent coalition of industry, commerce, and states assures a continuing outpouring of legal challenges to the EPA's climate warming regulations and no imminent truce of the battle within and outside Congress to blunt the second Obama administration's regulatory attack on domestic climate warming emissions.

Conclusion

Something profound, and as yet but vaguely conceived, happened to political cognition in the latter third of the 20th century. To this phenomenon we have ascribed the inadequate word *environmentalism*. The artifacts of this movement are the most visible and, ultimately, the least important aspects of it. Beginning with Earth Day 1970 in the United States and comparable political stirrings elsewhere in the industrialized world, a structure of domestic laws, institutions, and cultural practices has evolved in the United States to translate *environmentalism* into a social force and presence. This already large and elaborate national structure (the focus of most of this book) has become a national pediment, among many throughout the world, on which a new regional and international regime of environmental management (the focus of this chapter) is emerging. This incipient globalization of environmental management is extremely tenuous and as yet largely unproven, still more symbol than monument. Yet, it does exist, and it has never existed before in the history of human civilization. It is worth reflecting on the profound historical implications of an international protocol to manage climate change in the twilight of the 20th century.

At the beginning of the new century, however, a better perspective on the future path of environmentalism might be gained by looking beyond its current political and governmental architecture, important as that may be, to its implications for our evolving national conceptions of political time, space, and causality. From this perspective, one of environmentalism's most profound impacts has been to accelerate the way in which science is transforming public policy making. Environmental science, embodied in the technical underpinnings of current understandings of climate warming, ozone depletion, and intergenerational equity, is compelling policy makers to think in terms of policy problems and impacts, of the consequences of present decisions and future undertakings and on a time scale almost unthinkable a few decades ago and unavoidable in the future. The genie of anticipatory environmental science is out of the bottle and, like the secrets of nuclear power, cannot now be ignored, however disconcerting it may be. Although our national political language has always been afflicted with vaporous rhetoric about "the future" and "concern for future generations," science today is providing policy makers with the intellectual tools and a scientific metric for characterizing the future impact of present public decision making that impose a responsibility quite new to public life.

Added to this increasingly sophisticated ability to describe and anticipate the environmental consequences of present policies, environmentalism has also made us aware, sometimes acutely, of the need to think deliberately about the long-term risks of technological innovation. As the U.S. experience with nuclear power amply demonstrates, it is not only the scientific risks of technology development that need to be appraised but also the institutional risks—the questions about whether we have, or can develop in appropriate ways, the institutional means of managing satisfactorily the technologies we create domestically and internationally.

Most important, the evolving impact of environmentalism on our politics and culture has made an especially persuasive case, for those who will listen, that we are beginning a new century not only with the technological ability to destroy the cultural and biological conditions for the survival of human life on Earth but also with the capability to alter the genetic foundations of human life and thus consciously shape human evolution in materially and spiritually beneficial ways. Environmentalism at its best is a challenge to develop the moral and ethical sensibilities to leaven this power with an enlightened stewardship of Earth.

Suggested Readings

Chasek, Pamela S., ed. *Global Environmental Politics.* 4th ed. Boulder, CO: Westview Press, 2006.

Conca, Ken, and Geoffrey D. Dabelko, eds. *Green Planet Blues.* 4th ed. Boulder, CO: Westview Press, 2010.

Edwards, Paul N. *A Vast Machine: Computer Models, Climate Data, and the Politics of Global Warming.* Cambridge, MA: MIT Press, 2010.

Hulme, Mike. *Why We Disagree About Climate Change.* New York: Cambridge University Press, 2009.

Pachauri, Rajenda K., and Andy Reisinger, eds. "Climate Change 2007: Synthesis Report." (Contribution of Working Groups I, II, and III to the FAR of the IPCC.) IPCC, Geneva, 2008.

Susskind, Lawrence E. *Environmental Diplomacy: Negotiating More Effective Global Agreements.* Washington, DC: Island Press, 1999.

Notes

1. "Zoos, Aquariums, Wrangle With Teaching Climate Change," available at www.eenews.net/Greenwire/customize/2012/8/27 (accessed September 20, 2012).
2. Bill McKibben, "President Obama's Big Climate Challenge," Environment 360, Yale School of Forestry and Environmental Studies, November 5, 2008, available at http://e360.yale.edu/content/feature.msp?id=2082
3. Andrew C. Revkin, "Polar Bear Warns Obama About Climate Failure," *New York Times,* December 10, 2009, available at http://dotearth.blogs.nytimes.com/2009/05/07/polar-bear-protection-updates
4. Richard A. Matthew "Is Climate Change a National Security Issue?," *Issues in Science and Technology,* September 2011, available at www.issues.org/27.3/matthew.html (accessed January 20, 2012).
5. IPCC, "Climate Change 2007: Working Group I: The Physical Science Basis, IPCC Assessments of Climate Change and Uncertainties," 2007, available at www.ipcc.ch/publications_and_data/ar4/wg1/en/ch1s1–6.html (accessed May 15, 2010).

6. Ibid.
7. "Highlights From Climate Change 2007: The Physical Science Basis—Summary for Policy Makers," Pew Center on Global Climate Change, available at www.pewclimate .org/ . . . /IPCCSummary050407_050407_143632.pdf
8. Among the many sources for data concerning the CRU affair, those especially useful include the compendium of CRU e-mails, available at www.eastangliaemails.com/ emails.php?eid=295&filename=1047388489.txt; "Global Warming: Debunking Misinformation about Stolen Climate Emails in the 'Climategate' Manufactured Controversy," http://www.ucsusa.org/global_warming/science_and_impacts/global_warming_ con trarians/debunking-misinformation-stolen-emails-climategate.html; UCS, "Global Warming, 2009," www.ucsusa.org/global_warming/science_and_impacts/global_warm ing_contrarians/debunking-misinformation-stolenemails-climategate.html; Ronald Bailey, "The Scientific Tragedy of Climategate," *Reason Magazine*, December 1, 2009, available at http://reason.com/archives/2009/12/01/the-scientific-tragedy-of-clim (accessed February 16, 2010).
9. Annenberg Public Policy Center, "'Climategate': Hacked E-Mails Show Climate Scientists in Bad Light but Don't Change Scientific Consensus on Climate Warming," December 10, 2009, www.factcheck.org/2009/12/climategate.
10. Philip Shabecoff, "Global Warming Has Begun Expert Tells Senate," *New York Times*, June 24, 1988, A1.
11. Jill Jaeger and Tim O'Riordan, "The History of Climate Change Science and Politics," in *Politics of Climate Change*, ed. Tim O'Riordan and Jill Jaeger (London: Routledge, 1996), 5.
12. Quoted in Calvin Sims, "Poor Nations Reject Role in Warming," *New York Times*, December 13, 1997, A7.
13. Matthew L. Wald, "Fighting the Greenhouse Effect," *New York Times*, August 28, 1988, sec. 3, 1.
14. Committee on Energy and Commerce, "Climate Change Legislation Design White Paper: Appropriate Roles for Different Levels of Government," Washington, DC, February 2008, available at http://energycommerce.house.gov/Climate_Change/ white%20paper%20st-lcl%20roles%20final%202–22.pdf.
15. Adapted from "State Legislation From Around the Country," Pew Center on Global Climate Change, available at www.pewclimate.org/what_s_being_done/in_the_states/ state_legislation.cfm (accessed February 12, 2010).
16. Pew Center on the States, *Climate Change 101: Cap and Trade* (Washington, DC: The Pew Center, 2008), 1–4.
17. Ibid.
18. Ibid. See also, U.S. EPA, Office of Air and Radiation, "Cap and Trade," January 18, 2010, available at http://epa.sownar.com/airmarkets/cap-trade/index.html; Eileen Claussen and Robert W. Fri, *A Climate Policy Framework: Balancing Policy and Politics* (Queenstown, MD: The Aspen Institute, 2004); A. Denny Allerman, Paul L. Jaskow, and David Harrison Jr., *Emissions Trading in the United States* (Arlington, VA: Pew Center on Climate Change, 2003), pt. III.
19. David Biello, "Burying Climate Change: Efforts Begin to Sequester Carbon Dioxide From Power Plants," *Scientific American*, September 22, 2009, available at www.scientific american.com/article.cfm?id=burying-climate-change#comments.
20. Among the 152 multilateral environmental treaties and agreements adopted by the United States through 1990, 20 were signed between 1921 and 1959, 26 during the 1960s, 49 during the 1970s, and 48 in the 1980s. (Marvin S. Soroos, "From Stockholm to Rio and Beyond: The Evolution of Global Environmental Governance," in Environmental Policy in the 1990s, 3rd ed., ed. Norman J. Vig and Michael E. Kraft [Washington, DC: CQ Press, 1997], 283.)

21. For the history of international environmental negotiations, see Lynton Keith Caldwell, *International Environmental Policy: Emergence and Dimensions,* 2nd rev. ed. (Durham, NC: Duke University Press, 1990).

22. See, for example, Jill Jager and Tim O'Riordan, *The History of Climate Change Science and Politics* (London: Routledge, 1996); Sonja Boehmer-Christansen and Jim Skea, *Acid Politics* (New York: Belhaven Press, 1991); Duncan Liefferink, *Environment and the Nation State: The Netherlands, the EU, and Acid Rain* (New York: Manchester University Press, 1996); Oran Young, *International Governance: Protecting the Environment in a Stateless Society* (Ithaca, NY: Cornell University Press, 1994).

23. Boehmer-Christansen and Skea, *Acid Politics,* pt. II.

24. Caldwell, *International Environmental Policy,* 14.

25. "Four U.S. Senators Lobbying in Kyoto," *Washington Post,* December 3, 1997, A35, A42.

26. Boehmer-Christansen and Skea, *Acid Politics,* 19–20.

27. Marc A. Levy, "International Co-operation to Combat Acid Rain," in *Green Globe Yearbook 1995,* eds. Helge Ole Bergesen and Georg Parmanis (New York: Oxford University Press, 1996), 63.

28. See Richard Elliot Benedick, *Ozone Diplomacy: New Directions in Safeguarding the Planet* (Cambridge, MA: Harvard University Press, 1991).

29. Levy, "International Co-operation to Combat Acid Rain," 60.

30. On the role of science in international climate diplomacy, see Bert Bolin, "Science and Policy Making," *Ambio* 23 (February 1994): 25–29; Peter Haas, "Introduction: Epistemic Communities and International Policy Coordination," *International Organization* 46 (winter 1992): 1–35; Joseph Alcamo, Roderick Shaw, and Leen Hordik, eds., *The RAINS Model of Acidification* (Boston: Kluwer Academic, 1990); John E. Carroll, ed., *International Environmental Diplomacy: The Management of Transfrontier Environmental Problems* (New York: Cambridge University Press, 1988).

31. John Cushman, "Polls Show Public Support for Treaty," *New York Times,* November 11, 1997, A1. See also "Public Backs Tough Steps for a Treaty on Warming," *New York Times,* November 28, 1997, A36.

32. David W. Moore, "Americans Tepid on Global Warming Accord," The Gallup Poll Tuesday Briefing, April 13, 2004, available at www.gallup.com (accessed April 16, 2004).

33. "Polls: Water, Warming, Travel, Youth, and Green Guilt," *Environmental News Service,* April 23, 2007, available at www.ens-newswire.com/ens/apr2007/2007–04–23–03.asp (accessed May 1, 2007).

34. Quoted in Jon Cohen and Jennifer Agiesta, "On Environment, Obama and Scientists Take Hit at Polls," *Washington Post,* December 18, 2009, available at www.washingtonpost.com/wp-dyn/content/article/2009/12/18/AR2009121800002.html

35. Quoted in Juliet Eilperin and Anthony Faiola, "Climate Deal Falls Short of Key Goals," *Washington Post,* December 19, 2009, 1.

36. UCS, "The Copenhagen Accord: Not Everything We Wanted, but Something to Build On," in *Global Warming, 2009,* available at www.ucsusa.org/global_warming/solutions/big_picture_solutions/the-copenhagen-accord.html.

37. Ibid.

38. Robert Stavins, "Assessing the Climate Talks—Did Durban Succeed?," *An Economic View of the Environment,* Belfer Center for Science and the Environment, Harvard Kennedy School, available at http://www.robertstavinsblog.org (accessed November 27, 2012).

List of Abbreviations

ACES	American Clean Energy and Security Act
AEC	Atomic Energy Commission
AFO	animal feeding operation
ALF	Animal Liberation Front
ANWR	Arctic National Wildlife Refuge
ARRA	American Recovery and Reinvestment Act
BCA	benefit–cost analysis
BLM	Bureau of Land Management
CAA	Clean Air Act of 1970
CAFOs	concentrated animal feeding operations
CAGW	Citizens against Government Waste
CAIR	Clean Air Interstate Rule
CBD	Center for Biological Diversity
CCS	Carbon Capture and Sequester
CEQ	Council on Environmental Quality
CERCLA	Comprehensive Environmental Response, Compensation, and Liability Act of 1980 (Superfund)
CFCs	chlorofluorocarbons
COP 15	Fifteenth Conference of the Parties to the UNFCC
CPSC	U.S. Consumer Product Safety Commission
CPSRA	Consumer Product Safety Reform Act
CRU	Climate Research Unit
DDT	dichlorodiphenyltrichloroethane
DINP	diisononyl phthalate
DOE	Department of Energy
DOI	Department of the Interior
EIA	U.S. Energy Information Administration
EIS	environmental impact statement
ELF	Earth Liberation Front
EOP	Executive Office of the President
EPA	U.S. Environmental Protection Agency
EPAct	Energy Policy Act of 2005
FAR	IPCC Fourth Assessment Report

FPL	Florida Power and Light
FWPCAA	Federal Water Pollution Control Act Amendments of 1972
GAO	Government Accountability Office (until July 2004, Government Accounting Office)
GHG	greenhouse gas
IPCC	Intergovernmental Panel on Climate Change
IRIS	Integrated Risk Information System
MCL	maximum contaminant limit
MEF	Major Economies Forum
MPCA	Minnesota Pollution Control Agency
NAFTA	North American Free Trade Agreement
NASA	National Aeronautics and Space Administration
NEPA	National Environmental Policy Act of 1969
NFMA	National Forest Management Act
NIEHS	National Institute for Environmental Health Sciences
NIMBY	"Not in My Backyard"
NO_x	nitrogen oxides
NPL	National Priority List
NPS	National Park Service
NRC	Nuclear Regulatory Commission
NSR	new source review (Clean Air Act of 1970)
NWPA	Nuclear Waste Policy Act of 1982
OCS	outer continental shelf
OIRA	Office of Information and Regulatory Affairs
OMB	Office of Management and Budget
OPEC	Organization of Petroleum Exporting Countries
OSMRE	Office of Surface Mining Reclamation and Enforcement
OSTP	Office of Science and Technology Policy
PCBs	polychlorinated biphenyls
PSD	prevention of significant deterioration
RARG	Regulatory Analysis Review Group
RCRA	Resource Conservation and Recovery Act of 1976
REDD	reducing emissions from deforestation and forest degradation
RGGI	Regional Greenhouse Gas Initiative
RIA	regulatory impact analysis
RPS	Renewable Portfolio Standards
SAR	IPCC Second Assessment Report
SARA	Superfund Amendments and Reauthorization Act of 1986
SDWA	Safe Drinking Water Act
SMCRA	Surface Mining Control and Reclamation Act
SO_x	sulfur oxides
SUVs	sport utility vehicles

TAR	IPCC Third Assessment Report
TCDD	2,3,7,8-tetrachloridibenzodioxin
TMDL	total maximum daily load
TRI	Toxic Release Inventory
TSCA	Toxic Substances Control Act of 1976
TVA	Tennessee Valley Authority
UCS	Union of Concerned Scientists
UNCED	United Nations Conference on Environment and Development (The Earth Summit)
UNFCCC	United Nations Framework Convention on Climate Change
USTs	underground storage tanks
VOCs	volatile organic compounds
WCED	World Commission on Environment and Development
WIPP	Waste Isolation Pilot Project

Index